A Public Peace Process

A Public Peace Process

Sustained Dialogue to Transform Racial and Ethnic Conflicts

Harold H. Saunders

palgrave

First published in hardcover in 1999 by St. Martin's Press
First PALGRAVE™ edition: September 2001
175 Fifth Avenue, New York, N.Y. 10010 and
Houndmills, Basingstoke, England RG21 6XS
Companies and representatives throughout the world.

PALGRAVE is the new global publishing imprint of St. Martin's Press LLC
Scholarly and Reference Division and Palgrave Publishers Ltd (formerly
Macmillan Press Ltd).

ISBN 0–312–21939–3 hardcover
ISBN 0–312–29338–0 paperback

Library of Congress Cataloging-in-Publication Data
Saunders, Harold H.
A public peace process: sustained dialogue to transform racial
and ethnic conflicts/Harold H. Saunders.
     p.   cm.
Includes bibliographical references and index.
ISBN 0–312–29338–0
1. Conflict management.   2. Ethnic relations.   3. Race relations.
I. Title.

HM136.S25   1999
303.6'9—dc2198–48410
                                                                        CIP

A catalogue record for this book is available from the British Library.

Design by Letra Libre, Inc.

First paperback edition: September 2001
10 9 8 7 6 5 4 3 2 1

Printed in the United States of America

To all those, known and unknown, who have dared to make a public peace process their own and have helped shape it as a citizens' instrument for peace

To Carol—beloved partner in life

To Mark, Robin, Cathy, Caryn—who must teach the peacemakers of the future

To Emilie and Ward—the generation who will shape the "citizens' century"

Contents

Acknowledgments

B ecause this book emerges from many interactions in different times and places, it was put together in a way that reflects that experience. Although the thesis is mine and I alone have written all but parts of Chapter Eight and the whole of Chapter Nine, the work reflects close interactions with many colleagues. Of course, responsibility for the final presentation is mine.

Since 1981, my deepening involvement with the Charles F. Kettering Foundation has made its cutting-edge research into the nature of politics an integral part of my thinking. I almost feel that Kettering President David Mathews is a co-author of Chapter Three, "Citizens' Politics in Civil Society." I have used many of his concepts and formulations. The programs in community politics developed and tested by colleagues at Kettering—particularly James Wilder—have become a central part of my thought. The opportunity to carry their insights to faraway places and back has been a privilege and a priceless gift to me. I have also valued highly the freedom to conceptualize in my own way their insights in the form of the "citizens' political process" described in Chapter Three. Despite our closeness, this book should not be read as a statement of the foundation's views; the thinking here is mine, rooted in my own experience.

Randa Slim, colleague at the Kettering Foundation for eight years, participated in most of the international sustained dialogues with the former Soviet Union since 1989 and with Tajikistan since 1993. She also managed the Kettering Foundation's International Civil Society Exchange and International Civil Society Workshop. Lebanese by birth, with a Ph.D. in psychology from the University of North Carolina at Chapel Hill, she has worked intensively in the field of conflict prevention and resolution. We have co-authored two articles on this work. Her insights have been important to me.

My closest Russian colleagues in sustained dialogue are Gennady Chufrin, co-chair of both the Dartmouth Conference Regional Conflicts

Task Force and of the Inter-Tajik Dialogue; Vitaly Naumkin, president of the International Center for Strategic and Political Studies; and Irina Zviagelskaya, vice president of the center. Through their deep knowledge and widespread contacts in Central Asia they have provided the structural foundations and interpretive insight that underlie the Inter-Tajik Dialogue. Gennady and I co-authored the article "A Public Peace Process" mentioned in the Preface and cited in the Introduction; this shared work is part of the foundation of sustained dialogue described in Chapter Six, which elaborates the five-stage process of sustained dialogue.

In countless ways my Tajikistani colleagues in the Inter-Tajik Dialogue are present on many pages in this book. Chapter Seven is their story, but their insight, intelligence and dedication to peace in their country are touchstones that have been with me at many moments as I have formulated my own thoughts.

Three colleagues in Baton Rouge, Louisiana—Jan Bernard, Reverend Jeff Day, and Reverend Fred Jeff Smith—have collaborated with me to produce Chapter Eight, the story of the efforts in that city to improve race relations through sustained dialogue on several levels. In reality, all the participants in the sustained dialogue between the African American and white communities there are co-creators of that analysis.

In Chapter Nine, Galia Golan of Hebrew University in Jerusalem and Zahira Kamal of the Palestinian Authority in the West Bank describe their experience individually and together in dialogue at the heart of one of the world's longest and most intense deep-rooted human conflicts.

Beyond the work specifically directed at producing this book, I owe debts to many others in my past. Most of these cannot be named, but some groups and individuals must be singled out for special thanks.

First: I remember with deep respect and thanks many of the Arabs, Israelis, Soviets, Chinese, Indians, Pakistanis, Kashmiris, Estonians, Tajikistanis, Armenians, Azerbaijanis, Karabakhsi, Native Americans, African Americans, whites and immigrants to the United States from a number of ethnicities. Each brought her or his own complex of fears and hopes to the dialogue room. They enriched my life immeasurably, both personally and professionally. Their feelings and thoughts suffuse these pages in ways I can no longer identify.

Second: Since the mid-1960s, a handful of committed scholar-practitioners have worked outside government with citizens from groups in conflict in order to understand more fully the dynamics of deep-rooted human conflicts. I have learned especially from the following.

A pioneer among these was Herbert C. Kelman, professor of social relations at Harvard University, from whom I have learned much about the conduct and purposes of nonofficial dialogue. As a social and political psychologist, he developed his series of one-time "problem-solving workshops" among Israelis, Palestinians and other Arabs to help participants gain insight into their relationship. In 1990, he began a new sequence of workshops bringing the same participants back together over a number of meetings.

I am particularly grateful to two friends who introduced me to important psychoanalytic and psychological concepts. Vamik Volkan—a Turkish Cypriot by birth, psychoanalyst and founder of the Center for the Study of Mind and Human Interaction in the University of Virginia Health Sciences Center—pioneered the application of psychoanalytic insight to the behavior of groups in conflict. Joseph Montville, a former foreign service officer, systematized insights from the fields of psychoanalysis, psychiatry and psychology and brought them to the attention of the U.S. diplomatic establishment as well as those outside government dealing with people in conflict. Their concepts helped me to articulate what I had learned from experience and am still learning.

The work of John Paul Lederach, founding director of the Conflict Transformation Program at Eastern Mennonite University, has also been particularly helpful both because of his sensitivity to the cultures of those with whom he works—his "elicitive" approach—and because of the spiritual, and therefore human, roots of his efforts to help people deal with conflict.

With deep respect for all those colleagues and friends from whom I have learned so much, I have invited and incorporated their contributions over the past decade in a variety of panels, seminars and written comments. I no longer always know what I owe to whom. I hope that this book builds with sensitivity on their work and that my experience and this book may join theirs as a contribution to citizens trying to end destructive conflicts.

Recognizing that a comprehensive framework must be large enough to provide space for approaches and insights across disciplines, I feel that I have added my own experience as a diplomat to the psychological insights of those scholar-practitioners.

Third: In the period from January 1987 through June 1991, while I was a visiting fellow at the Brookings Institution in Washington, D.C., I turned intensively to the formative thinking that provided the foundation for this book. That work was funded by grants from the Ira and Miriam Wallach Foundation, the United States Institute of Peace, the John D. and Catherine T. MacArthur Foundation, the Carnegie Corporation of New York and the Ford Foundation. I want to express my appreciation for that support. I am also grateful to then-president of Brookings Bruce MacLaury and to the director of international studies at that time, John Steinbruner, for their welcome, their encouragement and their support.

Fourth: I want to acknowledge the cooperation of publishers in the following way: I first developed a set of observations about our changing world and the concept of relationship in two papers: "Beyond 'Us and Them'—Building Mature International Relationships," a draft monograph prepared in 1987–1988 under a grant from the United States Institute of Peace in collaboration with the Kettering Foundation; and a version of that paper published as a work in progress, "Beyond 'We' and 'They'—Conducting International Relationships," in *Negotiation Journal* (Vol. 3, No. 3, July 1987), pp. 245–277. I am grateful to the editor of that journal, the late Jeffrey Z. Rubin, for his encouragement to publish in those pages on several important occasions. The discussion of the concept of relationship was refined for "The Arab-Israeli Conflict in a Global Perspective," in John D. Steinbruner, ed., *Restructuring American Foreign Policy* (Washington, D.C.: The Brookings Institution, 1988), Chapter 8. A fuller presentation appeared as "An Historic Challenge to Rethink How Nations Relate," in Vamik D. Volkan, Demetrios A. Julius, and Joseph V. Montville, eds., *The Psychodynamics of International Relationships, Vol. 1: Concepts and Theories* (Lexington, Mass.: Lexington Books, 1990), Chapter 1. This approach was also applied to "The Soviet-U.S Relationship and the Third World," in Robert Jervis and Seweryn Bialer, eds., *Soviet-American Relations After the Cold War* (Durham, N.C.: Duke University Press, 1991), Chapter 6. The epilogue to a revision of my 1985 book *The Other Walls: The Arab-Israeli Peace Process in a Global Perspective* (Princeton, NJ: Princeton University Press, 1991) more fully sets the Arab-Israeli peace process in the context of international relationships as political processes. The concept of relationship was most fully developed in *The Concept of Relationship: A Perspective on the Future Between the United States and the Successor States to the Soviet Union* (Columbus, Ohio: The Mershon Center, The Ohio State University, 1993). In each case, observations about our changing world and the concept of relationship are stated in somewhat the same form—sometimes verbatim—as the necessary starting point for analysis. Each publisher agreed to this practice and gave the appropriate permissions at that time. These thoughts, much more deeply developed in light of much further thought and experience, built the initial foundations underlying the approach developed in this book.

Fifth: I must express my thanks to a succession of wonderful colleagues who have helped for over a decade in the production of the long sequence of building blocks that led to a final manuscript. At the top of that list in many ways stands Louise Skillings, who typed the many early formulations and versions of my thinking as it evolved in the four and a half years I spent at The Brookings Institution. After I came to work full time with the Kettering Foundation, I was helped by a series of young colleagues—Melissa Camacho, Richard Fisher, Daniel Plattner, Shavonna Maxwell, Joseph Mata, Phillip Lurie and Bryan Kurey. To all, for their support and highly professional work, I say a warm thank you.

Sixth: I am deeply grateful to St. Martin's Press, particularly in the persons of Karen Wolny, Mary Cooney, Meg Weaver and Alan Bradshaw, for their enthusiastic reception of my manuscript and their meticulous but gentle guidance through the editing and production processes.

Finally, above all, I want to place in bold relief the unique support and collaboration of my wife, Carol. Not only has she cheerfully supported me as I turned several vacations into writing retreats, but she also became a most insightful editor in the largest and most creative tradition of that role. Over the years, I have come to prize those few who have given me the great gift of putting themselves into my mind and helping me to think beyond my capacity. She is at the very top of that list. For all of these and countless other reasons, I express my deepest gratitude for her love and support and for her patience with me.

Harold H. Saunders
Washington, D.C.
December 7, 1998

Preface: A Personal Essay

The Human and Intellectual Roots of Sustained Dialogue

This book is a conceptualization of experience. It presents a framework for action by people mired in deep-rooted human conflict who want to change their conflictual relationships. That framework takes form in a multilevel peace process for ending violence, changing relationships and building communities with the capacity to resolve differences peacefully.

Because this conceptual framework is rooted and developed in experience, I want to give readers some insight into that experience. We are better understood when others know where we are "coming from."

Why write about concepts? Working with national and world leaders for four decades has taught me that the lenses (concepts) we use to bring our world into focus and give it meaning determine how we act. We will not change our behavior to meet the challenges of a new millennium until we change our conceptual framework. I have chosen to confront the obstacle of outmoded concepts head-on.

My rooting this book in a conceptualization of experience is an assertion that experience is, in many cases, the most valid way of learning and knowing. That assertion is a challenge, in company with an increasing number of philosophers,[1] to a century of academic thinking that has revered the "scientific method" as the most valid source of knowledge. Where the purpose is changing conflictual relationships, insights rooted in experience will be more authentic than those from any "social science" investigation.

A Career Focused on Conflict Management, Peacemaking and Reconciliation

For more than 30 years, I have worked with people in deep-rooted human conflict. My involvement began in 1961 as a U.S. government official. It broadened and deepened after 1981 when I left government and began working as a citizen outside government.

In government from 1961 to 1981 on the National Security Council staff in the White House (1961–1974) and in the State Department (1974–1981), I was deeply involved in U.S. mediation of Arab-Israeli agreements. I flew on the Kissinger shuttles (1973–1975) and participated as assistant secretary of state for Near Eastern and South Asian affairs (1978–1981) in the mediation of the Camp David accords and the Egyptian-Israeli Peace Treaty (1978–1979). I was also involved over those years in the conflicts between India and Pakistan, between and within other Middle Eastern countries and, ultimately, in the Iranian-U.S. hostage crisis (1979–1981).

Shortly after leaving government at the end of the Carter administration in January 1981, I became a participant in the Dartmouth Conference—the longest continuous bilateral dialogue among American and Soviet citizens, which began in 1960. Though its plenaries ended with the Cold War in 1990, its work goes on through its Regional Conflicts Task Force—one of the main incubators of the perspective presented in this book. Since the early 1970s, the conference was sponsored on the U.S. side by the Charles F. Kettering Foundation.[2] At the thirteenth Dartmouth Conference plenary, in Moscow in November 1981, this question dominated the agenda: "What happened to détente?" The answers clustered in the fields of arms control and regional conflicts in which the superpowers competed through proxies, as in the Persian Gulf, the Arab-Israeli arena, southern Africa, Central America and Afghanistan. The conference leaders—Georgi Arbatov on the Soviet side and Norman Cousins and David Mathews from the United States— agreed to form a task force in each field to see whether probing deeply into Soviet-U.S. interactions there could shed light on the "central" Soviet-U.S. relationship.

In 1982, I became the U.S. co-chair of the new Regional Conflicts Task Force. The Soviet co-chair from the beginning through 1988 was Evgeny Primakov, who became Russia's foreign minister in 1996 and prime minister in 1998. While we analyzed Soviet-U.S. interaction in specific regional conflicts, our overriding purpose was to learn more about the deeper dynamics of the overall Soviet-U.S. relationship. That task force—with Gennady Chufrin, who succeeded Primakov as co-chair in 1989—held its thirty-third meeting in October 1998.

During part of this period, I was a part-time associate of the Kettering Foundation; in 1991 I joined the foundation full time as director of international affairs. What attracted me to Kettering in the early 1980s was the fresh insight emerging from its research into the nature of politics—not the politics of governments and institutions, but the politics that happens when citizens come together in the relationships they form to solve their own problems. This work brought thinking about human beings back into the study and practice of politics. It was the definition of politics that I had felt to be at work in the Arab-Israeli peace process in the 1970s, though I did not fully understand it then.

From this experience, I have formulated the premises that underlie the conceptual framework presented in this book. My purpose here is to suggest how they evolved, one building on the other. Five stand out.

THE HUMAN DIMENSION

The human dimension of conflict must become central to peacemaking and building peaceful societies. Only governments can write peace treaties, but only human beings—citizens outside government—can transform conflictual relationships between people into peaceful relationships.

The study and practice of conflict prevention, conflict management and resolution, diplomacy, politics and peace-building will not be soundly based until the human dimension of political interaction becomes a full part of the operational picture. As long as policymakers focus primarily on institutions—states, governments and formal organizations—and on the tools of diplomacy, formal mediation, negotiation and elections, that picture will provide an incomplete basis for action.

I began to absorb this lesson forcefully after the October 1973 Arab-Israeli War. The date was November 7, 1973. I was accompanying U.S. Secretary of State Henry Kissinger on his first visit to Egypt for the talks with Egyptian President Anwar al-Sadat that laid the foundation for what became the Arab-Israeli peace process. Part-way through his talks with Sadat, Kissinger sent two of us[3] to Israel to report on those talks to Israeli Prime Minister Golda Meir and her colleagues. Shortly before our arrival, the full Israeli casualty figures from the war had been announced. In that small country, everyone knew someone wounded, lost or killed. One could virtually feel a biblical cloud hanging over the land.

When we first met Prime Minister Meir, she came over to me immediately. Knowing that my wife had died the day before the war broke out, she took my hand and said: "I am terribly sorry about your loss. I lost a lot of people, too. I guess we feel somewhat the same way." As her pain touched mine, I learned that, even though I was a government official, I would not be doing my job if I ever allowed myself to forget that, in this and other deep-rooted human conflicts, I was constantly dealing with people in pain. The human dimensions of this conflict were, in many ways, more real and more complex than the diplomatic and the juridical. A few years later, I learned how ethnic and national groups go through or get stuck in their own processes of mourning.

During this period, nonofficial dialogues began between Arabs and Israelis and then between Israelis and Palestinians. Some were initiated by Israeli and Arab individuals; several Palestinians were assassinated by fellow Palestinians for participating. Other dialogues were initiated by third parties. As time went on, I became increasingly familiar with these interactions.

From its very beginning in January 1977, the administration of President Jimmy Carter pressed hard to resume the Arab-Israeli peace process, which had been in a holding pattern in 1976 because of the U.S. presidential election. As 1977 wore on, progress slowed. Sadat became frustrated and apparently decided that the problem was partly human—not just diplomatic. He concluded, in my view, that the main obstacle was Israelis' conviction that no Arab leader would recognize a Jewish state in the Middle East. His stunning visit to Israel in November 1977 electrified the Israeli people. His speech to the Israeli parliament putting the human dimension of the conflict on center stage is quoted in Chapter Two.

In my personal world during these years, two documents of the former United Presbyterian Church in the United States of America placed the human dimension of peacemaking in a spiritual context. One is "The Confession of 1967," which addressed the theme of reconciliation as practical politics:

> To be reconciled to God is to be sent into the world as his reconciling community. This community, the church universal, is entrusted with God's message of reconciliation and shares his labor of healing the enmities which separate men from God and from each other. . . . God has created the peoples of the earth to be one universal family. In his reconciling love he overcomes the barriers between brothers. . . . The church, in its own life, is called to practice the forgiveness of enemies and *to commend to the nations as practical politics the search for cooperation and peace. This search requires that the nations pursue fresh and responsible relations across every line of conflict.*[4] (emphasis added)

Reconciliation was an appropriate theme in the 1960s when civil rights, the antiwar movement, the youth revolt against the Establishment and the sexual revolution tore many churches apart. My own Virginia church outside

Washington, D.C., with a number of military, CIA and other government employees, was particularly affected by the church's stand against the war in Vietnam. This was probably the first setting in which I used dialogue to try to hold a community together.

The second Presbyterian document is a study approved by the General Assembly in 1980 entitled *Peacemaking: The Believers' Calling.* It includes the statement: "Peace is more than the absence of war, more than a precarious balance of powers. Peace is the intended order of the world with life abundant for all God's children. Peacemaking is the calling of the Christian church."[5]

Although I do not agree with every point in these documents, they helped me place my work in a context defined partly by the spiritual life of the human being rather than only by states and governments. They encouraged confidence in consulting my own feelings as touchstones for judging my professional acts. They affirmed my inclination to see my own pain and hope as a bridge to other individuals—as I had learned in practical ways after my late wife's death and in the grueling professional effort to negotiate peace one difficult agreement at a time.

I was keenly aware, too, that other people much my senior also perceived a spiritual dimension in the assault on the barriers to peace. During their first full day at Camp David, President Carter, President Sadat and Israeli Prime Minister Menachem Begin issued the following statement:

> After four wars, despite vast human efforts, the Holy Land does not yet enjoy the blessings of peace.
>
> Conscious of the grave issues which face us, we place our trust in the God of our fathers, from whom we seek wisdom and guidance.
>
> As we meet here at Camp David we ask people of all faiths to pray with us that peace and justice may result from these deliberations.[6]

Recognizing the human dimension of conflict opened the door to seeing peacemaking as a process not limited to the work of governments. Important as that work was to me personally, it depended in fundamental ways on changes in human relationships—an arena well beyond the reach of governments alone. As that insight became more concrete, it enlarged the concept of the peace process.

THE PEACE PROCESS

The peace process—the operational framework for peacemaking—is a human or political, as well as a diplomatic and negotiating, process that works simultaneously on multiple levels.

The Arab-Israeli peace process is a series of mediated agreements embedded in a larger political process. It is in that larger process that relationships change. Until politicians and citizens act to change the political environment, formal negotiations have little chance. A seed will not sprout and flourish unless it is sown in fertile ground.

During the 1974 Kissinger shuttles, crisscrossing the Middle East on the secretary of state's U.S. Air Force plane—the plane on which Lyndon Johnson took the presidential oath in Dallas after the assassination of John F. Kennedy in 1963—we gradually recognized that the cumulative mediation of one agreement on top of another was generating a momentum that created a sense of possibility for change in the Middle Eastern political environment. We began using the phrase "the peace process." We realized, at least intuitively, that making peace ultimately required changing human relationships—that the peace process is a multilevel political and human process.

It was President Sadat's dramatic visit to Israel in November 1977 that changed the political climate there in a way that gave the Israeli government "permission" to try to negotiate peace with Egypt and opened the door to the beginnings of normalization. A senior Israeli diplomat who had been my personal friend since the mid-1960s had adamantly refused to believe that Sadat wanted peace. As we Americans flew between Egypt and Israel on the Kissinger shuttles, we told him that the Israelis could negotiate with Sadat. The day we arrived at Ben Gurion Airport outside Tel Aviv shortly after Sadat's visit to Israel, as this friend and I began the drive up to Jerusalem, he turned to me and said: "He really wants peace, doesn't he?" He expressed the changed perceptions of countless Israelis.

When in 1985 I wrote my conceptualization of the official Arab-Israeli peace process, I took the title of my book—*The Other Walls*—from Sadat's speech to the Israeli parliament to focus attention on the underlying human obstacles to peace. I subtitled the first edition *The Politics of the Arab-Israeli Peace Process* to underscore that the peace process included both official negotiations and the political environment created by citizens as well as leaders. At that time, however, I was still focusing mainly on the official peace process, not yet branching out to focus in depth on that level of the peace process in which citizens play the major role.

In 1993, Israelis and Palestinians formalized an official peace process when Israeli Prime Minister Yitzhak Rabin and Palestine Liberation Organization (PLO) Chairman Yasser Arafat shook hands on the White House lawn in Washington, D.C. It was my view that Israelis and Palestinians could not have taken this step had not countless Israelis and Palestinians met over the preceding 20 years. Some of these meetings were a continuation of the third-party-sponsored workshops begun in the 1970s, but many more were the interactions between Israelis and Palestinians rubbing shoulders in daily life. Military occupation did not prevent human beings from coming to know each other at close hand.

It was at one of the Israeli-Palestinian meetings in the California redwoods in July 1991 that I first coined the phrase "a public peace process." A group of highly placed Israelis and Palestinians outside government had agreed on a document that they hoped would move their two peoples closer to peace. Although that did not materialize then, their conference was another milestone in the long and broadening complex of meetings between the two bodies politic. And the citizens' role in the peace process now had its own name.

Sometime in the mid-1980s, I came to realize one reason I was so comfortable with the concept of the peace process as a human or political process of continuous interaction. When I was writing my doctoral dissertation in the Yale University American Studies Department from 1954 to 1956, I became familiar with social and political thinking that focused on the continuous processes of interaction among people in groups and the interactions among those groups themselves. What I wrote then surprises me now because it so explicitly presages words and thoughts that I was to use 20 and 30 years later:

> Twentieth-century thinkers have come to . . . interpret society in terms of a continuing evolutionary process rather than in those of rigid social structure. Whereas the eighteenth century had considered society a neatly balanced machine running according to natural law, current social scientists find the essence of society in a process of continual interrelationships, not rigidly structured, but in a constant state of flux. Although twentieth-century thinkers have rejected the literal analogy of the biological organism as a description of society, their concept of society is organic in that they perceive an evolving mutual interrelationship of parts rather than the attraction and repulsion of units which characterized the Newtonian thought of the eighteenth century. . . . The organic concepts of Darwinian evolution have supplanted the rigid laws of the Newtonian universe.[7]

In the mid-1980s, I began to think more about the theoretical constructs that underlay the study and practice of international relations. I concluded that the traditional "power politics" model—or "realist paradigm," as the scholars call it—did not describe the world in which I worked. I began to see the interaction of countries as a political process operating at all levels of bodies politic.

RELATIONSHIPS AMONG GROUPS AND
COUNTRIES AS A POLITICAL PROCESS

Relationships among countries or ethnic groups are a political process of continuous interaction between significant elements of whole bodies politic across permeable borders—not just relations between states and governments. It is in that dynamic process of interaction that relationships can be transformed.

We need to focus on the totality of interactions between whole groups—not just on the strategic chess game between states seen as "rational actors." I chose the concept of relationship to capture the dynamism of that total interaction. Academic and diplomatic colleagues told me I could not use an interpersonal word for this purpose. "States are different," they said. I continue to use it precisely because it embraces the human dimension.

Just as I was finishing *The Other Walls* in 1985, I began wondering why I so thoroughly disagreed with Secretary of State George Shultz's conduct of the Arab-Israeli peace process. He was an honorable, intelligent and committed public servant. He had come to office with a realistic perspective on the conflict. Yet his conduct of the peace process seemed narrowly diplomatic, unimaginative and mechanical—not dynamic, human and political.

A young man who was doing a mid-career fellowship with me at that time[8] said to me: "You talk about the peace process as you see it, and I will try to draw out your underlying assumptions. Then we will compare them with what seem to be the assumptions of the administration." The immediate result was a list of assumptions in two columns—one reflecting the traditional power-politics approach that focused heavily on states; the other reflecting a political process of continuous interaction among whole bodies politic.[9]

This work led to a series of analytical publications on the "concept of relationship." This shifts the focus in dealing with conflict from concentration on concrete issues dividing people to changing the overall relationship between them. It brings the human dimension into the prevention and resolution of conflict almost as a prerequisite to mediation or negotiation. After the dissolution of the Soviet Union in 1991 and the outbreak of major ethnic conflicts, we increasingly saw conflicts that were not ready for formal mediation and negotiation and could be dealt with only in terms of the human interactions involved. That led to the next lesson.

SUSTAINED DIALOGUE TO
CHANGE CONFLICTUAL RELATIONSHIPS

Just as governments have used diplomacy and formal mediation or negotiation as their instruments for dealing with conflict, sustained dialogue is the instru-

ment that citizens outside government use for addressing the human dimension of conflict to change their relationships.

The slowly accelerating work of nonofficial dialogue between Arabs and Israelis in the 1970s informed my work in the Dartmouth Conference Regional Conflicts Task Force. But that task force presented a particular challenge that no one else in the field faced: It was an ongoing group that met about twice a year over what has become more than a decade and a half. As Primakov urged in one of our mid-1980s discussions about our meetings: "We will begin the next meeting where the last meeting ended." In other words, there would be a cumulative agenda and a common base of knowledge, perception and common work that went well beyond the early experience in most other dialogues. The fact that we returned to meeting after meeting sharpened the challenge to think about what the meetings were producing and how the next meeting could produce more than the last. This pressure led us over time to see ours as a process that unfolded in stages.

When the Soviet Union dissolved, we in the task force decided to (1) focus on our relationship in its new form as a Russian-U.S. relationship; (2) conceptualize the process of dialogue that we had developed over more than 20 meetings; and (3) apply that process to one of the conflicts that had broken out on former Soviet territory. In April 1993, my Russian colleague and I co-authored an article, "A Public Peace Process,"[10] conceptualizing the process that we now call sustained dialogue as moving through the five stages presented in Chapter Six. We decided to apply it to the newly independent former Soviet republic of Tajikistan, as described in Chapter Seven.

Embarking on the Inter-Tajik Dialogue obliged us to further widen the angle of our lenses. Our Tajik colleagues could not talk about ending their conflict without talking at the same time about what kind of country they wanted to build as the violence ended. They needed to think not only about how to end a civil war, but also about how to lay the foundations for a peaceful society.

CIVIL SOCIETY AND PEACE-BUILDING

Peace agreements will not produce peace until they are embedded in a political process for transforming a broadening range of relationships over time—a process planted in the practices of a healthy civil society.

At the end of the 1980s, colleagues at the Kettering Foundation focused increasingly on the concept of civil society. They began exploring the possibility of a dialogue with colleagues in the Western Hemisphere, building on the Dartmouth Conference experience. We did not want it to be a quasi-governmental conference in which the rest of the hemisphere lined up in criticizing the United States. We recognized that citizens throughout the hemisphere—many of whom had recently emerged from under authoritarian governments—were freshly struggling with the challenges of strengthening civil society. A wise Colombian colleague[11] suggested that civil society become our focus. We convened the Western Hemisphere Exchange in 1989. In 1994, that became the International Civil Society Exchange with the addition of colleagues from Russia, Europe, the Middle East, Africa and Asia.

As we heard our Tajik colleagues talk about what kind of country they wanted when the violence ended, our earlier judgment was confirmed: The process of dialogue among citizens outside government for changing conflictual relationships must eventually merge with developing civil society to the point that citizens can talk together peacefully to resolve differences that affect their interests. This is why it has become imperative, in my mind, to bring together new reflections on how bodies politic interact with new reflections on the politics of citizens within those bodies politic. That thought is the genesis of Chapters Three and Four.

As we understood more fully the utility of dialogue within bodies politic abroad, we began thinking about sustained dialogue within the U.S. body politic. Although my experience has concentrated heavily in far-off places, our limited experience to date suggests that the greatest arena for application of the process in the future is racial, ethnic and communal conflicts right here at home. As we move down that path, I see sustained dialogue as one of many vehicles that will be used in strengthening civil society, reducing tension and nourishing cohesion in American communities.

It is from the experience of this personal pilgrimage in the company of countless fellow pilgrims that I invite readers to consider the process of sustained dialogue as an approach to dealing with the deep-rooted conflicts they face. The world desperately needs our combined efforts.

Harold H. Saunders
Washington, D.C.

Introduction

The Challenges of Conflict and Peace in the Citizens' Century

CITIZENS FACING TENSION AND CONFLICT

In 1972, a group of citizens in a Southern U.S. city formed an organization to improve race relations. In 1994, one of its officers reflected to me that, after two decades, a number of integrated civic committees had done much good work, close working relationships had been formed and trust had been built, but that, "in fundamental ways, the underlying relationships between the races have changed little." She concluded: "I guess we followed a strategy of doing the work together but not talking about the deeper relationships."[1]

A 1996 article in a U.S. weekly news magazine told the story of a rash of fires directed at the black community in Greenville, Texas:

> Like many towns of the New South, Greenville believed it had paved over the racial fissures that once divided its citizens. Whites hoped blacks had forgotten the sign that once spanned the city's main street: "GREENVILLE. THE BLACKEST SOIL. THE WHITEST PEOPLE." Blacks thought some integration meant whites had accepted them as equals. The fires have replaced those dreams.
>
> That's probably because racism was never buried very deep. The locals still talk about the white mob who burned a black man to death on the town square in 1908. When a sign hangs over your town proclaiming it home to the "whitest people," it's hard to forget even ancient atrocities.[2]

Good as the work of integrated civic committees in that Southern city was, they moved from brief talk to action without deeper reflection. The experience of community after community in the United States is that citizens either meet, talk superficially and jump to action—without stopping long enough to talk deeply about their underlying values, purposes and relationships—or they do not talk at all about those subjects. Americans as well as citizens in some newly independent countries are impatient to get results and reluctant to pause for a time of reflection about what they are really doing. Others simply shy away from talking about painful issues.

A different approach is possible. In Baton Rouge, Louisiana, the board of the Federation of Churches and Synagogues decided in early 1995 that the time had come to explore the possibilities of a deeper dialogue between the races. They learned of the process of sustained dialogue described in this book and, after exploratory talks with potential participants, began the sustained dialogue described in Chapter Eight. The focus was on how racism works in the daily lives of people.

In Syracuse, New York, a group of new immigrants from four Southeast Asian ethnic groups, second-generation Americans from several European countries and representatives of several Native American tribes came together in 1996 in sustained dialogue to improve ethnic relationships in a declining neighborhood. Through improved relationships, they hoped to make their neighborhood a happier and more upbeat place to live.

In Rapid City, South Dakota, a dialogue gradually took shape in 1998 among Native Americans and members of the area's racial majority. They have begun tackling some of the United States' most painful and deeply rooted relationships.

These groups are probing what happens in the space between them as they interact and how to change the interactions that burden their relationships with suspicion, contempt, mistrust, fear, hate and indignity. They are focusing on their relationships—the processes of continuous interaction among them. They are learning how to change those relationships.

In faraway countries, too, groups have come together in the middle of civil war, in the alienation and violence of deep-rooted intercommunal conflict and in the tense postconflict periods of attempting reconciliation and growing the sinews of cohesive and productive states. The change in the Franco-German relationship after World War II began, first, at the level of human reconciliation and only then was embedded in the new structures of the budding European community. As recounted in Chapter Nine, change in the Israeli-Palestinian relationship that began in countless dialogues—largely among citizens outside government—was first reflected in cooperative actions in the civil society; only after a decade and a half was that change reflected in official positions, declarations and agreements.

Each experience is unique, but the capacity of human beings to talk in depth with purpose about their relationships, while rarely developed with ease, seems available in most cultures to move from violence to workable peaceful relationships. How to channel that capacity through systematic and sustained dialogue is the subject of this book.

Unless citizens engage in this work, peace will have little chance. Human beings the world over cry out to end violent conflict and to build the practices, processes and structures of peace so they can live in safety, overcome poverty, bury discrimination and find dignity. Their starting point must be the formation of peaceful relationships among citizens who have to work together if they are to achieve those ends.

CITIZENS PREPARING FOR THE CITIZENS' CENTURY: THE AUDIENCE

This is a book for all who would engage as citizens in the works of peace— large and small. It is for all who believe that we must find a better way of conducting the affairs of humankind.

This book is written, first, for citizens outside government who want to build those peaceful relationships—whether in far-off countries or in nearby cities. It is written for citizens of various races, ethnic backgrounds and religious faiths whose differences have led to deep divisiveness, tension and even violence within or between their communities. It is written for those whose organizations are deeply troubled for human reasons and for citizens trapped by vicious civil war. It is written for citizens who are ready to reach out and transform relationships they can no longer tolerate, for citizens who say: "Enough! This situation can't go on any longer!"

This book is written, second, for the practitioners and scholars who develop, test and refine the instruments of peacemaking and peace-building that citizens use whether in their communities or between groups in conflict. Diplomacy, negotiation and mediation—the formal instruments of states, governments and officials—have been analyzed in depth. This book takes two steps beyond that traditional ground onto the ground where citizens do their work. As a first step, it presents a process of sustained dialogue among citizens outside government for transforming deep-rooted conflictual relationships that are not ready for formal negotiation and mediation. Next, it addresses the need to restore or create the sinews within society that have been torn apart by conflict but are necessary to the cohesion of a civil society and to the peaceful resolution of differences among citizens. This will be the work of citizens in the coming era and of the scholars and practitioners who are helping them develop the instruments they need.

This book is written, third, for citizens in government—among whom I have also served—who need to recognize that there are some things that governments do not do well; they need partners. As I often said to my colleagues in the State Department: "Your job is not just to make policy for the United States government but to make policy for the United States of America. If you saw your job this way you could turn loose a multitude of resources in the nongovernmental sector that could work in complementary ways with government to produce an imaginative and powerful policy for our whole country." The same is true at any level: Only human beings can change human relationships.

This book is written, fourth, for scholars of conflict resolution, political science and international relations, who are responsible for helping the next generations grind the lenses they will use to bring a very different world into focus. Perhaps they have the most difficult challenge of all: They have to redefine academic disciplines that have been engraved in stone over the past century. Many of them seem to believe that their careers depend on their adhering to the criteria of a passing era. Their rewards—appointment, tenure, salaries—often depend on not moving beyond traditional standards to chart really new ground. Some in the natural sciences, such as the molecular biologists, have had to redefine their disciplines so as to respond to new problems and opportunities. Most in the social sciences have yet to respond comparably to the fact that 350 years of the nation-state and concentration on institutional politics are giving way to what may well be called the "citizens' century."

In short, this book attempts to bring together in one framework the main elements of what we know about transforming deep-rooted human conflicts through sustained dialogue, whether at the national or at the community level. Others have written eloquently about particular parts of the process and about their approaches. I hope all of them will find a place here for their perspectives. More important, I hope citizens will find here encouragement and help as they face tension and conflict.

CITIZENS MAKING AND BUILDING PEACE: THE HUMAN DIMENSION

Only human beings can transform hostility into relationships of peace. There is a human dimension to starting and ending conflict, and building peace is also a human—not just an institutional—task. Conflict is not just a clash among institutions, as it has often been depicted traditionally, nor is peace made by governments alone.

The critical element is human beings in relationship—citizens in government and citizens outside government in the associations *they* create to do the work *they* need to do. Some of those relationships are constructive; others are destructive. By probing the relationships that fuel conflict, human beings can change them in ways that generate the capacities and relationships needed to build a peaceful society.

Profound change in our world—the beginning of a new era—compels us to go beyond traditional approaches to focus on this human dimension. We are in the throes of two simultaneous revolutions of historic proportions. Both shift attention from states, their governments and institutional politics to the key role of citizens outside government as political actors.

The more immediately visible of the two is the next wave in the democratic revolution that began in earnest more than three centuries ago with early attempts to limit the powers of the state by enhancing the power of citizens. The first steps toward parliamentary government in Britain, the steady growth of civil society in the American Colonies, the American Revolution and the Constitution of the United States with its Bill of Rights followed by the French Revolution dramatized the early steps along this path. The fall of authoritarian and totalitarian governments in the late 1980s and early 1990s opened a new chapter in this story, as citizens in far-flung countries turned to the institutions of democracy. In the United States, citizens' deepening lack of confidence in both their governmental and their nongovernmental institutions has triggered new thinking about the role of citizens in the practice of American politics.

The second revolution is the stunning acceleration of interdependence that now marks the interaction among whole countries, not just governments. Against a background of 350 years of seeing the nation-state as the organizing unit of international life, we now recognize that states and their governments are not the only—sometimes not even the primary—actors in international life. Through their associations, citizens outside government play decisive roles. Whole bodies politic—governments *and* the civil societies citizens build—interact across permeable borders. Instead of the linear progression of actions and reactions between governments, many elements of whole bodies politic are involved in a continuous process of interaction on different levels simultaneously.

The metaphor of the traditional view of interstate relations was the strategic chess game—your government makes a move, mine moves, yours moves—a rationally devised progression of steps. In contrast to that intergovernmental chess game, my metaphor for this multilevel process of interaction among countless interdependent elements is an inelegant one that stuck in my mind in 1980 when I headed the State Department's task force managing the Washington end of the Iran hostage crisis: a game of squash or racquetball with four players on a five-sided court with six balls in motion at the same time. It was a rapidly changing process with new events coming at us from all directions almost at the same time. That remains my image for capturing the continuous multiple interactions of whole human beings in whole bodies politic. The same multilevel interactions characterize life in communities.

Both revolutions throw the spotlight on the citizen—on the human, rather than only on the institutional, dimension of politics. They throw the spotlight on the citizen as a whole human being—not just on the citizen as a rational actor seeking her or his own advantage in a political-science or an economic model. This must be the focus in the new century.

States, governments and their institutions will continue to play the essential role they are constituted to play. But, after centuries of states and their leaders at all levels pursuing their own interests—enhancing their own power, seeking personal economic gain, building empires, trying to solve social problems, even committing genocide—and at the end of one of the deadliest centuries in history, citizens are disillusioned with government and are reenergized to curb the power of states. They recognize that the instruments of state, by themselves, are not adequate for fully effective governance; they can even be vicious and dangerous. Until the human dimension is fully added to the equation of governance, the world will not have the complete array of instruments it needs to end conflict and build peace.

There will always be some jobs that only states and their governments can do, but only citizens outside government who are positively motivated can change conflictual human relationships or build civil society. Those citizens need their own tools for those tasks. The purpose of this book is to help them fashion those tools.

CITIZENS HAVE POWER TO TRANSFORM CONFLICTUAL RELATIONSHIPS

If citizens are critical to making and building peace, how do they go about this work? How do they generate the capacity to change the course of events? What is their power? Citizens do have power, but they need to learn how to generate and use it.

This book presents a process of sustained dialogue in which citizens can explore answers to those questions. Citizens talking in depth together can become a microcosm of their communities, experiencing a change in relationships and then learning to design political actions and interactions that can change their larger bodies politic. I call them a "mind at work in the center of a community or country transforming itself."

Citizens' power to change conflictual relationships increases markedly when they learn to put themselves into the equation of governance by taking two conceptual leaps:

- The first is to broaden thinking about conflict and its resolution from a primary concentration on governments and institutions to focus on the human roots of conflict and on the overall relationships among groups of human beings like themselves in conflict—the dynamic political process of continuous interaction among them. It is in that human process, not in the official negotiating room, that conflictual relationships change. Relationships themselves are a dynamic process of continuous interaction among human beings functioning simultaneously at many levels.

- The second leap is to see politics not only as what institutions do, but also as what happens when human beings organize themselves to solve their own problems. It is to focus on the civil society they create as they interact. By focusing on the role of the citizen as an actor in the politics of that process of continuous interaction, we open a boundless source of imagination and instruments to change conflictual relationships.

In both cases, unleashing human capacity in the process of continuous interaction mines a resource not yet fully brought to bear on ending conflict and building peace.

The force of this wider perspective rises partly from the breadth of the human experiences that shape it—from countless communities in the Americas from Canada and the United States to Argentina and Chile, to the racial struggles of South Africa and the tribal and cultural violence elsewhere in Africa, to the intercommunal violence between Israelis and Palestinians, to the civil wars in Tajikistan and Georgia, to the interstate conflicts between Armenia and Azerbaijan or India and Pakistan, to the intercultural tensions within the East-Central European and Baltic states.

The lesson from experience in these far-flung places is clear: Governments face problems they cannot deal with alone, and citizens outside government have the potential to develop an array of capacities to deal creatively with the problems human beings confront. (It is worth noting that the word "potential" comes from a Latin word connoting power.) They even have as one of their instruments the potential—the often unrealized power—to reform government. Governments and citizens together must ultimately forge new partnerships, but that will be possible only as each strengthens and refines its own capacities.

The day when the potential of citizens is fully added to the equation of governance may still be far off. It certainly is not a widespread reality today. It is a possibility. But, given the fact that governments are overburdened—in many cases, to the point of paralysis or breakdown—we would be irresponsible not to focus on how citizens outside government can do their share in dealing with problems that, in the end, are theirs.

I began this as a book about conflict and changing conflictual relationships both between and within bodies politic—whether triggered by state leaders marshaling historic antagonisms between peoples, by citizens in revolt against repressive governments or by citizens in silent standoffs that block communities from solving their problems. That is still its focus. But, as my colleagues and I walked a distance down that road, we came to an intersection. Entering that intersection from another road were citizens concerned with going beyond the cessation of hostilities to rejuvenate or rebuild civil society. We welcomed them and have made common cause with them because we have learned in countless hours of dialogue that people cannot change conflictual relationships without hope that their lives afterward can be better than before. Ending violence is an essential step, but a peaceful society will not function until the sinews that bind it together across natural divisions are in place and healthy. It is in the work of ending conflict and building peaceful relationships in civil society that citizens create and learn to use the power they can generate.

I write at the end of a century of world war, unprecedented genocide, weapons of mass destruction; a century of Joseph Stalin, Adolf Hitler, Pol Pot, Saddam Hussein, Slobodan Milosevic; a century in which innocent people by the millions have been slaughtered. I am also aware of the inhumanity of one citizen to another. I have no illusions. But I write in the conviction born of personal experience that there *is* a better way to conduct the affairs of humankind and that this better way must be fashioned, in significant part, by citizens outside government in the hope that those inside government will follow their lead. To do that, citizens must come to know the power that they can create.

A PUBLIC PEACE PROCESS: THE CITIZENS' INSTRUMENT

This book lays out a political process that citizens outside government can use to generate the power to change conflictual relationships into relationships with the capacity to build peace. It places in political context and defines "a public peace process"—a process built around sustained dialogue in which citizens can create the power to change their communities, their countries or their regions.

A public peace process[3] is a sustained political process through which citizens outside government come together in dialogue to design steps for changing conflictual relationships in ways that create the capacities to build the practices, processes and structures of peace. The longer-term goal is to immunize the society against the recurrence of violence. As an instrument of citizens outside government, the public peace process stands apart from the formal mediation and negotiation of governments and, at its best, can complement, support or even energize the official peace process.

The idea of a peace process seems to have originated in governmental peacemaking, but citizens outside government have gradually taken their place on the stage. We must now think of a multilevel peace process involving officials and their negotiations *and* citizens and their dialogues in civil societies, where citizens develop the relationships, the practices and the processes of peaceful societies.

Those of us who flew on U.S. Secretary of State Henry Kissinger's diplomatic shuttles in the wake of the 1973 Arab-Israeli War first named what we were engaged in "the negotiating process." The strategy behind Kissinger's mediation of three interim agreements between Egypt and Israel and Israel and Syria in 1974 and 1975 was to build one agreement on another to generate a spreading sense that peace was possible. Soon, we realized that our name for that process was too narrow. We were really helping produce a series of mediated agreements embedded in a larger political process. It was in that larger political process that countless interactions—direct and indirect—took place. It was in that larger political process that relationships changed. We began calling that whole process "the peace process"—a political process of interaction on many levels to transform conflictual relationships.

Citizens early became a part of that peace process. In the years since, the official peace process in the Arab-Israeli arena has continued. Signing one agreement after another, governments have continued to change the public's sense of the possibilities of peace. But we have also seen a proliferation of dialogues among citizens outside government. Meeting in countless places for numberless human reasons, citizens from both sides have come to see each other as human beings, have found common ground and have decided to risk living at peace. In the words of one Israeli, such meetings created "a critical mass" of people in the Arab—especially Palestinian—and Israeli bodies politic who eventually gave their political authorities permission to try peace. Despite the inevitable ups and downs in the process, no one can say that nothing has changed since 1973. Citizens have played a critical, if hard to define, role in generating profound change.

Through those years also, American and Soviet citizens were locked together in the Cold War. In 1959, President Dwight Eisenhower asked Norman Cousins, then editor of the *Saturday Review,* to start a dialogue between Soviet and U.S. citizens so there would be a channel of communication between the nuclear superpowers when government relations soured. These Soviet and U.S. citizens first met in 1960 at Dartmouth College in Hanover, New Hampshire, the place from which the Dartmouth Conference took its name. Over the next three decades until 1990, that ongoing dialogue met in plenary session 17 times and in task forces on more than 40 occasions. We learned only in 1993 that Soviet Communist Party Chairman Nikita Khrushchev had approved Soviet participation in 1960.[4] When Mikhail Gorbachev began to change the Soviet system after 1985, most of the speeches and articles that came to make up "the new political thinking" were written by Soviet citizens who had participated in the Dartmouth Conference and a handful of other such dialogues.

Thus, systematic dialogue among citizens outside government on the relationship between countries goes back at least to the late 1950s, its importance sometimes sanctioned, encouraged and even generated by heads of state who realized the limitations of governments acting alone. As President Eisenhower said in 1959 on British television: "I like to believe that people, in the long run, are going to do more to promote peace than our governments. Indeed, I think that people want peace so much that one of these days governments had better get out of their way and let them have it."[5]

Gradually over those years, a small number of scholar-practitioners developed systematic processes of dialogue among citizens.[6] They experimented with different emphases and approaches in workshops with Israelis and Egyptians, Israelis and Palestinians, Lebanese, factions in Northern Ireland, British and Argentineans, Greek and Turkish Cypriots, Indians and Pakistanis, Armenians and Azerbaijanis, Tajikistanis, citizens and Russian-speakers in the Baltic states, Americans and Chinese and ethnic groups in American cities. Working to understand more fully the dynamics of deep-rooted human conflicts, these practitioners have developed tools for changing conflictual relationships through dialogue among citizens. In one workshop after another, by means of intensive interaction, they have led participants to insights into their conflicts that paved the way for changing their relationships.

Each practitioner applied her or his own name to the various approaches developed—interactive problem-solving workshops, psychopolitical workshops, track-two diplomacy, supplemental diplomacy, multitrack diplomacy, interactive conflict resolution.[7] In 1991, I came to call this work of citizens "a public peace process." Intending no judgment on others' terminology, I wanted a name that clearly identified the actors as citizens outside government ("public" as contrasted to "diplomatic") and emphasized the political work of citizens under the umbrella of a comprehensive multilevel peace process.

The important point is that this work by citizens have its own name. For centuries, scholars and public servants have studied the channels and instruments through which states and their governments work—force, diplomacy, mediation, negotiation, economic sanctions and incentives. The process through which citizens outside government do *their* political work must be dignified by its own name, as well as by serious study. Because the world now depends on citizens more and more, citizens need to know how to develop and use their capacities most effectively, and governments need to know how to help citizens as much as citizens need to know how to help governments.

The public peace process brings the human dimension into thinking about how citizens outside government can prevent or end violence in ways that lead to building peaceful societies. This is the work that former U. N. Secretary General Boutros Boutros-Ghali called "post-conflict peace-building."[8] This work of building peace is the second crucial element in the public peace process after ending violence.

Focus on building civil society has been the contribution of other pioneers in the political realm who, since the 1960s, became concerned with excessive reliance on governments to do what citizens outside government themselves must do. These practitioners began working with citizens and communities to enlarge their capacities to solve their problems. In the United States, much of the recent energy and experience was generated, first, in the civil-rights movement of the 1960s and in the protest against the Vietnam War. The disillusionment with big government in the United States was born partly of the same experiences and was reinforced by the Watergate debacle in the 1970s. As the Vietnam War wound down and Americans seemed to retreat within themselves, some Americans worked to perpetuate the spirit and experience of citizen capacity that they had known and believed was essential to reviving democracy.

When authoritarian and totalitarian governments elsewhere in the world began giving way to democratic pressures in the late 1980s, citizens of those countries began looking for ways to educate citizens as political actors. They quickly realized that simply voting for a democratic government would not solve their problems—that working democracy depends on an active citizenry. They began studying and amplifying the work on civil society that had been launched by their experiences.

It is worth taking a moment at this early point to define "civil society." It refers to that area of life and work between personal and family relationships on the one hand and government on the other—the public area in which citizens outside government do their work. It is the arena in which the associations citizens form and many less formal nongovernmental organizations work.[9] In contrast, states are legal entities that exercise sovereign power within defined borders and conduct formal relations with other such bodies; governments are the executive institutions through which the powers of the state are exercised.

It may also be useful to distinguish "civil society" from some other common terms. When the U. N. Charter was written at the end of World War II, "nations" referred to the population defined by habitation within a state—the "nation-state." At the end of the twentieth century, "nation" often referred to a "people" defined by a distinctive language, culture and historical experience, as in the phrase "national self-determination." I have chosen to use "state" for the formal entity in its traditional legal sense and "country" for the land, the totality of the population, the society and the economy within the boundaries of a state and under the authority of its government. "Public," in my vocabulary, refers to the citizenry outside government. "Body politic" includes the government, the civil society and the processes of interaction between them—the totality of citizens within government and citizens outside government.

This attention to the politics of citizens is essential to transforming violent relationships into the relationships necessary for building peaceful societies. It deepens the reservoir of insights from which those engaged in the "public peace process" can draw. That process can be organized by citizens.

AT THE HEART OF A PUBLIC PEACE PROCESS: SUSTAINED DIALOGUE

At the heart of the public peace process is "sustained dialogue"—a systematic, prolonged dialogue among small groups of representative citizens committed to changing conflictual relationships, ending conflict and building peace. It is more structured than a good conversation; it is less structured than formal mediation or negotiation. It has purpose, destination and product. As a microcosm of their bodies politic, participants absorb events in the communities around them and together learn to design ways to change the relationships that cause conflict. The five-stage process that I call "sustained dialogue" is described in Chapter Six of this book.

The deep-rooted ethnic, racial and religious tensions and conflicts between and within states that demand the world's attention on the eve of the twenty-first century are normally not ready for the solutions of institutional politics—formal mediation, negotiation, elections or referenda. They require an approach that probes the human roots of conflict and changes relationships in enduring ways. They require a conceptual approach that draws on insights from a broad range of disciplines.

This book lays out a framework large enough to invite voices from many experiences and academic fields. Work on how relationships between states are changing must converge with the study of community politics and civil society. Work that has focused on conflict between states needs to blend with the study of conflict within communities. Work that has focused on resolving conflict needs to meld with insights into developing democratic thought and practice and building civil society. Work on the behavior of groups needs to be set alongside study of state behavior. Work on the processes of continuous interaction within and between groups needs to be developed further, along with studies of institutional decision making.

This is a book about whole human beings in whole bodies politic. One of my aims is to break loose from the fetters of disciplines that have become too narrow to be helpful in our rapidly changing world.

The method of sustained dialogue presented here goes beyond traditional approaches to conflict. Formal negotiation and mediation will remain important in the eventual resolution of conflict at official levels, but a larger political approach often needs to precede, undergird or follow these traditional methods. People in the many conflicts that proliferate today, who are often not ready for formal negotiation and mediation, can, however, talk about their differences in systematic dialogue, even with adversaries. When they do, they are acting as human beings—citizens—working together in the political arena outside government to determine whether destructive relationships can be changed. This book attempts to strengthen their capacity to perform this public task in the political arena.

Because many of today's conflicts—both between and within countries—seem beyond the reach of governments, the world now urgently needs additional ways of moving them toward peace. The moment has come to consolidate the extensive developmental work in dialogue that has been done by scholar-practitioners and citizens and to build a comprehensive framework from those foundations. With great respect for the pioneers in this work, I have written this book as a contribution to a comprehensive strategy for citizens outside government to use in trying to end destructive conflicts and to build the structures of peace.

I am not urging everyone into a single framework. On the contrary, I recognize the richness of each approach. But, in my view, no approach will achieve its full potential to change conflictual relationships or to build peace if it does not generate in citizens outside government the capacity to act in the political arena where government is not able to act. That requires serious attention to the capacities of human beings to act politically in the human sense of that word.

In the United States, practitioners in community politics focus on the concept of "public space."[10] This is safe space—both literal and psychological—that citizens create apart from government. It is defined more by what happens there than by the specific physical location. It is defined by the interactions that take place there. It is space in which citizens express what they value in their communities, interact in deliberating on hard choices among options for changing their communities and work together to devise ways to achieve important goals despite their differences. It is space in which citizens build their own associations to accomplish their work. These are organizations that go beyond the family but are not governmental; they are part of the civil society; they are "public."

In that context, sustained dialogue is one of the instruments of citizens in a safe public space who are going about the difficult work of changing conflictual relationships and designing peaceful ones. It is in public space that public peace processes are born and nourished. In these dialogues, the groundwork for long-lasting, participatory institutions can be laid. Once relationships are changed in that space, a minimum level of trust is established, thus promoting increased capacity and willingness to act together in new relationships in joint problem solving.

The public peace process—with sustained dialogue at its heart—is a process through which citizens outside government can move from recognition that a conflict is intolerable through designing and implementing steps in the political arena to move parties from conflict to peace. It is a process for moving from a sharply fragmented society to a civil society within which people connect with each other in new relationships to resolve their differences peacefully.

A RESPONSE TO THOSE WHO RESIST THE PUBLIC PEACE PROCESS

Some colleagues will resist my adding a focus on the human roots of conflict or citizens' politics to the study of either domestic or international conflict. They will say that citizens are powerless to deal with such conflict or that citizens are apathetic, indifferent or incapable of mastering the problems in multi-issue conflict. Traditionally, conflict has been considered the exclusive domain of interior and foreign ministries or university departments of law, political science and international relations.

In today's world, many conflicts cannot be understood without reference to the human beings fueling them, and many governments have either been unable to deal with deep-rooted human conflict or have collapsed in the face of it. Often, the problem is not that citizens are not engaged but that they get their minds around issues in ways that are different from the reasoning of officials and experts. Citizens may instinctively have a fuller capacity acting as whole human beings to work with ambiguous and complex situations than experts who dissect and fragment the elements of those situations to simplify analysis. Citizens find authenticity in experience; experts often seek it in "scientific research." Citizens take an organic view of life's complex interactions, while experts often single out specific issues for isolated study.[11] An essential part of our task is to change our conceptual lenses so all of us can begin acting more effectively. Changing those lenses may be the most difficult task.

I do not argue in this book that the role of the government is necessarily diminished, but only that government is not the sole actor—or even the most effective actor in particular circumstances. Having been privileged to work in the U. S. government in one of its most creative moments—the Kissinger shuttles and the Camp David accords—I would still argue that theories that focus on the state as the only actor deprive both governments and citizens of powerful instruments for dealing with conflicts or building peace. When theory so obviously fails to lead to effective action, it is time to consider whether new perspectives might be helpful. One reason the Arab-Israeli peace process worked as well as it did in the 1970s, I would argue, is that it reflected at least instinctively the beginning of a larger conceptual framework.

Other colleagues may object to my emphasis on the process of interaction—on overall relationships—among whole groups. One outstanding social psychologist once wrote on a chapter I had drafted using the idea of an overall Soviet-U.S. relationship: "I've paid you the ultimate compliment of assigning your paper to my graduate students. But I'm still not convinced." Because I respected his work so much, I told him I really wanted to understand what was unconvincing. "I think your focus on relationship is right on target," he replied. "But I can't figure out how to fit it into a social science research design. It's too complex." That is my point: To work effectively in the world that is becoming, we must move beyond traditional academic disciplines and bureaucratic departments.

Still other colleagues will object to my bringing perspectives on domestic and international politics together in the same book. Starting from an international base, I have sat in countless dialogues with people in both domestic and international conflicts. I have learned that it is often not possible to end a conflict, whether within or between states, until those in conflict decide what kind of relationship they want and need as they build their futures. As they begin talking about what kind of region, country or community they want, without meaning to they have become one of the early associations of a new civil society—intranational or international. They are using the instruments of politics to move from conflict to peace.

Even in established democracies, the shared meanings that once undergirded relatively coherent national identities have fragmented to some degree and in some sectors. That fragmentation undermines the role that even materially powerful countries can play in the international community.

The United States, for instance, has its own racial and ethnic tensions that periodically erupt in violence. Much as Americans avoid the subject, the United States also continues to experience the deepening of class fault lines. The influx of Asian and Hispanic immigrants and the increasing activism of Native Americans have added other ingredients to the mix. And Americans continue to struggle to create equitable, productive and personally satisfying new relationships between men and women. Until Americans discover their identity that is taking shape and define a coherent purpose in the world for the people and the government of the United States together, the quality and strength of U.S. leadership will be in question.

"Along with other observers of American life, I am troubled by the growing power of the forces dividing Americans from one another, fragmenting our culture, causing us to grow apart," writes Daniel Yankelovich, one of the United States' leading analysts, tracking social, political and economic forces and measuring shifts in people's values and beliefs. "[T]o a surprising extent a certain kind of dialogue can counterbalance the worst effects of the isolation and fragmentation that threaten to overwhelm us. It can create better understanding among people with divergent views, help to overcome the mistrust that increasingly separates Americans from their institutions (e.g., government, business, the media, educators), connect cultural, professional and business interests, bring leaders and their constituents closer together, and create new possibilities in personal relationships and community."[12]

This book, therefore, draws both from institutional and human and from intrastate and international experience with the purpose of opening the door to a new marriage of insights into the politics of changing conflictual relationships and building peace. The public peace process must be both the engine and the product of that marriage.

SOME COMMENTS ON WHAT FOLLOWS

Focusing on how citizens outside government can act effectively to do the work that only they can do, this book has two purposes. The first is to put into their hands a practical instrument for changing conflictual relationships within their civil societies, for changing the course of the larger body politic by their own peaceful means and for creating the shared meaning that must undergird a coherent body politic. The second is to put citizens outside government in a position to play the role of full partner with governments when complementary action is necessary. My aim is to provide them with the tools to play that role so competently that they can even compel governments to work with them when necessary.

With those purposes in mind, the book falls informally into two parts. Chapters One through Four suggest how changes in our thinking about conflictual relationships, citizens' politics, international relations and peace all shine a spotlight on the human dimension of conflict, its prevention and its resolution. Chapters Five through Ten present the process of sustained dialogue as the public peace process—how dialogue differs from normal political debate; how a dialogue develops; three stories of dialogue changing relationships; and how one judges the effectiveness of the public peace process. The Epilogue suggests that sustained dialogue taught in American—and other—schools could become one vehicle for transforming our fragmented, confrontational and self-centered society. Young citizens could experience the power for good that comes from relationships among diverse peoples with a coherence of purpose that can grow in dialogue.

Chapter One

~~~~

The Peace Process: A Conceptual Framework

A Larger Conceptual Framework for the Citizens' Century

Helping citizens transform conflictual relationships into relationships that can end violence and build peace requires a larger conceptual framework than those commonly in use as the twentieth century closes. It requires a dynamic framework that reaches well beyond present academic or bureaucratic compartments to embrace whole human beings as political actors in whole bodies politic that are continuously in flux. It requires a framework large enough to bring together insight into both ending deep-rooted human conflict and building the political practices, processes and structures of peace—whether within or between bodies politic. As the next three chapters show, cutting-edge thinking about conflict, politics and international relationships in our changing world is opening the door to a larger approach to making and building peace.

The framework presented in this book is "the peace process"—a multi-level political process that involves people at all levels of the body politic. Within that process, the official and the public levels of the peace process, as well as governmental political institutions and citizens' groups in the civil society, all interact continuously.

As described in the Introduction, the name "peace process" seems to have been born in the early 1970s in a series of officially mediated Arab-Israeli agreements embedded in a larger political process. Most writing on the Arab-Israeli peace process and other such peacemaking efforts has focused on formal mediation and negotiation at the official level. I myself in the mid-1980s conceptualized the Arab-Israeli peace process from the experience of a former official participant, concentrating on actions of governments to remove the human, as well as the practical, obstacles to peace. Now, with the benefit of intensive further experience outside government with human beings in conflict, I focus this book on the larger political process that surrounds official talks and actions.[1]

Why is a conceptual framework important? How people define critical concepts and their worldview begins to direct how they act. Concepts such as power, interests, citizen, body politic, relationship and civil society are important because they are the lenses that people use to bring the world into focus—to give events meaning. They shape the tools citizens use to act. Since the seventeenth century, the prevailing concepts have been defined mainly in terms of states, governments and institutional politics. If citizens outside government are to play the role they must play in "the citizens' century," they need their own conceptual lenses suitable for today's world.

Traditionally, "power," for instance, was defined in narrow, largely material terms as the ability to force someone or a group to do what he, she or it does not want to do. In the U.S. civil-rights movement of the 1960s, in the largely unarmed Palestinian uprising against Israeli occupation in the late 1980s and early 1990s and in East-Central Europe in 1989, however, citizens with little material power changed the course of history. Their actions suggested that we might appropriately redefine power as the capacity to change the course of events. Citizens outside government can generate such power when they connect with other citizens in associations to combine a wide range of political capacities and influences. But they need to understand power in a way that makes it accessible to them. They need to understand that the relationships they form generate the power they need to achieve their objectives.

Citizens, practitioners and scholars all need a larger framework that includes the fullest possible range of actors and instruments that can interact to produce change. No one actor alone can make and sustain peace today. We can no longer think only of what states do to each other. We now see relationships among states and groups as a political process of continuous interaction between whole bodies politic. That includes citizens outside government as well as in government. Only when they see themselves in the largest possible framework can citizens act with full capacity to change the course of a body politic.

Where does a conceptual framework come from? In its most powerful and practical forms, it is a mix of experience and concepts pragmatically—not theoretically—defined. It is a conceptualization of experience.

My framework has evolved as I found myself at a juncture of experiences and academic disciplines that are not normally brought together. These are described in Chapters Two, Three and Four. I find that only by bringing together insights from a broad range of disciplines and experiences can we explain the changing world in which we try to reach our goals. Only such a convergence of insights can produce conceptual lenses wide-angled enough to see the citizen as a whole human being—not just as voter, officeholder, taxpayer, consumer of government services or statistic in opinion polls.

I arrived at the framework presented here by traversing my own path. It is not so important that others buy my framework as it is that they have one that reflects their own experience.

THE ROOTS OF A FRAMEWORK FOR CITIZENS

The conceptual framework presented here builds from the citizen up rather than from the state down because this dimension of the peace process has been widely neglected. Because this book seeks to fill that gap, its starting point is deep-rooted human conflict and the capacities of citizens to end it in ways that lay foundations for building peace. This approach is not intended to denigrate the necessary work of government but to add the capacities of citizens outside government to the overall work of making and building peace.

The world at the doorway to the twenty-first century is not dealing effectively with conflict. Yet, the conflicts that have erupted and proliferated will disrupt national and international peace and security for decades to come if the world does not learn how to deal with them. They threaten to undermine states—even the most advanced. They will block our goals of ending violence and pursuing the new international agenda of broadening respect for human rights and needs and establishing forms of governance that enable their fullest and fairest political expression within countries.

Why has the end-century world made such a poor start? It is not just that the Cold War ended so suddenly and unexpectedly—important as that was. More important, concepts such as state, power, politics, conflict and interests have not caught up with the nature of present conflicts or with the contexts within which they take place. Until we grind new conceptual lenses, we will continue to act ineffectually. That is why I have devoted the next three chapters to rethinking the key elements of our conceptual framework.

After a century marked by world wars among states, state genocide, the end of empires and the fragile balance of nuclear terror between superpowers, it is not surprising that we still see the world through state-focused lenses. Yet, much of the conflict that seizes our attention today is deep-rooted human conflict that takes place within states and communities and often reflects the breakdown of state and local authority.

The causes of these conflicts are numerous. Many explode not from competition between institutions over material goods; rather they are fueled by basic human needs. Although some intergroup conflicts that demand response are truly ethnic in motivation, the phrase "ethnic conflict" is not large enough to frame most of them. These conflicts are racial, religious, clan, tribal, regional, historic and class, as well as ethnic, in origin.

To understand these conflicts requires shifting focus from state action to how citizens outside government act and interact. Whatever their roots, these conflicts involve groups of human beings. Such conflicts do not necessarily respond to instruments of state, such as force, mediation, negotiation or elections. People do not negotiate about their identity, fears, personal security, historical grievances or other human needs. Their acceptance and security come not from government alone but from their relationships with other human beings as well. These fundamental relationships have to be changed.

Often, governments cannot solve intra- or international problems until citizens change their behavior or relationships. Historic wounds must be healed; misperceptions must be refocused; shared interests must be recognized alongside inevitable differences; in short, enemies must transform stereotypes into human beings with valid human claims. This work cannot be done in negotiating rooms or their antechambers.

Resolving these deep-rooted human conflicts, which include some conflicts between states, is not a task states perform well. Ending such conflicts requires looking not only to the machinery of government, but also to the civil society, in which citizens work to build the kind of society that will provide what they need. Neither officials nor theorists, for the most part, seem sensitive to what can be accomplished in civil society. It is there that human beings come together to pursue and protect what is valuable to them; it is there that they discover the power that emerges from acting in covenant with other citizens who value comparable goals.

By one definition, when citizens work together to solve problems that affect common interests or to reach shared goals, they act politically. When citizens act together across international borders to pursue shared interests, civil societies interact; they are engaged in international politics.

Among critical issues in civil society are these two: how groups that have different views and needs can form peaceful relationships and how they can build political processes within which to resolve their differences peacefully with regard for the interests of each. Dealing with conflict requires addressing the human roots of conflict while building the associations of civil society and the political structures in which power can be safely shared, differences resolved with mutual respect and peaceful relationships built.

Dangerous as interstate conflicts will always be, deep-rooted human conflicts embroil whole bodies politic when state authority is not yet established, has lost legitimacy or has been virtually swept away. Even when state authority exists, the absence of shared purpose among citizens can paralyze effective government action.

Scholars and practitioners are only beginning to consider the power that citizens outside government can create when they work together, for both constructive and destructive ends. It may be, in many circumstances, that a public peace process will have more impact than the attempted negotiations of official bodies. Which tools will be most useful will depend on circumstances, but the world clearly needs a larger tool kit than is available to those who focus only on states and their capacities and, thus, do not bring the human dimension into their analysis of conflict or its resolution.

At the same time, governments have agreed, through such international documents as the U.N. Charter and the Helsinki Final Act,[2] that the rights of human beings within states are the proper concern of the family of nations. But these governments have barely begun to address how the community of states helps put a state back together after a conflict caused when a government abuses its people or when citizens tear a country apart from the inside and slaughter one another. International law has traditionally focused primarily on protecting the sovereignty of states, not the human beings within them. Traditional legal standards of international behavior have, for instance, underscored the unacceptability of military intervention or political interference in another country's internal affairs. While respecting those understandable principles, the international community needs to develop more fully effective ways of thinking and acting in the face of the frequent contradictions between a concern for protecting the sovereignty of states and a concern for protecting the rights of human beings within states.

Neither governments nor citizens outside government—even in the supposedly advanced democracies—have really begun to think in terms of whole bodies politic. They focus mainly on governments and on citizens as voters, *not* on different actors in a whole body politic, each doing what each is uniquely qualified to do.

In that context, neither governments nor citizens realize the capacities that partnership between them could generate. Mutual mistrust is strong. Sharing of strategies is minimal. Governments have not learned that the components of civil society may be better equipped than they are to deal with conflicts generated in the human arena. At the same time, citizens outside government need more systematic ways of connecting their efforts with political authority where that will increase effectiveness—or even overhauling government when that seems necessary. A comprehensive peace process involves all elements of the whole body politic.

Traditional thinking about conflict within states and their cities has focused on what government programs can do to prevent it or quell it. As citizens develop and conduct processes to change their own conflictual relationships and to build their own structures of peace in civil society, their challenge will be to weave into their scenarios the capacities that governments can uniquely bring to bear so that the resources of the whole body politic may be deployed in the common interest.

One of the central challenges addressed in this book is to bring human beings and their politics into the work of changing the conflictual relationships often responsible even for conflicts between states. Citizens alone may be able to begin changing those relationships in order to prevent or end conflict; governments alone may be able to embody those changes in reshaping official relations or government policies. Citizens alone can create the relationships that produce a strong civil society and provide the sinews of economic development—both essential to building a peaceful society not prone to violent conflict. Citizens in and out of government need to restructure their relationships so they can work together to create power for constructive change.

This book proceeds from the need to strengthen the capacities of citizens outside government to contribute, in their way, to ending violence and building societies more immune to its outbreak. The idea of a peace process offers a comprehensive diagnostic and operational framework for this work.

THE PEACE PROCESS IN A WHOLE BODY POLITIC

A conceptual framework is simply an aid to getting one's mind around a problem. It poses a systematic sequence of questions: What are the causes of, and relationships behind, this conflict? How can I approach this conflict given my resources? What specific steps can I take? Because it provides participants with a reservoir of concepts and methods, a conceptual framework helps deepen understanding of where change might be possible and how it might be brought about. The framework—the peace process—is laid out below; the concepts are fleshed out in the chapters that follow.

Thinking in terms of a peace process operating among groups in one body politic or operating between whole bodies politic permits one to devise an approach to conflict prevention, management and resolution in a particular situation. Only such a comprehensive framework is large enough to keep one's mind open to the complex factors involved in a conflict. Only such a framework allows practitioners to draw on the broadest reservoirs of insight and to choose the widest range of appropriate instruments.

The peace process fully conceived is a complex of interactions at different levels and in different arenas of one or more bodies politic designed to change conflictual relationships over time. No one person or group alone can manage such a complex process, but thinking in terms of the overall peace process can provide a framework for analyzing the roots of conflict and designing a variety of complementary steps that can gradually change the relationships that underlie the conflict. Then individual actors can implement whatever actions are possible for them. Keeping the whole process in mind enables each actor to find complementarity among actions wherever possible. It can also provide a context in which to judge what is missing from the process and what is being accomplished; Chapter Ten applies this framework to evaluating a sustained dialogue.

Shaping a peace process requires working through three successive interrelated frameworks: First is the "diagnostic, or analytical, framework," within which parties probe (1) the relationships underlying the conflict and its causes; (2) the dynamics of the conflict itself; and (3) the components of the body politic as they interact in the conflict and as they could play a role in its resolution. Second is a broad "strategic, or operational, framework," within which parties decide how, in large terms, they will tackle a conflict—how they will connect with a conflict given their resources. Third is a "tactical framework," within which parties choose a specific approach to some element of the conflict—targets and points of intervention, a method, a purpose and a plan for how the work could contribute to an overall movement toward peace. Following is a skeletal outline of the peace process.

The Diagnostic, or Analytical, Framework

Analysis of the conflict itself involves probing (1) the relationships and causes underlying it; (2) the dynamics of the interactions and its present stage of evolution; (3) the range of actors who might be involved in peacemaking; and (4) the societal context in which they operate.

The first step in diagnosis will be to ask: Who is doing what to whom and why? Behind the factual answers to those questions is this deeper question: What are the real relationships among the conflicting parties? Probing for the real *relationships* underlying a conflict identifies more precisely the parties to the conflict. Those relationships can be analyzed in terms of six elements that operate in any relationship: (1) identity, both physical and psychological; (2) interests, both material and human; (3) patterns of interaction, including communication; (4) power, both material and relational; (5) respect for others' limits; and (6) perceptions and misperceptions. Each of these can be used as a diagnostic tool for identifying *causes* of a conflict; each can open a window and a way into a relationship; each can be defined carefully enough to permit efforts to change interaction in that area. Understanding the complex mix of elements at work gives insight into the nature of the conflict and ways of addressing it. This concept of relationship is laid out more fully in Chapter Two.

To add the dimension of time, it is essential to recognize that most conflicts evolve through a dynamic that can be described in stages such as the following, in which: (1) because of unfulfilled needs and interests, a dispute is brewing; (2) parties who see little prospect of meeting their needs resort to violence as a last recourse; (3) eventually, violence leads to stalemate and an ultimate realization that neither party to the conflict can achieve what it needs through violence; (4) a de-escalation of violence begins and leads to efforts to end violence by agreement and to resolve the conflict on a broad and lasting basis; and (5) as parties to a conflict look toward agreement on fundamental issues, they begin working on building or rebuilding the society torn apart by the conflict. This framework for analyzing the dynamics of a conflict enlarges the traditional field of conflict resolution by adding this fifth period of rebuilding the connective tissue that enables citizens to work together when necessary across the natural lines of difference, dealing with those differences peacefully.

The analysis of the relationships underlying the conflict will have identified key actors in the conflict. As attention turns to ending the conflict, it is important to recognize the contribution of *potential* actors in a peace process. They may work in five arenas from across the whole body politic and among interested outside parties. In these arenas: (1) governments and international organizations pursue an *official process* of conflict resolution, often using forms of mediation and negotiation or economic or military pressures supplemented by official acts to generate public support; (2) groups outside government sometimes work in such close collaboration with government that they are really pursuing a *quasi-official process* (an example is the Oslo dialogue between Israelis and Palestinians that led to an agreement between the Israeli government and the Palestine Liberation Organization in 1993); (3) citizens outside government engage in what I call a *public peace process* that is unconstrained by official positions and may address both officials and the larger civil society; (4) citizens working in a wide array of associations in the *civil society* pursue actions designed to reconnect elements of the civil society that have been alienated and fragmented by the conflict so as to restore the connective tissue necessary to bridge the normal divisions and reestablish a functioning society; and (5) actors from *outside the immediate area of conflict* reflect interests and capacity for intervention in a larger national, regional or international context.

Since this book focuses on citizens outside government in the public peace process, a fuller comment is desirable on one of their contributions to building peace: strengthening civil society to build peace. A functioning society includes a variety of associations and informal relationships that connect people across the divisions that characterize any body politic. An intrastate conflict often severs these connections and drives people into their own groups of like-minded persons bound together in confrontation with adversaries. The connective tissue, the sinews, the ligaments that made a whole body politic work are torn apart. Mediators may negotiate the terms for ending violence, but they rarely pay attention to reconnecting the torn tissues that might help the body politic function again as a whole.

An analysis of what tissue needs to be reconstructed and approaches to restoring it is an essential part of peacemaking and peace-building. As parties to a conflict talk about what kind of peaceful society they want, the peace process offers a context large enough to include this essential area of work beyond the traditional scope of conflict resolution. The political processes and concepts behind building a peaceful civil society are dealt with more fully in Chapter Three.

Within this analytical framework, it is possible to determine the nature of a conflict and the particular points at which relationships may be most open to change. It is also possible to determine where and with what actors in the body politic it may be most useful to work.

The Strategic Framework

Strategy is the link between analysis and action. Using the comprehensive conceptual framework of the peace process for analysis of the relationships and dynamics at work within a body politic in conflict, each potential actor in a peace process designs an approach to the conflict. This requires choices about (1) what relationships might be changed; (2) how causes of the conflict might be defined and addressed with the protagonists; (3) what stage the conflict has reached and what constraints and opportunities that timing poses; (4) which protagonists the peacemaking effort will focus on and which other actors could complement planned peacemaking approaches; and (5) how to stitch the body politic together again. These choices will reflect judgments about how change can be effected and how specific instruments might produce that change. These choices add up to a strategy for addressing some part of the whole conflict.

A strategy for the overall peace process would include the broadest possible combination of efforts to address the full array of pathologies in the strife-torn body politic. Each party needs to define a particular approach to a part of the conflict that reflects its own interests and capacities, keeping in mind the potential interaction of that strategy with others.

A key element in designing a strategy is recognizing explicitly how success in that strategy would affect the overall movement from violence to peace. No one actor's strategy can achieve peace, but it is possible to say what each is intended to contribute. Often it is not possible to be precise at the beginning, but only to describe the initial steps with the understanding that midcourse adjustments will be made in the light of experience. Each conflict is unique, and such uncertainty will be the norm. Evaluation of such work is itself an unfolding process.

The Tactical Framework: The Internal Dynamics of a Process

Once a broad approach is defined, an actor will choose instruments that seem most likely to accomplish the chosen tasks. These will reflect the particular capacities of the actor.

Instruments of Intervention

Different instruments of intervention are appropriate for addressing different problems and protagonists at different stages of the conflict and in different kinds of conflict. Military intervention is essential to peacekeeping and peace enforcement; formal mediation and negotiation are necessary to produce binding agreements between official authorities; forms of sustained dialogue may be the only useful approach for citizens outside government dealing with deep-rooted human conflicts; a quite different array of instruments will be appropriate to citizens outside government working to build the elements of civil society—nongovernmental organizations and spaces for resolving differences peacefully. One instrument may be useful at one stage and not at another or in one kind of conflict and not in another.

Stages of Intervention

Each method of intervention has its own stages and dynamics—movement through a sequence of steps or phases in addressing the elements of the conflict on which the instrument focuses. These stages provide one of the contexts for judging progress.

For instance, a peace process at the official level and a public process of sustained dialogue among citizens outside government may evolve through somewhat the same sequence, although each process will have its distinctive features. Chapter Six describes the five-stage process of sustained dialogue. Formal mediation and negotiation evolve through a comparable progression. The citizens' political process is laid out in Chapter Three. Other instruments—for instance, a sequence of training sessions on some aspect of conflict resolution designed to help two sides learn to work together—will have their own internal progression.

The advantage of a process laid out in stages is that it enables those managing the process to assess continually how the work is going and what needs to be addressed next. It is necessary, of course, to understand that these stages are not rigid and that participants will move back and forth among stages as they revisit earlier assumptions or tackle new problems.

This picture of the multilevel peace process may seem complicated. It is not intended to be applied in slavish detail. It makes the essential point that seeing the interactions among the full range of key actors and levels in a body politic opens the door to previously untapped resources for changing conflictual relationships. What is important is the process itself—the potential that lies in the continuous mutually reinforcing interactions and the power that can be generated from them. The idea of a peace process is more important than the details, necessary as they are.

A BRIDGING WORD

With this framework of the peace process in mind, the next three chapters fill the reservoir of concepts essential to conducting the public peace process. My purpose is to provide participants in sustained dialogue a sense that relationships and communities *can* be changed and to make available a range of ideas about how such change can be accomplished by citizens working within the political processes through which they interact.

Chapter Two

Changing Conflictual Relationships

RELATIONSHIPS—NOT JUST INTERESTS AND ISSUES

In seeking peace, governments negotiate around interests and issues; citizens focus on relationships. The peace process embraces both, but, until relationships are changed, deep-rooted human conflicts are not likely to be resolved. The power of citizens is most fully realized and demonstrated in the capacity to build and to change relationships. Governments rarely demonstrate that capacity, and they can be overwhelmed for lacking it.

In the first nine months of the administration of U.S. President Jimmy Carter in 1977, Carter's diplomatic team, under Secretary of State Cyrus Vance, worked steadily to develop terms of reference to resume the Geneva Middle East Peace Conference, first convened after the Arab-Israeli War of October 1973. As time passed and one diplomatic formulation after another failed to remove obstacles, President Anwar al-Sadat of Egypt, with little warning, announced that he was prepared to go to Jerusalem—where no Arab leader had visited formally since the State of Israel was established in 1948—to try to break the logjam. It was one of those rare initiatives by a political leader to change the relationship between peoples, but he appealed to citizens—not to government—to accomplish that change.

President Sadat took a negotiating position that Israeli Prime Minister Menachem Begin flatly rejected, but he fundamentally changed the foundations of the Egyptian-Israeli relationship. He did so not by dealing with legally defined issues but by recognizing the basic obstacle—that few Israelis believed any Arab leader would make peace with Israel and accept a Jewish state in the Arab Near East. Sadat's dramatic political act in flying to Israel threw their assumption into question. One portion of his speech to the Israeli Knesset (parliament) focused on the human dimensions of the relationship. After noting the concrete issues that faced the two governments, he stated:

> Yet, there remains another wall. This wall constitutes a psychological barrier between us, a barrier of suspicion, a barrier of rejection; a barrier of fear, of deception, a barrier of hallucination without any action, deed or decision.
>
> A barrier of distorted and eroded interpretation of every event and statement. It is this psychological barrier which I described in official statements as constituting 70 percent of the whole problem.
>
> Today, through my visit to you, I ask why don't we stretch out our hands with faith and sincerity so that together we might destroy this barrier?[1]

Sadat had recognized that there would be no Arab-Israeli peace until the overall relationship between the two peoples had begun to change.

Eleven years later, Soviet leader Mikhail Gorbachev stood at the podium of the General Assembly of the United Nations. Although he addressed diplomats representing the family of nations, he spoke with particular attention to an American people who still doubted his sincere intention to change the relationship between the two superpowers. "Is he for real? Can a Communist ever change?" Americans asked each other again and again.

> And finally, since I am here on American soil, and also for other obvious reasons, I have to turn to the subject of our relations with this great country. . . .
>
> No one intends to underestimate the seriousness of our differences and the toughness of outstanding problems. We have, however, already graduated from the primary school of learning to understand each other and seek solutions in both our own and common interests. . . .
>
> We in Moscow are happy that an ever increasing number of statesmen, political party and public figures and—I want to emphasize this—scientists, cultural figures, representatives of mass movements and various churches, and activists of the so-called people's diplomacy, are ready to shoulder the burden of universal responsibility.
>
> In this regard I believe that the idea of convening on a regular basis, under the auspices of the United Nations, an assembly of public organisations, deserves attention.[2]

Like Sadat, Gorbachev acknowledged the capacity of citizens outside government when he recognized that the superpower relationship would not change until the relationship between citizens in the Soviet and U.S. bodies politic changed.

Most traditional approaches to conflict and its resolution have dealt with it as a contest of material power driven by material interests. Formal mediation and negotiation have sought either to divide the materials in dispute or—in more recent thinking about negotiation—to find a solution that satisfies as many of the specific interests of each side as possible in what is called a "win-win" solution. Such negotiations will continue to be essential in countless circumstances.

Fresh thinking about conflict, however, recognizes that, when deeprooted human relationships are at the heart of a conflict, that conflict may not be ready for formal mediation or negotiation. Simply negotiating the surface symptoms of the conflict—the issues over which groups seem to fight—will often lead only to a temporary cessation of violence. Human beings need a different method for changing deeply conflictual relationships. Since the focus in these situations is on the relationships underlying the problems rather than primarily on the issues involved, it is essential to begin with a working concept of relationship—its elements, its dynamics and how these can be changed.

THE CONCEPT OF RELATIONSHIP

A word used to describe any new concept may cause discomfort, but often the problem is not so much with the word chosen as with the unfamiliarity of the ideas one is trying to capture. In the end, the solution is often to pick a word that is rich enough to absorb new meaning and then to define it in its new dimensions.

At first hearing, "relationship" is such a commonplace word that we hardly notice it, but, when we stop to think about relationships that sustain us as human beings, we begin to feel the power and depth of the concept. We are born into relationships, and we depend on close relationships—parent, sibling, spouse, friend, partner, colleague, spiritual beings—for our survival, our physical and emotional nourishment, our intellectual and spiritual growth, our material achievements, our pleasure, relief of our pain and our growing old.

We also know that we think differently in a relationship from the way we think about "us and them" or "I and you." Thinking as "we" produces a recognizable shift of mental gears—a change in the way we *interact*. When we use the concept of relationship to capture a dynamic, continuously changing process of interaction between people, it connotes the potential of transformation by changing the way people interact—by focusing on the interaction itself. This is a difficult idea to grasp, but it becomes real if one thinks, for instance, of how individuals in a marriage continually think about the quality of the ways they interact in an effort to enrich their marriage—a relationship with characteristics that are more than the sum of the characteristics of the two partners.

"Relationship" also has the disadvantage of not translating well into other languages, largely because the idea of using it to describe the process of continuous, multilevel interaction among states or groups is unfamiliar or even uncomfortable. Russians suggest "interdependent relations" or "comprehensive pattern of interactions." The Chinese have a strong concept of interpersonal relationships, but, when they use that word in the phrase "international relations," it lacks the connotations suggested here. Even in English, specialists are not accustomed to hearing a word that normally refers to personal interdependence applied to whole groups or countries.

My response is that the world is changing; that the concept of political institutions acting rationally does not adequately explain how this world works; that the old tools of statecraft are not always effective in today's world; that groups of human beings often behave in ways that evolve from their own human defenses. For all of this, we need a new vocabulary.

Perhaps the problem in accepting any word in this context is that we are still thinking of states and power politics or institutions; we are not yet looking through lenses that focus on the political—even human—process of continuous interaction between significant elements of whole bodies politic.

The very commonness of the word "relationship" may be the key to its usefulness. It is not a grand theory of international or intergroup relations. It is an idea that human beings understand almost from birth. It is the context in which human beings bring together, apply and test in their intercourse with other human beings all of the insights about life that help them understand and act. Those insights may have been learned from parents and teachers, from experience, from books, from the laboratory. Relationship is the context in which we humans integrate them. If we are increasingly in a world in which people are more involved in the political process of interaction among whole bodies politic, then using a human word may provide a sounder basis for action in the real world than abstract theories about political institutions and governments.

Four other points are important: (1) There are different levels, kinds and qualities of relationship. Relationships may be good and bad—conflictual or cooperative, immature or mature, destructive or constructive. (2) Relationships are dynamic. They reflect kaleidoscopic shifts among external factors that affect them. They change character over time. They regress or mature and contract or enlarge their capacity to accomplish what needs to be done. A good relationship may sour, and a bad relationship may improve. (3) An overall relationship will involve many different interactions—or relationships—among subsets of people. That different use of the word may cause some confusion, but, as with many rich words, context will usually make the meaning clear. (4) Relationships are organic interactions not mechanistic exchanges.

Relationship is a condition more often than we recognize. Many slaves and masters had a close relationship, however unjust. Israelis and Palestinians were developing a relationship long before a peace treaty between Egypt and Israel was even considered possible. To be sure, it was a relationship between occupier and occupied—in many ways a destructive rather than a constructive relationship. But, by the end of the 1980s, it was closer than that between Egypt and Israel more than a decade after a treaty of peace legally established "normal" state-to-state relations. The Soviet Union and the United States also had an intense though potentially destructive relationship, and one can argue that not seeing this relationship in all of its complexities was partly responsible for the failure of efforts in the 1970s to achieve a relaxation of tension and to sustain cooperation.

Perhaps most important, the concept of relationship does not focus exclusively on states, governments and political institutions. In a world in which many conflicts seem beyond the reach of governments, the concept of relationship opens the door to a wider array of instruments for dealing with a wider array of conflicts. Thinking about changing relationships and all that they involve is far more challenging and potentially more realistic and more gratifying than designing wars and negotiations, important as negotiation may remain in some situations for ending violence.

SIX ELEMENTS OF RELATIONSHIP AND CHANGING CONFLICTUAL RELATIONSHIPS

Experience suggests that relationships combine six elements. Each in itself is complex. The overall mix—the continuously changing interactions—affects a relationship's character and quality. The combination of those elements shifts continuously with time and circumstances as the pieces in a kaleidoscope. Changes within each element and changes in the combination of elements help explain why a relationship changes. Most important, those changing ingredients and combinations provide points of entry for those who would intervene to change conflictual relationships.[3] Following is a discussion of each of the six components.

Identity of the Parties

Probing and understanding the character of parties in a relationship involves understanding not only their physical characteristics but also the experiences that have shaped their views of themselves and of the world.

Each party in a relationship is described most simply in terms of observable characteristics, such as a group's size, geographic base, social and political structure, constitution if any, ethnic and demographic composition, resources and functions. Physical characteristics and position of a country or a group are important elements of identity because they affect its approach to the world around it.

But *human experience* is also critical. From the start of life, an important part of identity is formed in relationship by setting one's self off against others and making clear who one is not. We do not fully understand partners in a relationship until we understand how each perceives itself in contrast to the other. Beyond that, what experiences have shaped a person's or a group's worldview and their ways of acting in relationships with others? Any traditionally persecuted group will have its own compelling answer. Within a broader range of developmental experiences, particularly traumatic experiences often give rise to feelings that assume dramatic proportions in the life of a group and go far toward explaining its relationships, especially with groups thought to have been responsible for those experiences. How a group remembers those experiences and transmits them to succeeding generations may be more important than objective factors in shaping present relationships.[4]

At this unusual and intense moment in history, a number of group identities are in the process of rediscovery, formation or redefinition. Some of those will be shaped through interaction with others. Working through dialogue to affect those interactively derived perceptions of self in relationship to others can provide a fruitful area for trying to change a traditionally conflictual relationship.

A Coexistence of Interests and Needs that Lead to Interdependence

The present moment requires a richer concept of national interest and a broader picture of how group interests are defined if the concept is to be a realistic guide to policy-making or action. A relationship starts when two parties are drawn into the same space by their interests. As we probe those interests—what each wants to achieve and avoid and, above all, why—we begin to see deep-rooted interests that would rarely appear on a government's list of national interests. As a relationship grows, parties may identify goals and interests that neither could achieve without the other. That is the point at which interdependence is felt. Some scholars would say that this interdependence is the defining element in a close relationship—even a conflictual one.[5]

Most of us in the professional ranks of government or in the academic field of international relations were taught to think of *objective* interests—tangible and measurable. For instance, how much of a resource does a nation need or what geographic features strengthen defense? These are basic. But my experience in U.S. government policy-making suggests that a purely analytical statement of interests is rarely an adequate touchstone for a leader's policy.

Interests are defined *politically* as well as analytically. Besides receiving the bureaucracy's analysis of interests, a U.S. president will go into the political arena to sense how Americans see those interests, how intensely they feel and why. He will try to learn not just what their concrete interests are, but also what they value. Citizens inject their own domestic needs and personal values into a definition of the national interest. Probing that human dimension of interests reveals the deep-rooted fears, hopes, wounds, values and perceptions that form people's sense of what is threatening and of what is vital to protect their identity.

As people come closer and closer, we also see interests as *a function of relationship*—the makings of interdependence. To begin, in a conflictual or competitive relationship such as the Cold War relationship between the Soviet Union and the United States, parties may use a zero-sum calculation whereby one defines what it wants at the other's expense or what it wants to deny the other. In a more cooperative relationship such as a marriage, parties may use a positive-sum measure whereby pursuing one party's interests may produce a gain for both. Eventually, each party recognizes that its ability to realize its own interests depends in some way on the actions of the other.

The stakes over which ethnic conflicts are fought are often not objectively defined interests but interests defined in human and political terms in which identities are at stake and historical grievances drive groups to passionate crusades. When it is possible to bring one party to understand through dialogue another's deeply felt interests and hurts—imagined or real—then relationships begin to change. Governmental diplomacy will rarely create conditions for bringing interests defined in that way to the surface, yet in them lies a significant opportunity to change a conflictual relationship.

A Process and Pattern of Continuing Interaction

At the heart of any relationship is a continuing series of interactions over time; a single exchange—for instance, with a store clerk—does not produce a relationship. Whatever the quality of a relationship, the frequency, intensity and character of interactions over time teach each party to modify its actions in the light of what it learns about the other's likely responses. Three more detailed insights may help us understand more fully the interaction between bodies politic.

First, interaction is *complex*. Even the interaction of state institutions involves both the intertwining of issues in shaping perceptions within a body politic and the breadth of interaction among policy-making and policy-influencing communities. For example, in 1979–1980, the Soviet invasion of Afghanistan shocked Americans and roused such deep distrust of Soviet commitment to peace that President Carter withdrew a key nuclear-arms agreement from the ratification process in the U.S. Senate. Soviets argued for several years afterward that Carter could have separated the action in Afghanistan from arms control, but Americans persistently and vigorously responded that Carter had no choice, given the intensity of popular reaction. The two objectively different issues became intertwined through the human question: Can the Soviets be trusted to live up to agreements? A similar exchange took place with the Chinese government after its suppression of dissidents in Tiananmen Square in Beijing in June 1989; millions of Americans had watched tanks kill students and insisted that the president react. Issues interact, and actions and issues interact.

As those interactions become more complex, each country influences the other's behavior in more ways. We usually track changes in how governments interact, but only rarely do we track how bodies politic interact, even though that interaction may provide the largest context for change. Beyond studying the power, capability, positions, expressed interests and decision-making structures of states, we need to probe the complex political processes through which issues and people interact. Since policy-making reflects its political environment—even in an authoritarian government—we must factor those processes and their interactions into conducting and changing relationships.

Second, the medium for interaction is a *political process with multiple elements* that becomes a context within which change in a relationship can take place. Change does not always result primarily from a linear series of actions and reactions between governments. Change also evolves through a cumulative, generative process of continuous, multilevel interaction that can change perceptions by changing experience and create opportunities that did not seem to exist before.

Third, a relationship's quality depends heavily on *communication* between those involved. Historically, governments and leaders have provided most of the communications between peoples. Beyond diplomatic exchanges, there can be a depth of communication among human beings that reveals deep-rooted interests, perceptions and misperceptions, priorities, identity, purpose and political dynamics. Now we are beginning to see the possibility of adding to governmental channels nonofficial dialogues that can broaden the range of interaction, sharpen understanding, deepen communication and partly replace adversarial interaction and contests of force as a means of resolving differences. Sustained dialogue can complement or even replace formal diplomacy as a way of communicating to redefine problems. Citizens outside government can often communicate more directly than official representatives. Beyond those face-to-face communications are the proliferating opportunities to "talk" by a variety of electronic means.

Change in a relationship may result, in part, simply from understanding the patterns of interaction and developing ways of changing them. In a process of sustained dialogue, participants can actually design a scenario of interactive steps that will gradually make bodies politic aware of a changing pattern of interaction. Participants will identify actions that could cause the other side to believe that they can be more trusting of a constructive response to their actions.

The Nature and Working of Effective Power

As noted in Chapter One, power has usually been seen as a combination of tangible assets—economic, military, geographic—that one uses physically. Power in a relationship has been measured for centuries as a rough balance or imbalance of these assets. It has been thought of as the means for producing a desired outcome, even against another's will, by taking what one wants or by forcing a negotiation in which what is wanted would be conceded. It has been thought of as control or as "power over." The question now is: What insights into a relationship would flow from different ways of thinking about power? What happens if power in its traditional forms does not produce predictable results? I am not suggesting that traditional forms of power are irrelevant. I am suggesting that, if power is thought of not as control but as *the capacity to change the course of events or to make things happen,* it may be wise to think of different ways power may operate in a relationship.

Nuclear weapons raised questions about the limits on using military power. From Vietnam through Afghanistan to Lebanon, we have found examples of the limits of military power to accomplish political purposes. Even the complex Soviet-U.S. nuclear relationship came to be regulated not by the balance of physical power but by the general doctrine of deterrence, which was essentially a doctrine based on assumptions about how minds interact.

Although states are often described as immune to *human considerations,* the fact is that great disparities of military and economic power may not explain why change takes place or when. Egyptian President Sadat's trip to Israel in November 1977 may have done more to change the course of events than either superpower could have by withholding aid or trying to tilt the military balance against Israel. Appeals to conscience on behalf of human rights proved more powerful in producing change in South Africa than superior police power. Ethical principles constrained the British use of force in India in response to Mahatma Gandhi's nonviolence. Reconciliation as in the U.S. decision to help Germany and Japan rebuild after World War II proved a better way to peace than the prolonged punishment meted out after World War I. In each case, principle played a role in offsetting an imbalance of material power.

Power often emerges from political relationships. Events in East-Central Europe in 1989 dramatized that the power to bring about change sometimes lies with those who have no raw power. Power emerged from relationships among people who challenged government on grounds of legitimacy and effectiveness, and those in authority decided not to use force in the circumstances that citizens, in part, generated.

In short, the power to change relationships may emerge from bringing people together in different ways. Citizens outside government can create this kind of power. In sustained dialogue, for instance, once participants have designed a scenario of interactive steps to change relationships, their mutual commitment to try to put that scenario into action generates power with the potential for change. Military power will not cease to be important, but it may not be the vehicle for changing relationships in deep-rooted human conflicts.

Limits on Behavior

We have traditionally defined the limits of one state's behavior toward another in terms of such principles as noninterference in others' internal affairs or nonintervention on another's territory. These principles were crafted to protect the sovereignty of the state. They defined sovereignty partly in mechanistic terms of absolute control over what crosses national borders. These principles remain important, but, in a highly interdependent world, such statements by themselves are often inadequate guides to action.

At a minimum, groups accept some *regulation of physical interaction.* Sometimes, the imperative of avoiding fatal confrontation introduces a shared interest in a minimal level of regulating conflict. As two groups interact over time, implicit "rules of the game" develop—a sort of tacit regulation of behavior. As a relationship further develops, two parties can begin actually to write a "code of conduct" or "principles" for an explicit regulation of interaction. Each of these efforts played a role in Soviet-U.S. attempts to avoid nuclear war.

Underlying tacit or explicit practices that regulate behavior are *psychological limits* sensitive to the human dimensions of interaction. Those limits define when one is "stepping on another's toes" or "touching raw nerves." Limits must reflect what each party sees as threatening its sense of identity, integrity and self-esteem, as well as its concrete interests. In the United States, African Americans, Hispanics, Asians, Native Americans and whites, men and women are increasingly—though still inadequately—aware of words that cause each other pain or slight another's dignity.

As interactions change, the question is whether there are new *principles* that demonstrate respect and provide protection for the identity and integrity of each body politic in a relationship. As the world community in the late twentieth century increasingly asserts its right to express an interest in how governments treat their citizens, the emphasis has shifted from principles designed only to protect the rights of states to principles that also focus on the rights of human beings.

As relationships are probed, it may be that new practices will emerge more appropriately from a dialogue about necessary limits in the interaction between participants' groups than from trying to redefine traditional principles of international law. Changing limits in practical and meaningful ways can change relationships.

Evolving Perceptions

Learning what shapes the perceptions of each body politic toward the other can be critical. Each party will start with certain preconceived ideas of how a person or a group of the other's background, role, race, religion, ideology or nationality could be expected to behave. These stereotypes are common. As interactions multiply, each party's behavior may reshape the other's perceptions. A relationship may change as solutions to problems become possible, but, until people perceive it as changing, they may act no differently. On the other hand, working in what we perceive as a sustainable problem-solving relationship can transform cooperation, policy analysis and the tools we use to achieve our aims. An effective problem-solving relationship can prove so useful that it is perceived as a valuable interest that must be protected for its own sake.

Even in a constrained relationship, cooperation on issues of vital importance is possible, but perceptions of hostility may limit cooperation past the time when fuller cooperation would otherwise become feasible. Two parties can be locked into an ongoing interaction by a shared problem such as nuclear weapons or common geography (for example, Israelis and Palestinians living in the same homeland) that requires them to work together. But they may fear, hate, mistrust, even "demonize" each other. Until those human concerns are met and individuals perceive that the relationship might become constructive, it will remain constrained.

Even when feelings of hostility fade and some cooperation is seen to be possible or desirable, the perception of a durable relationship does not develop quickly, is often tenuous when it does, can rarely be complete and can continue to grow or go sour again. A positive perception may begin with working together guardedly to deal successfully with a common problem.

As a problem-solving relationship evolves, so do perceptions. Those changing perceptions emerge from a sense of acting from at least some comparable human values. These growing perceptions are tested through talking, thinking and working together rather than only observing each other from a distance. When partners work together to diagnose situations, envision alternatives and analyze obstacles and design courses of action, they can test the other's intent and their perception of it.

In a deepening relationship, *thinking together about acting to change perceptions* becomes possible. Groups have experienced developing together a scenario of interactive steps designed to change perceptions of a relationship and thereby enlarge their capacity to cooperate. This requires a different kind of conversation from the conversations of officials focusing on government-to-government issues. People need to talk together explicitly about the perceptions that constrain their capacity to act together and about how to change them.

Attempting to change a relationship in this way requires working from a full picture of what is involved, ranging from deep human fears and hopes, through cultures that shape behavior and worldviews, to the hard calculations of security and state decision making. It requires thinking in a larger political context and using a broader array of instruments—presumably peaceful—to change perceptions of the relationship and its potential for positive accomplishments.

FOCUSING ON THE OVERALL RELATIONSHIP

In sum, relationships embrace all six elements in changing combinations. The characteristics of each relationship reflect a particular mix. Focusing on individual elements can highlight causes of a conflict. Focusing on the whole set of elements and how it might be changed opens the door to a wide range of actions. In any case, focusing on the relationship itself differs significantly from focusing primarily on one state's policies toward another or one group's behavior toward another.

If we focus on the *whole* relationship between bodies politic, we will bring to light all that accounts for a conflictual relationship. This focus can open the door to a variety of ways of changing a relationship, can prevent good relationships from souring and can build peaceful problem-solving relationships.

Having probed the elements of a conflictual relationship in detail, we are ready to move into the strategic and tactical work of designing a peace process. The analysis of the conflictual relationship will have suggested a range of possible actions and their timing. It will have suggested where efforts might be concentrated to change the relationship.

If power is the capacity to affect the course of events, then power may come from the effective conduct of the process of political interaction that alters understanding and perceptions, probes to the deeper roots of conflict and finds political steps for building new relationships to cope with new problems. Such changes may be planned, for instance, in the course of sustained dialogue—the public peace process.

Some argue that this organic approach may not help in a totalitarian system or in any situation in which the people play little role in policy-making. That is true to some degree, but, even when policy-making is centralized, human beings make policy, and their thinking reflects the ideas of those around them. Even though outsiders may not see who influences policy, most leaders have to take account of constituencies and policy discussion of some kind. Second, though change may be slow, the world of the future will see people outside government steadily more involved. Events in 1989 and the conflicts that have erupted since should be argument enough that it would be unwise not to enlarge our conceptual framework.

TIMING AND INTERVENTION

Much of the literature on formal mediation and negotiation focuses at some point on the stages through which violent conflict evolves. An important purpose of that work is to analyze the moments when protagonists are more or less resistant to efforts to end the violence. William Zartman has introduced the terms "hurting stalemate" and "ripe for resolution" or "ripeness" to capture the thought that parties to a conflict must conclude for their own reasons that the costs of continuing the violence outweigh the costs of ending it.[6]

Scholars have described the progression of conflict in a variety of ways,[7] as noted in Chapter One. This progression of stages may well affect the readiness of officials to start movement toward formal negotiation; it affects sustained dialogue among citizens outside government less than officials. Indeed, there are significant examples of cases in which governments stood back and allowed nonofficial dialogues to produce insight into whether they could afford the risk of beginning formal negotiation with an enemy. When officials admit they are hurting and express a willingness to negotiate, they often pay a price for exhibiting what could be seen as a sign of weakness; a citizen outside government is simply judging as an individual that present or potential costs have risen too high and that it would be folly to continue. All it takes is a half-dozen individuals on each side ready to reach out to the other.

ACKNOWLEDGMENT, CONTRITION, FORGIVENESS AND RECONCILIATION

The concept of relationship as detailed above is offered as a diagnostic tool both for getting inside destructive relationships to improve them and for sustaining good working relationships. The transformation from an adversarial relationship to one capable of solving shared problems together requires some emergence of trust, at least in particular areas of the relationship. Examples include the control of nuclear weapons in the Soviet-U.S. relationship or an agreement on "turf" between city gangs. Such limited improvement—useful as it may be—does not imply a fuller transformation or reconciliation in the relationship. That is another step.

The ultimate transformation of a relationship involves putting the past into a manageable perspective so that it no longer blocks development of a fully cooperative and peaceful relationship. We refer to that transformation in human terms as "reconciliation."

Much late-twentieth-century thinking about transforming violent relationships into peaceful ones has focused afresh on the role of acknowledgment of a wrong done, contrition or confession and forgiveness. I recall a Palestinian refugee in a refugee camp outside the historic town of Jericho before the 1967 Arab-Israeli War. "I can go up to the hills overlooking Israeli-occupied Jerusalem and look over into the part of the city where I grew up and see my family home," he said. "You have to understand how a dispute is settled in Arab culture," he continued. "First, the person who committed a wrong acknowledges that a wrong has been done. Second, compensation for the wronged party is agreed. Third, the compensation is turned over to the wronged party. Fourth, in an act of nobility, the wronged party may turn back the compensation." Returning to the loss of his home during the war following the establishment of the State of Israel in 1948, he was implying that he knew he would never get his home back. "I just want somebody to acknowledge that I've been ill done to," he concluded sadly.[8]

Many of the moving stories about the gradual reconciliation between the French and Germans after World War II include accounts of dramatic individual apologies by participants on both sides. The embraces that followed were expressions of forgiveness. Many of these exchanges took place at Mountain House in Caux, Switzerland, a place for bringing together people in conflict established by the Moral Re-Armament movement in 1946.[9]

The same problem has arisen on a large scale in countries such as Chile, Argentina, Ecuador, Guatemala, El Salvador and South Africa, in which long periods of repression and intercommunal warfare left a legacy of atrocities. A common practice has become the establishment of "truth and reconciliation commissions" to develop credible accounts of the wrongs done and lists of the wrongdoers. When wrongdoers confess what they have done—often following orders of a repressive government—they may be forgiven and left free. A leading professor in the University of Central America in San Salvador, where six priests on the university faculty and administration were assassinated, made the point to me in a private conversation: "The timing of an amnesty is critical. Only if amnesty is granted after the confession of wrong is the amnesty a healing act. Only then can the amnesty be a genuine act of forgiveness."

Near the end of World War II, hundreds of Polish officers were murdered in the Katyn Forest as the Nazi army retreated from Soviet territory. For decades, the official Soviet position was that the Nazis had killed the officers, even though the Poles knew that the advancing Soviet forces had annihilated them. After the end of the Soviet Union, Russian President Boris Yeltsin compiled the Soviet files, including the order to commit the massacre, and had them handed over in a public ceremony to Polish President Lech Walesa. Walesa reportedly wept.[10]

In the sustained dialogue among citizens from different regions and parties during the civil war in Tajikistan described in Chapter Seven, one participant said: "Let's all forgive each other and get on with building our country." He proposed a shared project of establishing a memorial to those on all sides who had been killed during the violence.

Although the process of acknowledgment, contrition, forgiveness and reconciliation is deeply human, it has crept into official policy in the demands of East Asian governments, as well as aggrieved citizens of those countries, for Japanese apologies and restitution for atrocities committed by soldiers during World War II. Germany offered large-scale economic assistance to Israel as acknowledgment of the horror of the Nazi Holocaust and to create the foundation for a normal diplomatic relationship.[11]

A Bridging Word

As participants in the public peace process design ways of taking their experience in changing conflictual relationships beyond a dialogue group into the larger body politic, they need to understand the tools available to them there. Having absorbed the broader approach to conflict afforded by seeing the overall relationship between conflicting groups, they next turn to the processes and instruments of change that become available when they look beyond political institutions to the politics of citizens coming together to solve their own problems.

Chapter Three

―――※※※―――

Citizens' Politics in Civil Society

CITIZENS—NOT JUST INSTITUTIONS—AS POLITICAL ACTORS

As citizens outside government ignite conflicts within and between bodies politic or work to end them, the politics through which they act and the civil societies in which they act become critical arenas for changing conflictual relationships. Enlarging our conceptual framework and the array of resources for preventing and ending violence and building peace depends on broadening our present focus on political institutions to add a fresh look at citizens as political actors.

Most study of intrastate politics has focused on formal political institutions and processes, such as parties, elections, referenda, interest groups, media, opinion making, lawmaking, executive policy-making and judicial proceedings. Most studies of international relations include intrastate politics only when citizens influence government policies for managing those relationships.

Today, study of institutional politics does not provide a complete picture of the origins of conflict or the resources for preventing or ending it. Study of institutional politics certainly does not provide a complete inventory of resources essential to building societies that can bring the full capacities of the whole body politic to bear on meeting the needs of people and building peace.

Peoples around the world are rethinking the nature and practice of politics. They are exploring their own forms of civil society and "democratic" governance. Where they must cope with violent conflict, small numbers of them are rethinking their role in ending it and in preventing its recurrence. Where they see the need to broaden and deepen civil society, they are creating their own associations across the lines of recent conflict.

It is becoming increasingly evident that a group of citizens engaged in sustained dialogue over a span of time can become what I call "a mind at work in the midst of a society remaking itself." It can become the designer and even the partial implementer of a strategy that includes steps toward changing relationships and strengthening a new society and economy.

CIVIL SOCIETY: A CONTEXT OF PEACEMAKING AND PEACE-BUILDING

A whole body politic includes, first, government and quasi-governmental bodies—highly organized nongovernmental organizations that implement programs often authorized or funded by government. But it also includes the civil society—that vast area between individual, family and personal relationships on the one hand and government on the other. It is the arena of public life in which citizens outside government form the relationships, associations and less formally structured nongovernmental organizations they need to do the work they must do. It is in this arena that the public peace process works.

Politics is not just about governments and political institutions, but also about how all elements of a body politic interact to solve common problems, protect shared interests and pursue common aims. Politics is not just about zero-sum contests among organized groups for control of governmental power; it is also about how elements of whole bodies politic interact to set a direction and generate will, authority and capacity to achieve goals. It is not just about electing officials or changing their minds, passing laws or enacting programs; it also involves the choices citizens in and out of government make about the purposes and direction of the community in light of what they value. Politics is not just a linear series of governmental decisions, actions and programs; it is a multilevel organic process of continuous interaction among people and groups. Beyond government, it involves building relationships within which citizens expand their own experiences of how issues, choices and values are connected within a body politic. It is the context in which they develop their capacities to accomplish the tasks their interests define.

As citizens talk about ending conflict, they find themselves unable to separate that subject from talking about what kind of community, country or region they want and how to make it different from the one in which the violence broke out. Initially, they are not negotiating; they are thinking and talking together to design changed relationships and new ways of acting together peacefully. They are practicing politics at its fundamental level—what happens when people in community come together to deal with the problems that threaten their interests and to set their direction toward the future. They are working in the political arena—in public space. This is the political, as contrasted to the mediated or negotiated, resolution of conflict. They are engaged in the public—not the official—peace process. Above all, they are engaged in politics within civil society.

If this is how citizens outside government instinctively begin work to end conflict, our larger conceptual framework must incorporate what we are learning about the fragmentations and reconfigurations of civil society that underlie conflict and its resolution. Peace-building and immunizing a society against renewed conflict require both strengthening, restructuring or restoring the relationships that fragment as conflict looms and then reconnecting them to make peace.

Most academic analyses of the prevention and resolution of conflict focus on the dynamics of conflict itself—its causes, escalation, stalemate and settlement—as well as on the decision making of the parties to the conflict. Formal mediation and negotiation address the issues, interests, symptoms, power balances and costs of violent conflict. Most nonofficial workshops try to change the underlying human relationships that often cause or fuel conflict or block its resolution. All of those approaches are important, but by themselves they overlook resources critical to moving from violence to peace. They leave out an essential part and, thus, cannot put all of the pieces together to develop a complete picture.

To add the missing part, consider what happens in a civil society as violence breaks it apart into warring units and as genuine peace rebuilds and reconnects them. Envision the following unfolding situation.

First, a functioning society includes a number of relationships and networks. Some are formal organizations; others are informal associations. Many serve the purposes of spanning fault lines—ethnic, racial, religious, vocational, economic, social—that normally divide people in a society and of providing spaces where people from different groups come together. These are spaces in which perceptions can be changed and differences can be accommodated peacefully. In democratic societies, most of these organizations are generated by citizens outside government. In totalitarian societies, most have been spawned and controlled by a single dominant quasi-official political party. When totalitarian rule collapses, those organizations are dismissed, and in some cases the initial vacuum is filled by armed groups vying for control.

Second, as a society fragments through internal conflict, whatever social units survive—tribes, clans, regional groupings, ethnic groups, ideological movements, criminal networks, armed organizations—coalesce into like-minded "alliances" against an adversary. Relationships between unlike groups that may have existed to pursue shared interests across fault lines are torn apart. The society is largely fragmented into opposed groupings. Confrontation and violence are the media of exchange.

Third, mediators bring leaders of opposing factions together to negotiate agreement on ending the violence. They address tangible issues and interests. They may even produce agreement on a transitional division of power and on elections. They may arrange to begin reconstruction of physical damage. Then the mediators go home. They cannot change human relationships. They do not normally think of the need to regenerate those groups that span the fault lines in a peaceful society or the political processes through which they interact. The agreements they produce are often like skeletons without ligaments, sinews, flesh, nerves or blood vessels.

Meanwhile, a few citizens outside government during a violent civil conflict may have begun dialogue across the lines of conflict—a public peace process that can pave the way for official talks and provide ideas when the official peace process stalls. Participants in such dialogue build relationships across the fault lines of the society, as well as across the lines of violence. They create organizations in the civil society to help refugees return home. They create their own organizations to teach peaceful political practices to citizens outside government. They begin to regenerate connections between the coagulations of warring groups—to build the sinews of nascent cohesion in a society that needs to build peace. Citizens' groups outside the country offer education in the practices of building those boundary-spanning organizations and in the philosophy and practice of developing the associations that can build civil society.

Without the building or rebuilding of civil society, efforts to prevent or resolve conflict work only on the surface. They address the issues in conflict—not its human roots or structures. When they probe the relationships underlying conflict, they do not project changes in those relationships into the unfolding design of the fabric of civil society and a whole body politic. Work and theory on resolving conflict must be enlarged to include rebuilding civil society.[1]

Even in countries with long experience of civil society and democratic practice, such as the United States, leaders and people are struggling to recapture lost arts and practices of citizens' politics in civil society. So much attention has been given to the role of government that the roles of citizen, civil society, public and public space have slipped out of the political limelight. People in many societies feel fragmented. Many suffer a diminished sense of shared meaning that once gave coherence to their bodies politic. Many experience or fear internal violence that could threaten their fabric.

EXPERIENCES IN DEMOCRATIC POLITICS
AT THE END OF THE TWENTIETH CENTURY

In the mid-1980s, a growing number of Chileans chafing under military dictatorship began the movement that culminated in the "vote no" campaign that toppled the authoritarian government of General Augusto Pinochet. Citizens came together against the dictator, and, in December 1989, Chileans elected their first democratic government in 17 years.

By the mid-1990s, frustrated Chilean citizen-leaders were lamenting that citizens believed that they had fulfilled their duty by electing a democratic government and thought that they had no further responsibility. They expected the government to solve their problems. When it did not, they were disillusioned with democracy because they concluded that their vote was worthless and that politicians often do not keep their promises to represent citizens. Like their neighbors in Argentina, citizen leaders in Chile say their overriding problem is to cause fellow citizens to see that even a democratically elected government cannot do its job unless citizens do theirs.

In 1994, during a meeting of the International Civil Society Exchange, one of the leaders in part of the movement against Pinochet reflected with frustration on the attitudes of Chilean citizens:

> When we had Pinochet, of course, all these people had power because everybody was joined against Pinochet. But today, everyone is fighting for their own interests. They are not acting together with anyone, so I don't know what we can do. . . . The politicians need votes, and that's why they would like to have relations with their citizens. But they don't want to have very active citizens who have their own ideas, their own actions, their own decisions or their own conversations.[2]

This experience was repeated in country after country in the early 1990s. In historical perspective, the late 1980s may well appear as the start of the next historic wave of the democratic revolution that began to gather momentum in the late sixteenth century. But it has been an uncertain start. As the Chilean story suggests, an unfolding of three successive experiences—faith in democratic institutions, citizen disillusionment and then a coming together—seems to have marked these years.

Faith in Democracy

People emerging from totalitarian and authoritarian systems understandably placed their faith in the institutions of democratic government. They believed that written constitutions, the principle of one person/one vote, free and fair elections, decision by majority and representative government would guarantee just and effective government and assure their freedom and well-being.

It was natural that people who had known elections not at all or only under rigid control by a single totalitarian party would put their hopes in open elections contested among many parties and that they would rely on new written constitutions to spell out the rules of new political systems. For reasons that only deeper study of culture and experience may explain, many seemed to believe that a system described on paper thereby becomes a reality. Their experience did not equip them initially to recognize that these mechanisms alone—without supplemental political processes to keep them honest and effective—could leave the field open to other practices that undermined the very democracy they thought they had attained.

It was natural perhaps for some politicians to kindle the flames of ethnic antagonism to win elections and exclude opponents from power. Those politicians chose to see parliaments as the arena for contests of power rather than as places for finding common ground on which to cooperate in solving common problems. Criminal elements filled vacuums in these new systems.

It was shocking, though not unexpected, that the absence of experience in the peaceful democratic resolution of differences led a frustrated Russian President Boris Yeltsin in October 1993 to call out tanks to shell a rebellious parliament. It was perhaps natural that the government of the newly independent former Soviet republic of Tajikistan should seek legitimacy in a draft constitution written by lawyers and diplomats and modeled on constitutions in other countries by trying to force it into effect so quickly as to exclude a significant part of the population that had been displaced by civil strife. People from different regions of that country placed hope in elections without assurance that winners and losers could then compromise in ways that would serve the interests of all rather than lead winners to usurp power and losers to open the fault lines of the next civil war.

Even in established democracies in North America and Western Europe, citizens—at least since the Depression of the 1930s—increasingly placed their hope in the machinery of elected governments to resolve their problems. From 1933 on, for instance, Americans looked more and more to programs of the federal government to deal with the problems of their country, with the notable exceptions of the civil-rights movement and the movements against the Vietnam War and nuclear war.

Disillusionment

Although even brief experience with the machinery of democracy has left many citizens disillusioned, some of them are gradually realizing that democratic institutions by themselves cannot deal with all of the problems citizens want resolved. Although initially they knew little of the politics needed to make those institutions work, some have begun to realize that the mechanisms of democratic government cannot work effectively without the active political participation of citizens themselves.

The disillusionment is worldwide. As of this writing in 1998, a negotiated peace and cabinet government had yet to restore fully functioning democracy to Lebanon, an elected government had not produced a polity without corruption in Argentina and a new constitution and parliament in Russia had not produced effective government or blocked the onrush of Mafia-style elements to exploit a weak government and a deregulated economy. In the United States, the bitterness of partisanship often paralyzes the legislative process. Citizens believe that elected and appointed officials have closed them out of the political process. They see government as "gridlocked" and officials as going their own ways, deaf to the interests and voices of the citizens who elected them. U.S. citizens are angry and want little to do with institutional politics.[3]

Against the background of this disillusionment, however, citizens' groups in a few places began working to make the experiences that changed governments in 1989 and the early 1990s a permanent part of democratic practice by helping citizens learn the arts and skills of active citizenship. The International Civil Society Consortium for Public Deliberation, for example, connects the Inter-American Democracy Network, a similar network in East and Central Europe and Russia and budding networks in the Middle East, Africa and Asia. Other groups—such as CIVICUS and CIVITAS—also bring together workers in the field.[4]

Working Together

As citizens and governments, both slowly and grudgingly, recognize the need for a more active citizenry and more responsive government, the next step will be to recognize the need for a new partnership between them. They will come to understand the potential complementarity of their actions.

This experience is still limited, but it begins to point in several possible directions. Just as analyzing conflict in the setting of civil society opens new resources for changing conflictual relationships, bringing together in mutually reinforcing ways the resources of both government and civil society—the whole body politic—could markedly increase the capacity to prevent and resolve both intrastate and interstate conflict.

Accumulating experience from dealing with conflict provides more and more insight into the interaction between official and public peace processes. Much of this experience was unplanned. As experiences multiply, it should become possible to attempt interactions as part of a strategy for dealing with conflict.

The 1992 agreement that ended the violent internal conflict in El Salvador, for instance, set up a commission of citizen leaders outside government to generate and oversee the laws that would implement the provisions of the agreement on political practice. This National Commission for the Consolidation of Peace (COPAZ) provided a link between the citizens who had fueled the violent conflict and the newly constituted government.

Citizens and scholars alike are beginning to emphasize the important connection both between the strength of civil society and economic development[5] and between economic development and a strong partnership between civil society and government. Vaughn Grisham of the University of Mississippi tells the story of the small city of Tupelo, Mississippi. Over more than five decades since the late 1930s, Tupelo moved from being the poorest city in the poorest county of the poorest state in the United States to enjoying a per-capita income at least equal to that of Atlanta, Georgia, in the mid-1990s.

Perhaps the most basic principle in Tupelo, Grisham explains, is that local people must solve local problems, but since most local communities—especially poor towns like Tupelo—lack the technical and financial resources to address those problems properly, they have sought partnerships beyond themselves. Joint ventures, Grisham recounts, have brought together the private sector, represented by the Community Development Foundation, which promotes locally developed businesses, city and Lee County governments, the Tennessee Valley Authority (TVA), the local newspaper, the International Business Machines Corporation, two community colleges and a branch of the University of Mississippi. Tupelo's citizens gained a reputation with government officials of having prepared their projects with the utmost care and of turning to government only after exhausting all local resources. "Since Tupelo's projects would probably succeed," Grisham concludes, "they would make government partners look good."[6]

Those climbing out of the destruction of civil war with little trust in the competence or goodwill of their government are beginning to recognize that their countries will be made whole only when citizens in the civil society take the initiative. That initiative includes both building new practices and relationships among themselves over time and reforming government so it can play its complementary role.

RECAPTURING THE MISSING THREAD IN DEMOCRATIC THOUGHT

As people in many countries invent, rediscover or redefine politics, their experience reveals that reforming political experience requires not only changing the form of government, important as that may be. They are gradually learning that the political equation has two sides: Government is one, to be sure; the other is putting a responsible public of active citizens into politics.[7]

Critical to this task of injecting or reintroducing citizens into the political equation is recapturing a part of the democratic memory that has faded from center stage for many years—totally obliterated in places like the Soviet Union or China and eased aside by attention to big government in countries like the United States. Political thinkers such as Jane Mansbridge and David Mathews[8] in the United States recall that there are two significant threads in Western democratic thought—not just one.

The more familiar line of thought has dealt in path-breaking ways with the mechanics of democratic government—voting, representative government, majority rule, written constitutions, bills of rights, government by law, protection of minorities, political parties, parliaments, measurement of public opinion and channeling its influence to government, freedom of the press and now instant electronic communication between leaders and citizens. All of these are crucial as peoples lay their paths toward new ways of practicing politics and structuring government. At the same time, some Americans have noted that this system is adversarial because it depends on debate and confrontation, one side winning and the other losing.

In this view, the citizen has been seen mainly as a law-abiding voter and taxpayer—often a consumer of government services—who elects representatives to solve society's problems. The voter judges those solutions at the next election. But today, many in the United States and elsewhere are increasingly asking whether representative government can work without the partnership of active citizens in directing, complementing, undergirding and sustaining its efforts.

The other thread of democratic thought began in the forums of ancient Greece and Rome and, in U.S. experience, the town meeting. This poses a picture different from the politics of the adversary proceeding—the confrontation between political parties, the conflict between opposing groups and the stylized political shouting matches between opponents. In forums or town meetings, citizens come together to talk about the problems that hurt their interests, to make choices and to establish common ground for dealing with them. This approach has focused on a politics of dialogue and deliberation among citizens who take responsibility for change and form associations to achieve common purposes—associations that make up civil society. The citizen is seen as a political actor with the capacity, working in relationship with others, to change the course of events.

Ideas like government through representatives, open competition among interest groups and voting as a means of holding officials accountable are very much part of American politics. Yet, these are not all of the ideas that Americans have about what should happen in politics. "Somewhere en route from the Greek polis to the British hustings to the New England town meeting to the airwaves of the twentieth century—somewhere along the way," says Mathews, "[Americans] seem to have lost the occasions in which people come together as a public and define the public interest in a way that gives direction to government and common purpose to public actions."[9]

Probing the feelings of citizens in the United States in the early 1990s revealed that they saw themselves as excluded from politics by a professional governing establishment that included both institutions of government and other organizations such as lobbies, political action committees and even the media.[10] During the 1992 presidential campaign, U.S. presidential candidate Bill Clinton spoke frequently of "giving America back to Americans." But that slogan left open the questions of whether American citizens were ready to take America back and whether governments were willing to take citizens into the process of governance. It left open the question of whether a new partnership between government and citizens outside government was possible—whether Americans are ready to create or redevelop a whole, coherent body politic.

The United States: A Case in Point

The people who created the United States had a civil society for more than 150 years before they had a state or a constitution. As Hannah Arendt noted in her comparison of the American and French revolutions, the inhabitants of the American colonies had created a politics of their own long before the American Revolution. John Adams said the inhabitants were "formed by law into corporations, or bodies politic." Those associations took the shape of gatherings in town halls or other meeting places "to deliberate on the public affairs." Arendt quotes Adams as saying that it was "in these assemblies of towns or districts that the sentiments of the people were formed in the first place."[11] On the eve of the American Revolution, the town meetings were stitched together in a network for political action as the "committees of correspondence." Those committees connected the deliberations of the town meetings in most of the colonies.

From the experience of the town meetings came the starting point for governance in what became the United States of America. After waging the war for independence, the citizens of the new country began writing the documents of self-government. "If the king were no longer the authority for government," Mathews asks, "who was? The same town meetings that had played such a decisive role in the Revolution," he says, "had a very clear answer to that question: the people of the town meetings were in charge." Ultimately, the role of people in dialogue gave rise to Thomas Paine's observation that "a constitution is not the act of a government, but of a people constituting a government."[12] Or, in the words of the Constitution itself: "We, the people of the United States . . . do ordain and establish this Constitution."

In this tradition, one might note the well-known mid-nineteenth-century observation of Alexis de Tocqueville on the propensity of Americans to create associations to deal with their interests and problems:

> Americans of all ages, all stations in life, and all types of disposition are forever forming associations. There are not only commercial and industrial associations in which all take part, but others of a thousand different types—religious, moral, serious, futile, very general and very limited, immensely large and very minute. Americans combine to give fêtes, found seminaries, build churches, distribute books, and send missionaries to the antipodes. . . . Finally, if they want to proclaim a truth or propagate some feeling by the encouragement of a great example, they form an association.[13]

Citizens did not wait for government to resolve their problems, he observed, but rather came together to form associations to do what needed to be done.

Toward the turn of the twentieth century against a background of rapid and heavy industrialization and urbanization, Americans asked with distress what was happening to the strong tradition of individualism that de Tocqueville had also noted. The freestanding, almost heroic, citizen shaping her or his own future seemed all but lost in the increasingly impersonal and fast-growing cities and factories of a dramatically changing country. And the frontier was closing.

As a new breed of political and social observers—some beginning to call themselves "social scientists"—studied the political dynamics of the new

America, they found reason to focus on the small group as providing the space where individuals come together to deal with the larger society, not directly or alone but in relationship with each other. These groups were defined by the pattern of interactions among the persons within them around common concerns. Then these groups themselves came into relationship with one another to achieve common purposes. Today, we see them as the elements of civil society.

While much of this thinking at the national political level gave way to the focus on big government and the anti-Depression programs of the New Deal in the 1930s and the war effort of the 1940s, social thinkers kept alive the attention to the small group—family, church, social group, workplace, interest group, task-oriented civic association—as the place where character is formed and fulfilled. These were the "mediating structures" that provided the meeting ground—now we might refer to it as public space—where individuals came together to do the public's business.[14]

These two traditions in democratic thought are complementary; they need each other. They are not mutually exclusive; both the machinery of democracy and citizens as political actors are essential. There are some things that governments cannot do and some things that only citizens can do; conversely, there are some things that only government is given the authority to do. Democratic governments cannot create their own legitimacy. They cannot define their own purposes, chart the basic directions they are to follow, set the standards by which they will operate or make and sustain tough decisions over time unless the people support them. Democratic governments need broad public support if they are to act consistently over the long term.

Some political thinkers suggest that the Constitution itself is not just a basic legal document; it is also a political process. In the United States, that was true from the beginning: First, compromises were reached on great issues through dialogue; next, a document was agreed upon; then the document was submitted to the people for deliberation in communities, and they insisted on ten amendments before they would consent to ratification. Subsequently, the continuing reinterpretation of the Constitution through more than two centuries is living proof of a process that some have called a process of a people continuously reconstituting themselves.

The meaninglessness of written constitutions that did not emerge from genuine political compromise and were not rooted in public political processes has been highlighted in the twentieth century by the constitutions of totalitarian governments. While sounding very much like the constitutions of genuinely democratic polities, they had no real effect on the continuing practices of governments. The Soviet Union under Joseph Stalin is only a most dramatic example.

THE CITIZEN AS POLITICAL ACTOR IN CIVIL SOCIETY: THE CITIZENS' POLITICAL PROCESS

Two ideas are essential in giving new life to this second thread of democratic tradition: First is the concept of the citizen as a political actor; second is the concept of civil society as the complex of associations that active citizens form and through which they interact with other groups to do their work. Since the politics of citizens is a process of continuous interaction among people and associations, one way to get inside the dynamics of that process is to lay it out as a progression of interacting ideas and actions—a citizens' political process. It is through that process that a disparate collection of citizens forms itself into an engaged public with its members having the capacity together to change the course of events. It is by working within that process that citizens generate the power to bring about change.

The power of citizens lies partly in their effective conduct of that political process. The sequence of work outlined below is comparable to the sequence of negotiation and of the sustained dialogue described in Chapter Six. In the citizens' political process, the task is to create public space in which they can come together to make the choices and form the relationships and associations within the civil society that they need to solve their problems in the larger body politic. In the peace process, the purpose is to change the relationships that underlie conflict, so in that case there must be deeper probing of the dynamics of the relationships themselves. But the progression of these processes is probably comparable because they reflect how the human mind works in approaching a difficult situation.

Following are the stages through which the citizens' political process seems to evolve and the concepts that underlie it. To speak in terms of a process with a sequence of stages is not to present a rigid template for action. It is simply to open the door to thinking about connecting individual actions to achieve larger objectives. It provides a conceptual framework for sharpening strategy and tactics. Each stage reflects the broadening and deepening of a process of interaction—relationships—among citizens.

Stage One: Coming Together around a Problem

At the beginning of this process, a citizen concludes that a situation hurts her or his interests badly enough to require change. Seeing a connection between personal interests and the larger situation, the citizen reaches out to other citizens whose interests may also be hurt. A group of citizens with comparable concerns decides to come together to talk about the problem that affects them so seriously. This step can take time: The problem may seem daunting; citizens may worry about the reaction of others or even be afraid of those who oppose change; a widening circle of talk may be needed to create a critical mass of people who are ready to come together for systematic talk. One or two key persons may take the lead in precipitating a decision to meet; on other occasions, a large enough group to make people feel comfortable may have to grow. At some point, they decide the time has come to talk. Exactly what precipitates the citizen to move into the political arena is a primary subject for deeper inquiry.

Even from these early interactions begin the associations—the relationships—of which de Tocqueville wrote. These may be as transitory as the time required to perform a particular civic task, or they may endure across generations. Some have little organization; others have officers, bylaws, legal status, accounting systems and chains of command. In their essential definition, associations have this characteristic in common: Their borders are marked by the patterns of interaction around the common concern that brings their members together. That dynamic process of interaction and the interdependence that gives it reason are the essence of the human relationships that are the sinews of these associations and of the civil society of which they become a part.

Beyond the internal interactions that define individual groups are the interactions among groups themselves. Much of the new thinking about politics grows out of a sense of how important relationships are in politics. So many fundamental problems have proved to be problems of relationships that some citizens' organizations have concluded that basic change can be made only by fundamentally changing the working relationships in the community—the ways people habitually deal with one another. The idea is not to have good, happy or trusting relationships. The idea is to construct relationships that can solve problems whether the individuals involved like and trust each other or not.

"Associations are held together by a force that governments and institutions often find in short supply—the simple but powerful force of the promises people make to one another, their covenants," says Mathews, continuing:

> Covenants are the . . . glue that holds [associations] together and makes them work. . . . A covenant contains certain principles for structuring the way peo-

ple work together. In covenants, the partnerships are voluntary; no one can be forced. Each party remains independent; no one is asked to merge her or his identity into some collective melting pot. People are not asked . . . to like one another. They just have to be willing to work together. The [association's purposes] have to be agreed upon mutually. . . . The partners 'own' the association; they are not employees or clients. Partners need not have equal resources. . . . [Yet] everyone has to treat everyone else in the relationship as an equal . . . [b]ecause everyone is dependent on the agreement of others, and everyone has a say in what the associations' purposes are.[15]

All of this work by citizens takes place in "public space"—the physical and psychological space where every citizen can feel he or she belongs, which is not anyone's territory.[16] This space owned by the participants as citizens is different from government space; it is space where citizens meet for deliberation and dialogue on problems important to them. All are safe here. It is psychological in that participants experience the views and feelings of other citizens in a way that creates a new context for personal thought. It is also different from the private sphere. In the latter—personal life with family, friends, associates, identity group and local community—one expects belonging, similarity and loyalty. In larger public environments, it is more productive to expect diversity of interests and views and to learn how to deal with those differences in constructive problem solving.

Stage Two: Mapping the Problem, Naming It and Framing Choices

When the group first sits together, participants need to spend time talking about the situation so as to identify its important dimensions, the relationships that cause it and the interests affected by it. We call this "mapping" the problem—laying out its main elements. At its most effective, mapping begins with individuals telling their stories to relate how a problem affects their lives and what is important to them. They will provide the ingredients for a definition of the problem from the viewpoint of the citizen, not the expert or the government.

An important part of this stage of their talk is to put the problem in a perspective that reflects why and how it threatens what citizens in that group value. Unless they define or name the problem in a way that accurately reflects their connection to it—why it hurts their most important interests— their efforts to deal with the problem will not be as effective as they could otherwise be.

Often implicit in citizens' name for a problem is their answer to such questions as: What kind of community would we like? What alternative to the present situation would we like to move toward? How does this situation affect our getting there? Answers to such questions can range widely, depending on different citizens' philosophies about a better society. That is why naming the problem in a way that each participant can live with is essential in building the common ground necessary to start tackling the problem.

When the group has characterized the problem in a way that reflects the connection of this problem to their interests, they need to probe its dynamics in such a way as to frame their choices for dealing with it. Citizens, however, do not frame choices as experts do in terms of technical solutions; they frame choices in terms of what they value and a general direction in which they want to move. Again, just getting this far may take time. These are complex tasks that are intellectually challenging because they demand personal soul-searching as individuals listen deeply to the feelings of others. This stage ends when those involved have defined the problem they must deal with and identified their choices among ways of tackling it.

Stage Three: Deliberating and Setting a Direction

When they are ready, citizens meet to deliberate. To deliberate is not just to "talk about" problems; to deliberate is to agonize within oneself and with others over the pros and cons of each choice they have framed. Often more than one choice contains elements a person values, so difficult trade-offs must be made. As they weigh with others the choices they have identified— that is, as they deliberate—they deepen their understanding of the consequences of the options for themselves and for those whose cooperation is critical in dealing with the problem. Their deliberation gradually identifies common ground from which they can move to action. That common ground provides the starting point for defining the broad direction in which they want to move together to create a situation all can live with. It does not signify total agreement—just enough agreement to undergird shared purpose in a particular situation.

If citizens genuinely grapple with their choices together, they will begin to change the quality of their relationships. They will not necessarily agree about everything, but they will emerge with a sense of where their aims are common and what is tolerable and intolerable for each significant actor. And they will understand why. They will begin considering their commitments to engage in the common task of dealing with the problem at hand. It is the mutual promises they may decide to make that will bind them in whatever associations they eventually form to accomplish the particular task they decide to pursue.

Deliberation involves choice. Citizens must choose before they can act. In its most basic form, taking responsibility for their own fate begins with citizens recognizing that they have choices. Recognizing their power to choose does not imply that they are not subject to external forces beyond their control. Choices come from the way they deal with those circumstances.

"There are two ways to understand the process of making choices," says Mathews. They reflect how citizens view their own role. "Conventionally," Mathews continues, "the public's choices are understood to be decisions about the various solutions that the political system generates. Politicians and governments propose options . . . [that] are usually very technical and involve complex pieces of legislation. The public isn't the source of such options; citizens are just expected to choose among those that politicians, governments and interest groups offer—in much the same way as consumers choose merchandise off the shelf."

But choices are also made about more fundamental issues. "The most basic choices citizens make are about what kind of community and country they want. These choices aren't the same as preferences for one solution or another. People really can't select a particular solution until they have made more fundamental choices about purposes. The primary political challenge, from this perspective," Mathews concludes, "is to answer basic questions like, What do we want for our community? What do we want our community to be?"[17]

Basic choices force people to consult their deepest motivations. Making choices is hard work; citizens have to "work through" their initial reactions of confusion over conflicting interests until they are in control again and can deal with unpleasant realities. The alternative to making public choices is likely to be relatively uninformed, knee-jerk reaction.

The ultimate experience in deliberation is determining whether there is political will to pursue the course chosen. At the end of a deliberation, the final choice is: Do the consequences of doing nothing outweigh the anticipated results of the course the group has chosen, or not? If the consequences of maintaining the status quo are more serious than attempting the course chosen, there is presumably the beginning of a will to move ahead.

In some ways, the most essential resource in a community is political will: the commitment of its citizens to work on a problem until they have it under control. "The idea is to join existing interests, and the energy associated with them, in order to create a larger public will," Mathews writes, "This way of thinking about generating will is quite compatible with the new thinking about building functional political relationships. In both cases, the strategy is to get people to see the connections among their interests to produce 'combined energy.'"[18]

Political will has certain qualities. It is the will of many—not of everyone, but of enough people to get the job done. It is more than the perseverance of a few. It certainly means more than fanatical devotion to one cause. Will connotes staying power or determination, not just initial popular support. Usually people have to be willing to make sacrifices. Political will goes deep into a body politic; it is not a superficial enthusiasm. Communities can create political will by linking together inclinations, motivations and interests that already exist rather than attempting to create something new.

In a large body politic such as the United States, government will need a sense of the public's judgment on issues that reach beyond associations in which face-to-face dialogue is possible. In these cases, the questions become: What makes the people a public? If we are not simply talking about a mass of people voting, what more is a public than a mass of people or a collection of interest groups?

If the question could be answered in just one thought, says Mathews, it might be this: People become a public through the connecting process of deliberation that sets a direction for public policy, builds common ground from which to move, designs the relationships and interactive steps necessary for change and generates the will to work for change.

Stage Four: Planning a Course of Complementary Actions—Scenario-Building

When participants have determined the general direction in which they want to move, they must then figure out how to get there. One way to do this is to work through these four steps:

- List the obstacles to moving in this direction. These are not just obvious physical or political obstacles, but also underlying human obstacles such as misperception, fear, hatred and longstanding grievance. Often, cancerous relationships are greater obstacles to solutions or peace than the most serious practical issue.
- List steps for removing those obstacles. Again, these steps will include practical solutions to practical problems, but they must also include steps to change relationships that block such solutions. Sometimes it is more important to find steps to allay fear—even unjustified fear—than it is to find technically sound solutions.

- List the actors who can take those steps. Often, this exercise will reveal the need to bring others into the process. It may also reveal that the burden of action is unfairly distributed and cause participants to go back and review their work on obstacles and steps to deal with them.
- List those steps beside the name of the actor who will take them in a sequence that makes it possible for each actor to take the steps he or she needs to take. This is the point at which participants assess what actions depend on prior actions or on supportive responses. Often, what seemed impossible before the sequence began now seems possible. As steps accumulate, a sense of momentum is generated by the interactive quality of the sequence.

The product of this work is sometimes called a "scenario" because one action builds on another, much like the actions in an unfolding drama. Or we speak of "complementary actions," a powerful accumulation of interactions that reinforce one another. Unlike institutional action, complementary action is not directed toward a single objective in a planned way. Rather, it is more organic and repeating, like a jazz group in which each player supports the others within an overall theme but is free to improvise and express individual style without following a conductor.

Stage Five: Acting Together

Once a scenario of complementary actions has been developed, the group must decide whether and how it will put that scenario into action. Often, the options include moving insights from a relatively small group out into the larger community through the associations to which members relate.

Some have criticized thinking of this kind, arguing that it ignores a central concept of politics: power. However, this framework does not ignore power; it recognizes broader bases for power.

Power is commonly thought of as control over hard resources—money, institutions of government, instruments of force, legal authority. By that traditional definition, power transactions are normally a zero-sum calculation, in which people believe that there is a fixed amount of power and that the only way to get power is to take it from someone else.

Mary Parker Follett, an unusually versatile thinker in the first half of the twentieth century, noted that power could either flow in one direction as "power over" or be experienced in an interactive lateral way as "power with." Power, in her view, grows out of people relating to each other in ways calculated to achieve a common purpose. A phrase that has been used to describe this "power with" is "relational power"—power that grows out of people relating to each other in ways that produce a result. Power in this sense has to be created and re-created and enlarged—and it can be. From this perspective, power that is "given" by somebody to "empower" others is not real power. Citizens must generate their own power.[19]

As citizens act, a critical continuing dimension of their work is constant thoughtfulness about whether their work is producing the results anticipated. Continuous assessment of failures and successes leads to midcourse corrections as a natural thought process in an unfolding experience. It makes civic learning an integral element in a strong civil society. This thinking on evaluation is developed more fully in Chapter Ten.

The purpose of thinking in terms of a political process such as this is to enable citizens to place their actions in the larger context of a political strategy with a sense of direction, destination and potential accomplishment. Through this process, they can systematically generate the power they need. This process is *their* instrument for change, *their* version of the instruments of governments such as legislation.

A citizens' political process such as this has historically been the wellspring of democratic politics. Without deliberation and the capacity to work in association, people are just people—a collection of individuals, inhabitants—not a public. They have no connection or relationship to one another. Unless they become a public in this particular sense of the word, citizens are incapable of giving common direction to government. Without public deliberation, governments are left without public direction and legitimacy.

At the end of the twentieth century, across the world, new forms of associations are emerging. These organizations are about problem solving and more; they are dedicated to changing the way politics operates, to changing the character of politics. Their creed is reflected in Czech President Václav Havel's words: "It is not that we should simply seek new and better ways of managing society, the economy, and the world. The point is that we should fundamentally change how we behave."[20] Before we can change how we behave, however, we have to reshape the concepts that determine how we think and see.

BUILDING CIVIL SOCIETY

As of this writing, a neat strategy for building civil society had not been worked out. But research was beginning to suggest some of the components that would need to be part of such a strategy.

First, the civil societies that seem to have worked have been rich in the availability of public spaces. Citizens have created a variety of contexts in which they interact. Their purposes for coming together may be many—ranging from the recreational to civic improvement—but always they strengthen the habit of talking about common interests and working together when necessary to achieve common purposes. The important characteristic is the habit of interacting. Experiences in the citizens' political process described above and in sustained dialogue can help build this habit.

Second, the civil societies that seem to have worked have been characterized by citizens who formed connections with one another to pursue common goals. These relationships first take place among citizens as they form associations to pursue their goals. Then associations come together in networks. These societies are tied together by complexes of interlocking networks. Some of these span the fault lines that normally exist among unlike people—the racial, regional, ethnic, class, religious and historical antagonisms that appear in some form in most societies. As societies emerge from the fragmentation of civil violence, such associations can be built consciously to span society's fault lines.

Third, these networks provide a steadily growing experience in a pattern of continuous interaction that becomes the context for gradual development of what Robert Putnam calls a "normal generalized reciprocity." As citizens observe each other's behavior—the predictability and the reliability of how each interacts with others—trust grows, and the glue of potential cooperation is added to the social mix. This reservoir of predictable reciprocity becomes part of what Putnam refers to as "social capital."[21] It is also an essential ingredient of sound relationships.

Fourth, the civil societies that seem to have worked have demonstrated a continuing hunger for learning and growing. That kind of learning comes not from textbooks, but from the experiences and rewards of succeeding or failing in working together to accomplish tasks that both advance interests and produce the incentives to try again.

These observations do not provide a sure prescription for creating a functioning civil society; in any case, that takes a long time. They do suggest steps that citizens can take to begin generating the experiences, the habits and the capacities for starting to move in that direction. Those steps are embodied in the citizens' political process outlined above.

A BRIDGING WORD

Citizens around the world are angry or disillusioned with institutional politics, but they are only barely beginning to recognize the missing element that is needed to complete the democratic political equation: their own role as political actors. They are still working to crystallize a conceptual framework that would sharpen their perspective on themselves as key figures in the development and nourishment of vibrant civil societies. As they move further along in that task, their frameworks are likely to be built around processes and concepts such as those described here.

In this chapter, we have focused on the relationships citizens form to do their work as political actors and pinpointed those relationships as the principal source of the power on which citizens draw. In Chapter Four, I introduce the concept of relationship in international affairs to capture the political process of continuous interaction between significant elements of whole bodies politic across the permeable borders of countries.

As we restore the missing thread of democratic thought to its rightful place and look at international relationships through new lenses, we also come face-to-face with a phenomenon experienced in one place after another: that domestic politics and international politics are converging in ways rarely recognized before. This convergence in mutually enriching ways opens the door to a broader range of approaches to conflict and to building institutions in the wake of conflict that can immunize a body politic against its recurrence.

Chapter Four

——~✦✦~——

International Relationships
Across Permeable Borders

RELATIONSHIPS AMONG WHOLE BODIES POLITIC—NOT JUST STATES

We are living through a profound shift in how we understand international relationships. This shift is taking place not because the Cold War ended. It reflects fundamental changes in how countries relate on the eve of a new century as viewed in the 350-year perspective of focusing on the nation-state as the organizing unit and principal actor on the international stage.

In the system of the past three-and-a-half centuries, theories of international relations have depicted states as amassing economic and military power to pursue objectively defined interests in contests of physical power with other states. This mode of interaction has been called "power politics." The metaphor has been the strategic chessboard. Each state has been seen as a rational actor plotting its government's moves on that chessboard.

A reflective look at the world from the brink of the twenty-first century will not argue for setting that picture aside; it *will* question the completeness of such a picture. A more complete view will broaden the present focus on how states come to decisions and how they act *on* each other. It will use a wider-angle lens to include, first, the many actors in addition to state institutions that affect international relationships and, second, the processes through which those many actors, including governments, interact *with* each other. It will focus on the overall relationship between whole bodies politic, not just on what governments do to each other.

In a wide-ranging conversation in April 1977 well before the historic 1978 meeting at Camp David was conceived, U.S. President Jimmy Carter and Egyptian President Anwar al-Sadat were reflecting on the nature of peace. Carter was arguing for a definition of peace between Egypt and Israel that would involve the complete normalization of relations between the peoples of the two countries. Former Israeli Prime Minister Golda Meir had once said: "When I can shop in the markets of Cairo, I will know there is real peace." Former and later Israeli Prime Minister Yitzhak Rabin put it in another picture: "When we can play basketball against each other, we will know there is real peace."

"That kind of peace," Sadat responded, in effect, "is for the next generation." His point, repeated on a number of occasions, was that governments can sign peace treaties, but governments cannot decree normal relationships between peoples. For instance, Egyptians will go to Israel on vacation when they feel like it. They will not feel like it until they are proud of their peaceful relationship with Israel—until they believe that their peace has led to peace and restoration of land for others. Time and time again during negotiation of the Egyptian-Israeli Peace Treaty, members of the U.S. team argued: "The quality of the normalization of relations will depend on the quality of the overall peace process—the progress in bringing Palestinians, Jordanians, Syrians and Lebanese into the process."[1] The peace process has been a series of mediated and negotiated agreements embedded in a larger political process in which relationships changed slowly.

As it happened in the negotiation and implementation of the Egyptian-Israeli Peace Treaty, the approach was a combination of both men's views. The treaty itself included an annex on the normalization of relations. It gave juridical permission for people in the two countries to develop normal relationships. But for years after the treaty was signed, Israelis called it a "cold peace" because much of the hoped-for normalization did not happen. Egyptian citizens were not ready for it.

In short, one of the most important instruments of statecraft—a treaty of peace signed by leaders and ratified by parliaments—could not be fully followed through without the participation of citizens. Trust is not established by the acts of government alone; it is built over time through a growing network of interactions and relationships among citizens who are engaged together in solving problems and pursuing common interests. That truth is slowly and painfully being placed on the agenda of the study and conduct of international relationships in the closing decade of the twentieth century: Citizens play an essential role in the political processes through which bodies politic interact; international politics is not an affair of states alone.

Compelling evidence all around us demands a shift in the framework we use to understand our world and to act in it. Refocusing our conceptual lenses is a first step toward dealing more effectively with conflict. Concepts from the past, too narrowly defined, block the path to more imaginative action tomorrow.

THREE OBSERVATIONS ON A CHANGING WORLD

Three observations about our changing world suggest some of the thoughts that provide a starting point for a new conceptual framework for understanding more fully how countries relate on the eve of the twenty-first century. Readers will have their own formulations and emphases. I use these observations to begin to form a common outlook.

Government Cooperation

States and their governments increasingly face problems that not one of them can deal with outside relationships with others—in some cases, relationships with other states, but, in many cases, new relationships with their own citizens. These intense and complex relationships involve political processes of continuous interaction among interdependent participants. Those processes must be understood in their own right.

Unilateral action by government seems less and less effective. During the Cold War, the superpowers learned that neither could provide security for its people without cooperating with its adversary. The concept of "common security" was articulated by citizens outside government to express the seeming contradiction that the people of one superpower could not be secure unless they helped the people of the other feel secure.[2] Other governments also faced weapons that make war prohibitively costly and learned that building their own power and acting alone could not guarantee security for their people. Many countries are torn by intercommunal conflicts that can only end when neighbors build new human and political relationships.

Beyond security, other challenges that reach across borders are familiar: the interactions of a global economy; pervasive instantaneous communications and electronic access to vast stores of knowledge and new thinking; rapid transport of people, products and weapons; disease; ecological systems; environmental degradation; fallout from nuclear accidents. All cause us to rethink the capacity of the so-called sovereign state and to recognize the permeability of state borders. All dramatize changing threats to national security, as well as new opportunities for cooperation if states will rethink the nature of their sovereignty.

Events in distant parts of the world affect perceptions and actions in other places almost immediately. Not only do problems cut across national borders; more centers of influence—both state and civil—affect events. Interaction of involved parties on many levels and fronts at the same time often poses problems beyond one state's control.

Finally, mounting concern for the rights of individual human beings within sovereign states has steadily become a factor affecting relationships among states. Governments still jealously guard the principle of noninterference in relations between them and their people. Yet, the legitimacy of one government's concern for the rights of individuals in another sovereignty has been established in such interstate agreements as U.N. documents and the Helsinki accords, as well as in the watchfulness of such nongovernmental organizations as Amnesty International and Asia Watch and election observers monitoring voting in the Philippines, Nicaragua, Haiti, Zambia, Cambodia, the Dominican Republic, Mexico, Palestine, Yemen and numerous other countries. Questions about the rights of Soviet Jewry, Palestinians under Israeli military occupation, Bosnians under Serbian attack or blacks in South Africa have affected relations between states.

In sum, state institutions must still maintain foundations for action and for organizing and directing official resources to accomplish goals, but politics among interdependent countries is more than a transmission belt for military and economic power. It is also a process of interaction among bodies politic in which power to produce results may itself be generated from within that interaction as interested groups combine to tackle a problem. A world in which problems cut across borders and no one state can be in complete control requires a focus not just on the decision making of states, but also on the political processes through which concerned groups generate a capacity to work together to deal with problems. New ideas of sovereignty formed in new relationships may become part of the solutions to previously intractable problems. Those political processes—the relationships among actors—demand careful study in themselves, beyond the decision making of individual actors.

Citizen Involvement

Citizens outside government are increasingly involved in the conduct of international relationships. The groups they form within their bodies politic to do their work make up civil society. As they interact to form those groups and as the groups themselves interact, they generate the capacities—the power—to change both governments and the course of events. As they interact with other such groups across permeable borders, they play a part in shaping international relationships.

Governments have encountered an increased popular role in many ways. Israel had to deal with an essentially unarmed popular resistance in the West Bank and Gaza in the late 1980s—a challenge that military leaders said, almost from the beginning, had no military solution. Popular movements changed the national direction and international relationships of Chile, Argentina and Nicaragua. The democracy movement in China in 1989 that triggered the military crackdown around Tiananmen Square changed Sino-U.S. relations because of the reaction of U.S. citizens to the events on their television screens. The dramatic events in East-Central Europe captured world attention later that year. Some of the "ethnic" conflicts that broke out following the dissolution of the Soviet empire were often the work of people outside constitutional government. Some Russians worry about interaction between Islamic movements in Iran and Afghanistan and the Islamic peoples of Central Asia and Russia itself; Americans worry about a potential flood of refugees from south of their border if conditions there become intolerable. Public representation at the Earth Summit in Brazil in 1992 drew on other constituencies. Few of these movements depended entirely on material power.

Increased popular involvement also reflects a widely growing belief that relationships between governors and the governed are much less productive than they should be. People ask whether government is failing—or even whether government is dead. Looking beyond their own borders in this world of sophisticated weapons, in which people are more aware of dangers from day-to-day interactions and are more in touch, citizens ask whether governments are capable of providing security and building peace. More and more, people believe that they must harness their own political power in new ways to tackle chronic social and political problems. To accomplish this, they are thinking about politics in creative, noninstitutional ways. Interaction among citizens is proliferating.

In well-established countries, too, leaders are realizing that solutions lie beyond the power and proficiency of government alone. They lie in new ways of practicing politics that turn loose and help focus the energies of citizens outside government on resolving their own problems and building their own futures. The power of individual incentive is being recognized in China and the post-Soviet countries after years of reliance on central planning and direction.

Focusing on groups of people, as explained in Chapter Three, also causes us to think about politics not just as what politicians do, but also as what happens when citizens outside government work together through the associations they create to deal with their problems. It causes us to think about the civil societies those associations form. It opens the door to recognizing that elements of civil societies increasingly interact across borders. It requires awareness of a politics in which insight begins with knowing whole human beings—not just statistical voters or numbers of troops in a military balance.

Because of the revolutions in communication, transportation and information, what one leader says or does in her or his own country can be heard, seen and assessed by another's constituencies almost immediately. Beyond leaders, peoples in many nations are more aware of each other as human beings and not just as institutional abstractions, thanks to sister-city programs, innumerable cultural and educational exchanges, international sports and tourism.

This phenomenon is far from universal. People from developing nations often remind us that most of them—as well as the poor in more economically advanced countries—are far from participating in their bodies politic or enjoying the luxury of this kind of interaction across borders. Indeed, we in the United States are concerned about the emergence of a "permanent underclass." While these disadvantaged people are sadly right, even among the poor, radio and television and the print media reach across some barriers to create international interaction. Even in the poorest countries, rebellion against government has not depended on expensive travel.

As more people experience or affect international relationships, incentives mount to understand countries and governments at least partly as groups of people. Such understanding requires that we no longer explain how countries relate only in terms of transactions between state institutions but that we introduce a human dimension into our analysis. Increasing engagement of people in domestic and international politics demands new awareness of the human roots of interests, priorities and conflict in relationships among countries. Fear, suspicion, rejection, mistrust, hatred and misperception are often greater obstacles to peace than an inability to resolve technically definable problems. Conflict has many roots, but some of today's most intense conflicts will not be dealt with fully by focusing on states and governments.

As the role of citizens outside government increases, interaction among public agendas in civil societies plays a larger part in relationships between countries. Those agendas reflect the "gut reactions" of the citizens of one country to the perceived character and intent of others. In different ways in different systems, they can impel or constrain policymakers. We begin to look beyond an abstract state system and to question the proposition that states are to be analyzed as institutions quite different from the groups of human beings who influence, make, implement and sustain their policies.

In sum, as we focus on the process of interaction between whole bodies politic—that is, between civil societies as well as governments—rather than mainly on transactions between state institutions, our picture of the international system changes. As we add human beings to the study of relationships among bodies politic, we recognize that the politics of relationships among countries have roots deeper in human concerns and needs than is recognized by interests defined by governments alone. Power in relationships among countries may ultimately be more compelling when it grows out of human need—physical and psychological—than when it is based on weapons and money. Because those individual human needs and perspectives express themselves in civil societies, international life must include space not just for interstate transactions, but also for the interactions among elements of civil societies as well.

Broadening Concepts

The familiar concepts of international relations such as state sovereignty, power and national interests do not—as presently defined—adequately describe how countries relate in our interdependent world, and the traditional instruments of statecraft such as military power and negotiation do not reliably produce the results we expect of them.

In making this point, I am *not* arguing the end of the nation-state; nor am I arguing that force will cease to be a major factor in the foreseeable future. I *am* arguing that these concepts, as traditionally understood and normally practiced, are not defined broadly enough for today's world. We need to place those concepts in the environment of a changing world so as to begin transforming them for the tasks at hand.

"States" will continue to be the primary organizing unit in international life, and "governments" will normally continue to speak authoritatively for states in relations with other states. But now we see that governments are often not the only, or even the most effective, agents for resolving problems; the institutions of so-called sovereign states confront problems they cannot resolve acting by themselves. Even countries that have relied on highly centralized systems recognize that, in many instances, only the energies of citizens can deal effectively with certain problems.

Increasingly, we will also focus on "civil societies"—a concept not usually included in writing about international relations. This concept will call attention to the broadening role of citizens in shaping not only the character

of their countries, but also relationships with other countries, and in accomplishing changes that governments acting alone cannot make happen.
Some of the most telling differences among societies over time have come
down to the degree to which such associations among people within a society exist to give larger fabric to their lives together.

The "political arena" is not just the place where elections and decisions of
government take place; it also includes the "public space" in which citizens
deliberate on their country's direction in relationships with others and, increasingly, citizens in the bodies politic of different countries interact across
state borders. We are beginning to think of international civil society and international public space. As that public space grows in the years ahead, we
will probably need to rethink the nature of state borders themselves—not so
much their existence, necessity or legitimacy but exactly what they do or do
not define, confine and exclude. In this book, I am not positing a world
without borders but, rather, a world in which borders serve different, but
still useful, purposes.

"Power," "authority," and "capacity" are not fixed economic, military and
legal resources lodged only in institutions and exercised or allocated only by
existing laws or by government policies. Power has been defined as the ability to force another party to do what it does not want to do. As stated in earlier chapters, I believe it is more realistic and useful to think of power as the
capacity to change the course of events.

Today, the most powerful weapons the world has ever known cannot be
used by leaders of conscience, and, even when force is used, it may not produce the expected results. In the 1940s, a nonviolent movement ended
British rule in India. The American and Soviet experiences in Vietnam and
Afghanistan are not unique. Israel learned that superior weapons could not
exterminate the Palestinian national movement. In the winter of
1987–1988, changes in the Israeli-Palestinian relationship came not from
the armed power of a state but from the civil disobedience of an unarmed
people. Television screens pictured Palestinian youths throwing stones at
young Israelis wearing the uniform of the Israeli Defense Forces; cameras
captured those Israeli soldiers beating Palestinian youths on the ground with
sticks and stones, not fighting them with planes and tanks. Clearly, factors
other than material power changed the course of events. If we are interested
in change, we must focus on what produces change.

Even strong states are less and less able to prevent instant oral, visual and
written communication from crossing their borders. In an interdependent
world, people are interacting across permeable borders whether governments
want them to or not. In internal conflicts in which authority has broken

down and some citizens claim the right to engage in their own act of self-determination, the state alone is increasingly less able to provide security or to preserve a coherent body politic. The permeability of state boundaries—important as those boundaries remain in defining the identities of some groups and in organizing certain activities—and the failing capability of government cause us to rethink what constitutes capacity for change.

Power can also be created from nonmaterial sources—for instance, the power that grows from commitments among citizens acting within strong relationships. If power is the capacity to change the course of events and if relationships among countries are a political process of continuous interaction, power may come as much from the effective conduct of that process as from controlling or using military force or economic sanctions or incentives. Significant sources of power reside in the bonds of civic associations and commitments of mutual support in achieving common purposes. The roots of power may often be relational rather than physical or juridical. The capacity to accomplish goals does not depend only on action by government; the independent, but complementary, actions of various elements in a body politic may be far more effective if they are inspired and guided by a shared scenario. Power may stem from the connectedness between issues and groups.

"Interests," as suggested in Chapter Two, are defined not just analytically and objectively, but also politically—that is, in human terms. They are defined not just by the analytical arms of government, but also in the body politic reflecting what citizens value. We have been taught to think of interests as measurable. But a political definition of interests also reflects human identity, values, fears, hopes and choices among rival claimants on resources; it reflects not only individual interests, but also interests of the larger community and body politic. Defining "interests" is further complicated when—as in conflicts such as the East-West standoff between "mortal enemies" during the Cold War—interests are defined as a function of a relationship. What can we not accomplish without help from the other? What do we feel we must deny the other? Or: We are who we are because we are not the other.

We have already noted how "military force" has not produced the results we expected of it in Vietnam, Afghanistan or Palestine, but think also for a moment about "negotiation"—the peaceful alternative to the use of force. The intensive Arab-Israeli peace process in the 1970s demonstrated that negotiation alone does not initiate change. Change is initiated and shaped in the political arena.

Negotiation may define, capture, crystallize, consolidate and give impetus to change that has already begun, but, until political leaders or interacting citizens have transformed the political environment, negotiators are unlikely to succeed. Even if they reach a technically sound agreement, it may not be fully implemented or have the consequences intended without the support of the body politic on both sides.

Mediation and negotiation remain indispensable instruments in many situations, but they achieve their potential only when they are embedded in larger political processes. Many deep-rooted human conflicts are not ready for formal, governmental mediation or negotiation. Often, parties to those conflicts cannot define issues for negotiation. Besides, people do not negotiate about their fears, historical grievances or identities. Conflict at that level must often be dealt with through processes among human beings working together in the political arena without reference to authorities.

Moreover, traditional government-to-government negotiations have normally assumed that two parties who are at least equal in status and legitimacy, if not in power, meet to engage in a joint effort to resolve conflict by agreement. In many conflicts among groups, neither is a state; the conflicts are intercommunal. Because the issues in dispute are often indivisible—existence, survival, identity, acceptance—they are not negotiable at the outset. Such issues cannot be dealt with before recognition in human terms and commitment to peaceful coexistence; only then can practical arrangements defining new relationships be spelled out in negotiation.

Negotiation is just one instrument of peaceful change; change is often initiated in the political arena, not necessarily first in the antechambers of the negotiating room. Problems may be solved not just by agreement or compromise, but also by using a variety of political instruments. Whether or not resolution of problems is negotiated, the political process involves creating common ground for a range of possible actions that seem politically permissible within a community that has struggled with its choices.

In sum, as we see the limits of traditional concepts of international relations in our changing world, we recognize that enlarging our understanding of them can make peaceful political instruments available to us that have normally been excluded from the study and professional conduct of relationships among countries. New ideas about the politics of international relationships may offer an array of instruments for affecting the course of events. We may speak less of power politics and more of power from politics. Our attention may focus not only on the results we may want to achieve, but also—and maybe first—on building political relationships and changing political environments in ways that will make it possible to produce and sustain those results.

Some diplomatic or academic colleagues say to me, in effect: "I'd like to think the world has changed enough to make that possible, but I just don't see it. Force is still widely used, and most states still do not reflect citizens' views in making foreign policy." That is true. The point is not that the world has changed completely. The point is that evidence of change has been all around us for some time. Standing on the bridge between two paradigms as a new millennium approaches, we would be unwise not to act in recognition of elements of the future that are already with us and not to begin developing a worldview that will enable us to act creatively in that future while we go on dealing with the present. When old pictures blur and old tools do not always work, the time comes to search out more effective ways of thinking and acting.

THE STARTING POINT FOR A NEW CONCEPTUAL FRAMEWORK

While I do not claim originality in these observations, the conclusions I draw from them differ from the usual. They open the door to a different way of thinking about how countries relate. Practitioners and scholars in a wide range of disciplines are already redefining familiar concepts and enlarging definitions of the tools used to bring about change. My aim is a conceptual framework that will enable us to begin integrating this rich collection of insights into thinking about conflictual relationships. If we do not, we will deprive ourselves of tools for guiding change peacefully and creatively.

As I said at the beginning of this chapter, the traditional power-politics framework for the study of international relations might be captured in a formula such as the following: Leaders of nation-states amass economic and military power to pursue objectively defined interests against other nation-states in zero-sum contests of material power. As I have argued, that state-centered formula does not fully explain interactions among countries today.

I find the following formulation more descriptive of the world in which we live: *Relationships among countries and groups are increasingly a political process of continuous interaction among significant elements of whole bodies politic across permeable borders that sovereign states no longer fully control.* That interaction involves an intertwining of issues, actions and perceptions operating simultaneously in all directions on many levels through many channels.

The word I use to capture that political process of continuous interaction—the total pattern of interactions between whole bodies politic—is the simple human word "relationship," which I have explained in Chapter Two. We must focus on the *whole* relationship between *whole* groups of people and recognize that it is *whole* human beings who are part of those groups and affect their policies. And we must focus on that political process of interaction—the *whole relationship*—at many levels involving both governmental institutions and groups of human beings.

As civil societies develop and citizens outside government increasingly influence and participate in cross-border relationships, change often takes place through that interaction on many levels at once rather than mainly through a linear series of government actions and responses. Looking beyond the power and policy-making of states and their governments acting on each other, we need to see the overall relationship between whole bodies politic. In that context, we need to provide new channels for those interactions among civil societies that have not normally been seen as part of the international system.

Shifting focus to that political process—the continuous multilevel interaction between significant elements of whole bodies politic—incorporates two important dimensions of experience into our thinking about foreign affairs. Initially, we pay more attention to the larger domestic political environments in which citizens reach fundamental value judgments about peace, war, negotiation, economic development and trade. Next, when we turn to that political environment, we begin to see how those judgments are influenced by external events and, therefore, how perceptions and the course of change may be affected by political action across borders rather than only by contests of force.

If we see power as emerging from the political ability to conduct the interactive process between groups imaginatively, we open the door to focusing on political—therefore, peaceful—ways of changing conflictual relationships. We even dare think of political strategies for transforming conflict.

MOVING ON

In Chapters Two, Three and Four, I have argued that our evolving thinking about conflict, about politics and about international relationships increasingly introduces the human dimension into our understanding of what making and building peace require. I have fleshed out the concepts we need to take full advantage of the framework provided by the idea of the multilevel peace process.

In the chapters that follow, I shift the spotlight to the primary instrument available to citizens outside government in changing conflictual relationships—dialogue—and focus particularly on the process of sustained, systematic dialogue that I call "a public peace process."

Chapter Five

The Dialogue Process

A DIFFERENT APPROACH TO CONFLICT

Sustained dialogue—an interactive process designed to change conflictual relationships over time—is different from the usual public-policy discussions and from formal mediation and negotiation. First, it focuses on the dynamics of the underlying relationships that cause divisive problems, not just on the problems. Second, it focuses on changing those relationships, not just on choosing a policy direction or on dividing material goods or power in dispute through formal mediation or negotiation. It is designed for groups, communities and organizations in deep-rooted human conflict or tension whatever the cause—ethnic, racial, religious, historic, material or personal.

Some people in conflict reject dialogue because they think of it as "just talk without purpose or destination." Others immediately think of mediation, negotiation or arbitration. Still others believe they would be able to resolve conflict if they could just hold a free election.

Sustained dialogue is more structured than a good conversation or study-group discussion and less structured than a mediation or negotiation. It perseveres over time. It has purpose and destination and the possibility of generating power to accomplish goals. Its purpose is to provide an experience in changing relationships within the dialogue group. Its destination is to design a plan for changing relationships in the larger community. It can produce a shared sense of what kind of community or country current antagonists would like to build together to serve the interests of each.

If power is the capacity to change the course of events, one product of sustained dialogue is to create power. Members of a dialogue group can design together a scenario of interactive steps to be taken in the political arena to change perceptions and to augment the possibilities of working together toward objectives that meet shared needs.

WHAT DIALOGUE IS—AND IS NOT

Dialogue is a process of genuine *inter*action through which human beings listen to each other deeply enough to be changed by what they learn. Each makes a serious effort to take others' concerns into her or his own picture, even when disagreement persists. No participant gives up her or his identity, but each recognizes enough of the other's valid human claims that he or she will act differently toward the other.

Dialogue differs sharply from exchanging views, discussing, explaining, declaiming, debating or persuading. It contrasts to positional bargaining, to the adversarial proceedings in courtroom litigation and to the oppositional debate in a democratic parliament. In those approaches, solutions to problems are argued; the aim is to make the best argument possible. Many communities embroiled in such debate become engaged in "solution wars"[1]—adversarial arguments over favored solutions.

Dialogue and deliberation stand in sharp contrast to these adversarial approaches. Some classic distinctions go like this:

In the words of David Bohm, a physicist and philosopher who turned his attention to the importance of dialogue in human relationships:

> Contrast [dialogue] with the word "discussion," which has the same root as "percussion" and "concussion." It really means to break things up. It emphasizes the idea of analysis, where there may be many points of view, and where everybody is presenting a different one—analyzing and breaking up. . . . Discussion is almost like a ping-pong game, where people are batting the ideas back and forth and the object of the game is to win or to get points for yourself.[2]

In dialogue, on the other hand, one's mind opens to absorb new views, enlarge perspectives, rethink assumptions and modify judgments. In debate, one listens to find flaws in others' points so as to attack them and to defend one's own point of view. In dialogue, one puts forward ideas while suspending judgment on them in the expectation that others' thoughts will deepen them; together, two sides assume many approaches to an answer and work toward common ground. Debate assumes one right answer and invests only in pressing and defending it; dialogue assumes the possibility of an answer better than any of the original points. Debate narrows views and closes minds; dialogue can build new relationships.[3]

Daniel Yankelovich develops the role of dialogue in building relationships, a central thesis of this book:

> In philosopher Martin Buber's classic work "I and Thou," Buber suggests that in authentic dialogue something far deeper than ordinary conversation is going on. The I-Thou interaction implies a genuine openness of each to the concerns of the other. In such dialogue . . . I fully "take in" your viewpoint, engaging with it in the deepest sense of the term. You do likewise. Each of us internalizes the views of the other to enhance our mutual understanding.
>
> To Buber we owe the stunning insight that, apart from its obvious practical value (most problem solving demands mutual understanding), dialogue expresses an essential aspect of the human spirit. Buber knew that dialogue is a way of being. He recognized that by performing the seemingly simple act of responding empathetically to others and in turn being heard by them, we transcended the constricting confines of the self. Instead of saying, "you or me," you hear yourself saying, "you *and* me." The act of reaching beyond the self to relate to others in dialogue is a profound human yearning. If it were less commonplace we would realize what a miracle it is.[4]

In confrontations and even in adversarial democracy, there is a struggle of assumptions, with power determining the outcome. Assumptions are built from experience; they become part of identity as experience and assumptions together are programmed into memory. Clusters of assumptions nourish cultures and subcultures. In dialogue, we suspend our assumptions to listen to others. To quote Bohm again:

> [We] realize what is on each other's minds without coming to any conclusions or judgments. . . . We . . . weigh the question a little, ponder it a little, feel it out. . . . If we can see what all of our opinions mean, then we are sharing a common content, even if we don't agree entirely. . . . Accordingly, a different kind of consciousness is possible among us, a *participatory* consciousness. . . . We would be taking part and communicating and creating a common meaning. . . . Society is based on shared meanings, which constitute the culture.

In dialogue, thought and communication are often at the tacit level; fundamental change will come at that tacit level.[5]

Inherent in dialogue is the potential for growth, change, movement and direction. As individuals incorporate others' views into their pictures of a situation, their own perspectives are enlarged. By working to get into the minds, interests and feelings of others, each participant changes. The ultimate purpose is finding some common ground, not domination of one view over another or even total agreement. As partners in dialogue enlarge common ground, they thereby change their relationships. An outcome of genuine dialogue—without expecting any participant to give up part of her or his own identity—is to create a picture of the overall relationships that affect capacities to serve important interests. As each party takes others' interests, fears, hopes and concerns into account, the parties come to define their interests as what they can live with—not their optimal interests—in order to reach the cooperation with others necessary to achieve what all parties absolutely need.

As philosopher Bernard Murchland explains:

> Political meaning is disclosed . . . when the citizen enters into dialogue with other citizens, not primarily to persuade them of anything but to find out what is on their minds, what their concerns and interests are. . . . In this way a common world, a public world, is created. . . . [Hannah] Arendt puts it clearly: through conversation "we become equal partners in a common world and together constitute a community." We can converse precisely because we see things differently; we can find common ground when we are able to talk to one another. This is the political meaning of deliberation.[6]

In the Dartmouth Conference Regional Conflicts Task Force, the co-chairs often began discussions by asking each side to present its view of the other's interests. In time, we shared insights on the effect of such factors as fear of the other's system, feelings of inferiority or different use of concepts in policy-making. In that setting, a few Soviet and U.S. citizens gained a deeper insight into why each group thought and acted as it did. As a Russian colleague reflected in our tenth-anniversary meeting in 1992:

> This process involved taking into account the positive elements of what my partner had to say. This was not always easy. One reason was that, early on, I was not sure what my American colleagues were saying. But gradually, their comments began to penetrate my consciousness.[7]

Dialogue is dangerous; it often involves risks. Unlike negotiation, in which delegates often withhold such information, dialogue requires participants to reveal to others their deepest interests, hopes and fears. That can make one vulnerable. Dialogue sometimes requires a participant to give up important human defenses that define her or his own identity as it contrasts to the identity of the "other." One such mechanism in a conflictual relationship is dehumanizing or even demonizing the enemy. Giving up that characterization requires us to accept the enemy as a human being with feelings, pain, hopes and interests comparable to ours. It involves recognition that the other has legitimate interests when we have flatly dismissed the other's interests as unworthy of respect, diabolical or intent on our destruction. It may even require one human being to recognize her or his own responsibility for part of the other's pain.

Dialogue, Negotiation and Conflict Resolution

Dialogue also differs in significant ways from formal mediation or negotiation. The hoped-for product of mediation or negotiation is a concrete agreement. The aim of dialogue is a changed relationship. The currency of negotiation is defining and satisfying material interests through specific jointly agreed arrangements. The outcome of dialogue is to create new human and political capacities to solve problems. Negotiation requires parties who are ready to try to reach agreement. Dialogue can be fruitful by involving parties who are not yet ready for negotiation but do not want a destructive relationship to continue. Negotiation deals with goods or rights that can be divided, shared or defined in tangible ways. Dialogue may change relationships in ways that create new grounds for mutual respect and collaboration.

Since the early 1960s, the study of negotiation, mediation and other methods of resolving conflict has grown significantly, especially in the United States. Most of the academic emphasis and financial investment in that early period focused on formal mediation and negotiation. Beginning in the later 1960s, as mentioned in the Introduction, the pioneering work of John Burton, Edward Azar, Herbert Kelman and then Vamik Volkan began drawing attention to the human needs and behaviors that underlie conflict and may be far tougher obstacles to its resolution than any of the tangible interests that lend themselves to negotiation. These pioneers focused on delving into causes of conflict, finding ways of healing its wounds and identifying ways of taking such healing beyond the small group into the larger body politic.

By the 1990s, the world's leaders and its citizens needed the broadest possible range of approaches to resolving conflict. Many of the so-called "ethnic" or deep-rooted human conflicts that have increasingly demanded the world's attention since the early 1990s can be dealt with only in the political arena through methods other than formal mediation or negotiation.

Everyone who deals with conflict needs to concentrate both on surfacing insight into the causes of conflict and on moving from that insight to formal public policy for changing conflictual relationships. Building that bridge from the relatively private insight to the public and even governmental arenas is one challenge this book addresses. Dialogue, mediation and negotiation may each play appropriate, even simultaneous, roles in a larger political process for the resolution of deep-rooted human conflicts. The dialogue approach described here is potentially complementary to the other methods, not exclusive.

Sustained dialogue is not the only method of creating new spaces and processes for changing relationships. The fact that sustained dialogue is the focus of this book is not intended to ignore excellent work being done by others with much the same purpose.

Practitioners using methods other than dialogue have found, for instance, that they can use an extended series of training sessions in approaches to conflict resolution as a vehicle for bringing people closer to the point at which they can do public work together. The Institute for Multi-Track Diplomacy in Washington, D.C., has, over several years, conducted an intensive series of training experiences involving Greek and Turkish Cypriots. "Alumni" of these sessions have created their own centers for conflict resolution, including communication between the communities. Participants in such projects learn much about their relationships.[8] Instinctively, they may even be diagnosing their relationships in somewhat the way suggested in Chapter Two, although they may not talk explicitly about relationship.

Another Washington-based organization, Search for Common Ground, in the early 1990s began an ambitious project to bring together participants from all over the Middle East in a series of continuing working groups to begin developing networks of relationships across boundaries. Organizers modeled the project on the Conference (now Organization) of Security and Cooperation in Europe (OSCE), a European network created in 1975 that was designed to multiply relationships at different levels of society across divisive borders in Europe. Recognizing that the OSCE effort took at least 15 years to mature, John Marks, founder and president of Search for Common Ground, intends the Middle East project to continue for a comparable period. One of his organization's unique emphases in other areas, including Macedonia and Rwanda-Burundi, has been the use of television panels bringing adversaries together to change perceptions across the lines of conflict.

To be more specific about the niche that sustained dialogue fills, let me compare it with one other nontraditional approach to intrastate conflict. "Collaborative problem-solving" is used in New Mexico to bring together over time ranchers and environmentalists—groups with two different identities—to try to work out understandings on practical problems that divide them. They engage in dialogue, and they sometimes talk deeply about what they value, but their aim is to reach pragmatic solutions. Sustained dialogue, on the other hand, is designed to provide one of those rare spaces in which people can call time-out from everyday problems to ask: "What are the real problems in our relationship that make issues seem so intractable?"

While we human beings tend to start most conversations by talking about practical problems, sustained dialogue systematically puts a second item on the agenda: the underlying relationships that daily interactions reveal if we probe them. The differing premise of sustained dialogue is that serious problems are unlikely to be resolved for the long term by practical agreements—that they will be resolved only as deeply conflictual relationships are changed.

Sustained dialogue is not offered as an approach useful in every situation. It is intended to provide a space in which protagonists in deep-rooted human conflict can address what divides them in a systematic way with a practical purpose and destination. The purpose is providing a place where people can experience a change in their relationships; the destination is taking that experience into the larger community. It is intended as a complement to the increasing number of efforts to engage citizens in the work of resolving their differences productively and peacefully.

The point is not to judge one approach or another but to develop and to make available the processes to probe conflictual relationships as deeply as participants feel meets their needs. My purpose is to introduce in depth one of the spaces and processes available—a process of sustained dialogue that users may take as far as they wish in pursuing the public peace process.

Diplomacy, mediation and negotiation have been the objects of extensive study. Dialogue has not. In fact, sustained dialogue is rarely—if ever— thought of as the essence of a political process that can transform relationships. That is a gap this book seeks to fill.

Dialogue, Democratic Deliberation and Civil Society

In distinguishing dialogue from other approaches to the resolution of conflict, I want to recognize further the similarities and differences between dialogue and the democratic process of deliberation that is essential to building or strengthening a peaceful polity. As I pointed out in Chapter Three, citizens in deliberation in the town meeting, taking the fullest possible account of human, social and political needs, weigh carefully in dialogue the consequences of possible courses of action to meet those needs. The ways of talking and listening are the same in both dialogue and deliberation. The difference between deliberation and the process of sustained dialogue presented here is that deliberation on issues of public policy tends to concentrate on issues and on choices among possible directions to move in dealing with them. Sustained dialogue focuses on the dynamics of the relationships underlying the issues and on ways of changing those relationships so groups can work together to deal with specific problems.

Electoral politics, legislation, diplomacy, mediation, negotiation—these are the institutions and instruments of state. Sustained dialogue to change conflictual relationships and deliberation to set a course for dealing with complex public problems are both processes for citizens outside government. Deliberation and sustained dialogue are the contexts in which citizens outside government do the work that only citizens can do.

In the mid-1990s, those engaged in responding to the challenges of building democracy and those attempting to move deep-rooted human conflicts toward peaceful resolution realized that they labor in neighboring fields. Both groups found themselves struggling to develop creative responses to a collection of challenges that might be put under the heading "problems of governance, civil society and the political resolution of conflict." In approaching those problems, dialogue and deliberation walk hand in hand while each tackles different dimensions of the challenge.

SUSTAINED DIALOGUE AS A POLITICAL PROCESS
TO CHANGE CONFLICTUAL RELATIONSHIPS

However revealing one session in a dialogue may be, dialogue is unlikely to change relationships fundamentally unless it is sustained over time. Only through repeated interactions do people come to feel safe enough to open themselves to a degree that may be painful or respectful enough to give an opposing view a careful hearing.

As noted above, the initial purpose of dialogue is for each participant to reveal to others the deep-rooted feelings that lie at the core of conflict. A sustained dialogue goes beyond this initial purpose to permit participants to think through together what actions can be built from those insights to actually change conflictual relationships in larger bodies politic.

The purpose of the following chapters is to present for discussion, testing and further development a process of dialogue that marches steadily and with purpose from recognition that a conflict requires attention through a series of stages that gradually transform a conflictual relationship and eventually generate the capacity to act together in the larger political arena to end conflict and build constructive and peaceful relationships.

A dialogue sustained over time can produce such a transforming political process. Sustained dialogue is a political and psychological process, first, for changing relationships within a group that is a microcosm of conflictual relationships in the larger body politic and then for designing a political process to change those relationships in that larger community. Sustained dialogue can create the power to change.

This book describes a five-stage process of dialogue, lasting over weeks, months or even years. Chapter Six presents the process—with each stage given attention in a separate section. Following is an overview.

Stage One: Deciding to Engage

Individuals, either from a party in conflict or from an interested third party, talk to a number of people involved in the conflict to identify those who want to change the dynamics of the relationship, to end the conflict and to build a future in which parties to the conflict can work together from defined common ground. This stage ends when a small group of citizens representing the principal parties to a conflict agrees to talk about the causes and remedies for the tensions between them.

Stage Two: Mapping and Naming Problems and Relationships

The parties sit together for the first time to start talking about their relationship and the causes of tension. This stage could begin with participants telling their stories about how the conflict has affected them. In the Inter-Tajikistani Dialogue group, the co-moderators asked: "What do you see as the causes of the civil war?" The purpose in Stage Two is to encourage people to talk broadly enough about the conflict so that they "map" its larger and deeper dimensions—both the surface issues and the relationships that cause them. Gradually, they move to define or name the problem or problems they are most concerned about. This stage ends when the group seems ready to enter an in-depth dialogue on specific problems they have identified.

Stage Three: Probing Problems and Relationships to Choose a Direction

It is essential for the moderator(s) to keep before the group the dual agenda that is the essential characteristic of this dialogue process. In addition to whatever concrete subject is being discussed, the second question is always: "What are the relevant dynamics of the relationships that cause this problem and must be changed to resolve it?" In Stage Three, the group works its way through five tasks:

- It confirms its definition of the problem.
- Participants probe the problem(s) that they have agreed they most need to work on in a way that helps bring to the surface the dynamics of the relationships that are responsible for creating the problem and must be changed if it is to be dealt with.
- Participants identify possible directions to take in tackling the problem. The purpose at this point is not to lay out a detailed course of action; that is the work of Stage Four. The purpose here is to frame the broad choices.
- Group members weigh those choices and try to come to some sense of direction that they believe should guide their communities' next steps.
- When the group has weighed the choices and seems to lean toward moving in a certain direction, the moderator asks: "Do you feel the costs of moving in this direction are less or greater than the costs of doing nothing?" The answer should reveal whether a will exists to shift gears and to begin talking about how to move in the desired direction.

Stage Four: Scenario-Building—Experiencing a Changing Relationship

Participants are asked to recall the direction in which they would like to move and then to engage in the following tasks in sequence:

- List the obstacles—human and practical—to moving in this direction.
- List all of the reasonable steps that might be taken to remove those obstacles.
- List those who can take each of those steps.
- Put those steps into an interactive scenario so that the second step responds to the first, and the third step builds on and reinforces the second, and so on.

The process in which the individual parties in a group work together to design actions that meet the other's needs is itself a demonstration in microcosm of how change might be designed in the larger body politic. In experiencing this process, participants internalize the possibility of change because they themselves have experienced change in collaboration with the adversary.

Stage Five: Acting Together to Make Change Happen

The participants discuss among themselves what can be done to put that scenario into action. To begin, they must assess conditions in their bodies politic and capacities for change. They may need to add preparatory steps to their scenario.

One caution cannot be underscored heavily enough or repeated too often: Any framework built around stages suggests more order than is possible in any human process. These five stages are not rigid, and the process is anything but neat and orderly. One stage does not fully end before the next begins. Participants may often move back and forth among the stages when they need to update a changed situation, rethink an earlier judgment or tackle a new problem, or their minds may just be "all over the place" when they are groping for focus. When they do return to an earlier stage, it is at a more profound level because they are continuously deepening their experience in relationship throughout the course of the dialogue.

Organizing thinking about this process in a series of stages simply provides a continuing checklist for those involved to realize what they may be skipping over, what they must concentrate on to deepen the dialogue and what building blocks they must lay down to achieve their objective. For instance:

- A group may well find in Stages Two or Three that some crucial voices are missing, so someone will go back to Stage One to recruit additional participants.
- A well-developed group will regularly return to Stages Two and Three as the dialogue moves along because the members need to redefine key problems or define new problems they want to work on as the situation develops.
- When a group is designing a scenario of interdependent steps in Stage Four, participants may want to return to the questions they addressed in Stage Three to probe the dynamics of relationships more deeply for further insight into steps that might change their interactions.
- Group members may jump quickly to solutions. Recognizing that they have skipped over probing the dynamics of underlying relationships that cause the problems can help them pull back in a way that will eventually enlarge their options.

Since the human mind and human interchange wash back and forth across depths of feeling—rehashing historic grievances, defining problems afresh and imagining a better future and concrete political work to bring about change—one must allow for fluidity. At the same time, one must keep in mind that a serious process has a destination and that conceptualization of the process in stages helps keep its leaders aimed toward that destination.

Picturing the dialogue process in terms of the stages through which it can deepen and change a relationship can be a diagnostic tool. It helps those engaged see what needs to be done at each period of the dialogue, what is required to make the transition from one level of dialogue to another, what may be premature at a given moment and what foundations must be laid upon which to build a new relationship. The five-stage process can also help measure how far a dialogue has gone, identify obstacles to progress and assess how far the dialogue can go.

In describing the process in terms of stages, I repeat and underscore these points:

- The stages are not rigidly delineated sequential steps. Groups often move back and forth among stages of feeling and analysis.
- The process does not move quickly, neatly or logically. Absorbing new ideas and approaches takes time. Repetition and redundancy are often essential.
- The time spent in each stage will vary from group to group. Some groups experienced in the process may telescope the stages. Others may reach a certain point and not move beyond it for some time.

Despite these cautions, I have found again and again that keeping a sense of the whole process in the back of our minds provides valuable touchstones for checking the progress of a dialogue. Are we skipping important steps that will cast us on the shoals of misunderstanding later? Why are we stuck? What might be the unspoken obstacles, and how can we surface them? How can we consolidate what we have achieved and make a transition to the next, deeper stage of dialogue?

The framework presented here does not provide answers in all situations; each is unique. My hope is that it will suggest a way of thinking that can produce imaginative responses to whatever challenges the reader may face.

RESISTANCE TO DEEPENING RELATIONSHIPS: GETTING STUCK

Participants should expect to get "stuck" at particular points in a sustained dialogue because some subjects are scary to talk about in depth. Most often, these points occur as a group tries to move from one stage to the next. Both individuals and the group will need to mature and gather courage to step across some thresholds. These points are identified and discussed in the detailed presentation of the five stages in Chapter Six, but some broad comments may be helpful here.

The variety of possible resistances is as wide as the number of situations confronted, so there can be no comprehensive guide for responding to all possible situations. The best approach is to establish a constructive attitude toward a group's resistance to movement.

Perhaps the most useful thought to keep in mind is this: Treasure the participants' resistance to moving forward because you will learn much from it. It is not a nuisance or a hindrance but a concentrated opportunity to unlock another door leading to further progress.

Resistance is an almost inevitable response to the possibility of change at every stage. People are often reluctant to change for good reason. The most productive approach is not to try to persuade participants to give up their reluctance by saying: "Trust me. It will be OK. You are safe in this group." The most productive approach is to demonstrate our understanding that a person's reasons for resistance are real for her or him: "You wouldn't feel that way without good reasons. Let's try to understand your reasons." Accepting participants' reasons without judgment and working together to analyze them gradually enables participants to feel safe enough to move to the next level of dialogue and relationship.

Psychologists have learned that their most important work is helping clients understand their internal obstacles to change by unraveling them as they come up. It is counterproductive to try to ignore them.

Becoming frustrated with such obstacles is the greatest enemy of those who would move dialogue forward. Both moderators and participants can learn from resistance to moving ahead what is really going on in a dysfunctional relationship. An attitude of patient exploration of causes is most likely to produce useful insights.[9]

The time between meetings is often the period when participants work through their resistance to moving to new levels of dialogue. There is a special quality about thinking over a problem without time pressure when one can talk over aspects of the situation with friends. Often, groups that are at an impasse at the end of one meeting will return to the next ready to move forward.

SOME HUMAN EXPERIENCES IN DIALOGUE

In addition to warning moderators that they must be prepared to get stuck at critical moments along the way, it will be useful to identify some of the other psychological phenomena they may encounter. Vamik Volkan and

Demetrios Julius have distilled from their work in Cyprus, in the Arab-Is-raeli conflict, in the Baltic states and in other areas of conflict an extensive collection of these experiences.[10]

Each group brings to dialogue an identity that embodies a wide range of experiences over time. Among these are what Volkan and colleagues call "chosen traumas" and "chosen glories."

> Chosen traumas refer to the shared mental representations of humiliating events where losses occurred and could not be effectively mourned. Chosen glories recount the shared mental representations of events of success or triumph. Both are often mythologized and passed from generation to generation, although historical hurts are stronger markers of a group's identity than the mental representations of past glories. Losses associated with chosen traumas cannot be mourned and the humiliation and hurt cannot be resolved. Therefore such traumas are handed down in the "hope" that they can be mourned, resolved or avenged in the future. This handing down, however, functions to perpetuate feelings of victimization, entitlement and the desire for revenge rather than successful mourning and resolution. Traumas experienced many centuries in the past are still active in the identities of some groups. . . . Our experience has shown that in the beginning of a workshop, the adherence to these chosen traumas is often the greatest obstacle to initiating meaningful dialogue.

Sometimes in the early meetings of a group, moderators observe a vying between groups over who has suffered more—what Volkan calls a "competition of historical grievances." Unproductive and time-consuming as these exchanges may seem on the surface, participants need to put their feelings on the record and to feel that they have been heard. While moderators need to avoid taking sides, they must absorb some of the emotion and, when possible, cause each side to begin taking in what they hear from the other.

Often, this competition of grievances is compounded by current events that seem to substantiate one group's claims of the other's harmful behavior. Because recent events are "echoed" in opening remarks of a dialogue, Volkan refers to this as the "echo phenomenon." These comments need to be addressed and put into perspective. In a sustained dialogue, events between meetings often usefully fall into this category.

Sometimes, drawing on a current experience, some participants will seize on a minor event and magnify it to major proportions so that this threatens to divert the dialogue from major issues. Often, participants are "displacing" onto the lesser event their feelings about fundamental grievances. The challenge to the moderator is to acknowledge the feelings about the "mini-conflict" and also to help the group see that it reflects the larger issues and that participants need to avoid becoming mired in the lesser problems.

Sometimes, participants will state as fact what they believe to be the beliefs of members of the other group. Asking participants to engage in an exercise to identify the others' perceptions can provide useful insights, but, when participants do it on their own, they are often "projecting" onto others elements of their own behavior that they would rather disown. When this is obvious, it can be helpful for a moderator to suggest that one side is imputing to the other what it wishes or fears the other side would believe.

Throughout a prolonged dialogue, moderators will see participants draw close to each other and then pull back, then draw close again and, after a time, pull back—a pattern Volkan calls the "accordion phenomenon." It is important to recognize that some coming together may be premature or may represent more pressure than participants can absorb—as when the accordion is squeezed together. The pulling apart reintroduces the realities of the situation and permits participants to regain perspective.

One feeling that accounts for two groups pulling back from each other is the anxiety that closeness creates as parties become uncomfortable at perceiving themselves becoming more like their enemy. In these circumstances, participants sometimes focus on minor differences to protect their "separate" identities. Some trivial point may threaten continuation of the dialogue. A moderator may need to help the group understand that agreement on one point or perspective does not lead to loss of identity.

Underneath seemingly rational discussion of problems, one often finds that unseen factors prevent rational solutions from being carried out. Often, these "hidden transcripts," as Volkan calls them, reveal the dynamics of underlying resistance. As these become apparent to moderators, they may find it useful to articulate what they think they hear and check their interpretation with participants. This can cause participants to reflect on what may be going on under the surface.

Throughout a dialogue, unresolved mourning of past losses may block a change in relationship. "Mourning is a psychological response to loss, and is exhibited by both individuals and groups," Volkan says. "When we mourn, we accept the loss or change and adapt to new situations." But some traumas—such as the losses Jews suffered in the Nazi Holocaust—may be too great to mourn in a short time. As these traumas are passed through generations, "the inability to mourn the loss and the inability to work through the humiliation may lead to a certain shared ideology," Volkan continues. "For example, new generations may hold onto an ideology of entitlement, i.e., we have been hurt enough—now we should be given what others owe us." Where a moderator or a participant senses this lack of mourning, bringing the need to the surface for all to think about may help begin the mourning of these losses and the consequent acceptance of reality. Sometimes, both sides have suffered losses in common tragedies.

Through dialogue, each group can begin to recognize the feelings and perceptions of the other. The rigidity of their own pictures loosens. Each group becomes more able to listen. In many cases, the telling of personal stories can play a vital role in compelling others to pay attention to facts they would rather ignore. As participants modify their own pictures of reality, they may begin to see past behavior as counterproductive.

TURNING TO THE FIVE STAGES OF SUSTAINED DIALOGUE

In the next chapter, we turn to detailed presentation of each of the five stages. Please remember: They are presented to describe a sequence of tasks and the progress of relationships. No one will follow the course laid out here word for word; those who would use this process will need to internalize it and to make it their own instrument in the unique circumstances of their own dialogue.

The potential user will find in the Appendix a manual for organizers and moderators of dialogue. There, the process is presented in a practical form, addressing concrete problems and suggesting specific approaches to the conduct of meetings.

This may look like a complicated process. It is. Not only that. People can be painfully frustrating—even offensive and dense—in an experience like this. But the dialogue process is also exciting, challenging and immensely rewarding as participants move deeply into it and feel relationships change. Those who lead will grow as participants change; they will make this process their own, sculpt it creatively to their use and contribute their own experience to its enrichment.

Chapter Six

Sustained Dialogue: A Public Peace Process

I n this chapter, I explain the five-stage process of sustained dialogue and the reasoning behind each stage. In the Appendix there is a manual addressed directly to potential organizers and moderators that presents this material for practical use. It offers specific suggestions for planning and running meetings, for breaking logjams when groups get stuck and for bringing groups to points of closure around particular problems. In addition, there is a short brochure that is useful in explaining the process for the first time to potential organizers, moderators and participants. Here, you will find an overview and the thinking behind each stage in the process.

The stages represent a progression of tasks—both practical and psychological. As I have said, they will not be followed rigidly; participants can jump forward or circle back among the stages; no group will proceed exactly as any other group. The stages provide a framework, a checklist or a set of suggestions and touchstones for those who are stewards of this process.

Sustained dialogue is, above all, a dynamic process. It is a process of continuous interaction not only among participants in the room, but also between participants and their environments outside the dialogue room. It is a process with direction—a process that produces change within the room and enables participants to design change in the larger body politic.

As a process with direction and purpose, it requires individuals who understand it as a process and who can guide it, making the most of its potential. In laying out and explaining the workings of the process, I offer potential users the means to help get their minds around the process. My hope is that they will make it their own and craft it to the needs of the citizens with whom they work. Ultimately, they will make their own contributions to the ongoing refinement and development of the process.

STAGE ONE: DECIDING TO ENGAGE

"Enough! We Can't Go on This Way"

A Brief Overview

Persuading citizens to talk across lines of conflict—getting a dialogue started—is, in the words of most who work in this field, the task that is "easiest to describe but hardest to do." Talking to a seemingly insensitive or even hostile group or talking to the "enemy" can be seen as senseless or even traitorous. Governments that do so risk vehement backlash. Citizens, in some situations, risk assassination. Even in nonviolent situations, individuals can find it scary to talk with people who they believe discriminate against them, do not care about them or even hate or harm them. In U.S. communities, minorities often feel safer not risking reaching outside their racial or ethnic group any more than necessary.

Underlying the discomforts, fears or dangers that sometimes confront potential participants in a dialogue is a deeper problem. The critical moment comes when they acknowledge that they can no longer live with the situation—that they must act to change it. Each can find many reasons not to face up to the need for change. For each, the critical step is seeing and acknowledging that the costs of not acting will be greater than the potential costs of acting. Once possible participants step across that threshold, the next hurdle is accepting the idea that sustained dialogue can be an instrument of change. Reaching that moment of realization and commitment is the challenge of Stage One.

The Many Faces of the Challenge

Before tensions erupt, few individuals want to acknowledge the need for preventive dialogue—trying to change a difficult relationship before it deteriorates into crisis or violence. Often, the problem is to see that a long-term problem would be less costly to address in the near term than after violence has erupted. While this early period is the easiest time to get people together, the need then often seems least compelling. "We're doing OK. Don't rock the boat."

When a relationship has become violent, it is difficult to persuade either side that it can talk with the other. The need for talks to end the violence may be clear, but, often in a test of force, neither side is willing to give up any advantage it feels it may have. One may see no recourse at this point except to let fighting parties exhaust themselves before trying to begin talks, but that argument goes against the grain for those who believe too high a price has already been paid.

Dialogue to work out new conditions for postconflict life together is obviously needed. But what is essential at this stage is dialogue not only about ending tension or violence, but also about changing fundamental relationships as a foundation for building constructive and peaceful relationships for the long term.

Bringing people to dialogue—the task in Stage One—requires addressing five questions:

- Who will take the initiative?
- Who has the will and the capacities to engage in dialogue?
- Who can overcome the resistance of potential participants to meeting and talking with persons they fear, suspect or dislike, and how can they overcome it?
- In what space—under what conditions—will the dialogue take place?
- Who can precipitate the decision to make a meeting happen and how?

Potential participants must be willing to commit their time and energies to a series of meetings over a considerable open-ended period. They must also understand that such dialogue is different from other meetings: Participants will focus on their overall relationship for the purpose of improving it rather than focusing only on concrete issues that divide them.

Those trying to make a meeting happen must think in terms of the several tasks above, as well as convening, funding and moderating. Sometimes, an organizing or convening team of several members—each with particular abilities or contacts—will work together to make a dialogue happen. It may take some time just for this team to form itself, since different organizations may have to make decisions and come together around them.[1]

Who Will Take the Initiative?

A dialogue can start in one of two ways: Either concerned individuals from within the communities in tension can seek out like-minded people in the other community, or an interested person or group from outside the field of tension can try to bring people together.

From Within. Sometimes a person or a group inside one community takes the initiative, or individuals from each group cautiously reach out to the other. The advantage of this approach is that participants take ownership of their dialogue from the beginning.

Experience shows that, as long as two parties avoid accepting joint ownership of their dialogue, they can slough off responsibility for progress or lack thereof onto a third party. When one or two persons reach out to members of an adversary group, they will usually speak from serious concerns or commitments that they believe the other persons share.

Whatever the exact situation, a dialogue is formed as a few individuals talk quietly together and carefully reach an understanding that a dialogue group will form. In dialogues between Soviet and U.S. citizens and Chinese and U.S. citizens, one side originated the idea, discussions took place, and the other side decided whether or not to join. After the 1967 Arab-Israeli War, when Israel occupied the West Bank and Gaza Strip and removed the barbed wire between Israel and its Palestinian neighbors, contacts in all walks of life took place. Most of these were not systematic dialogues, but a few were; others involved such activities as regular interaction among professionals to deal with practical problems or economic relationships. In U.S. cities, one pattern seems to be that a group or an organization in a community already concerned about intergroup tension will decide to deepen its work through sustained dialogue.

From Outside.   Since it is often difficult for groups to come together on their own, a catalyst from outside may be needed. A well-developed body of thought describes the value of a professionally trained, sensitive third party in overcoming resistance to taking the first step—from unwillingness for fear of losing face to unwillingness to acknowledge one's need for help and change.

Once meetings have begun, a third party can "absorb" much of the emotion that would otherwise be directed from adversary to adversary, as well as help perceive common ground that the parties to dialogue may not see themselves in the heat of their commitment to their own positions. This third-party role in nonofficial dialogue differs from formal mediation in a negotiating situation in that it aims at probing beneath stated positions to determine the underlying elements and relationships in conflict rather than producing a solution in written form. That differing role is consistent with the way in which the purpose of such dialogue differs from the purpose of formal mediation or negotiation.

A Combination of Functions.   The issue is not whether a bilateral initiative or a third-party role is the correct approach but, rather, what mix at particular times during efforts to start a dialogue is most appropriate to that situation. In some complex situations, the two approaches have worked side by side.

When I was explaining the bilateral dialogue between Soviet and U.S. citizens—the Dartmouth Conference—a colleague asked: "But who performs the third-party role?" After some thought about the experience of a decade, I replied: "The co-moderators organized the meetings, agreed on the agenda, assumed joint responsibility for advancing it and became stewards of the process." After the Cold War ended, the same Dartmouth Conference Task Force on Regional Conflicts as a third-party team launched a dialogue among factions from the civil war in Tajikistan.

Similarly, in 1995 staff of the Charles F. Kettering Foundation shared their experience abroad in sustained dialogue with a white pastor in Baton Rouge, Louisiana. Already deeply engaged in a citywide effort to improve race relations, that pastor, eager to deepen his work, sought the support of his Federation of Churches and Synagogues and then reached out to a black pastor; together they identified and brought together participants and co-moderated the meetings.[2]

How a third party explains why he or she is there is critical; potential participants can be very suspicious of what personal gain a third party might seek from involvement. The best approach is to explain simply and straightforwardly why one cares.

The Convener. The identity of the convener—whether an individual, a team or an organization—can make a big difference. One possibility is respected co-conveners from within the communities in tension. Another is one person or organization from within or outside trusted by all. If there is an outside convener, a backup team with broad experience across communities can provide knowledge and impart a neutral character.

Who Will the Participants Be?
In putting together a dialogue group, a guiding principle is that this group becomes a microcosm of the communities and relationships from which participants come. Members absorb events that take place in the bodies politic around them and "process" them within the dialogue group. As individuals agonize within themselves over coming to terms with the uncomfortable views of an adversary, they preview—first internally and then with the group—what change in the larger community would require.

The task is to find sensitive and reflective individuals who are able and ready to talk. In a sort of "fact-finding mission," one might start by speaking with two- or three-dozen people but, for the initial dialogue, select about a dozen who represent main perspectives in the communities, being aware that there are divisions within groups as well as between them. It may not be possible to enlist a fully representative group at first, but it is usually better to begin the dialogue than to seek perfection. The initial aim is to select a core group whose members can work together and stay together over a prolonged period. The long-term aim is to expand the dialogue experience into the community to lay foundations for changing relationships. In addition to identifying good participants in the dialogue, these preparatory talks also help define key problems and identify the relationships that create them, as well as how each group sees both.

Participants must be individuals who are respected and listened to in their communities, not just those with titles or positions. Participants come because of who they are as persons, not as formal representatives of any organization. Where individuals hold organizational positions, it is often best if they work at the number-two level, where they are listened to by top decision makers but are less visible and more free to listen and to share—less compelled to defend or posture. It is most important for all participants to understand that they speak only for themselves.

Whatever the participants' roles in the community, one human characteristic is essential: Each must be willing to listen to others' views and feelings—not just to pronounce her or his own position. This normally rules out extremists and fanatics, although at some point their views have to be taken into account. One difficult choice at the outset may be between including some individuals who may be a destructive element in the dialogue or leaving them out initially in order to establish some common ground at the center of a relationship before attempting to deal with extremes on either side.

Often, participants believe that there is a destructive relationship or situation that demands attention that governments are not likely to give in a timely manner. They may simply be curious about what motivates the other group(s) in the conflict, or they may feel a serious mission to engage with them. They may be willing both to engage the other side(s) and to draw others from their own group into a dialogue.

In addition to willing participants from each side, comparable partners must be found. Each individual must believe that the quality of the interaction will justify any risk. All must believe that serious dialogue is possible among authentic representatives—in the nonofficial sense—of each group who are of comparable abilities and standing in their communities. Normally, one does not engage officials in nonofficial dialogue, although occasionally there may be good reasons to try to involve officials in their personal capacities. Thus, the organizer's problem is to find individuals who may have relationships with government itself or who would be influential in moving nonofficial organizations.

Whatever collection of motives brings them to the dialogue, participants must also normally have some kind of political permission to engage in a systematic dialogue. Casual or accidental conversations are one thing; a dialogue over time is another. If they are truly representative, participants may believe that this "permission" comes from consensus in their community. A few courageous individuals may brave disapproval. In the case of individuals living under military occupation or governmental authority not sympathetic to their cause, government approval in the form of visas or permits to travel may be required.

Who Can Overcome Resistance?

Perhaps most frequently, one may find only individuals who do not see the need for dialogue and are reluctant to relate to other parties to tension or conflict. Precipitating a sense of need is key. Some parties feel safer with a known situation, difficult as it may be, or they are not ready to face the pain of others. They deny that a problem exists because they are not ready to deal with it. In such cases, one may need to wait for a traumatic event that increases pain or threat of pain beyond endurance. But the hope is to precipitate a sense of danger before the situation explodes. Unlike officials, citizens outside government do not have to defend a group interest in the status quo and can overcome resistance to dialogue with less risk.

Without drawing any pejorative analogy, the problem in these circumstances is somewhat akin to the problem that confronts many individuals in our society: How does one persuade an alcoholic or a drug addict to seek treatment? The answer of persons who counsel such individuals is that frequently there must actually be a physical trauma—loss of job or spouse, a serious accident or a patently self-destructive act—to cause the person to hit bottom and seek help. More subtly, the trauma may be internal as an individual gradually becomes overwhelmed by her or his self-destructive behavior and can no longer cope with the related feelings.

In social or political situations, it is often difficult to persuade individuals of distantly impending trauma through intellectual argument alone. The art may be to find a way of dramatizing a distant threat through metaphor in the present. One Israeli captured a sentiment that often serves this purpose when he said with tears in his eyes: "I worry about my grandchildren living in Israel if we do not act now." Or even an American Jew reacting to human-rights violations by Israel expressed his fear of anti-Semitic backlash in the United States when he said: "When Israel acts like this, I worry about the future of my son as a Jew in America."

Even when people say, "But we do talk," the challenge often is to get them to realize that their talk does nothing to address the problems in their relationships that cause trouble between them. To serve their own self-interest, groups may have learned to work together on common projects or in workplaces. But they have carefully avoided talking about underlying tensions in their relationships so as not to disrupt minimal necessary cooperation.

If tensions are already escalating, some might think that they have already invested too much in pressing their side's positions to "capitulate" now. They might see talking to the other community as "selling out." The challenge is to cause people to see that they and the other community are interdependent and that it serves everyone's interests to engage in a systematic dialogue.

When tensions have already erupted, persons on both sides may believe that time is on their side or that tensions will have to subside. Some may even need conflict to define their identity. The problem is to convince people that tensions, if not dealt with, usually deepen rather than disappear with time.

Ideally, individuals chosen for a dialogue will be influential, but they should not be burdened with the expectation that they can or must take decisive action. The realistic aim is to gather a group of people who together can become a microcosm of the relationships that need to be changed so they can explore those relationships and think as a group to design ways of changing them. Group members will not deal with how their initial experience can be transformed into results in a larger political arena until they are well along in the process.

Once an organizer has identified willing, comparable and ready partners, those potential participants will still need to be satisfied that the conditions for their dialogue will be sensitive to their concerns and will not disadvantage them in any significant way. They require a direct and full description of the space in which the dialogue will take place and what will happen there.

What Are the Conditions for the Dialogue?
The Compact or Covenant.   The concept and characteristics of public space or safe space underlie efforts to assure individuals that they have a voice in setting the conditions for the dialogue. Participants need to understand that they will meet in space "owned" by all of them, in which all will agree to the specific conditions that will prevail there.

As discussed in Chapter Three, this is a space set aside for dialogue among citizens, not for negotiation. It is also a space in which the purpose is to probe together the underlying elements of the conflictual or tense relationship between parties, not simply to restate familiar positions and demands. The quality of behavior and discussion in this space is expected to be quite different from the confrontational characteristics of interaction in a conflictual situation. All involved should make every effort before the dialogue to create a frame of mind that will bring people into this space with willingness to try something quite different from what they may have experienced previously.

Most important perhaps, the space will be defined by certain ground rules that make it feel "safe." These should be agreed upon in advance. Participants need to know what will be expected of them and what they may expect of others as a basis for judging whether they want to get involved. Talking about these ground rules will also help organizers assess the capacity of potential participants to listen to others and to work with them. It is also an opportunity for organizers to underscore that the group will deal with both concrete problems and the dynamics of the relationships behind the problems. It can help them gain some sense of potential participants' capacity to respond to that dual agenda.

To highlight the importance of these ground rules, conveners may want to prepare them—as adapted to the situation—on a separate paper to discuss them individually and with the group when it first meets. That paper could be titled, for instance, "Purpose and Character of the Dialogue," "Covenant" or "Compact." (Please see accompanying sample covenant.)

The Place.   Often the place is a critical factor. Sometimes, only a faraway, neutral site can help the parties feel safe. In other situations, participants may welcome direct exposure to each other's community or body politic. Sometimes, a familiar and neutral domestic setting will be best. The choice will depend not only on the preference of the participants, but also on factors such as personal security or the need for seclusion from the media or other potential intrusions on the privacy of the dialogue.

Purpose and Agenda.   Beyond the question of behavior within the space will be the critical questions: What is the purpose of coming together? What will be discussed? This task is often described as "defining the problem" or "agenda setting." At this stage, there are limits to what the group can do and what it should attempt; the purpose is simply to begin a dialogue. The best statement of purpose is the simple one that begins the covenant itself. But some very difficult problems will demand attention.

COVENANT

- The purpose of this dialogue is to work on changing the relationships among the groups with which participants identify.
- There will always be two items in the agenda: the particular problems participants need to talk about and the underlying feelings and relationships that cause these problems.
- Because of the importance of this work, participants commit themselves to meet regularly over a period of months—at least four to five hours in each meeting, although international meetings may last two to three days. The duration of the series will be open-ended. Participants will wait until they are well into the dialogue to agree on when to finish the series of meetings.
- Participants represent only themselves. They reflect views in their communities, but, in these dialogue sessions, they do not formally represent organizations or groups.
- Participants will observe time limits on their statements to allow genuine dialogue.
- Participants will speak from their hearts as well as from their minds.
- Participants will interact civilly, listen actively to each other with attention and respect, not interrupt and allow each to present her or his views fully.
- Because participants will need to speak about the feelings and relationships behind the specific problems that bother them, feelings will be expressed and heard with mutual respect. Participants will try to learn from these expressions.
- Participants will try to respond as directly and as fully as possible to points made and questions asked. Each will make a real effort to put herself or himself in others' shoes and speak with sensitivity for others' views and feelings.
- To facilitate serious work, participants will listen carefully to the issues and questions posed by the moderator and try to stick to them.
- Nobody in the dialogue will be quoted outside the meeting room.
- No one will speak publicly about the substantive discussion in the dialogue unless all agree.

Some participants may press to identify substantive starting points in advance. Each party has its own picture of the problem, the situation or the relationship. It is essential for those convening the meeting to identify these starting points individually and to identify what is complementary in those pictures that would justify a dialogue. Probing those pictures can begin awakening in each party an awareness of the other's views. Often, each side will, before meeting the other, define a problem without reference to the other party's picture of the problem. Sometimes, each party acts as if the other does not exist, or neither acknowledges that it is part of a relationship.

However important such soundings may be for organizers and moderators, a detailed agenda can grow only out of the dialogue itself. If participants press for detailed terms of reference in advance, the appropriate response is that the purpose of the dialogue is to probe the overall relationship in a fresh way. Getting bogged down in drafting a detailed agenda can preempt the dialogue itself if either party tries to incorporate in the terms of reference a definition of the problem that requires concessions from the other about how the problems will be addressed.

Drafting detailed terms of reference may be appropriate preparation for negotiation, but not for nonofficial dialogue in which the starting point is human, not legal. Because in the end it is self-interest that will bring participants to the table, all parties will need some assurance before entering the dialogue that their concerns will be addressed. The art is to find a way of expressing that assurance that does not get ahead of the dialogue itself.

Group Size.   A critical factor in determining how a group will talk will be its size. Sometimes, someone will have called an academic conference or a large public meeting in an effort to begin a discourse. Such groups are not suitable for dialogue, but they may be a prelude. Typically in such meetings, there will be two- or three-dozen people in a conference or even several hundred in a town meeting and little opportunity for any form of communication other than a sequential statement of views as people raise their hands. There is often little direct interaction. For parties who are leery of the greater intimacy of dialogue, this may be the only acceptable way to begin an exchange. But, as parties get to know one another, each may recognize the value of a more intensive exchange in a smaller group. Sustained dialogue can begin only when a small group of about 12 is committed to stay together through many meetings. David Bohm suggests that "a group of about twenty to forty people is almost a microcosm of the whole society,"[3] but, in situations of acute tension, I find that about a dozen to start is enough to manage.

Transition: Who Can Make a Meeting Happen?

Any list of tasks such as those presented in this chapter is intimidating and suggests a more systematic approach than will be the case in the real world. But they need to be handled in some way before a dialogue can begin.

When the groundwork has been laid, it is necessary to precipitate a decision to meet. A compelling need to begin meeting may arise from numerous possible causes:

- Serious discussion may be enough.
- A visible worsening of the situation—even a traumatic event—may dramatize the need to talk.
- One of the parties may create a new sense of possibility by showing sensitivity to the other's concerns, accepting a shared responsibility for the conflict, expressing concern about a shared future or recognizing a common agenda.
- A third party may offer inducements to meet, such as the prospect of a kind of involvement that each party may regard as advantageous in balancing the scales to improve its situation.
- Conveners may simply issue an invitation after they judge there has been enough preparatory talk to offer realistic hope of a positive response.

Stage One culminates when agreement to try dialogue is reached. This agreement will also need to set time, place, convening authority, financial responsibilities and ground rules as appropriate.

The Moderator

(For the sake of simplicity, the word "moderator" appears from now on in the singular; this formulation includes the possibility of co-moderators.)
The persons who have completed the tasks in this stage to make a meeting happen may or may not include the person who moderates the meetings. Quite often, different experiences and abilities make different individuals appropriate to each job. If the task of moderating falls to someone else, that person should be briefed fully on the experience in Stage One. If the moderator has not played a role in organizing the dialogue, it may be wise for the organizers not to settle on a moderator until they have a sense of how potential participants feel about who should moderate. In all cases, organizers will do well to have some potential moderators in the back of their minds to test them subtly with potential participants.

The unique character of each group will suggest particular qualities in a moderator. However, some qualities seem essential:

- sensitivity to the human dimension of problems—why people hurt, what participants as human beings really need, why people may be

understandably angry—and the ability to relate to participants on that level rather than treating them as trainees to be instructed;
- commitment to the overall purpose of reconciliation between groups that have real grievances against each other;
- the ability to convey genuine caring and commitment at a human level;
- realistic expectations for the pace at which people can change;
- some depth of experience with related problems and ability to conceptualize that experience so as to draw on it in this group;
- the ability to help people see common elements in their experiences and views;
- sensitivity to the cultural uniqueness of the groups involved;
- the capacity to design agendas that build from previously expressed ideas to advance and deepen the process;
- a sense of political process—an ability to see the whole picture, keep a destination in sight and not take sides;
- the ability to help participants organize their thoughts;
- respect from participants as a caring person and as an experienced professional.

A word of perspective on the process. The person chosen as moderator may have played roles in other processes. However:

- This is not like moderating a community forum or policy discussion. This process is sustained over a longer period of time. Participants focus not just on problems but, even more importantly, also on the relationships that cause them. In focusing on changing relationships, the moderator will need to welcome expressions of emotion within reason and try to help the group learn from them. The moderator will share in the experience of the dialogue.
- This is not mediation. While many of a mediator's abilities may be helpful in this process, a mediator is usually asked to help participants reach a specific agreement about one defined problem or complex of problems. Sustained dialogue involves the full range of problems that affect the relationships involved. Its purpose is to change relationships so participants can deal with whatever problems arise using whatever peaceful methods seem appropriate.
- This is not negotiation. People in deep-rooted human conflict have little to negotiate, at least initially.

- The moderator should not approach her or his role as a teacher or trainer. This is neither an academic seminar nor a skills-building exercise, although participants may learn a lot from how a moderator conducts herself or himself, poses questions, draws on broader experience, expresses care and concern and demonstrates respect and sincerity. At most, the moderator should share experiences as an equal.

Separate Meetings with Each Team?

Before the first meeting, the moderator may meet separately with the individual groups or subgroups in the dialogue.[4] Such meetings can:

- begin to develop a relationship of mutual trust and respect if the moderator can show the capacity to be understanding and supportive without bias;
- provide the moderator direct initial insight into what is on each group's and individual's mind;
- provide a preliminary sense of who are leaders, idea producers, negative factors and reconcilers in each group;
- identify the most divisive issues and glimpses of common ground;
- provide a preview of potential sources of resistance to deepening working relationships;
- reinforce the ground rules and forge alliances to make them work.

A Practical Note

As dialogue begins, the moderator will find it essential to take good notes or arrange for a rapporteur. As soon as a meeting ends, someone must write an interpretive analysis of the group's progress, the obstacles it faces and a useful takeoff point for the next session. These notes provide moderators an opportunity to review main thoughts and feelings and think about the flow of the interaction. The purpose is not just to record who said what. In fact, it is important not to have a paper with names of speakers that could embarrass anyone if it were accidentally to reach people outside the group. But a stimulus to reflection on what has happened in the group and a point of reference for taking stock are critical.

STAGE TWO: MAPPING AND NAMING
PROBLEMS AND RELATIONSHIPS

"THE PROBLEM WE REALLY HAVE TO WORK ON FIRST IS . . ."

A Brief Overview

Stage Two normally begins with the first formal meeting of the whole dialogue group, although in a few cases the group may have met to discuss a series of meetings. The main task is to bring to the surface both the full range of significant problems and the dynamics of the relationships that cause them. The objective is to define—to name—the specific problem(s) that require priority in-depth attention.

We speak of "mapping"—or drawing a mental picture—of that complex of critical problems and relationships. This is a time of exploration—of encouraging participants to say what is their minds. In this computer age, we could say it is a time of downloading. For that purpose, the discussion must be wide ranging. Only at the end of this stage are participants asked to focus an agenda for in-depth probing of one issue at a time. Since developing a full picture of some problems and the depths of the relationships behind them may be painful, Stage Two will probably last through several meetings.

This stage ends only when natural resistance to probing key problems is overcome, and the group says, in effect: "What we really need to work on first is. . . ." Participants need a definition of the problem(s) they want to probe that is both concise and yet broad enough to encompass the full range of perspectives and feelings in the group. That statement, when it comes, is the high point of Stage Two.

Establishing the Character of the Dialogue

To set the tone and particular quality of the dialogue, the moderator will keep certain continuing aims in an ever-present "back-of-the-mind agenda." He or she must look constantly for opportunities to move this underlying agenda forward.

First, to give character to this public space, the moderator must help participants consolidate the understanding on ground rules that were suggested in the previous stage. The principles in the "covenant" or "compact" should be reaffirmed, if only informally, by the whole group—or at least the group should be reminded of them. Establishing them in practice takes time. Some participants sitting down together for the first time can hardly look at each other.

Dialogue begins with a period of learning to talk with civility, to pour out concerns without abuse and to listen to what others are saying. Participants slowly get to know others in the dialogue—their experience, needs, interests, hopes and fears. Such knowledge will not come easily or quickly; all that is said will not be absorbed on first hearing. But no knowledge will be possible unless the character of genuine dialogue is understood and the practice established.

Sustained dialogue requires new habits. Learning to talk analytically with civility, rather than polemically or positionally, takes time and effort among those who have spent lifetimes suspecting, mistrusting, dehumanizing or demonizing each other. Probing beneath the surface is not easy because it reveals vulnerability.

Natural tension exists between the need to press for a civil and sensitive exchange with time for all to speak and the need for all to feel that they have had an opportunity to be well heard. This tension may exist especially in some cultures in which "getting down to business" right away or forcing compliance with time limits—as would be normal in Anglo-Saxon cultures—is considered insensitive by participants, especially when parties to conflict may never have had a chance to be heard outside their own groups. As time goes on, asking speakers to be brief, agreeing on the sequence of subjects, keeping speakers to one subject and allocating time among topics may become more feasible. A moderator should insist on temperate language and tone but should not cut off expressions of feeling or create a sense that a speaker's thoughts are not valued. It helps if the moderator can model a disciplined use of time, mode of expression and focus.

The character of a dialogue can be established only by practice, not by a single pronouncement. A moderator must use statements as they are made to draw participants into a common approach, to build relationships among them and to create sensitivity for one another. A conversational mode comes slowly.

In addition to what participants may have agreed upon in the compact, they will also define this space by what they believe they achieve here. It is essential, especially in a first meeting, to make the experience in this space one that participants value enough to come back. The space may be valuable because there is nowhere else for opponents to talk and to listen. In addition, creating some common ground can reinforce the value of the dialogue.

No one should expect too much this early. Common ground may involve only a common desire to end tension or destruction and to establish security or an agreement on what problems must be dealt with first. Finally, although this is more the work of the next three stages, a moderator must keep in mind that "the fundamental point of a public space is to create an environment where no one is an 'outside expert'—everyone has an explicit stake and interest, and needs ownership."[5]

The second underlying objective of paramount importance throughout the dialogue—but essential to stress at the outset—is to generate awareness of whole relationships. Because this dialogue differs from other meetings, a moderator may occasionally ask: "What does this point reveal about the underlying relationships between your groups?" Since interactions and interdependence define relationships, it is important whenever possible to cause participants to notice them. If a group is to learn how to change a relationship, it must see how one group depends on another to fulfill even its own interests.

Another way of making this point is to note the following contrast: Experts and officials will talk about technical ways of resolving technically defined problems, and they may find imaginative solutions. But those solutions may be of little use unless placed in a political context in which people are concerned with whole relationships and with more than one problem and in which they must consider the interaction between unlike problems. That is not something experts do easily. Many discussions do not get beyond the experts' agenda because experts rarely focus on the relationships behind the problems. Citizens are freer to talk more naturally about what blocks a fuller relationship. They reach beyond the governmental agenda to discover what forces block or impel change. The focus on relationship—whatever concrete subject may be discussed—separates this kind of dialogue from a negotiation among technicians or officials.

Third, to enhance a sense of relationship, a moderator must find ways to help participants become aware of each other as human beings and to dispel abstractions and stereotypes. Dialogue requires that each person develop respect for the other participants and some trust that the dialogue is sincere, not mere maneuvering.

"Storytelling" can be a powerful way of introducing a human element into the dialogue. It can transform enemies into human beings. Asking individuals at appropriate moments to tell their own stories can often project authenticity and power in ways that no analytical statement could. Storytelling can often become the only experience vivid enough to cause some participants to recognize the reality of others' problems and pain. Others seem compelled to listen—with a respect they would not give to a formal position statement—to the story of someone who has suffered or has had a transforming experience.

Participants must face the stereotypes they hold. To sustain conflict, one side often dehumanizes or demonizes the other. The challenge is not to avoid statement of these misperceptions but, rather, to use them to probe for deeper causes and needs. One person's stories can cause others to doubt their misperceptions.

Fourth, to bring each person alive to the others as human beings, the moderator must—rather than fear expression of strong feeling—seek ways to channel this feeling into fuller understanding. One person showing pain, anger or a sense of injustice, if kept within reasonable limits, can challenge stereotypes, force others to pay attention and begin to enlarge others' understanding. It is not a true dialogue if the feelings of parties who are in conflict are not expressed. A moderator needs to acknowledge that expressions of feeling are understandable in this situation. The moderator's task is to ask what participants can learn from them about the dynamics of these relationships.

While it is essential to prevent the expression of anger, grief or blame from blocking further productive discussion, each person must take those feelings seriously and incorporate them into a larger picture of the relationship. One approach is for a moderator to pause after a participant alludes to a traumatic experience or shows emotion, to call the group's attention to the importance the speaker attaches to what he or she said and to invite the speaker to share that experience or feeling more fully. Listeners will normally show respect for a person in pain.

Fifth, at a more analytical level, the moderator must help participants learn to delve beneath initial positions to underlying interests. Each must learn not just to state what her or his interests are, but also to explain why those interests are important—to open the deeper feelings, values, motivations and fears behind them. Each needs to understand why a problem is important in human terms.

Finally, the moderator will need to find appropriate moments—"teaching time-outs"—throughout the dialogue to introduce certain concepts so that participants will learn to use them to enlarge their ways of thinking about problems. This is best done at moments when the discussion provides a good example of how a concept can be used to put a problem in a new context. Being explicit is important so participants consciously gain a new political tool. Among those concepts are: (1) public space; (2) dialogue as a method of discourse different from argument, debate, diplomatic exchange, mediation or negotiation; (3) the idea of an overall relationship between groups; and (4) diverse self-interests.[6]

The Tasks of Stage Two

Beyond these underlying objectives of the moderator, three tasks need to be accomplished in Stage Two:

- mapping the problems and relationships, which will absorb most of the time;
- defining or naming—narrowing and sharpening—a small list of problems to probe in depth (these are the subjects that the group thinks demand priority focus);
- making the transition to Stage Three.

Mapping the Problems and the Relationships

The first task as the dialogue begins is to stimulate discussion of the situation that prompts the dialogue—its problems, irritants, injustices, dilemmas, habits, misunderstandings and practices that reflect sources of difficulty, conflict or opportunity in the relationship. This will take a significant amount of time, and, just as one thinks the group is ready to move on, it retrogresses. Sometimes, the retrogression takes the form of diverting discussion to other issues, but it may be evidence that the group has not overcome its resistance to moving on.

Each person shares her or his views of a problem and tries to understand differences. The purpose is to develop as full a picture of the whole situation from as many viewpoints as possible. Participants might explain the main problems they face and how these problems threaten their group's interests. They might also identify the important relationships responsible for creating these problems that need to be changed.

These opening comments will include a mix of analytical and emotional statements about events in the more distant past and in recent time. Although lengthy recitals of history have to be limited, everything people need to say has some relevance in their minds and is part of the picture.

Mention of interests can provide one of those moments early in the dialogue for saying a few words about the *concept* of interests. Two points are particularly important:

- Each person in the dialogue comes with diverse interests. This diversity is useful because it helps each understand what is really important to others and why. Knowing others' interests can become a resource for solving problems as common ground among interests emerges.

• Interests are not only tangible and measurable; they also include individual and group identity, fears and aspirations. They reach to the core of what individuals value as human beings.

Participants in deep-rooted conflict have a lot to say. They must be given time to say it. What they say becomes the pool of insights and ideas from which they will eventually draw in trying to change relationships. Brief as the description of the task is, moderators and participants must allow it the time it deserves.

Naming Problems for Priority Attention

When a relatively full picture of key problems and the relationships behind them has emerged, the moderator will begin shifting gears to bring this stage to a close. The task is to cluster problems and to select a small number—one overriding problem or several of equal weight—for the group to talk about in greater depth.

To start this transition to the next stage, participants need to address questions such as these: Given the problems you have identified, which are the ones you most want to work on in greater depth? Given the realities of the situation, which problem do you need to work on first?

The aim is to produce an agreed-upon short list of the problems the group considers most important and to define them thoughtfully so their definition captures the most important concerns of all. The purpose, until now, has been to identify a broad range of problems and the relationships underneath them. This has been a survey, or "mapping." In contrast, in the next stage (Stage Three) the group will take one problem at a time and probe it deeply and systematically. That probing requires defining the problem carefully.

It is important for the larger purposes of the dialogue that the subject or subjects identified be ones that require—along with substantive elements—revealing discussion of the relationships involved. Such probing will lead eventually to thoughts about how some of those relationships might be changed by actions in the political arena.

Many discussions do not go much beyond this initial exploratory level, if they get even this far. Often, funding is available for only one meeting. Sometimes, organizers are content to discuss the same topics governments are discussing, and, since they do not have authority to negotiate, they are limited in how far they can go. Others are content with an exchange of information or a research experience and do not envision a relationship as a process that can be explored and deepened over time in a group that is a microcosm of the whole body politic. The main reason dialogues stick at this level is that they focus only on topics, not on the overall relationship, and consequently they do not overcome the resistance to moving to a deeper level of dialogue.

Transition: Overcoming Resistance to Sustained Dialogue

This is a point at which a group may well hit an impasse. Much more difficult than reaching agreement on topics for future dialogue may be overcoming remaining resistance to a sustained exchange on problems that participants know will involve their reaching out to opponents in ways that acknowledge the legitimacy of some of their opponents' views. After a vigorous discussion, participants may lapse into silence, go off on tangents, talk around a problem—that is, take whatever tack they can to avoid the subject.

A moderator may want to conduct a short trial run to see whether the group is ready to move on by asking participants what elements of the problem they have agreed to focus on and would now be ready to probe. He or she should press just far enough to determine whether the group is ready to explore new ideas—that is, to go beyond fixed positions.

Resistance to deepening the dialogue can result from a number of feelings. Some participants are unable to accept that others have serious needs or, even if they do, cannot reexamine their own positions in the light of others' needs. Other participants may realize that the discussion could trigger such deep feelings of injustice, grievance and anger that they fear lashing out in a way that frightens them; they may feel that the risk is not worth taking. They may be afraid of the emotions they know could be released. Still others may fear that reaching out could cause their own group to ostracize them.

Overcoming such resistance can be a critical element in the transition to Stage Three. The options below describe two ends of a spectrum of possible approaches.

Option One: "Take a Walk through History." Some colleagues argue that the most effective way to overcome resistance is to stop and deal with it head-on. They ask each participant to describe key events leading to the present. Each side listens to the other's experience in a situation that was traumatic for both. One might say: "I didn't know that's how it looked from your side." Another may acknowledge partial responsibility for what the other suffered or even apologize. An aggrieved party may even forgive. Through what Joseph Montville calls "a walk through history," psychological wounds can be healed in an "acknowledgment-contrition-forgiveness transaction."[7] As Vamik Volkan writes, until "chosen traumas" and "chosen glories" are brought to the surface and acknowledged, they will continue as hidden obstacles to reconciliation or to constructive work together.[8]

The advantage of this approach is that it tackles resistance at its heart, potentially clears the air and may even open the door to basic changes in relationships. The argument is that only by bringing the deep-rooted causes of conflict to the surface and dealing with them in a healing way can one truly remove the obstacles to dialogue and problem-solving relationships.

The danger is that reopening an exchange of recriminations by rehashing history will bog down the dialogue and even risk an outburst of emotion that could destroy it. Once that kind of exchange begins, in the worst circumstances it could become impossible for a moderator to put the dialogue back on track.

Option Two: Address Obstacles through Concrete Problems.   An alternative is to march ahead with dialogue on the practical problem(s) identified as the focus for continuing probing while actively seeking moments when feelings might be dealt with constructively to solve a particular problem.

In many instances, parties to a conflict profess readiness for deeper dialogue, but, when faced with the need to accept an agenda that other participants could accept, they fear that reaching out to another group will require them to surrender prematurely a part of their position. Often, the approach of negotiators is to try to split the difference between two positions. The approach in dialogue could be to stop and probe the fears behind the resistance to see whether they can be dealt with by talking them through with other participants—not with a full-blown "walk through history" but with a modified approach of seeking deeply rooted causes for the particular behavior of the moment. The argument *for* this approach is that it might minimize the danger of a destructive explosion; the argument *against* it is that it might not accomplish what is necessary.

Another line of reasoning in this situation is to say that participants are still in Stage Two, in which the task is "mapping" the elements of the relationships involved, and are not yet ready for a systematic attack on these obstacles—a full-blown "walk through history"; that would be the task when they have made a full transition to Stage Three and have built deeper relationships with each other, as well as stronger foundations for such work.

Yet another variation on this option is not to press ahead in the current meeting but to wait and see whether participants come to the next meeting ready to move ahead. I have seen dramatic examples of how using the time between meetings to allow experience to settle and be processed accomplishes more than tackling a problem head-on.

In Stage Two, the value of the dialogue has been its wide scope in making sure that each party's interests and concerns are included in the dialogue. Now, with the bare beginnings of an enlarged and partly common picture of the situation and its relationships in individual minds, the group should be prepared to move to Stage Three, provided participants feel and articulate an interest and a commitment to continue. They must agree to move to more precisely defined problems with the particular purpose of pursuing the dual agenda: discussing concrete problems for the purpose of understanding the whole relationship.

The Products of Stage Two

The first products are the moderator's judgments that (1) resistance has been sufficiently overcome; (2) the quality of the dialogue has begun to change—the participants can now talk *with* each other instead of just stating their views; and (3) they show readiness to settle down to an in-depth discussion of specific problems, one at a time. It is essential that participants show readiness to think honestly about the implications of others' interests for their own positions. Until they can, they are not ready to move solidly into Stage Three.

Second is a clear definition and understanding of one to three concrete problems to be discussed in depth one at a time. This should be a more-or-less agreed-upon list.

Homework Assignment

It often proves useful to provide participants a way of channeling their reflections as they evolve between meetings. At this stage, the moderator might present one of two requests to participants. If the group seems ready to move on: Would each of you come next time with a carefully worded statement of the problem(s) as each would describe it (them), along with a list of the important ways in which these problems affect you? If it still seems difficult for participants to reach out to each other: Would each of you try before the next meeting—as fully and honestly as possible—to describe why you do not feel comfortable opening up?

STAGE THREE: PROBING PROBLEMS AND RELATIONSHIPS TO CHOOSE A DIRECTION

"THIS IS THE WAY WE NEED TO MOVE"

Beginning groups will enter this stage in natural progression from Stage Two. Groups that have been at work longer often circle back from later stages to tackle a new problem or an old task in a changed situation. These groups will normally pick up at the end of Stage Two to name the new problem or just pick up here by quickly defining or redefining the task they must work on now rather than go back to the beginning of Stage Two. Their experience in the dialogue will provide the practical context and the sense of their relationships that they need as background. In either case, the group will begin the real work of Stage Three with a reasonably precise statement of the problem(s) it wants to work on.

Definition of the problem the group intends to work on is at first a tentative setting of goals, against which a group later assesses its progress or makes midcourse corrections. Recalling the presentation of the peace process in Chapter One, we can say that the dialogue group has begun its diagnostic—or analytical—work in Stage Two. Participants will deepen that work in Stage Three and move into thinking about strategy. I make this point here because, when we turn in Chapter Ten to the work of judging progress, it will be important to remember how deeply group members have been engaged in developing together a rough analytical framework within which to work. The definition of the problem in Stage Two and the setting of a direction in Stage Three are bridges from the group's early analysis to a strategy for ending violence and moving toward peace.

A Brief Overview

The tasks in this stage are (1) to use in-depth probing of specific problems to reveal the dynamics of the conflictual relationships that cause those problems and (2), on the basis of that work, to frame possible choices among approaches to changing those relationships so the group (3) can weigh those choices to set a general direction for action. At the end of Stage Three, participants will decide whether they have generated the will to work toward changing those relationships.

The dialogue can move beyond this stage only when participants feel a compelling need for change because they see their situation becoming intolerable and their relationships less able to turn that situation around, and when they accept personal responsibility for change. The end of this stage may well be a period of internal struggle for participants; they may strongly resist going beyond this point—sometimes because they fear it is too dangerous.

The Process Agenda

To accomplish these tasks, the character of the group's work together needs to change. The transition from Stage Two is not likely to have been neatly accomplished, and regressions are normal. But, while a moderator can expect to face this continuing challenge, the time has come to press harder for setting a new pattern.

At the start of each meeting, the moderator, as the steward of the dialogue process, has the opportunity in an opening comment to consolidate and advance the pattern and the substance of the interaction within the dialogue. These are rare "teaching moments" that help participants become more conscious that they are engaged in a process with a character, a purpose and a sense of direction—not just another talk. Repetition is an important part of the teaching because participants often ignore these comments and revert to their customary ways of talking. Because the moderator is, at the start of each new stage, trying to shift gears, it is especially important that he or she speak explicitly to make the shift clear and then be as active as necessary during the dialogue that follows to consolidate the shift.

First, the mode of discourse needs to shift from explaining to genuine *dialogue* about a problem recognized as affecting each party's interests. The talk in the opening sessions was necessarily closer to statement and explanation than to dialogue. Participants had a lot of thoughts and feelings they needed to pour out. The discussion was often an analytical exchange of viewpoints. They talked *to* each other rather than *with* each other. Now, each person needs to listen more carefully and consistently to others and to engage their thoughts in response—not just to make individual statements. The purpose is not so much to present or to persuade but to explore what others think and feel and why.

The shift to a new way of talking together needs to be made explicit. Participants must be aware of the shift. It may come slowly, but, if the moderator articulates it, he or she will find participants repeating the point after a time. There may be a moment at the opening of a meeting for the moderator, drawing on Chapter Five, to reflect again on how dialogue differs from other modes of discourse. As the dialogue proceeds, the method of this stage—probing one subject at a time—will provide a natural context in which participants will need to seek clarification, to hear alternative views, to weigh choices together and to think through the complexities of the problem before moving on. By exploring systematically what is on others' minds and the implications for each group member, participants can lay the foundations for thinking together in a problem-solving relationship.

Second, this is the moment to dramatize the dual agenda: the concrete problem plus the underlying relationship that causes it.

The starting point for dialogue this time is the subject the group agreed to work on first at the end of the last meeting. The discourse needs to shift from a scattershot spray of problems to a shared, systematic, disciplined *probing of one problem at a time*. Only by sticking to each subject until some closure is reached can the group achieve a sense of useful accomplishment and build a solid foundation for continuing dialogue.

At the same time, a serious effort to probe the *relationships behind the problems* must begin. The flat-surface capacity of the wide-angle lens used in Stage Two to map the full terrain of problems must give way to the probing, three-dimensional capacity of the CAT scanner. Again, this may require talking about what it means to focus on the overall relationship(s) among parties to a conflict, drawing on the analysis in Chapter Two. The discussion should be used to open doors in three directions:

- As participants refuse to hear or respond to others, express anger or reject arguments out of hand, the moderator must use some of these occasions to encourage individuals to reflect on their reactions. This is part of dealing with resistance left over from the transition out of Stage Two and a window into the dynamics of key relationships.
- If participants recognize that they have defined their task too narrowly—that, in focusing on a near-term problem, they have excluded a longer perspective they need—the moderator should encourage enlarging the definition of the problem. That is one way to begin building a bridge to the next agenda.
- Above all, the moderator must help participants understand that probing the relationships behind the problems is the paramount task—and then help them do that probing. Only when progress has been made in thinking in terms of whole relationships can the group move on to Stage Four, in which the task is to design ways of working in the political arena to change key relationships.

Accomplishing these tasks will require a more directive style of moderating than in Stage Two. Whereas the moderator may have adopted a permissive style in early meetings to allow everyone to feel heard, he or she now may need to press participants to stick to the subject at hand, to respond directly to others' points and questions and to try to explain underlying interests, which are not always easy to articulate. It will require repeated efforts and perseverance to accustom participants to think and talk about relationships and to engage in serious dialogue.

The moderator owes it to the group to warn that the chair will play a more active role. Since the shift to genuine dialogue and to a focus on relationships themselves is so important to the future work of the group, the moderator should ask the group's understanding of more frequent interventions.

The Working Agenda in Outline

The agenda in Stage Three is a heavy one. In outline, group members need to work through five tasks:

- confirming as quickly as possible the definition of the problem they intend to work on;
- probing the problem that they have agreed to start with in a way that brings to the surface the dynamics of the underlying relationships;
- framing, with the moderator's assistance, broad choices for possible directions to take in tackling the problem;
- weighing those choices and working to come to some sense of direction to guide their communities' next steps;
- assessing where present relationships are leading—the consequences of doing nothing—and determining the need to change them by confronting the fundamental questions: Are the consequences of doing nothing worse than the consequences of trying to move in the direction we have been discussing? Do we have the will within the group to design ways of changing the destructive relationships that stand in the way of movement?

Confirming the Definition of the Problem

An agenda was agreed on in general terms at the end of Stage Two, and participants were asked to define the problems more precisely between meetings. Intervening events may have shifted their perspectives, and they will have had time to think in more detail about how different approaches would affect their interests. They must now produce quickly a concise statement of the problem.

This exchange could become complicated as participants begin discussing elements of the problem. What was an intellectually agreeable subject generally stated in the wrap-up of a previous meeting might now appear in its real-world complexity as participants discuss it in light of their individual interests.

This is the point at which the moderator needs to introduce discipline. He or she needs to be sure a definition of the agenda is agreed upon and to prevent the discussion from going off in all directions.

Strong feelings are likely to flare up even in defining the agenda. As soon as this happens, the moderator should control some but choose others to begin opening up the dynamics of the interactions involved. In time, participants will learn to handle sharp differences so that—even when disagreements lead to acrimony—dealing with them constructively can move relationships to a still deeper level. These combined exchanges help them experience and understand more clearly the full pattern of interactions that make up the totality of their relationship. But the moderator has to move gradually. At first, the task is simply to start participants thinking in these terms. Sometimes, it may be worth asking whether a participant would be willing to talk about why a subject makes her or him angry, to say at whom the anger is directed or to identify what relationships are involved.

Probing Problems and Relationships

As participants prove able to deal with the idea of relationship, the moderator would do well to have in mind the checklist of the components that make up a relationship discussed in detail in Chapter Two. The purpose is to help identify the groups involved in the problem; how they have experienced each other in the past and developed their self-images in relationship with each other; how each defines its interests and why and whether they share interests; whether the groups normally interact by fighting, bargaining, posturing, talking; how power works in the relationship; what limits they observe in dealing with each other; how each perceives the other and why.

Obviously, all of these subjects are too much to deal with at one time. Attempting too much can overload the circuits. The moderator will have to choose only those questions that are pertinent in a particular exchange and useful in bringing out underlying ways of thinking about relevant relationships. Since the discussion of the substantive agenda can go on for some time, a number of opportunities will present themselves.

At some point, the moderator will have to sense that participants have de-veloped a complete-enough working picture of the aspects of the problem they are dealing with and of the relationships involved to permit them to move on. Because their picture will necessarily be imperfect, the moderator may want to offer a summary that will be good enough to work from. For instance, I have often developed a sharply defined list of the elements of a problem drawn from the dialogue. It omitted some points but helped participants focus their dialogue. To deal with relationships in one dialogue, I wrote and read to a group a list of ways in which each side feared the other. It covered enough important points to give participants a rough picture that they could refine and develop themselves.

Framing Choices among Possible Directions for Action

The next task is to move from a good-enough working picture of a problem to framing the main choices the group identifies as ways of dealing with that problem. The purpose here is not to decide on a detailed course of action but to give group members a chance to weigh their choices in approaching the problem. Those choices need to reflect what each party to the conflict especially values. This framing of the choices need not be formally done, but enough work needs to be done to give participants a sense of the pros and cons of each approach so they can at least set a general direction for action.

As participants talk about a problem, they may naturally fall into talking about how to deal with it, so the moderator's task may be limited to helping the group draw those comments together. If that has not happened, the moderator will want to ask what participants see as possible ways of dealing with the problem.

Often, as citizens discuss a problem and how they might deal with it, they throw out a range of possible actions. As the informal list of those actions grows, the moderator will find that they are falling into clusters that reflect particular mind-sets. Grouping those possible actions may help participants begin to see how they might frame their main choices. In a dialogue, this process can be as elaborate or as informal as the group wants to make it. The important point is that the group's thinking provide a basis for moving to the next level.[9]

Weighing Choices and Setting a Direction

Once participants have talked enough about a problem and the kinds of steps that might be taken to deal with it, they come to a point of deliberating on possible approaches. They may agree on a particular approach. Or, in talking about the consequences of possible approaches for the interests of individual parties to the conflict, they may further refine the choices. Or, at this point in their relationship, they may not be able to agree completely on an approach, but they may identify some common ground that provides a basis for initial steps. Simply agreeing on a range of refined choices at certain points in a conflict may be a significant contribution to public and official thinking.

The acts of identifying and weighing choices necessarily help group members think, talk and work differently together. Such is the very nature of dialogue.

The minimal purpose of this work is to provide a basis for moving the dialogue to a yet deeper level. In some circumstances, what is accomplished at this moment in a group's experience could be shared with other citizens or officials verbally or in writing if the options are framed and the consequences laid out in a systematic way.

Determining a Will to Change

Generating the will to change is the ultimate goal in Stage Three. Only the participants can do that, but a moderator can set the stage so they can explore their own readiness.

At some point, participants will recognize that what logically should be done cannot be done as long as the present state of relationships persists. But changing those relationships even in the limited ways necessary to accomplish near-term goals may not be easy. Change will require a judgment that more would be gained than lost by attempting change.

Where Are These Relationships Taking Us?   One way to move toward a judgment that change is worth the cost is to bring the group to a pause for assessment—assessment of the state of present relationships as the group has discussed them and reflection on where those relationships are taking the situation. Each group will need to reflect on how likely developments will affect its interests, its capacities to deal with the situation and the ability of the two groups to work together in those situations in which outcomes depend on some collaboration.

Is Change Possible? What Would It Require?   Next, it is necessary to assess whether there is enough common ground to allow working together just enough to deal with the immediate situation and whether the costs of change are affordable. The dialogue should have enabled the parties to see whether their respective self-interests can be different without, in all cases, being mutually exclusive. While the parties will not necessarily find identical interests, they may begin to identify those interests that are compatible enough to permit some degree of cooperation for a limited purpose.

Specifically, participants need to ask whether change is possible—whether those involved have the will to change the relationships that would have to be changed to produce the result they desire. More precisely, they need to identify the elements in those relationships that might be changed. They need to think about exactly how they and their groups might contribute to the desired change.

If the group gets this far in its thinking, it is close to imagining together a picture of the changed relationships that would serve the interests of each party to those relationships—at least for the limited purpose of dealing with the narrowly defined problem on the agenda. In weighing the advantages and disadvantages of each kind of relationship, the group is working toward the basis for a constructive relationship—a relationship with foundations that make it able to deal with the problems it must deal with. As dialogue deepens, participants find it increasingly possible to talk about why they do or do not value particular relationships; what is strong or weak, good or bad about them; and whether and how they might change for better or worse.

At some moment, a moderator might find it revealing to ask what each party's interests require from present relationships. In some cases, an honest participant might explain why some people in her or his group may have an important need to continue a conflict because they define their identity in terms of that conflict or they stand to gain from it in some other way. In other cases, participants might be honest about how the continuing conflict negatively affects human values. As this conversation deepens, it becomes possible to talk more precisely about their interest in changing relationships.

The question now is whether the group dares to go beyond exchanging ideas and assessments to design steps for putting them into practice—whether individual members judge that the need for change is compelling enough to pay the price of change. Can they make the hard personal choices involved in deciding to talk with the adversary about ways of trying to change existing relationships?

Attempting Transition to Stage Four: Overcoming Resistance

The main task in bringing Stage Three to closure and moving to the next level of dialogue is to determine whether all participants are ready and able to think and work together in an operational way. Do group members really show the will to take that next step and begin talking among themselves about how to design change?

This is perhaps the most difficult transition in the whole process. Often, in a first burst of enthusiasm, participants will express determination to move ahead, but, when faced with the demands that step will require, they will back off. To take the next step, participants must shift from being adversaries—however civilized they may have learned to be with each other—to becoming coworkers. That is asking a lot, and it can be frightening.

Despite stories that dramatize pain caused by the present situation, some participants—deep down—may actually find practical advantages in it. In particularly tense situations, opposition and confrontation may elevate some individuals to positions of leadership they probably would not enjoy to the same extent if the confrontation ended. Others might lose a livelihood, a way of life or unusual material gain. At a minimum, living with a situation one knows—even if it causes some pain—may provide certainties, whereas moving to an unknown situation could leave individuals uncertain of their capacity to meet the challenge.

Enemies may genuinely fear what the adversary represents. They may really believe that the other side is so committed to holding or gaining power in self-defense that no real change in the relationship is possible. If there is no possibility of compromise, the only alternative might seem capitulation that would threaten what is most valued.

Cooperating with an adversary requires giving up one's worst picture of her or him. That worst picture may boost one's own self-esteem. Each of us defines her or his own identity in terms of not being someone else—for example, our enemy. Giving up that worst picture may cause uncertainty about who we are.

These are only a few of the factors that may be at work. They are mentioned here only to stimulate thought. Since a moderator may be able to go only so far in a discussion with the whole group together, this may be another occasion for separate meetings with individuals or subgroups.

The Products of Stage Three

The products of this stage are: (1) the experience of an increasingly direct and probing dialogue that deepens and begins to change relationships within the group; (2) a new body of insight into the perceptions, feelings, and conceptual frameworks of others; (3) an outline of how present relationships between the parties need to change to produce conditions that might lead to a more desirable way of dealing with problems; and, above all, (4) a judgment that the costs of continuing the present situation and relationships outweigh the costs of trying to change them. The critical product—and Stage Three cannot end without it—is the generation of a will to change.

Homework Assignments

If the group is not ready to move on, participants might be asked to think seriously and to write before the next meeting a statement about why it is still difficult for the group to work together to design change. Is the situation still not painful enough? What would have to happen to persuade them and other members of their groups that the situation cannot be allowed to go on any longer?

If the group is ready to move on, participants might be asked to get a head start on the work of the next stage by writing three lists:

- obstacles to moving in the direction participants seem to prefer;
- steps that might overcome those obstacles;
- steps each group would need from the other to enable it to take the steps it must take.

STAGE FOUR: SCENARIO-BUILDING— EXPERIENCING A CHANGING RELATIONSHIP

"What Might an Action Plan Look Like?"

A Brief Overview

The framing of choices and the deliberation on them in Stage Three to choose a direction for action will have brought to the surface a number of interactive steps to help deal with concrete problems and change relationships. In Stage Four, the task is to develop those possible steps and that sense of direction into as detailed an action scenario as possible to be a practical basis for considering what action might be possible.

The purpose in this stage is no less than planning to change relationships. The specific aims are twofold: to bring members of the group into a new way of thinking together about how to generate the change they would like to see happen and to design an actual scenario for change. The ultimate task of the participants as a microcosm of the larger relationships involved is to project the change they are experiencing into the larger community. That is the work of Stage Five, but that possibility will be in the forefront of participants' minds from this moment on.

Scenario-Building: The Vehicle for Change

The vehicle for change is a task that requires participants to work together to design a scenario of interactive steps to change relationships between their groups. Figuratively, participants are no longer sitting across the table talking to each other. As individuals, they are sitting side by side thinking together about how to change a situation and the relationships that cause it. In doing so, they themselves experience what the relationship will have to become in the larger society if the desired changes are to be accomplished. Participants experience the internal obstacles to change and agonize over how individuals and groups in their communities might overcome those obstacles.

In addition, participants come to understand that an improved relationship need not be dangerous. They see that building a constructive relationship does not eliminate all negative factors but can generate the capacity to deal with them peacefully. Creating that self-generated political capacity can become the main product of this experience in transforming their relationship and lay the foundation for extending it into the larger body politic.

The Scenario-Building Experience

We call the task used in trying to bring about this transformation "scenario-building." Participants are laying out a complex of interactive steps much as a playwright lays out the interactive moves in a drama. The key to creating these scenes in a drama is the genuineness of the interaction. In the dialogue, that interaction begins with thinking together to design the impact of interactive steps. Participants almost become coconspirators in designing steps aimed at changing perceptions and reactions in their respective groups.

First, they are asked to list the main obstacles to moving in the direction they envisioned at the end of Stage Three. These obstacles range from the most deep-rooted misperceptions and fears to more tangible causes and issues of difference.

To achieve more than a superficial listing of obvious physical roadblocks, the moderator can use the elements of relationships presented in Chapter Two as a resource for pressing participants to probe beneath the surface. Participants will certainly identify practical obstacles, such as the positions of opposing parties, the lack of resources and the opposing objectives of different groups. But they will also need to probe for the underlying human dimension of those obstacles—human fears, historic grievances, misperceptions, stereotypes, wounds from the past and human interests. Often, these are greater obstacles to changing relationships than objective components of a situation, for which there may well be technical solutions. Some of this work may have been done in Stage Three and can be brought back into the conversation, but there will also be opportunities to deepen the discussion.

Second, they list steps to help erode or remove those obstacles. These steps must work at economic, social, political, military, legal and human levels. Responses at the practical political level will be fairly obvious. These steps will include concrete measures to change conditions that one group finds unjust or harmful. Responses to some of the underlying human fears, grievances and animosities will require actions that come to mind less quickly. These human factors are not thought of in official political life as often as concrete issues. Steps to deal with them may include public statements or acts that symbolize contrition and forgiveness—recognition of harm that has been done and apology for it—or simply an acknowledgment of another group's suffering. Participants should list as many steps as possible in order to generate a cumulative impact over time.

Third, participants identify who might take those steps, engaging as broad a cross-section of social elements as possible while keeping in mind what is possible given present conditions and capabilities in their bodies politic. Often, the first attempt at a list of actors reveals that participants are naming steps for others to take—none that they themselves will take responsibility for initiating. The exercise has little real meaning until participants themselves are personally engaged. They will not experience the cost of changing critical relationships until they struggle with those costs inside themselves.

Fourth, participants arrange these actions in a sequence that takes advantage of reinforcing interactions among steps. Scenario-building recognizes that it will not always be possible to move to a new situation all in one step; a series of reciprocal and interactive steps may be necessary.

Given political realities and human sensitivities, some actions clearly need to be taken before actions by the other side are possible, and others cannot be taken unless a positive response by the other side is reasonably assured. For instance, Party A says it could take Step One if Party B could take Step Two; Party B says that is possible, but only if Party A would respond with Step Three or Party C would support movement by taking Step Four.

This is the time when participants should be encouraged to explain their groups' constraints in taking steps, what they need from others to enable them to take the necessary steps, and why. Will prior agreement on the whole scenario be necessary in providing the assurance to get it started? The interdependent and interactive character of these moves leads participants to think of these steps as they depend on one another. As awareness of interdependence increases, relationships change. This part of the discussion may significantly expand the list of steps and permit steps to be clustered to build a sense of momentum.

When the interaction operates in public, its effect depends not only on the interaction, but also on public recognition of what is taking place. The participants as authors of the scenario need to build into it the moment when the media, scholars, politicians, analysts and citizens begin to notice and talk publicly about the fact that something different is happening. The authors need to name the trend they want others to perceive so others can begin acting to accelerate it. As more and more people become engaged, they enlarge the interaction between groups.

Since this interaction and interdependence are the essence of relationship, participants learn from their own deeper thought and experience the nature of the relationships that are essential to their achieving their goal. This part of the exercise is worth a good deal of time.

The Products of Scenario-Building

The scenario developed will not be neat or complete the first time around, but there are two important products. The concrete product is a first cut at a plan of action that could actually be implemented. It will provide a foundation for the group's work in Stage Five. Less tangible but more important is the fact that participants gain from their personal experience a sense that it is possible to enlarge the political capacity to deal with problems by changing relationships in ways that protect the identity of each party. They experience what it is to think in the context of relationship and to use the interactions within a relationship to begin changing it. It is important for members of the group to articulate what they have experienced so they can build on that experience in the larger body politic.

It is not an overstatement to say that, through this experience, a small group of citizens can design ways of changing a relationship. That is not to say that any group has the capacity to engineer such sweeping changes, but it is possible for a group to imagine how such changes might come about. Those involved confront a problem and design change, not as negotiators or mediators but as individuals thinking and imagining together in an increasingly close relationship. They do not give up their individual identities; indeed, those identities remain important parts of the experience. But they do begin to think about how those identities may be more fully realized if a conflictual relationship can be transformed.

The transformation is underway when the participants begin to think in terms of "what we can do" or "what I must do to enable you to do what I want you to do" rather than "what you must do." This is a qualitatively different way of thinking from the norm in governmental exchanges, in which each side thinks it must press its own position and demands. That constraint explains the occasional impulse of diplomats to go for "a walk in the woods" or to explore the potential of official negotiating parties to encourage nonofficial groups to discuss in greater depth than officials can the obstacles to changing a relationship.

Participants experience both the constraints and the opportunities in planning to act together. Often, it is not possible at a given time to change a relationship dramatically, so participants must be content to move one step at a time. Such steps can open the way for others. These steps are sometimes called "confidence-building measures"—a concept akin to scenario-building.

Transition: What Action Flows from This Scenario?

Most nonofficial dialogues do not get this far. It has not been customary in international relations or tense communities to think of trying to change the dynamics of underlying relationships. It is particularly difficult for nongovernmental groups to find funding for the kind of sustained dialogue necessary to reach this point. To have gone this far, such groups will have consumed many days over a prolonged period working on a cumulative agenda.

When a group has completed a draft scenario, a participant will ask: "What can we do with what we have produced?" Some of them will take their new insights to the communities where they are influential or even to policymakers. Others will take their fresh understandings of adversaries' views into their own political experience and organizations. Still others will believe that demonstrating how parties to the conflict can work together is a useful model for others who seek ways to deal with practical problems.

Beyond those applications, participants may want to move to purposeful action. But it is a delicate issue for a group to determine how it can contribute to action while preserving its capacity to think together about continuing problems in the relationship free from the entangling obligations of action.

The transition to this discussion begins when someone asks: "What do we do now? Are we going to stop with just talking?"

This is not a transition for a moderator to press; it should be left very much to the participants. A decision among adversaries to try to act individually or together is a momentous, dangerous and, perhaps, impossible step. With good reason, many groups' members think that they have completed their task if they can simply model a different way of relating and share the insights from the experience with a few key colleagues. It may be enough that the ideas begin to circulate among those in the larger body politic who are looking for ways out of a painful and deteriorating impasse.

At one end of the spectrum, dialogue participants face a question that many citizens outside governments face: How can a group like ours have any impact at all? That is a broad question that can be answered only in the specific situation. Or they may simply not be able to muster the time, concentration, energy or resources to do more than to engage in their own dialogue. At the other end of the spectrum, they may fear being branded traitors for working with the enemy. All of these feelings have their own legitimacy. But for some participants, a moment comes when they ask whether they do not have a responsibility to turn what they have experienced to practical use for the benefit of a whole community or country afflicted by conflict.

Once participants have engaged in scenario-building, it is difficult to say which is the more important product—the political scenario that can lead to a sequence of actions or the experience of strengthening a relationship among those who have developed the scenario. These two products converge if those who design the scenario involve themselves in its implementation.

Participants have experienced the change in their own relationships as they thought together to develop a scenario. Beyond that is the potential experience of acting together, responding together to the consequences of actions, finding new solutions, making midcourse corrections and eventually experiencing the success of having arrived at an objective. They arrive knowing that the objective could not have been achieved if the relationship for achieving it had not been built early in the process. But the deliberation on whether and, if so, how a group moves to that new level is a subject participants will probably need to ponder and perhaps talk over with a few colleagues outside the dialogue in their own communities before the next meeting. If they are ready to think about implementation, they will face the most difficult task of all. That is the challenge of Stage Five.

If participants judge that the time is not ripe to do more than share what they have done with a few colleagues, they have the opportunity to circle back to Stage Three and pick up one of the other problems they wanted to work on or, even more likely, new problems that have emerged with the passage of time. As they do, they will take with them both the insight into the relationships gained so far and the significantly deepened relationships within the dialogue.

A Word about Evaluation

In defining a problem for priority attention at the end of Stage Two and the beginning of Stage Three, the dialogue group established a first benchmark for judging its own future work.

Producing an interactive scenario is evidence of the group's ability to work together in a new way and is of substantive value in itself. It is worthwhile at a moment of achievement such as this for a moderator to invite each member of the group to write a short statement of how the dialogue has affected her or his life.

At the same time, this is also a moment of setting new goals. Those will become new milestones for checking further achievement.

These points underscore the nature of evaluation itself as an unfolding process. At this point in a dialogue, it is important enough to note the changes in the dialogue group's own capacities, but the group cannot yet be judged for not having had an impact on the larger community. Now that it has begun laying out possible steps to be taken in the body politic, it sets the stage for that judgment at a later time.

Homework Assignment

Between meetings, participants might be asked to write down what they think they can do with this scenario. More broadly, they might review their expectations for the dialogue and what more they would like to accomplish.

STAGE FIVE: ACTING TOGETHER
TO MAKE CHANGE HAPPEN

"WHAT CAN WE REALLY DO?"

A Brief Overview

One of the most difficult challenges in this work is to take the transforming insights and experiences generated within a small dialogue group into the larger community to change relationships there. The work in this stage goes well beyond what was done in Stage Four. Then, within its safe space, the group was designing steps to overcome obstacles to changing relationships. Participants were thinking about what should be done. Now they must think about what actually can be done. They will discover the significant difference between thinking in the relative safety of a dialogue room about what ought to be done and actually deciding whether and how to persuade others to take such steps. Now in Stage Five, the group must decide what—if anything—it can do to put into practice the scenario it has designed.

In the context of the peace-process framework, the group was doing its analytical work in Stages Two and Three. Designing a strategy began in earnest in Stage Four. The strategy is enlarged in Stage Five, and a tactical plan is laid out, but not before another round of analysis—now with a direct operational purpose.

The challenge of enlisting a multiplying number of actors can be daunting. Participants must consider two questions about the social context in which their design would be implemented: Do conditions exist that would permit people to attempt safely the range of activities that would be required? What is the character of institutional life in the community that would provide the instruments for implementing a scenario? This question has two aspects: Do citizens themselves demonstrate the inclination and the capacity to organize themselves to take action? Do "boundary-spanning" associations exist that provide channels for cooperation across lines?

At this point, participants are taking an inventory of the context in which they must work and of what resources they have to work with. If they decide that there is a realistic possibility of moving to action, they must refine the strategy begun in their scenario and begin devising a tactical plan for the new task of engaging the necessary individuals and institutions. How will they "plug into" the institutional life of the community to generate implementation of their scenario?

They will also need to decide what the role of the group itself will be. Will the group act as a group, or will individuals act apart from the group to put the plan into the hands of others?

The moderator will need to take into account that individuals are facing both the possibilities and the dangers of acting. They need to proceed carefully; they may need another interval between meetings to think about what they would be getting into and to take soundings in their own communities.

Assessing Conditions and Capacities for Implementation

To begin, the group needs to deal with two sets of questions: Is the situation in the community/country such that an attempt to change seems workable? What capacities and resources can the group marshal?

Conditions

Perhaps without talking much about the subject, participants will have instinctively taken into account the context in which implementation would take place. But now they need to go through a more systematic assessment: What conditions in the society are favorable or unfavorable for the actions proposed? Is change possible? How safe would it be to take those steps proposed?

The process of sustained dialogue is designed for use in conditions ranging from active civil war or tension between communities in an otherwise peaceful society to a situation in which citizens are thinking about strengthening civil society. Always, it is necessary to ask what the risks of implementation would be.

Capacities

Beyond assessing basic questions of possibility and security, one way to help put doubts into perspective is to ask participants to consider their own capacities to marshal resources for change. Often, as individuals think about the associations and networks of which they are a part, they begin to see what results old and new relationships might produce. They may begin to visualize what citizens outside government can accomplish simply by committing themselves to work together. That will be even more true if some are already in influential positions.

In sum, participants will need to consider such questions as these: Do the basic conditions of personal security exist that will permit individuals or groups to feel safe in taking the actions suggested? If not, what prior actions must be taken to generate such conditions? Are there citizens and associations already in place to work with, or do those capacities need to be created before change is possible? What can participants personally—or organizations and groups they relate to—do to carry out parts of the scenario they have developed?

The answers to these questions will suggest the starting point for a course of action leading toward implementation of the scenario participants have designed.

Some Examples

Two examples may help make these tasks more concrete. The moderator may be able to draw on experience more relevant to her or his particular dialogue.

Israel-Palestine

In 1991, a group of Israelis and Palestinians met in nonofficial dialogue—one meeting among numberless nonofficial meetings that began in the mid-1970s. Together, group members wrote, signed publicly and distributed a document they titled "Framework for a Public Peace Process."[10] They named it so because a fabric of citizens' associations was well developed, and they wanted to call attention to a supportive network of associations and interactions with the cumulative purpose of changing the fundamental relationship between the two communities.

Estonia

In 1995, inhabitants of Estonia—a former republic of the Soviet Union, which reestablished its independence in 1991—struggled with the problem of tense relationships between ethnic Estonians and Russian-speaking inhabitants, many of whom believed they were being denied Estonian citizenship as preparation for driving them out of the country. As they worked to overcome these differences peacefully, individuals from existing institutions such as research institutes, universities, government ministries, schools and churches began to design programs for dealing with the relational gulf between the communities. Although a number of highly professional and dedicated individuals committed themselves to this work, they were among the first to acknowledge that, initially, the infrastructure did not exist for spreading such programs throughout the two communities and that the first task was to focus on developing that infrastructure. An important step was creation of the President's Roundtable, bringing together members of parliament, representatives of the Russian-speaking population and individuals from other minorities. The Center for the Study of Mind and Human Interaction at the University of Virginia conducted a series of meetings to demonstrate ways in which the two principal groups could probe the dynamics of their historic relationship and begin to design programs and projects to change their relationships. This process focused primarily on developing insight into the psychodynamics of the relationships involved.

A Strategy for Implementation

Having worked through their assessment of conditions and capacities in the society, participants are ready to determine what opportunities and instruments exist for implementing their scenario. To start laying out a strategy for implementation, participants must ask such questions as:

- Are conditions ripe for launching the first steps of the scenario? Or are some preparatory steps necessary?
- The scenario identified people and groups who might take the steps described. Are those people or groups able and ready to take such steps? If not, can those groups be persuaded to act? How? If existing groups seem, in the light of the assessment, to be inadequate, can they be changed in some ways?
- If preparatory steps are necessary, can some of those steps be taken interactively so as to begin changing relationships even in this preparatory period? Could those steps be added as a new beginning of the scenario?

The group may find at this point that some of the steps required for changing tense relationships converge with steps that would develop or strengthen civil society. This insight may be useful because it can open the door to another body of thought and other resources.

In some situations prior to the evolution of a more developed civil society, the only option may be to work through existing institutions or organizations such as agencies of government, political parties or established educational institutions. Even in highly developed civil societies, perhaps the most usual objective of nonofficial dialogue has been to influence government policies. Often, participants in such dialogues have been chosen because they are close to policymakers.

Beyond working with existing institutions is the objective of influencing the direction of established nongovernmental organizations or associations where they exist or of creating them where they do not. Some nongovernmental organizations serve essential functions in the society that are almost quasi-governmental. Others in their missions put significant distance between themselves and official policies, but their operating practices give them a character and degree of stability that make many of them seem part of the Establishment. Still others are loose associations of citizens that have come together to accomplish a particular purpose and have very little permanent structure.

This public arena outside governmental structures provides the greatest opportunity for citizens to bring people together to pursue their purposes. Dialogue participants need to determine who might take what steps and how those who must take those steps might be persuaded to take them.

What Responsibilities Will Participants Assume?

Once participants have a sense of what steps need to be taken to persuade larger elements of the society to act, members of the group need to pause and talk seriously about what course they as individuals and the group as a whole might take. Participants might consider a range of options such as the following, though these are laid out here only as a framework for the moderator to have in mind, since the options need to come from participants:

Option One

Individuals might make what personal use they can of the ideas generated in the group. This approach may already have been pursued by some participants. It involves sharing insights with government officials or discussing possible actions within participants' individual organizations. That, of course, can continue.

The advantage of this approach is that it is the most feasible and can happen in a variety of ways with minimal cost. The disadvantage is that impact is limited.

Option Two

Participants might act individually or as a group according to a plan agreed upon by the group to distribute its detailed scenarios systematically to appropriate authorities in government and in public organizations or to publish them without lobbying such authorities to act. Further action would be left to others. The rationale of participants would be the importance of preserving their capacity to reflect on the changing situation without becoming bogged down in action. They would confine themselves to calling attention to growing problems in the relationship and to designing new scenarios for heading off such problems or taking advantage of them.

The advantage of this approach is that the group would keep itself free by not immersing itself in the details of action, and participants would minimize their own exposure. The disadvantage is that the normal experience is for governments to ignore citizens outside government—to accept suggestions politely but to lay them aside quickly.

Option Three

The group might constitute itself as an action group. It would actually assume responsibility for making steps in the scenario happen. Even if it were not itself the agent of action in all cases, it would undertake efforts to encourage governments or other organizations to take the steps involved. It would assume responsibility for persuasion itself.

The advantage of this approach is that the same individuals who have thought through a problem and reached some judgment about what needs to be done would be building on their experience to get that job done. The disadvantage is that the group would then become absorbed in a course of action and could well lose the capacity to step back and reflect on the way relationships are evolving. The character of the two kinds of groups—reflection and action—is quite different, although an ideal might be a group that combined the capacities for both.

Option Four

The group might remain a place in which scenarios are generated but also invite officials into this space for periods of time so as to equip them with the means of acting. One such step might be to draw individuals from action organizations into workshops with participants in the dialogue to experience designing a political scenario.

Since it is often difficult to bring individuals into a group that has been together for a long time, a preferable alternative would be for members of the original group to create new groups in their own communities. As such dialogue groups proliferate, members could create a steering group to consolidate a scenario and encourage their groups and others to carry it out.

The mere act of proliferating groups is itself an important action. After almost two decades of such dialogue, Israelis and Palestinians recognized in the early 1990s that one consequence of dozens of meetings had been the creation of a critical mass of individuals who had had the experience—over and over again—of discussing fundamental issues in their relationship and actually resolving a number of differences on important problems. After a period of time, that critical mass of people was big enough to create a body of thought in their societies that caused a fundamental change in perception of the possibilities of a peaceful relationship.

At the same time, while that change in perception can be described as a long-term product, it may not produce decisive action in the near term. Depending on the vigor with which participants pursue actions within their own organizations, they could produce specific results. Somewhere there needs to be a group of people intent on making change happen through a series of steps in the near term.

Option Five

The group might enlarge the space for a time to include participants from government and/or conflicting groups. This would not involve the new participants in the dialogue as such but would provide an opportunity for members of the original group to explain insights from the dialogue. The purpose would be to open the door to new partnerships between governments and the public. The original group could preserve its ability to remain a space in which participants come together to think through basic problems and approaches to them, leaving action to be taken in other contexts when participants leave that space.

In this option, it would be possible for a dialogue group to create a subset of itself to discuss a particular problem. It could, for example, create a working group with membership designed to focus on a particular conflictual relationship, while preserving the integrity of the original group itself. This way, the base group would have both a capacity for reflection and an opportunity to work operationally to help others deal with their conflict.

To bring to closure participants' discussion of what they will do, they will need to decide:

- What must happen first? Who will do it? How will it be connected to the next step?
- What step must be taken in response? Who will take it? How will it be made clear that this step responds directly to the first step and deliberately opens the door to a following step?
- What steps can be taken to generate wider public awareness of changing behaviors?
- Will members of the group assure that the motivations behind steps are understood by all involved groups?

A Final Thought on Stage Five

The ultimate benefit from this stage is the experience of deciding together whether to take the plunge into attempted implementation. If participants decide to try, they will experience the further dividend of working together over time. Confronting unexpected obstacles in implementing a course of action together and designing ways of overcoming them would then further deepen understanding of the relationship. Even if their decision is more tentative, exploring the possibilities for action would bring them together in new ways.

Whatever the mechanism a group uses to put its insights into action, participants must not lose sight of their fundamental purpose: changing the relationship among the groups they come from. They must not allow themselves to be drawn into the details of individual actions to the extent of losing that essential perspective. They must remember that it is the *inter*action—not the action—that is most important. In that interaction, a relationship begins to change. The aim is not just to persuade one party to take certain steps; it is to motivate that party to take its steps with the conscious purpose of developing interaction with another party.

Keeping an eye on this overarching purpose can significantly change the way in which actions are taken. Many times in political experience, one party will have taken a step only to discover to its puzzlement that it has had no effect on the other group or the body politic; perhaps the others have not noticed it, or, just as likely, they have had their own internal reasons for not wanting to notice it. This has been the experience of many steps taken by Palestinians who, in the end, have been angered by the fact that not even Israelis who were given early notice of the meaning of specific actions used them to bring about a change in Israeli perceptions of the Palestinians.

The art, then, is both to design a scenario of interactive steps that makes sense analytically and—in the stage of acting together—to make sure that responses to such actions set in motion a cumulative interaction. This is not an abstract exercise. A relationship begins to change when one party—to use the words of my Russian colleague—is able to "penetrate the consciousness" of the other. A relationship begins to change when one group can cause the other to see it in a different way or hear it with new understanding. The purpose is to design actions that jolt Group B into taking notice that Group A's behavior is different from what Group B expected. Sadat's 1977 visit to Jerusalem is only a most dramatic example of opening the eyes of the other side.

Much has been made in diplomatic literature of "signaling." Actions by one side are wafted into the air much as the smoke signals of Native Americans. Little attention has been given to assuring that those signals are read—and read correctly—by those for whom the signals are intended. The stage of acting together gives primary attention to creating an *inter*action and using that interaction as the context within which change in a relationship is gradually brought about.

In Chapter Three, I discussed new thinking about community politics. It is at this point—in Stage Five—that thinking about politics in one body politic becomes relevant to changing the relationship between two groups or bodies politic.

In this stage, individuals coming from two bodies politic are together designing steps that will stimulate actions in each body politic that could change *citizens'* perceptions of each other. As they work together to generate actions that will change perceptions or even create the possibility of groups collaborating to change some aspect of the relationship, they must think in terms of how to generate a response from the bottom up. They will not be directing their actions primarily at governments; they will be attempting to persuade individual citizens and groups of citizens on each side to take the responsibility to change the way the two groups interact from the ground up. Because members of a dialogue group like this are citizens outside government, their actions must be designed to influence other citizens outside government.

Finally, as far as the dialogue process is concerned, please remember that it is possible—even after a group has reached this point—to circle back to Stage Three to define further problems and to move with them through scenario-building to action. If a group chooses to widen its circle of action in this way, it will work at deeper levels with much greater efficiency.

This raises the question: When does a dialogue group disband? The only real answer is: when it decides to. Practical answers seem to range across a spectrum. At one end, a group could come together to develop approaches to some deeply rooted but fairly precisely defined problems that bother a community. Having worked out a broad plan of action and having launched it, participants might decide—much as a blue-ribbon commission appointed for a particular task—that its work had been completed. At the other end of the spectrum, a group might work so well together that it would, over time, become a "mind at work" at the center of a community's life. It would work on fundamental problems and then on others as they arise, spinning off ideas and miniscenarios for dealing with them as they come up. In some cases, a group might almost become an institution of sorts—a kind of ongoing "council of elders." There is no right answer—only the participants' answer.

BRIDGING REFLECTIONS

Sustained dialogue provides a space within which relationships can be changed. Participants come to terms with each other's identity—not only where they are from, but also why they see the world as they do. They learn why others value what they value and begin to recognize where there is interdependence of interests. They begin to change their patterns of interaction, first by changing the way they talk with each other, then by recognizing that they have common problems and finally by learning to work together. They come to treat each other as equals even though they may come from groups of unequal power and position. As they gain respect for each other, they show sensitivity for each other's feelings. They gradually give up many of their misperceptions of each other. All of this happens in a psychological space that they create for themselves. Relationships change as participants change the processes through which they interact. They learn this through experience. Moderators can articulate what is happening and encourage specific changes.

This has been a long explanatory chapter. We turn now to three examples of how sustained dialogue has played itself out in the lives of people. In Chapter Seven, I tell the story of the dialogue among Tajikistanis from different factions in a vicious civil war. This has been the most intense laboratory in which the five-stage process has been tested and steadily refined. After more than four years and twenty meetings of this public peace process, official negotiations between government and opposition produced a peace agreement in June 1997. Participants in the Inter-Tajik Dialogue have moved to a new phase in their work—the "postaccord" phase—in which the focus is on building a peaceful society. In Chapter Eight, we turn to the somewhat later work of a dialogue in Baton Rouge, Louisiana, between members of the African American and white communities. This account— presented mostly in the words of three participants—tells the story of sustained dialogue adding a deeper human dimension to the practical work on race relations already underway in the community. In Chapter Nine, two women who have engaged in Israeli-Palestinian dialogue for years provide an account of their experiences that dramatizes the complexity and richness of dialogue.

Chapter Seven

The Inter-Tajik Dialogue

DIALOGUE IN A DIVIDED SOCIETY: A TWO-TRACK STRATEGY

In March 1993, a small group of Tajikistanis from different regions, nationalities and political movements sat down together in Moscow for their first dialogue. They have continued to meet every two to four months to the time of this writing at the end of 1998. Their purposes have been to help end violence in Tajikistan and to design ways of building the kind of society they agreed from the start that they all wanted—a "united, secular, democratic and peaceful" Tajikistan.

The meetings have often been difficult. Initially, some participants feared meeting adversaries. The lives of some were threatened because of their opposition activities, and they lived in exile. When the group first sat together, members found it difficult to look at each other. Angry words have characterized many meetings. Gradually, group members have learned to work together on some of Tajikistan's fundamental problems. For those non-Tajikistanis present, it has been an awesome experience to sit with citizens who are conceiving and building a new country.

Over time, some of them created their own organizations to begin developing the capacity of citizens to take responsibility for their future. To support that effort, the managers of the Dialogue included a plan for education of Tajikistanis in the work of deliberative democracy and building civil society within the framework of the multilevel peace process.

This concern for ending violence and building peace leads to a strategy of two interrelated processes: first is the unofficial process of sustained dialogue; second is a civil-society strategy that aims at strengthening and/or building institutions of civil society that transcend the traditional divisions

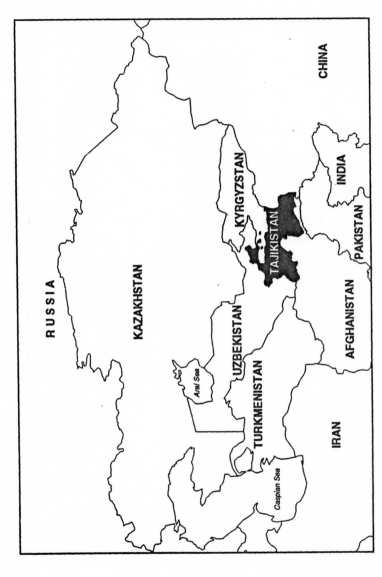

CENTRAL ASIA

RUSSIA

KAZAKHSTAN

KYRGYZSTAN

TAJIKISTAN

UZBEKISTAN

TURKMENISTAN

Aral Sea

Caspian Sea

IRAN

AFGHANISTAN

PAKISTAN

INDIA

CHINA

Adapted from the map base by Cartesia Software's Map Art.

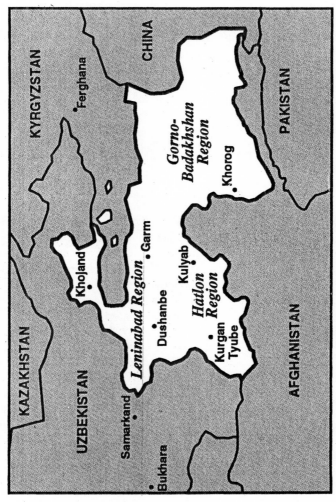

TAJIKISTAN

KAZAKHSTAN

KYRGYZSTAN

UZBEKISTAN

Ferghana

Khojand

Samarkand

Bukhara

Leninabad Region

Garm

Dushanbe

Kulyab

Hatlon Region

Kurgan Tyube

Gorno-Badakhshan Region

Khorog

CHINA

AFGHANISTAN

PAKISTAN

in the society and play a crucial role in reducing the mistrust that always exists in divided societies.

The Inter-Tajik Dialogue was formed under the auspices of the Dartmouth Conference Regional Conflicts Task Force.[1] With the end of both the Soviet Union and the Cold War, members of the task force decided to create a subgroup to use the process of sustained dialogue they had developed together to help bring peace to one of the conflicts that had broken out in states that had emerged from the former Soviet Union. After much thought, they chose Tajikistan—one of the poorest of the former Soviet republics—which had slipped into a violent internal power struggle within a year after declaring independence in 1991. The Dialogue has become the most intensive testing ground for developing and refining the two-part strategy. For that reason, it is the best current case for demonstrating how this strategy for managing conflict in divided societies works.[2]

BACKGROUND: THE CONFLICT IN TAJIKISTAN

In August 1991, Tajikistan, along with other former Soviet republics, declared its independence. The country was immediately consumed by a struggle for power and national identity. Eventually, out of a population of 5.5 million, 25,000 to 200,000 are estimated to have died; perhaps one in seven were displaced from their homes or fled to nearby Iran, Afghanistan, Pakistan, Russia and other countries of the Commonwealth of Independent States (CIS). A formal peace agreement was signed in June 1997. Its implementation was still in progress at the end of 1998.

When in the Dialogue's first meeting a co-moderator asked for the causes of the conflict, participants agreed, first, that Tajikistanis were unprepared politically and economically for independence. Second, although there is a deep sense of Tajik culture reaching back over a thousand years to Persian roots, participants agreed that there is little sense of Tajikistani identity among the citizens of the new state. The people of Tajikistan have long based their identity on their region.

Before the Union of Soviet Socialist Republics took constitutional form in 1923, the area now called Tajikistan did not exist as a separate entity. When the Soviet Union incorporated additional republics a year later, the Republic of Uzbekistan, mainly Turkic speaking, covered the entire area of today's Uzbekistan and Tajikistan, with an autonomous region for Tajikistan. The inhabitants spoke mainly a Persian-based language. In 1929, the independent Republic of Tajikistan was created while the Persian-speaking cities of Samarkand and Bukhara, the ancient seats of Tajik culture, were left within Uzbekistan. Part of the predominantly Uzbek Ferghana Valley was included in Tajikistan. Later, Soviet leader Joseph Stalin's nationalities and collectivization policies settled many Russians in the Central Asian republics, including Tajikistan. All of these events—in addition to the Soviet policy of forcing creation of a Soviet identity—helped discourage development of a Tajikistani nation and identity.[3]

During the Soviet era (1923–1991), political power in the government and in the Communist Party in Tajikistan was in the hands of the elite from Khojand (called Leninabad in Soviet times). This area was more industrialized and Russified. Starting in the 1970s, the party leadership began to include in the governing structure members from the southern area of Kulyab. At the time, significant elements of the intelligentsia came from the southern areas, particularly the Garm and Gorno-Badakhshan regions. The intelligentsia urged that power should be shared among the different regions, thus setting the stage for the formation of opposition movements.

Tajikistan began its independence with an old-style Communist parliament. Then new political parties and movements emerged, including the Democratic Party of Tajikistan and the Islamic Renaissance Party. During the November 1991 elections, the opposition parties united to present an opposition candidate, but he was defeated in rigged elections.

The new regime, heavily populated by former communists from the Khojand and Kulyab areas, passed a series of repressive measures to try to prevent the opposition movement from having any kind of role in the governing structure. In May 1992, violent clashes occurred between opposition and government forces. The former Soviet, now Russian military still present in the country was reportedly involved in distributing arms to the government forces.

In an attempt to prevent further escalation of the conflict, the president put together a coalition government involving the opposition parties. This drew sharp reaction from the right-wing elements in the government, mostly from Kulyab and Khojand, who declared the new government invalid because the parliament, which failed to reach a quorum, did not approve it.

Following violent clashes between the two parties, President Rahmon Nabiev was forced to resign at gunpoint in September 1992. The speaker of the Parliament, Akbarshu Iskandarov, assumed power. With support from the democratic and Islamic parties, a coalition government was formed. The governments of Uzbekistan and Russia, believing that their national interests were jeopardized by the anarchic situation in Tajikistan, decided with the governments of Kazakhstan and Kyrgyzstan to send CIS peacekeeping forces to Tajikistan.

In December 1992, the parliament removed Iskandarov as Kulyabi militias entered the capital city, Dushanbe. The parliament elected Emomali

Rakhmanov, the leader of the Kulyab region, to succeed him. To consolidate political power, pro-government forces—reportedly with support from some Russian and Uzbek guards—conducted a campaign of executions, looting and terror against anybody affiliated with the opposition parties. This resulted in mass displacement of refugees to Afghanistan. The opposition leadership fled to Moscow and Tehran, Iran. The government imposed a further ban on the opposition parties and the media. From 1993 through mid-1997, despite several cease-fire agreements, sporadic fighting continued within Tajikistan itself and on the border between Tajikistan and Afghanistan, often involving Russian border guards.[4]

THE SUSTAINED DIALOGUE

In this context, the Inter-Tajik Dialogue was launched. It is managed by a team of three Americans and three Russians,[5] who may well be the first joint Russian-U.S. citizens' peacemaking team. The Russian and American co-moderators alternate in chairing sessions of the three-day meetings. Before each meeting, the team sets a tentative agenda and frames questions to be raised, but the final agenda emerges from what is on participants' minds in their opening session. At the end of every meeting, both a narrative substantive report and an analytical memo are drafted by the management team. The latter was shared with interested official bodies such as the U.S. Department of State and the U.N. staff, especially with the U.N. mediator, until negotiations produced a peace—as they did in June 1997.[6]

Stage One: Deciding to Engage
A team from the Russian Center for Strategic Research and International Studies visited Tajikistan in early 1993 to talk with more than a hundred Tajikistanis, to select a dozen participants and to acquaint the government with the proposed Dialogue. They found serious doubt among some potential participants.

It was important to the Tajikistanis that the invitation came from "an international movement"—the Dartmouth Conference. They have taken pride in calling themselves in their documents "The Inter-Tajik Dialogue within the Framework of the Dartmouth Conference."

Stage Two: Mapping and Naming Problems and Relationships
Dialogues 1–3 (March, May, August 1993) saw the Tajikistani group mapping problems and relationships. The relationships cut across regional, ethnic and political boundaries. Ultimately, the group settled into two camps:

one closer to the political philosophy of the government; the other closer to the democratic opposition. (As the Dialogue progressed, what became most defining was the particular political philosophy of individuals rather than hard and fast commitment to the formal government or opposition camps.)

The co-moderators began the first meeting with two questions: What do participants see as the causes of the civil strife? What do they see as "ways out"? These questions were vehicles for putting important subjects and relationships onto the agenda while establishing the principles and habits of a civil dialogue among individuals coming out of different factions in a civil war. In the second meeting, the co-moderators asked two further, related questions: What are the interests of the group(s) with which you identify? What kind of Tajikistan would you like to see develop over the long term?

In a sustained dialogue, what happens between meetings is often as crucial as what happens in meetings. Between the second and third meetings, military activity on the Afghanistan-Tajikistan border increased, and the Russian Security Council decided to name the southern Tajikistani border the southern security border of Russia. The Russian government reinforced its troops there under the CIS umbrella. As violence within Tajikistan increased, the government appeared unable to guarantee its citizens' security.

The third meeting was the first in which the Dialogue met at a conference site where all members could meet, eat and relax together under the same roof. An important voice was also added to the group: a vice chairman of the Democratic Party.

The group still needed to crystallize from the "mapping" of a range of problems and relationships a few key problems to probe in depth. Part way through, when participants still seemed unable to focus the conversation, one participant said: "We really need to work on starting negotiations between the government and the opposition on creating conditions for return of the refugees to their homes. No progress on other problems can be made until this problem has been solved."[7]

Recognizing that turning point, a moderator asked each member to write two paragraphs: first, an invitation from the government to major political groups to join negotiations, written to make opposition elements feel safe in accepting and, second, a response by opposition elements stating their understanding that members' security would be guaranteed and providing some reassurance to the government that it would not be threatened.

Participants found it virtually impossible to produce usable statements. The group had identified an immediate focus for the Dialogue, but participants still lacked the capacity to talk and listen in ways that permitted them to work together on common problems. With a bitter civil war still fresh in their experience, they could not yet reach out to those who represented what they feared.

Stage Three: Probing Problems and Relationships to Choose a Direction

Dialogue 4 (October 1993) showed a marked change. The discussion focused on how to begin a negotiation; it was a genuine conversation about the pros and cons of different approaches.

What accounted for the change? As would happen repeatedly, the time between meetings played a significant role. By October, all of the participants shared concern that the country was further fragmenting and that the government was unable to stem that tide. One participant had been fired from his academic post for his opposition views, and another had been twice threatened. Neither felt able to go home after the Dialogue. Even those with opposing views saw individuals they had come to respect become victims. Now that the group members had come to know each other as human beings and had absorbed enough experience together, they seemed able to turn to problems without polemic. One other dramatic event quickened the larger atmosphere of political crisis and fear: a week before the meeting, Russian President Boris Yeltsin shelled the Russian parliament.

During Dialogue 4, the group moved into Stage Three. Participants turned to the practical problems involved in starting a negotiation and the relationships underlying those problems: How could opposition forces be brought to sit together given their geographic dispersion and their ideological spread from moderate democrats to militant Islamists? Who would come to the table? Where are they? Would men "with blood on their hands" come?

Once again, the period between meetings was critical. Elements of the opposition met in Tehran in December, signed a declaration stating a common platform and established a formal Coordinating Center for the democratic opposition forces in Moscow. Two members of the Dialogue were signatories of the Tehran document, and four became members of the new Coordinating Center's eight-person steering committee.

On the surface, this may seem a direct response to the points made in Dialogue 4 about the difficulty of knowing how to involve the geographically dispersed and ideologically diffuse opposition in a negotiation. In actuality, it is not possible to prove any direct cause-and-effect relationship between the Dialogue and the opposition's decision, beyond the involvement of two Dialogue participants in that decision.

In Dialogue 5 (January 1994), pro-government participants quizzed opposition members at length about the meaning of the new opposition positions. An opposition participant responded in a low-key, reassuring way that caused a pro-government participant to say: "I think the government will be able to accept these proposals as a starting point. There is now the necessary basis for negotiations. We will report these proposals to the government."

During the meeting, the co-moderators produced two working papers. Each put in writing what participants had said so they could reflect on the observations of the moderators and check their accuracy.

One paper recorded principles that the co-moderators thought had been agreed on by participants, who promised to communicate them—along with the full explanation of the opposition position—to both the government and the opposition Coordinating Center in Moscow. Those principles described concrete steps that participants recommended be taken to begin negotiation.

The second paper recorded the fears on each side that blocked the capacity to work together. Pro-government participants seemed more comfortable with the predictability of a centrally controlled political order. They feared opposition democratic and militant Islamic groups who had taken control of the government by forcing a president to resign at gunpoint. The opposition detested and feared what they saw as a threat to personal security and integrity emanating from the reimposition of elements of the totalitarian Soviet system.

Stage Four: Scenario-Building—Momentarily

Dialogue 6 (March 1994) moved the group squarely for a moment into Stage Four. Since Dialogue 5, an envoy of the U.N. secretary general had arranged for a first round of negotiations to take place in April. Two members of the Dialogue would be on the opposition negotiating team, and one would be on the government team. Again, it is difficult to know what the information and papers developed during Dialogue 5 contributed to the government decision to negotiate. However, the participant appointed to the government team had briefed officials on the Dialogue. He was a citizen outside government—a professor and vice chairman of the Uzbek Association, an organization of the largest national minority. Participants in the government decision to negotiate and U.N. officials credited the work of the Dialogue with having played a significant role.

To contribute to the negotiation, participants in Dialogue 6 talked through two principal sets of interconnected problems. The first was how to state the purpose of the negotiation in a way that showed sensitivity to the needs of both sides for a solution of shared problems. The idea of stating a purpose for negotiations in this way seemed new to the group. They were accustomed to pressing for the statement of purpose to be in their own terms and to cater to the aims of their side rather than being stated in such a way as to establish a practice and basis of compromise. The second problem was to order the work of the negotiating teams so as to facilitate the negotiating process rather than blocking it at the outset. Again, the group learned a lesson: arranging the agenda for negotiation is a critical act.

The substance around which this discussion of procedure revolved had emerged from discussion during preceding meetings. Two of the most important subjects were: creating conditions for return of refugees, which required controlling and disarming unlawful armed elements, and producing a constitution that could provide the basis for a unified, democratic, secular state in which all important groups would have access to power. For the opposition, this required reorganizing the government to include them—a step the government would see as designed to unseat them. The hard discussion began when participants argued the order in which the negotiating teams should address these problems.

Opposition forces believed the government incapable of implementing any agreement and argued that first the government needed to be reformed. Eventually, they saw that this confrontational approach could produce a stalemate and block the beginning of broader talks because the government would see raising this subject as an opposition effort to replace it. After lengthy discussion, participants came to see that focusing first on creating conditions for refugee return would be acceptable to both sides and that they could approach government reform more gradually in a way that would not seem so threatening. They proposed that the negotiating teams establish four broadly based commissions to coordinate the necessary work. The commissions could, in effect, be the first practical step toward reorganizing the government to handle complex issues.

When the group turned to the timetable for the negotiations and the political process ahead, pro-government participants reported a government plan to publish a draft constitution in April, hold a referendum on the constitution in June and elections in late summer. The opposition saw this as a government effort to ram a new constitution through a ratification process while 700,000 Tajikistanis were still displaced and conditions in the country were not stable enough to allow serious discussion of the constitution or the conduct of an election campaign. After discussion, all participants agreed on a timetable that would rely on a working group under the negotiating teams to organize public deliberation on the draft constitution before a constitutional referendum.

By agreeing to work within the present governmental framework and to urge a longer process for discussion of the new constitution, participants addressed fears that threatened negotiation: the government's fear that the opposition would use the organization of the negotiations to reduce its power and the opposition's need to overcome exclusion from the political process.

How was this first joint memorandum produced? As participants talked, the moderating team—following the method used during the 1978 Egyptian-Israeli summit at Camp David moderated by U.S. President Jimmy Carter—recorded what seemed to be areas of common approach. After writing two drafts, which were translated into Russian and Tajiki and commented on both orally and in writing by the participants—partly after discussion among themselves without the moderators' presence—the co-moderators produced the finished paper, "Memorandum on a Negotiating Process in Tajikistan." It outlined the elements of a political process for uniting Tajikistan to be generated by the negotiators through working commissions.[8]

The important experience for the overall Dialogue process was that all participants worked together as a single team to produce a memorandum, using the draft memorandum to focus their deliberation. The participants and moderators passed the memorandum to the governments of Tajikistan, the United States and Russia, as well as to the opposition Coordinating Center, the U.N. envoy and the offices of the Conference on Security and Cooperation in Europe in Vienna and Warsaw. Three of the drafters actually participated in the negotiation. Opposition members said it served as a guide for the opposition's approach. But exactly what influence it had on the approaches taken in the negotiations by the two teams cannot be determined because of the many different people and factors at play in a complex interaction.

The fact that the Dialogue group had passed into Stage Four and experienced working together to produce a product of which they were proud moved the group into a new way of thinking and working together. Even though participants later circled back regularly to earlier stages to tackle new subjects or could not agree fully, they had passed a milestone. Their way of dealing with each other had changed.

Readers will note that the co-moderators did not literally pose the questions outlined in the description of Stage Four in Chapter Six. But the Dialogue group did address obstacles to movement in the negotiation, ways of overcoming them by meeting the deepest fears on both sides, recognition of who should take those steps and a sequencing that made it possible for each side not to pay an exclusively high price.

Readers will also note that the memorandum dealt with organization of an official negotiation rather than suggesting steps to be taken in the civil society. The important point is that participants introduced working commissions under the negotiating teams to oversee important political processes. Those processes would create opportunities for Tajikistanis from different communities and political persuasions to work together and with government in ways that might provide foundations for new national cohesion. Without naming it, participants were actually beginning to create a framework for civil society.

Stage Five: Acting Together to Make Change Happen

This is an appropriate point to say a word about Stage Five. In the case of the Inter-Tajik Dialogue through the end of 1998, the Dialogue led to action as individual members took its ideas, what they learned and the substance of the joint memoranda into their places of work—government, opposition councils, the negotiating room, journal articles and citizens' discussions. Because of unsafe conditions in the body politic, acting openly as a group was not possible. As suggested at the end of this chapter, conditions that may be created by full implementation of the peace agreement may make it possible for participants to act as a group in the future. But during this early period, they had to rely on what they could do as individuals nourished by their interactions in the Dialogue.

Dialogue 7 (May 1994) began shortly after the first round of U.N.-mediated negotiations in April. To the co-moderators' question, "Can such a nonofficial Dialogue continue alongside official negotiations?" participants answered quickly and unanimously, saying, in effect: "Yes. The six meetings before negotiations began contributed to the possibility of negotiations. We want to help them succeed." While group members wanted to avoid any appearance of trying to "substitute" for the negotiations, they expressed the belief that they could think ahead of the negotiations by considering the organization of the social and political processes necessary for implementing any agreements negotiated. That would include parallel political processes for reducing tensions and moving toward reconciliation. This was certainly the work of citizens outside government—a step into civil society without naming it as such.

Between Stages Three and Four

From that time on, the Dialogue participants described their focus as developing a "process of national reconciliation" that would erode the deep mistrust between the two sides that blocked evolution of relationships necessary to build "a united, secular, democratic, peaceful Tajikistan." Participants began to talk not only about issues under negotiation, but also about the politics underlying the interaction among groups in the body politic and the pacing of steps in civil society to deal with those issues.

In terms of the five-stage process, this meeting demonstrated how even a well-formed group will need to circle back to an earlier stage when it faces new problems. With official negotiations under way that were partly consistent with its document, the group moved to a more difficult overarching problem: how to deal with the larger questions behind the negotiation in a way that would contribute to an overall political process of national reconciliation. To do this, participants had to move back to a deeper mapping and probing.

The practical problems in the official negotiation included the opposition's demand that its representatives be brought into the government to improve the government's competence. They insisted on a "package deal"—that is, they would negotiate agreements on all issues but not sign any of them until the issue of power sharing was resolved. A related question was the short timetable proposed by the government for adoption of the constitution and holding elections. The Dialogue group's "Memorandum on the Negotiation Process in Tajikistan" had raised the possibility of a step-by-step process.

As Dialogue participants stated, the issue that would slow the pace or even block progress in the negotiations—the deep mistrust and fear between the two sides—was not on the agenda. Finding practical ways of steadily removing this blockage, and using the negotiations themselves partly for that purpose, began to emerge as one focus of the Dialogue's future work. Designing a political process for national reconciliation became the centerpiece of the meetings after Dialogue 7.

Dialogue 8 (June 1994) took place in the United States, so there was more than the usual opportunity for the U.S. participants to share their constitutional and political experience. Here the group made its first public appearance. It sat in a four-hour dialogue before an invited audience at the United States Institute of Peace in Washington, D.C., on the subjects of designing a political system to represent the interests of people from all major regions, political movements and minorities and taking the next steps in a political process to create such a political system.

Since the earliest meetings, the moderating team had wondered whether the Tajikistanis could ever accept genuine power sharing. One participant had explained: "Each region tries to gain control of the government in order to protect the interests of that region."

After the public session, Dialogue 8 itself began outside Princeton, New Jersey, with discussion of options for development of a framework for action over the next nine months. These involved the timing of the constitutional referendum and elections as related to national reconciliation and peace-building. The method for producing a memorandum in this meeting differed from that used to produce the signed "Memorandum on the Negotiating Process in Tajikistan" agreed upon in Dialogue 6. Instead of producing drafts of a text for participants' revision, moderators asked each side to write a statement of its own needs in beginning a political process.

Much common ground was agreed upon. One of the more important moments was the declaration of a pro-government member that he wanted to see members of opposition groups participate freely in the political process, but he had to live with the fact that the government had particular legal requirements to be met before the ban on certain parties and newspapers could be lifted.

Once each group had produced a draft document, each said that it had to state needs that went beyond the common ground agreed upon. Ultimately, how to include those separate views in a final document became the ostensible issue over which the group refused to agree. Finally, the group decided that these papers should be called "Working Papers of the Dialogue," not agreed documents. On the eve of the second round of formal U.N.-sponsored negotiations, which was less than a week away, both sides were uncomfortable about how their colleagues would view their "talking with the enemy" at a critical moment and could not move again to Stage Four.

Between Dialogues 8 and 9 (September 1994) a unique between-meetings event took place. A member of the U.S. moderating team and five Tajikistani participants during Dialogue 4 had drafted a grant proposal to the United States Information Agency to bring 15 Tajikistanis to the University of Nebraska at Omaha for a five-week course in public administration and civil society to be taught in Tajiki. The grant was approved, and the 15 came to the United States in mid-July. Following two days at the Charles F. Kettering Foundation in Ohio for an introduction to the concept of civil society, they went to the University of Nebraska. Several participants in that course were brought into Dialogue 9. For all, it was a unique bonding opportunity.

Shortly before Dialogue 9, the warring parties in Tajikistan agreed to a cease-fire. The government had also set a September date—subsequently deferred until November—for a referendum on the new draft constitution and for elections.

Dialogue 9 was planned to take stock and to design steps for taking insights and processes developed within the group into the larger body politic in the form of a political process that could lead to national reconciliation.

The purposes were to deepen a sense of political process within the group and to begin generating wider processes of dialogue beyond the group.

Talking in Stage Four: Scenario-Building— Experiencing a Changing Relationship
After Dialogue 9, the U.S. moderator wrote in his analytical memo:

> The third day of this meeting was probably the best we have had to date. Participants struggled together with how to move beyond bargaining over who makes the first move in changing the relationship between government and opposition toward an interactive political scenario of mutually reinforcing steps. They seemed to grasp and to grapple with the wisdom of not waiting for the other side to back down but rather putting together a series of interactive steps that would permit them to move ahead simultaneously on issues of concern to each side, building confidence as they complete each step.

This work placed the group more systematically than ever in Stage Four. To begin a process of "scenario-building," the U.S. moderator asked each member, as "homework," to list obstacles to a political process that would require a compromise among groups to agree on the normalization of relationships and political activity.

Participants returned with elaborate lists, including abnormal conditions created by the large number of refugees; the large number of weapons in the hands of the population; denial of elementary rights to citizens; widespread lack of confidence in the government; a low level of political culture; dependence of the present leadership on illegal armed units; and the opposition's belief that the government would not share power with other regions.

They struggled with the impasse that would result if each side insisted that steps to satisfy its needs be taken before steps in response to the other side's needs. They began to consider integrating steps for both sides into an interactive, step-by-step sequence of reciprocal moves.

They discussed what each participant could do to take the insights of the Dialogue into her or his organizations and into the larger body politic. While the discussion produced creative thoughts, Tajikistan was about to move into a period of great uncertainty created by the constitutional referendum and presidential and parliamentary elections. Again, participants judged that circumstances prevented action.

One U.S. team member asked: "In your minds, are there only pictures of one group winning, another losing? Could you not win in elections by the construction of coalitions or compromises? Will losers feel their only option is armed opposition? Each of you has interests that you share with other groups."

Back to Stage Three: Probing Problems
and Relationships to Choose a Direction

Dialogue 10 (December 1994) took place at a difficult moment between the constitutional referendum and presidential election in November and the parliamentary elections scheduled for February. The conduct of elections did not meet international standards, and the question was whether and how opposition elements could participate in the upcoming parliamentary elections. On a more positive note, also between Dialogues 9 and 10, the third round of U.N.-sponsored negotiations in Islamabad, Pakistan, had consolidated and extended the cease-fire and had led to a symbolically important prisoner exchange. The Dialogue group stayed in Stage Three without trying to move on in an uncertain situation, engaging in a useful postelection assessment that revealed deep differences—first at the analytical level, then at a deeper human level.

Participants agreed that the ratification of a constitution that could be amended was an essential foundation for evolution of a constitutional process. But conditions under which the government conducted the elections in some regions produced the judgment that democratic conditions did not exist and raised fears that the government did not want, or was not able, to promote democracy.

At a deeper human level, those of a traditional mind believed—at least intellectually—that a written constitution actually creates the conditions it describes. Others said from experience that, although a constitution grants rights on paper, in the real world one's life can be threatened when one acts as if those rights actually exist. These fundamentally different mind-sets produced heated exchanges.

Following the first day's "mapping" of postelection problems, a moderator asked: By what formula could power be shared through compromise across regions, political movements and minority groups? What kind of political processes would create conditions for the development of democracy? Some participants wondered whether Tajikistan was ready for multiparty democracy or whether it needed a transitional period of more centralized rule and a broadening of citizen experience before such forms of democracy were even a good idea. Some noted that Tajikistanis' experience with nongovernmental organizations (NGOs) was only beginning.

Dialogue 11 (March 1995) took place after the parliamentary elections, which had produced a parliament and government narrowly constructed from a power base in one region, the Kulyab. Participants from the opposition considered whether to accept the results of the elections or to fight them. After lengthy deliberation, they determined to consider the elections the starting point of a transitional period during which the situation could be gradually changed over time. Naming the period "transitional" permitted opposition members to work in the new situation rather than to fight it.

Participants continued to work in Stage Three, probing the dynamics—practical, political and psychological—of the new situation and laying out—but not agreeing on—the major components of a process of national reconciliation. They remained unable to determine whether both sides had the will to go down this path.

Back to Stage Four: Scenario-Building—Experiencing a Changing Relationship

Participants came to Dialogue 12 (June 1995) after another round in the official U.N.-mediated negotiations had failed to produce an agreement on a mechanism to oversee national reconciliation. The two extreme options in contention reflected an opposition desire to create a supragovernmental council of national reconciliation, on the one hand, and a more traditional proposal to create a consultative council of citizens to meet with the president and members of parliament in an advisory capacity, on the other. The government saw the opposition's proposal of a supragovernmental council as designed to supplant the government. The opposition saw the consultative council as powerless and therefore useless.

Toward the end of Dialogue 11 in March, the moderators of the Dialogue had distilled from the conversation about such a mechanism notes on the choices the participants suggested. The day before Dialogue 12 began, they distributed those notes with a request that participants study the options before the meeting.

Eventually, one participant came to the third option in those notes: creating a Coordinating Council for National Reconciliation *under* the negotiating teams to oversee implementation of the decisions from the official negotiations through four working groups. These groups would have the authority to marshal resources of both the government and nongovernmental organizations. In some ways, this option had roots in the "Memorandum on the Negotiating Process in Tajikistan," produced in Dialogue 6. This third option became the basis of the joint memorandum produced during Dialogue 12. In addition, that memorandum proposed creation of a Consultative Forum of the Peoples of Tajikistan as a space where a group of highly respected citizens—"elders"—could gather unofficially to talk about the kind of Tajikistan they wanted to see evolve. Dialogue participants hoped that such a group might stimulate discussion among citizens.

Participants had come to Dialogue 12 with a strong sense that it was time for them again to contribute to the negotiating process by helping design the transitional postelection period. They produced a "Memorandum of the Tajikistan Dialogue Within the Framework of the Dartmouth Conference on National Reconciliation in Tajikistan." This document, as usual, was reported to the government, the opposition and the United Nations. In July, Tajikistan President Rakhmanov and opposition leader Said Abdullo Nuri, meeting in Tehran, Iran, instructed the official negotiating teams to establish a Consultative Forum of the Peoples of Tajikistan. Their agreement was written in the hand of one of the Dialogue participants and signed by them. In August, the U.N. emissary incorporated that agreement in a protocol signed by the two leaders that laid out the full agenda for continuing official negotiations.

At that moment, they could not agree on the Dialogue's idea of a Coordinating Council, but the proposal remained alive. It became one inspiration for the Commission on National Reconciliation established by the June 1997 peace agreement with four subcommissions to oversee the implementation of that agreement.

At Dialogue 13 (September 1995), participants wrote a memorandum detailing how a Consultative Forum might be composed and organized, how it would accomplish its work and how it would interact with the government. It urged the negotiators to establish an organizing group to take the first formal steps in setting up the forum. In two subsequent meetings—14 (December 1995) and 15 (February 1996)—the Dialogue group refined its proposals and urged early formation of the forum. Through the first half of 1996, official negotiations were stalled, partly because of a shift of U.N. emissaries.

Dialogue 16 (May 1996) was the first to be held in Tajikistan. Meeting there required the president's approval. Numerous influential Tajikistanis expressed hope that our meeting would herald holding the official negotiations in the country as well. Participants were ready to be recognized publicly for what they were doing.

This meeting produced one of the Dialogue's most somber memoranda. It stated that the official negotiations were stalled because both negotiating teams were engaged in a struggle for power; that recent regional uprisings reflected citizens' feelings of exclusion from the political process by the narrow composition of the government; and that both government and opposition leadership had lost public confidence. It urged both sides to broaden their negotiating teams.

In October 1996, one participant, who was now a member of a joint (government and opposition) commission to oversee cease-fire agreements, came to Dialogue 17 with a description of how the commission had worked with field commanders in negotiating a regional cease-fire in a critical area. After hearing this account, another participant reflected: "The reason cease-fires have broken down is that they have been negotiated at the highest political level without reference to local citizens with the guns and the interests at stake. What we need is a multilevel peace process that connects the local and the official levels." The Dialogue participants composed a joint memorandum that stated: "It is necessary to broaden public participation in the efforts to achieve peace by developing a multilevel peace process in order to assure the widest popular involvement in achieving and implementing a nationwide peace agreement."

The group recommended in their joint memorandum that the official negotiating teams "further develop their practice of working on several levels simultaneously. Specifically: (1) They will use working groups of experts and advisors to involve field commanders in making recommendations on military and security issues. (2) They will also use such an expert group to involve local officials and administrators. . . ."

Dialogue participants again pressed for immediate establishment of the Consultative Forum of the Peoples of Tajikistan. They now saw the forum as a potential public space in which citizens outside government could contribute vision to the peace process. In their memorandum, they wrote:

> Participants believe that one of the main obstacles to peace is lack of a common vision about what kind of country the Tajikistani people want. . . . A central element in that vision must be an understanding on sharing power among the representatives of the regions, political parties, social movements and national communities in Tajikistan.
>
> These questions must be the first agenda of the Consultative Forum. A common vision shared by the citizens of the country is the necessary foundation for a negotiated peace agreement.

The group urged that the negotiating teams "invite suggestions from the Consultative Forum to broaden the involvement of citizens in the peace process." It recommended that the negotiations create a Committee on National Reconciliation "to oversee implementation of a peace agreement" and that the committee work through existing joint commissions and other boundary-spanning groups.

Finally, participants "encourage[d] the citizens of Tajikistan to strengthen and develop the growing network of citizens' associations and nongovernmental organizations." Noting with concern efforts by the government to restrict such associations by law, they continued:

> Dialogue participants also appeal to the government and the Majlis-i-Oli [parliament] to cooperate with citizens in writing and passing a series of laws that will constitute a legal framework that will enable these organizations to grow and to work effectively in building the civil society of Tajikistan.
>
> Recent developments have demonstrated the importance of agreements and achievements at the local level. Only associations of citizens outside government working within the constitutional framework can enlarge the capacity of citizens to play their necessary role in building new Tajik society.

From December 1996 through June 27, 1997, the official negotiations produced a series of agreements, culminating in the capstone peace agreement. The key elements in the agreement were creation of a Commission on National Reconciliation to implement the peace accords in a transitional period through four subcommissions, and an understanding that the government and the opposition would share power in this commission and in the government according to agreed formulae. The Dialogue can claim no specific credit for that arrangement, except to note that such a commission, the four working subcommissions and a transitional period had been major elements in its joint memoranda on repeated occasions.

The important point is that the "postaccord phase" had begun, and, with it, the Dialogue's focus gradually broadened to give increasing attention to building the civil society where democracy would grow, if at all. In Dialogue 19 (May 1997) participants refined their objective once again. In effect, they described it as "identifying the obstacles to democracy and ways of overcoming them." They had laid a foundation in their thinking for this work.

The Civil-Society Strategy and the Dialogue

Participants in the first four meetings of the postaccord phase (Dialogues 20–23 in October 1997 and February, June and November 1998) followed closely the work of the National Reconciliation Commission. Four Dialogue participants were commission members, so the interaction between the Dialogue and this quasi-official body intensified. At the same time, participants understood that—important as the work of the commission was in creating the constitutional, legal and practical conditions for democratic development—the development of a civic infrastructure was equally important.

This second track of strategy—development of civil society—involves working with citizens outside government, building on existing traditions of public talk and deliberation to broaden the public's participation in the body politic. The aim of this strategy is to establish or strengthen the "boundary-spanning organizations" that are essential as sinews of a cohesive country. These organizations involve individuals from competing groups in working together across the natural divisions in the society to achieve goals that would serve the interests of all.

Central to this strategy are the concepts of public space and civil society. Action designed in such space transcends region, nationality and party. Joining separate groups in common discourse links community interests to the larger public interest. A tradition of talk in public space exists in Tajikistan, as in most cultures. In most villages, an informal group of revered individuals or elders comes together in council to resolve disputes or to make decisions on pooling village resources for community purposes and dividing tasks among the different families in the village.

In Dialogue 23 (November 1998), participants paused to take stock of their achievements and to begin thinking of the Dialogue's role as the postaccord phase evolved. As a framework for their thinking, I suggested that they think of the activities that have grown out of the Dialogue in six areas.

The Dialogue Process

The Inter-Tajik Dialogue itself has become what I call "a mind at work in the middle of a country making itself." In Dialogue 23, participants began thinking about institutionalizing the Dialogue group to continue in that role, nourishing the framework of the multi-level peace process as a context for all groups working in the civil society.

Since 1995, Dialogue members have expressed the hope that dialogue groups could proliferate and become common throughout Tajikistan. In late 1996, the Tajikistan Center for Civic Education, founded in 1994 by a Dialogue member, began a series of "dialogue seminars" for discussion of the critical subject of regionalism. In 1998, the Center began planning such meetings in other regions to start building a network. If the Consultative Forum of the Peoples of Tajikistan is ever established, it could provide another space—in addition to the Inter-Tajik Dialogue—where highly respected citizens could come together to reflect on issues facing the country.

Nourishing the Official Peace Process

Since the official negotiations began in April 1994, Dialogue participants have played a role first in those negotiations and then in the National Reconciliation Commission. When the next government is formed, some of them will probably serve in official posts there.

They will have experienced in the Dialogue a unique opportunity to reflect on the budding political processes of their country—both the institutional processes and the nonofficial processes through which citizens outside government do their work. Their insight into the interaction between the official and the nonofficial spheres could help reduce the gap so common today between government and public.

Nongovernmental Organizations

Two Dialogue participants have already started their own nongovernmental organizations. Since the beginning of the Inter-Tajik Dialogue, the Russian-U.S. management team has built into the funding for the program a capacity to train individuals for work in such organizations.

One member of the Dialogue has chartered an operating-and-research foundation to probe Tajik culture for ideas that would undergird a Tajik style of democracy. Among its activities, it organized a series of seminars at Tajikistan State University on the rule of law, hoping to put on the public agenda issues of human rights and the rights and responsibilities of citizens in a democratic society. The Foundation has started the Independent University. It gives heavy emphasis to teaching in the field of management.

In support of the Tajikistan Center for Civic Education, the Kettering Foundation invited two young associates of the center to the foundation as international fellows to study the philosophy and methods of strengthening civil society. Kettering has also included others in its workshops.

The U.S. members of the team have worked with NGOs in the United States that sponsor projects in Tajikistan to urge them to build a civil-society-development component into their projects. For instance, projects for helping restore water and irrigation systems or rebuild homes destroyed during the fighting bring the staffs of these organizations into close working relationships with local authorities, who must make decisions with their communities. Representatives of some of these organizations with offices in Washington, D.C., drafted an unpublished working paper, "Framework for an NGO Strategy towards Tajikistan."

Conflict Resolution Education

In 1995, the university-based participants in the Dialogue asked the U.S. team to help them develop courses in conflict resolution. For a year, two U.S. team members met with them after each meeting of the Dialogue to review the range of subjects that might be covered. After two meetings in Tajikistan with a larger group of administrators and professors, the management team held a five-day workshop in St. Petersburg, Russia, built around a collection of readings assembled under the title, "Conflict Resolution and Building Civil Society," and translated into Russian.

In the academic year 1997–1998, courses and modules of courses were offered. A textbook was being written. A small book on the five-stage process of sustained dialogue was translated into Tajiki by the Tajikistan Center for Civic Education.[9] To provide the civil-society dimension, the Tajikistan Center for Civic Education translated into Tajiki Kettering President David Mathews's *Politics for People*.[10]

University Collaboration

As a direct outgrowth of the relationships developed around the Dialogue, the University of Nebraska at Omaha (UNO) established cooperative programs with the new Technological University of Tajikistan. They have hosted two Tajikistani groups of 15 participants each for courses of three to five weeks taught in Tajiki on public administration, civil society and conflict resolution. As of the end of 1998, UNO had sent some 30 professors to Tajikistan and had received a like number of faculty and students in Omaha.

Civil Society and Economic Development

At the end of 1998, a new arena for work was coming into focus. The Kettering Foundation was preparing to bring to bear unfolding research on the connection between civil society development and economic growth. As the Tajikistanis tried to launch their version of a market economy, it was important for them to understand the ways in which the constructive interactions of citizens in the civil society can increase the effectiveness of economic interactions.

The point of describing the scope of the Dialogue's impact in this way was to help participants see their function as a unique group capable of keeping in view the key elements of the multilevel peace process. As they talked about their future, they began to see the possibility of transforming themselves into an NGO with the function of supporting and connecting activities in these areas of work. If this happened, they would demonstrate the capacity of a group established in sustained dialogue to put what they have learned in the Dialogue to work for the transformation and growth of the country. They will not run programs; they will help those who do connect in complementary ways. They will plant themselves permanently in Stage Five: Acting Together to Make Change Happen, while demonstrating sustained dialogue as a way of life at the heart of a new country.

Chapter Eight

~~~~~

Baton Rouge: Dialogue on Race Relations

with William Jefferson Day,
Jan Bernard and Fred Jeff Smith

*A*uthor's Note: The first application of sustained dialogue—as presented in this book—to race relations in the United States began in 1995 in Baton Rouge, Louisiana. Agreeing to meet "for five hours the third Saturday of each month," participants have held 29 meetings as of this writing at the end of 1998.

Unlike the Inter-Tajik Dialogue described in Chapter Seven, which provided the only contact between the government and the opposition for more than a year, the soil was well tilled in Baton Rouge before the sustained dialogue began. The intensive prior work on race relations produced its own further insights into the dialogue process.

In mid-1989, the mayor-president of East Baton Rouge Parish, Tom Ed McHugh, then in his first term, had launched a series of town meetings on important subjects such as air pollution, the well-being of children, workforce development and crime. In late 1992, a few courageous citizens who constituted the core of the Town Meeting Committee decided that the subject of race relations in Baton Rouge should be tackled in the next town meeting.

This core group of citizens continued from one town meeting to the next as the preparatory committee. For each meeting, they added to the core a few members who could make special contributions to planning a meeting on the particular subject selected. In retrospect, in their lengthy, agonized deliberations they seemed to have worked through a progression of experience comparable to that of the sustained dialogue, once again suggesting that the five stages discussed in Chapter Six reflect a natural process for tackling a problem. The account that follows is organized to examine that point, even though participants at that time were not familiar with the five-stage process.

The town meeting on race relations, which was finally held in April 1994, led to the formation of a complex of civic committees under the umbrella of a movement called Going the Second Mile, which was designed to channel the energies generated in the town meeting into community-led action. With that experience ongoing, a decision was made to try to deepen interracial relationships through sustained dialogue.

The story of the six years from 1992 to 1998 is told here by three of the leading participants. Jan Bernard, executive assistant to the mayor-president, was convener of the Town Meeting Committee. Her background in broadcast journalism, coupled with a fervent belief in the capacity of citizens to change their community, pushed the project forward. Rev. Jeff Day, executive director of the Greater Baton Rouge Federation of Churches and Synagogues, participated in the process throughout, as well as in a black-white clergy dialogue within the federation that began in March 1992. He became co-organizer and co-moderator of the sustained dialogue. Rev. Fred Jeff Smith, pastor of the Greater Mount Carmel Baptist Church and also a member of the black-white clergy dialogue, is the other co-organizer and co-moderator of the sustained dialogue. The local YWCA, with its strong track record of racial awareness and programming, served as event coordinator for the town meeting.

The story that follows is told mainly in their own words, with some analytical sharpeners and sinews added by me to probe this progressive-dialogue experience for its lessons in our study of sustained dialogue. I have done so even to the point of analyzing their experience under the headings of the five-stage process, which the early participants had not heard of at that time. My purpose has been to test the thought that people engage in sustained dialogue—perhaps not so systematically as described in this book—as a natural way of tackling tough problems and that the five stages are simply a conceptualization of that experience.

THE TOWN MEETING

By the early 1990s, the issues of race, racial tension and racial nonunderstanding as well as blatant acts of institutionalized racism had surfaced as undercurrents eroding the civic health and concerns of this Southern community.

Political campaigns with particularly virulent racial overtones and the April 1992 riots in Los Angeles, California, in the aftermath of the Rodney King case, as well as an escalating murder rate in the city, heightened concern.

Four previous town meetings had generated widespread public interest among citizens in coming together to talk about public issues of immediate concern. But volunteers making up the core of the Baton Rouge Town Meeting Committee had previously chosen to dwell only fleetingly on race relations and its impact in the city as a whole. Some recognized a need in the community for shared courage and commitment to engage citizens in serious dialogue on race—an issue that pervades cities across the country and yet seemed too overwhelming, perhaps too personally painful, to tackle in Louisiana's capital city—that is, until September 1992.

Stage One: Deciding to Engage

That was when the core group, convened by Jan Bernard under the auspices of the Mayor's Office, started a process that some say changed their lives forever. It was a process of direct, honest, engaging dialogue on racism that released pent-up emotions, rearranged and, for a few participants, blew up personal barriers between them to create a renewed vision rooted in the word "community."

The core members of the Town Meeting Committee bore three factors in mind in adding to their group individuals who could be of special help in preparing a town meeting on race relations: Nominees had to possess either the courage or the tenacity to discuss race or to have shown previously some skill as community mediators. Imperative in the final selection was that the group be composed of a geographic and professional cross-section of citizens and be evenly balanced racially. The full Town Meeting Committee ultimately included individuals ranging from real estate agents to grass-roots activists, from charity workers to police officers.

This team of people intuitively "walked a walk" together that, years later, the author of this book saw as a process closely paralleling sustained dialogues in the Arab-Israeli peace process, in the Inter-Tajik Dialogue and in other important applications of sustained dialogue abroad. In the early 1990s, however, members of the Town Meeting Committee were simply inventing their own way of learning to talk about a painful, deep-rooted historical and human conflict.

Never in Baton Rouge had a formal, publicly hosted town meeting on this subject been held. Race is a topic most often discussed in office whispers, from academic lecterns or in single-race assemblies. Would the public in Baton Rouge come together around this subject? Would even a preparatory committee of unpaid volunteers stick together long enough to bring about a town meeting to explore this issue even for two hours in one night? Could a community come together in a safe setting, discuss race and go home with the peace of the town assured?

Stage Two: Mapping and Naming Problems and Relationships

The full Town Meeting Committee sat down together for the first time in January 1993. Their 15-month journey in exploration of the undefined "race issue" was to become a multilayered, often heated, discussion. It was marked by entangled past and present personal and civic experiences of volunteers succumbing to a heartfelt confession of "not truly knowing" one another. The date for the town meeting was changed three times, with the event finally taking place in April 1994. Ultimately, participants' interactions ignited a deeply rooted desire to build fuller community relationships across racial lines.

During January and February 1993, Jan Bernard, as convener, asked participants to begin the process by sharing what they thought the potential value of a town meeting on race would be and then to identify their greatest fear or barrier to progress on the race issue. All were asked to listen carefully as each spoke and to honor the confidentiality of members' comments. The convener asked that no individual cut off another.

This exploration of possibility and fear seemed to stun some members, who, for the first time in years of working together, heard their fellow volunteers talk in a human way about their hidden anxieties concerning racial understanding. Personal fears ranged from the individual to the collective—from possible employment retribution for speaking honestly about one's personal race experience to unearthing in a public assembly in Baton Rouge the silent rage of a multitude of victims of racism. The participants identified an array of possible goals described partly in spiritual terms: a desire for unity, for one people under God, for love between those who did not know each other and for more equity in the policies and actions of local institutions.

Even in the first meeting, participants seemed committed to moving forward. This exploratory experience of each individual doing a reality check of fears and possibilities unveiled a shared list of perspectives on the value of publicly discussing racism. For the first time, on a rickety flip chart, these citizens exposed their concerns about race. Ultimately, they agreed, the list of benefits to the whole community outweighed the risks taken by the citizens in approaching such a project. Participants appeared joyful at exposing their dreams of the pending town meeting.

When they had finished listing their fears and possible goals in April 1993, committee members were offered the opportunity to leave the group if they were uncomfortable with delving more deeply into the racial issue. No one did.

As the committee decided to go ahead with planning, the central challenge that emerged, through soul-wrenching discussion, was the need to come to some understanding on the definition of "racism." For much of 1993, Town Meeting Committee members, in effect, began a dialogue of their own, which gradually brought to the surface the underlying elements of racism as they experienced it. Meeting every two or three weeks in the spring and fall, with intermittent meetings in the summer, members felt exhausted by the end of the nearly two-hour sessions.

Inevitably, they moved through a series of advances and setbacks. Tears, anger and healing occurred as participants shared personal stories about their experience with racism. As they talked, committee members learned from telling and listening to these personal stories that they lacked a common language about "race." What was *said* was not necessarily what was *heard* by fellow committee members. They needed time simply to explore the full dimensions of the subject, which they had never really talked about in depth. They had to learn to talk about and to understand the real nature of the relationships involved.

Tensions within the group were both direct and indirect. As personal stories were told and challenged by fellow committee members, several participants expressed resentment about the openness or lack of control of the convener to "let such things be said" without constraint at the table. White males seemed the least threatened by the candid dialogue. Intense emotion triggered discomfort among some of the women of both races. African American males were the first to open up and "reveal" themselves. In the course of the 15 months of town-meeting preparation, perhaps three-quarters of the participants broke through to probe the core of their personal racial concerns. Stories ranged from employment discrimination and criminal behavior to institutionalized racial practices, with examples given on the deterioration of inner-city schools, police threats on stopped motorists and the practices of local money-lending institutions.

Repeatedly, progress gained in one session of the committee appeared to be lost in the next. Even though a few of the founders threatened to leave the table, none walked away permanently. Often, after discussion in one session stalled, at the next meeting stories went deeper in understanding. As the subject of racism was peeled gradually "layer by layer like an onion," participants began to permit disagreement, even hostility, among themselves to be expressed in dialogue.

Discussion fostered new understanding and more common language on what the word "racism" means to different people, but participants were not ready to settle on a single definition. Members decided the problem of racism was deep seated and discovered that personal experiences must be "burned off" and trust built up front in any discussion. They agreed that individuals, including members of the public at large, must first be given a safe space to discover their personal relationship to the issue of race before formal discussion could begin.

Perhaps one of the biggest breakthroughs on the issue came in an agreement to disagree on the formal definition of racism. Committee members agreed that the general public would come into the town meeting, just as *they* had come into the committee meetings, with diverse personal understandings of racism. They reached common ground in agreeing to use only a "talking definition" of racism the night of the town meeting because there was no start-up language mutually understood by different races in Baton Rouge upon which to base talk about race.

Beyond the recognition that each person's definition of racism lies deeply rooted in her or his experience, members also came to see one of the public's roles in dealing with race relations as looking at the personal manifestations of racial prejudice as they affected the welfare of the community: the institutionalization of racism. These, too, could be identified in the various experiences of committee members.

With few exceptions, committee members persevered throughout what several called a "season of reconciliation." Even when members related their fears in painful stories that sometimes included accusations accompanied by tears, the group was able to handle the high voltage. Because it was a relatively large committee, not all members spoke their thoughts; a few strong personalities could be counted on to sound their opinions on the subject at hand. Surprisingly, this most dangerous, deeply felt, heretofore taboo subject became an accepted subject among members, who, in many cases, had hardly known each other.

The group held its meetings in the mayor-president's conference room, next door to the Mayor's Office, a unique setting to discuss race relations. Past town-meeting topics were matters of public-policy concern to citizens, but they proved to be mild compared to this one. Yet, the integrity of the group was uncompromised. The deep feelings, remembrances of past family or racial suffering and the passionately held feeling that things were not right among blacks and whites drove the group to continue. Time, the memory of the recent political campaigns of David Duke with their heavy racial content,[1] the quandary of what to do about public schools, especially the contentious issue of busing—and how these issues would be racially exploited with another political run of demagoguery—spelled in capital letters: KEEP AT IT!

In this stage of mapping and naming problems and relationships, the talk in a dialogue group does not progress neatly. It is characterized by continued attempts to hear each other. Just learning to talk "race" and to contain the emotional and personality differences alone made steering the group toward defining the subject and setting a date for the town meeting an enormous challenge. Participants also had to decide what to tell peers at work and in other settings about the group's deliberations while preserving the confidentiality of the group's discussions. What are you all doing? Are you sure that Baton Rouge is ready for this? And, of course, What's going to come of it? Finding ways of dealing with such questions became shared work in the group.

Considering the five stages of sustained dialogue, as some participants later came to know them, it appears that this stage began to close in the early summer as committee members decided that they had the appropriate group to discuss the issue, that they would eventually agree on a town-meeting format and that they would succeed in bringing the political and business powers with them.

To this day, several committee members are in disagreement about many issues, but at a certain point they felt themselves on common-enough ground—built from their dialogue on the nature of the subject and on the need to push ahead with concrete plans for the town meeting—to proceed. Personal values had surfaced that drove the project to completion.

Against the background of their "mapping" conversations, committee members had come to identify the tasks necessary to move the project forward—what they really needed to work on. Those tasks were:

- developing a consensus on the talking definition of racism that would be used to start the town-meeting discussion around tables of 10–12 citizens each;
- formulating precise questions to focus discussion at the town-meeting tables—questions that would reflect the committee's own process of dialogue;

- taking steps for communicating to key community leaders that this town meeting *would* soon happen—an advance notice of the public assembly.

In the long process of identifying these tasks, committee members had learned to talk with each other in a way that permitted them now to begin focusing their work against the background of the changing relationships among them. As participants drifted in and out of deeper discussions on race, including frequent references to day-to-day occurrences in the community, the convener reminded the group of the need to get at "the town-talk questions." In previous Baton Rouge town meetings, the use of preformulated questions had proved to offer freedom for multifaceted discussion and equal treatment of participants—two vital ingredients for the topic of race. Upon agreeing to move forward on a working definition of racism, the group made a collective decision to craft questions to give the general public an opportunity to experience the process the Town Meeting Committee members themselves had worked through. There would be no attempt to draw the public to a consensus on what racism is and what to do about it—only an attempt to start the journey realistically.

Stage Three: Probing Problems and Relationships to Choose a Direction

Committee members gradually found themselves in deeper dialogue on these focused questions, knowing that they had to reach some closure on each if the town meeting was ever to happen. This focus itself led to deeper probing.

After one particularly painful discussion of racism in May or June 1993, the convener sent the entire committee a paper reflecting on the impact of human moods and emotions in leadership.[2] She added a personal observation on the intensity of guilt, shame, blame and anger that had paralyzed the committee's discussion. At the next meeting, the air cleared, and a renewed sense of personal commitment emerged. Participants once again made a noticeable effort to listen carefully to each other. The moods and emotions had shifted, and relationships among members had become strong enough so that tasks could be tackled and the consensus for holding the town meeting could be sustained. The dissemination of that paper seems to have helped precipitate the group's getting down to concrete tasks.

At this stage of the process, in particular, the words "trust" and "faith" were used frequently by all members of the working group. The word "trust" was used to remind colleagues of the need to protect disclosures and advance honesty among members. The word "faith" came to assure that progress was happening, even though the slow pace of concrete steps was frustrating. One member kept the whole team focused by constantly reminding members that the process of talking and learning from each other was as valuable as the product—the town meeting itself.

Stage Three of their work, as it might be called in retrospect, also brought a noticeable increase in private contacts with the convener. Members often shared personal concerns with the convener away from the meetings, discussing attitudes, distrust, accusations and, on occasion, actual love and deep, heartfelt respect for fellow members.

Great disparity in how individuals measured the value of the slow work on specific tasks persisted. Some knew progress was being made. Others asked: "Why take so much time here?" One participant kept bringing the group back to the point, refusing to tolerate repetition of the same story over and over and gently leading the dialogue back to the vision of the town meeting. The town-meeting date was changed no less than three times via full committee decisions, and the planning process was, in late September 1993, in its eighth month.

The group finished its first hard task when members agreed in early fall 1993 that the following words on racism would be used as a "talking definition" to introduce the subject the night of the town meeting: "Racism is the intentional or unintentional use of power to isolate, separate, and exploit others based on a belief in superior racial origin, identity, or supposed racial characteristics. Racism is more than just a personal attitude; it is the systematic or institutional form of that attitude."

Consensus on framing discussion questions for the tables came more easily as they were drafted and tested—first, against the committee's own internal experience of talking about racism; and, second, in four formal test groups in dispersed geographic locations in the community. These questions crystallized as relationships within the committee became solid: What does racism mean to you? What problems has racism caused for Baton Rouge? What do *we* want to see happen? What can *you* do?

Members clearly understood the value of persons telling their own stories and their own understanding of race. As with any of their previous town-meeting topics, they also knew the value of the community defining its own problems in its own terms.

The first and second questions would do just that. The crime town meeting in 1992 had taught them the value of allowing healthy community-based tension to be expressed in a managed fashion. Their own dialogue convinced them that the same was true on the topic of race and racism.

Lastly, the final two discussion questions opened the vision of possibility and the value of exploring racism in community terms so others could listen and join together in action to eliminate it. The committee members had designed the town-meeting questions patterned directly on their own work, which they had launched with an exploration of their fears and hopes for what talking about race could mean in terms of healing among persons and building as a community.

Having resolved the problems they could resolve within the group, committee members faced the decisive question of how to put their plans before key members of the community. They could just as well have judged that the community was not ready and retreated within themselves around further questions. But their experience together had generated the will to move ahead.

Stage Four: Scenario-Building—Experiencing a Changing Relationship

Ready now to take their first steps into the public realm, members had to consider the obstacles to a successful town meeting and how to remove them to the fullest extent possible. Identifying obstacles actually built a keener understanding and deepened solidarity among members.

By late fall 1993, the group had developed two lines of action to build the strongest possible public support for the town meeting. One course was to try to win the support of leaders in the community for holding the meeting; the other was to hold pilot meetings in widely dispersed geographic areas.

Because of the sensitivity of the subject, members believed that nontraditional community leaders—not just the people with titles and positions—needed to be told of the town meeting. In one particularly important meeting, the convener asked black members to list *all* people of influence to whom they would listen, while white members kept silent. Then she asked the white members to do the same, while black members listened. Members of each group said they had "never heard of" some people listed by the other. Some members openly declared a lack of trust for leaders on the other group's list. At the end of this process, the group had listed some 50 names. After discussing the list with remarkable candor and insight, members identified only 2 of the 50 persons on that list, one black and one white, as individuals to whom people of all races in Baton Rouge would listen without reservation or with whom they would join wholeheartedly to advance the community. Members had identified the true multiracial leaders in Baton Rouge in what was probably the most honest discussion of community leadership ever held in City Hall by a diverse group with "the gloves off." The group then developed a plan for briefing the 50 whom they had identified and the media through a presentation at a community leadership breakfast to be held later in the winter.

The committee also designed the pilot meetings that it planned to conduct with several groups around the city-parish to test the distillate of its conversations as embodied in its "talking definition" of racism and the related questions to be used at the town meeting.

As preparations became more precise, a formal vote within the committee in early 1994 produced a title for the town meeting: "WHAT COLOR IS COMMUNITY? Baton Rouge Talks About Race Relations." The title was intended to suggest that talking about racism is one way of building community.

One other preparatory task had begun to take shape in midsummer of 1993. "What are we going to do after the town meeting? What's going to happen then?" Rev. Jeff Day asked the question and was delegated, along with another member, to come back with a proposal. Holding a meeting of this magnitude with no way to channel its energies out into the community seemed to be the waste of enormous labors in preparation, as well as a sacrifice of a priceless opportunity to carry the conversation further. By late fall, committee members agreed that Going the Second Mile would continue the work begun in the town meeting. How it would be carried out would be decided after the town meeting.

Stage Five: Acting Together to Make Change Happen

As these gradual moves into the public domain began, committee members pledged to get people to come to the town meeting. Speaking before the city's annual community prayer breakfast on November 6, 1993, the convener asked members of the mixed audience to check their individual physical reaction to merely hearing the word "racism"; that reaction, she said, would be their answer on the value of talking about the subject in a Baton Rouge town meeting in 1994. "If in their bodies people sensed any form of discomfort—anger, tension, fear—when hearing the word 'racism,'" she said, "that was a sign that racism was worth exploration. Racism is often treated as a civic concern much the same way as child abuse," she continued. "People cringe. People avoid it. People lack understanding about it. Some people hide it. People can only heal if they talk about it."

The actual testing of the questions for the town meeting began in January 1994 in four locations. Simultaneously, several prominent business, civic and religious leaders tried to stop the project, pressuring both sponsors and individual committee members to call off such an event. Their efforts failed, and relationships tightened within the Town Meeting Committee.

The test groups proved successful. The committee refined the questions in the first two weeks of February and set a final date for the town meeting—April 26. Facilitators were rigorously trained on April 12 by committee volunteers supported by The People's Institute of New Orleans. Precautions were taken to address each of the original fears committee members had experienced. In training, table facilitators were offered a process that reflected the personal experiences of the Town Meeting Committee members during the previous year. Key ideas included directives such as:

- Patience with tolerance is a must.
- Declare it is okay to disagree on the definition of racism.
- Facilitators do not have to solve racism or table disagreements.
- Be aware early of the tone of the table and the volatility of the issue.
- Do not allow any personal attacks.
- Encourage the group not to take disagreements personally.
- Do not use words of violence.
- Revisit the three goals of the town meeting: to explore the issue of racism, to increase awareness, and to build hope.

A formal briefing of community leaders also accomplished its purpose. At the community leadership breakfast on April 12, as many as would fit into the mayor-president's meeting room of the civic complex were invited to hear the committee's plans. The group appeared to be taken with testimonies of committee members on what the process meant to them and what it could mean to Baton Rouge, and the earnest words of the mayor, clergy and a few others among the invitees provided an aura of hope in moving on to April 26.

On April 26 at 7:00 P.M., the committee members arrived with nearly 60 facilitators and more than 500 others for the town meeting. More than 50 tables were provided for participants. Planners looked at each other in growing amazement and awe as the Centroplex civic center filled up with citizens looking eager to get on with the work. Historic as the moment was, time was allotted for music to lighten the atmosphere. Those introducing the program personalities were keenly aware of their responsibilities, and they exuded a sense that "we've never done anything like this before, but let's get on with it."

The evening dialogue opened with a video that created discomfort in its historical context and data on racism but also primed the crowd for intense, respectful discussion. The video depicted scenes from the 1960s—scenes of civil-rights violence and cross-burning. These scenes were followed by a statistically grounded statement about then current racial hiring practices, financial figures, and positions held by people of color. There were also scenes of integrated classrooms. The tape itself was not used again after the town meeting. In the words of one attendee: "Baton Rouge would never be the same again."

"WHAT COLOR IS COMMUNITY? Baton Rouge Talks About Race Relations" lasted three hours. Utter strangers, though fellow citizens, sat in one another's company to discuss racism; voices soft and loud punctuated the air. To at least one participant, the meeting had the character of a long overdue family reunion, with all of the attendant perils most families experience when meeting after a long time. A full range of needs and expectations, often mixed with pain and tension, are part of such relationships. The town meeting showed clearly that race relations matter deeply to the citizens of Baton Rouge, and, though no attempt was made to change anyone's particular views on race, there was a sense that ground remained to be broken and cultivated in a sustained way to diminish racism.

At 11:00 P.M., an hour after the meeting ended, some participants still lingered in discussion. Between 200 and 300 people had signed up for a second assembly.

Years later, references to the lessons learned during the town-meeting preparation are still frequently made in Baton Rouge. The volunteers teach, coach and lead others when racism "hot buttons" get pushed. Many of the original town-meeting participants have also taken what they learned into their subsequent civic work and have paired together to lead other projects. One was a 1997–1998 initiative to follow up on the nation's work to help children in conjunction with America's Promise, led by General Colin Powell, which is designed to bring youth basic care, health, safety, education and opportunities to learn service. The Baton Rogue version—Community Action for Children—continues as of late 1998.

Relationships forged among the original participants in the racism dialogue are building community in Baton Rouge. Though unmeasurable, there is more of a concerted effort for multiracial leadership of community initiatives. Without question, key relationships grew among those who persevered to produce "WHAT COLOR IS COMMUNITY? Baton Rouge Talks About Race Relations."

GOING THE SECOND MILE

During the preparatory committee's consideration of how to find a way to channel energies from the town meeting, a Jesuit colleague of Rev. Jeff Day—Father Thomas Barberito, stationed in the inner city—quickly grasped the purpose and exclaimed: "Going the second mile!" The biblical metaphor captured what colleagues had been struggling with for months: how to turn the unrest, hate and sometimes violence that afflicts racial relations in America from retaliation and revenge toward peaceful resolutions.

The Gospel of Matthew quotes Jesus, in an extended teaching on ways to handle tense human relationships, as suggesting going beyond retaliation—an eye for an eye, a tooth for a tooth—by taking the unexpected step of assuming part of the antagonist's burden by helping carry it even one extra mile (in this biblical story, a Roman soldier's pack). The teaching turns on the change that can come in the one who has been wronged and who wants not to harm the enemy, but to see her or his release from hatred also.

Going the Second Mile was to become the medium for extending the work of the Town Meeting Committee and of the town meeting itself. Day announced to the town-meeting crowd that a meeting would be called in several weeks to reconvene those who might be interested in continuing the discussions.

The Town Meeting Committee had generally agreed that, whatever the outcome of the discussions at the town meeting, it seemed best to leave it to those who would volunteer to set the major contours for Going the Second Mile and to plan the follow-on effort. The committee agreed that the experience of organizing and directing the town meeting would be made available to the next participants and that a few colleagues from the committee would be available to assist with the work ahead.

The catalysts in this new phase were Day and Maxine Crump, a former television newscaster-reporter, past president of the local YWCA and organizational consultant who was a veteran in interracial dialogue. Day's experience in the black-white clergy dialogue and work in building an interfaith-interracial federation provided another dimension of bridge building in fostering peaceful relationships. Several persons who attended the town meeting joined them in planning sessions.

On June 14, the first follow-up meeting to the town meeting was held at the Catholic Life Center with about 200 people attending. A speaker presented a stirring overview of racism in America. Again, tables were prepared for the discussion of three questions, attempting to learn what was on participants' minds about racism and what kind of structure would be necessary to move the group into future dialogue groups. At the conclusion of the meeting, several options for immediate action were presented through announcements that groups were being formed to discuss and act on education, general civic concerns, government, youth, business and health care, public relations and the media, churches and synagogues and police-community relations. Almost all of the groups drew 6 or more interested persons, some as many as 20 or more.

By the beginning of 1995, at least four of the eight topic committees were continuing to meet and get better organized. Each of these four had a representative on the Coordinating Committee, which also included Crump and Day and three or four other volunteers. It helped keep all committees informed of each other's work.

The Second Mile offered two community-wide events: one in December 1995 in response to the uproar about the O.J. Simpson verdict; the other in early 1997 addressing how welfare and racism form a complex of ideas that stereotype welfare recipients as almost always people of color. A little more than a year later, when the public was talking about welfare reform—with a new national welfare policy in effect and with local concern mounting about how it would be applied in Louisiana—another public meeting was called to examine race and welfare policies.

The Coordinating Committee insisted from the first that Going the Second Mile would never be an organization; it would be a "movement," growing out of the commitments of participants, who would find a place on a topic committee and would then move with others into discussion and actions to reduce racism. The lack of an overall organizational plan no doubt turned some away, since no specific goals were set. Others seized the opportunity to engage in dialogue and shared work, satisfied that this itself was action.

Going the Second Mile became a gateway for the more than 500 citizens who had attended the April 1994 town meeting. For those who wanted to exploit the newly found energy to engage in continuing experience and dialogue on race relations, the opportunity to meet new people and a way to affect a few areas of civic life, it became a route for traveling together.

THE SUSTAINED DIALOGUE

By early 1995, those who had been involved in preparing and managing the town meeting and Going the Second Mile were gratified by the new doors that had been opened but felt the need to deepen the work that had begun. Those who attended individual functions or worked together in civic committees certainly experienced new working relationships, but they also experienced the same self-imposed constraints that Town Meeting Committee participants had felt when they first sat down together. They undoubtedly learned from working together across racial lines, but perhaps they did not learn as deeply as they could have because they did not talk directly about race.

A conversation in March 1995 between Day and two members of the Charles F. Kettering Foundation staff—James Wilder and Harold Saunders—opened the door to the possibility of a sustained dialogue on race relations. Kettering's staff had been frequent visitors in Baton Rouge, working with citizens in a variety of ways. The foundation was looking for an appropriate U.S. community in which to test the process of sustained dialogue that had been developed abroad. As the conversation deepened, the Kettering staff members met with the members of the board of the Greater Baton Rouge Federation of Churches and Synagogues to share their experience with the dialogue process and Kettering's interest in collaborating with an organization like the federation to learn from a pilot effort. The joint hope was to produce an experience in the United States on which others might draw in dealing with racial tension in their own communities.

The board decided to go ahead with the project as a way of amplifying the federation's own mission. Board members were intrigued by the opportunity to take advantage of the intensive experience with dialogue in peacemaking in other places. They believed it could deepen their own work in building peace within their own community.

To launch the project, Day turned to one of the other initial participants in the black-white clergy dialogue, Rev. Fred Jeff Smith, to be co-moderator of the sustained dialogue. Saunders returned to Baton Rouge in May 1995 to meet at length with the co-moderators. He had sent them the manual that appears in the Appendix of this book—it was actually written for them—to acquaint them with the process in detail, but he had also promised to talk through the process with them until they felt comfortable with it. He also met with the black-white clergy dialogue group.

Stage One: Deciding to Engage

The effort began in earnest throughout the summer of 1995. In setting out to enlist members from the black and white communities, the co-moderators agreed that they would have an equal number from each race, even though the community's population was about 65 percent white and 35 percent black. They thought that the clergy would be more than adequately represented by the co-moderators. They began their search for a cross-section of citizens who ran the gamut from liberal to conservative, Republican to Democrat to Independent, business leader to working person. No politicians, present or aspiring, were invited. They chose to exclude those with entrenched political or racial ideology.

To find the right participants, Day and Smith talked during the summer with three-dozen individuals who were personally known to them or recommended by those well known to them. In each of those conversations, they laid out their purposes and experience with the subject and their hope for a community in which race relationships could steadily become healthier.

They wanted the final group to include strong, articulate people who could more than hold their own in dialogue. They wanted those with firm convictions who could be expected to be open enough to others to show respect for them—literally, to take a second look. (Day constantly reminded colleagues about the definition of respect: to re-look or to take a second look. Taking off his spectacles, he emphasized the limits on vision if we see only part of the world.) In their conversations with participants, they talked, somewhat playfully, about how they and group members would be inspecting, retrospecting, and prospecting with one another. Throughout these exploratory meetings, the co-moderators believe, they overcame the temptation to people the group with replicas of themselves. To summarize the candidate search, they looked for people who:

- felt the urgency of improving race relations;
- were known by them or by trusted colleagues;
- shared hope for a broader discussion of race matters;
- would commit to a significant sacrifice of time: four to six hours a meeting every four to six weeks over months and perhaps years;
- would meet away from the concerns of work and family;
- shared the expectation that the dialogue group would come to conclusions and make decisions that would improve the quality of race relations in Baton Rouge. (The distant goal was that the group's experience might encourage other groups elsewhere in the United States.)

After evaluating their exploratory conversations with the initial candidates in light of these criteria, Day and Smith chose twelve people—six white and six black, seven men and five women—for membership in the initial dialogue group.

Stage Two: Mapping and Naming Problems and Relationships

Baton Rouge, the state capital, is home to two major universities: Louisiana State University and the predominantly black Southern University. The latter, though well known through the media, is about as unfamiliar to most whites as one could imagine. Pride in the school knows no bounds among alumni and friends. Southern's campus, for those who remember the civil-rights era in the 1960s and 1970s, became a flash point of conflict, leading to the deaths of two students. When a new student union was built, it was named the Smith-Brown Memorial Union, after those two students. The moderators chose that site for the first dialogue in October 1995.

The moderators envisioned a formal beginning with a fully catered meal. While participants courteously introduced themselves, eyed the agenda, responded to the printed question—What are your feelings about race relations in this community?—it became apparent that they required little prodding to open up.

The ten participants presented their ideas, hopes and fears for what the group was up against and what it might achieve. Only one person lamented the enormous sacrifice in time required to do this kind of work. With few exceptions, the perceived problems, the most serious ones to work on and expectations for change that the group identified at this first session varied little through the first two years of dialogue.

Both blacks and whites treated each other hospitably throughout the session, although for some, particularly black participants hearing white perceptions, the strain was evident. Everyone expressed some grief that conditions in the community normally prevented this kind of meeting. A question from one participant—"Why would I want to know you?"—though asked in a tentative, polite manner, echoed the unease that some felt as they tried to reach out to one another. At this first meeting, it seemed in retrospect, each person was aligned to some degree with those of like skin color. When a black member spoke of her desire to know whites, she said that her previous experience of being in race-relations groups gave her little encouragement that this would be more successful.

The political surprise of the day for whites was the keen resentment expressed by blacks that the white mayor of Baton Rouge did not live in Baton Rouge but in the predominantly white Zachary, which had a mayor of its own. For most white participants, this perspective on the racial balance in the community had been as hidden as the dark side of the moon. "The very political atmosphere is tilted away from us," black participants told their white colleagues, who responded: "We did not know you felt so strongly about this." Black revelations about their interpretations of political realities such as the mayor's residence have continued to surprise white colleagues. Black members' sometimes surprising comments gave white members deeper insight into how blacks perceive their disadvantages.

There were more surprises for whites, too, as black members engaged in a kind of "believe it or not" sharing about the variations within the black community. Worship styles in black churches differ markedly from each other, whites were told; they were invited to attend some of these so that their eyes might be opened to the rich complexity of the black community. One got the impression that, while blacks knew about white worship styles, their ways were largely mysterious to whites.

A young white mother of three children gained enormous credibility when she said that her children were in public schools. Because she had taken heat from her white upwardly mobile counterparts in the community for sending her children to public school, her testimony of commitment to public education impressed black members. Her commitment to the basic opportunity for all children in public education helped seal an early alliance within the group to stay with the dialogue. By the end of the first meeting, everyone had spoken in some way about personal pain over the separation of the races. Everyone offered some hope that the group might be able to stick together.

If the moderators' vision of a heterogeneous group needed vindication, the first session settled any concern that the mark would be missed. Lawyer, insurance salesman, engineer, hospital executive, educator, clergy—all injected different viewpoints that had nothing to do with skin color, but of course, each had her or his own experience with race. The engineer, always attempting to sketch a model, for instance, asked: "What will our community look like when we get there?"

If ignorance is the result of ignoring persons or things, then black citizens' feelings of being ignored by whites in the United States are largely substantiated. Because they were treated as property for the first 250 years of Western settlement in this North American continent, they are constantly pained at their fellow white citizens' failure to catch up with—and understand—what they speak about with such pain. This presents a challenge of utmost importance for the stability of civil society. The dialogue group has faced that challenge at each meeting.

The second dialogue occurred in November 1995 on the Saturday of the runoff election for governor between Republican State Senator Mike Foster and Democratic Congressman Cleo Fields. Fields was the first African American to be so close to the governorship since Reconstruction. Black participants began the dialogue with loud lamentations that white Democrats would desert Fields; in fact, black candidates in Baton Rouge find little support among whites. "Not even Colin Powell could win here! Why do Democrats not support their party candidate?" asked black participants.

Black participants seemed interested mostly in seeing whether Fields would get a respectable vote since they assumed he would not win. The dialogue became a debate over progress in race relations. "Show us a sign that we matter, count for something"—the black argument. "We do care, we want to work for the day when a black may win the governorship," replied the whites. The anxieties of the group were still at fever pitch when the meeting ended in the early afternoon, but both black and white members had made progress. When the meeting began, black members seemed to assume that a chasm of polarization would exist between them and white members. That sense of polarization diminished as black members realized that all whites were not supporting Foster; whites experienced something new in just talking about this.

Stage Three: Probing Problems and Relationships to Choose a Direction

In this dialogue, the transition from Stage Two to Stage Three was not clear-cut. It was more implicit than explicit. But, one way or another, participants were groping for ways to talk about race relationships.

Like members of the Town Meeting Committee, participants seemed to feel without saying so that what they needed to work on was sharing more examples of everyday black experiences with racism so they could probe more deeply the essence of racism. That became the pattern of each session—discussion in depth of recent happenings, either in the community or to individuals, and how participants felt about them.

What seems to have marked the transition visibly was the increase in participants' comfort level in sharing feelings with each other and in speaking frankly. "The transition from formality, noisiness and challenge to relaxed and quiet exchanges was marked," Day writes. In addition, the commitment to the dialogue process and to other members of the group seemed to deepen. Day again reflects: "Another apparent characteristic took the form of members following with keen interest another member's effort to find a new job, the birth of a child and concern over the welfare of a family."

The discussion ranged over a variety of experiences, feelings and reactions. As this became the pattern, members learned to focus on the relationships underlying the specific subjects discussed—whether housing, everyday conversations between persons or in the difference among worship styles. In session after session, these and other subjects have come up, but they have usually been used as starting points for understanding the racial relationships that underlie them.

Housing patterns in Baton Rouge have remained segregated with few exceptions. Mostly, the group spoke about the distress of blacks attempting to move into white neighborhoods or, even more disturbing, the refusal of whites to consider buying a black-owned house for sale in an integrated neighborhood. White colleagues listened in wonder as their counterparts spoke of how they handled the problem of running out of space. What to do about the inability to move? Simply knock out a wall, build another room. It was a revelation to whites to learn that they are perceived by blacks as seeing a house simply as an investment: Put the house on the market and move on with a hoped-for profit. Feeling ignored, even shunned, black members asked: What are people to do or think when they feel trapped in a neighborhood? The group found common ground in seeing that this dilemma for blacks prevents the possibility of making new relationships across racial lines. Some black households may really be an island.

One of the lighter conversations that occurs from time to time deals with how each group conducts conversations in a variety of settings. How curious it is, black participants say, to be told that "you are not like the others." They also cited a comment that comes up in nearly all introductions: "I know [a certain black]. Do you?" The awkwardness of not being able to talk with a degree of comfort keeps both groups uneasy, as if some formidable national (foreign), cultural walls are going to prevent communication. One insight into finding common ground in this matter, the co-moderators believe, is that people today want and need to communicate with each other in ways that this kind of awkwardness prevents. The patience of colleagues with each other as they discuss, sometimes role play, these situations, usually with humor, is one of the more pleasant parts of the dialogue. The group consensus is: Practice, practice, practice.

Perhaps because the moderators are clergy, the group members often run through a cycle of discussing religion. Several participants are active members of their churches; almost all speak with deep feeling about how faith is important to them. The search for an ethical way to develop a more responsive dialogue is, without question, a passion of the members. The varieties of religious response and feeling among black believers is always of interest to their white counterparts. White participants have felt considerable pain in learning that racism has played such a part in denominational life. They were astounded to learn that at least three major Southern groups seceded from their natural religious denomination over the issue of slavery years before the South seceded from the Union in 1861. Some whites in the dialogue even asked in distress how the Bible could be used to authorize slavery, Jim Crow laws and the more contemporary forms of segregation.

If, as has been said, religion is an expression of a person's ultimate concern, then it should not be surprising, Day reflects, that waves of religious feeling should pulse through the group. The common ground and interests that permeate every aspect of racial relationships, he suggests, are expressions of some kind of ethical code. This shared concern has enabled colleagues in the dialogue to find a common language that binds the group to search for more compassionate ways to work with each other.

Other currents flowing through conversations are the plight of public education, environmental racism and questions of economics. Each of these subjects provides an example of how discussion of a real-world problem can lead to dialogue on racial relationships that underlie it. Each one opens an economic issue: the opportunity to get ahead and, in the discussion of the environment, to get out of a poor community. The common ground that members of the group search for is fairness. The difficulty lies in defining environmental racism, for instance, as an obstacle to fairness.

The dramatic changes in public education have clearly focused the dialogue on reforming that sector. As of this writing in late 1998, a reform group of school-board members has presided for three years over the settlement of the nation's longest-running desegregation suit. The situation in Baton Rouge represents the only case in which the school board, the National Association for the Advancement of Colored People (NAACP) and the U.S. Justice Department have mutually agreed upon a plan. Under an agreement approved by a federal court, the school system has embarked upon a program to improve public education. The dialogue group follows news of progress and setbacks with intense interest. This issue, more than any other, has become a focus of sustained interest. It is still early to discern how much will there is to work together on a specific agenda to aid the reformation of the system.

When the South used to be referred to as "the place of the peculiar institution," slavery, there was little argument that the label was fitting. Generations beyond that, it may strike one unfamiliar with this Southern historical tradition that Americans should be discovering it so difficult to speak with each other about race matters. If slavery was "long ago" to whites, then it matters little in trying to bring about current racial understanding; if slavery seems "just ended"—albeit more than a century ago in 1863–1865—then, for blacks, that is rather recent, considering how long it has taken the racial attitudes of whites to mellow. To treat each other with respect, even to speak of each other's suffering with an almost reverent respect, is bridging the disrespect, the ignorance of each other.

One particular theme that resonates throughout the group is parental discipline, especially the strictness that black parents exercise. These revelations demonstrate the resolve of parents to enable their children not only to cope, but also to succeed, in a predominantly white world. White participants have expressed respect and awe toward black group members as they have learned that their black colleagues were taught as children not only to be good citizens, but also to be safe within their own persons because so many events taken for granted by white children were impossible for them, given the places and times that could prove dangerous for black children. One member had never stayed overnight with friends because it was "too dangerous; remember the lynching of young Emmett Till."

With these revelations has also come what one can only call humility toward each other—the willingness to let the person be who he or she totally is. That does not mean that there are no challenges, but these are couched in a frame that attempts to preserve two things: the integrity and honesty of the group and the respect that each member has for the other ("I think too much of you to let you get away with saying that; I can't let that pass").

Individual stories, especially characterizing how blacks have suffered from racism, reveal each group's perceptions. Black group members have heard stories from their white counterparts about how the struggle to affirm fairness to blacks is often scoffed at by their family or colleagues. White participants have heard stories of how slave voices even yet speak to these times, for the struggle of slavery and Jim Crow still causes pain to these black members ("How can we forget . . . ? You need to know . . . I . . .").

One participant sees an enlarging "we" in each "me" in the group. Since beginning on a formal note in October 1995, the group has gone beyond formality to informality: Friendships are flourishing, hilarity sometimes pervades the room at the expense of someone's obvious change; pleasure in eating meals together is obvious, with members taking turns providing food. Members embrace third Saturdays each month for dialogue to become more equipped to improve race relations and grow in friendships.

The dialogue group has remained in Stage Three for some time, probing for the deeper meaning and causes of racism, but, as of this writing, it is also struggling with the question of how to take its insights into the larger community. That struggle itself is bringing the group closer and closer to its own sense of racism and how to deal with it.

One thing the group has learned is not to rush into activity until it has dealt fully with the fundamental questions of relationship. While it may appear that the group should be about changing the society around them, the growing affection for each other that brings almost 100 percent attendance, gives evidence that work significant to the participants has been going on and has taken considerable time. The quest for a viable peace process among this kind of diverse group, beginning to learn to speak to each other about race matters, has a season all of its own. To that end, participants have shown a commitment to invest a significant amount of time regularly and to attend all meetings.

The group has made substantial progress in setting in place a "culture of learning from each other"—a culture characterized by respect. The group has developed the capacity to take a second look, to give another hearing to what participants have seen and heard from each. Beyond that, the group has established an "extensive field of concern"—the freedom of members to talk directly to each other about any matters that participants choose. It seems likely that group members will hear each other out in eventually dealing with the as-yet unaddressed issues of changing dysfunctional community racial relationships.

As of this writing, the group feels a strong urge to share what it has learned with the wider community, but some participants think the group still has deeper work to do. A few white colleagues are eager to begin a list of members for future sustained dialogue groups ("Each one of us can start one!"). While there is little disagreement that this is a worthy goal, others fear it may become a distraction from dealing with the more pressing and deeper issue in the group that is just coming into focus.

That deeper issue revolves around two strongly held feelings that group members are dealing with head-on.

Some black participants feel that the United States—and perhaps even the dialogue—is not as far along on the issue of race relations as many have hoped or as many observers seem to believe. In fact, looking back at the civil-rights movement of the 1960s, they argue that the country is regressing rather than progressing in efforts to achieve unity. Instead of being a "community making inroads of understanding," said one participant, "we have veered into disunity, disharmony and disrespect." At the heart of the problem, in the view of these participants, is the denial by many white Americans that racism is a serious problem and their use of a variety of tactical devices to avoid facing up to the reality.

This avoidance of the issue, said Rev. Smith, is "the great roadblock to progress in the dialogue on race relations. It is precisely why sustained dialogue is the most valid remedy to this problem I have so far come across. Town meetings and commissions on race are woefully inadequate to confront the deeply rooted issues that continue to keep America a divided nation." At the same time, he believes, until the dialogue group agrees on the priority that should be given to the issue of race relations in the community, it is hardly ready to act.

Some white participants feel that they do recognize that racism remains prevalent and is immoral but that black citizens sometimes make the mistake of seeing everything through racial lenses. They acknowledge that African Americans have been grievously wronged in the past and are still being wronged today, but they argue that the only constructive approach is to concentrate on building the future.

In concluding this chapter while the work is still unfolding, I cannot cite highly visible achievements. I can make the point that sustained dialogue after 29 meetings seems to provide a unique space in which these citizens have achieved the capacity to deal with this fundamental tension. Having come this far, they seem to stand on the threshold of an opportunity to demonstrate that dialogue can change interracial relationships and that participants in dialogue can together design interactive steps that could engage a whole community at all levels in changing itself. The story in Chapter Nine suggests that this can be done.

Chapter Nine

Bridging the Abyss: Palestinian-Israeli Dialogue

Galia Golan and Zahira Kamal

*A*uthor's Note: While the dialogues described below by Galia Golan and Zahira Kamal have not taken place explicitly within the framework of the five-stage process described in this book, the transforming essence of dialogue is breathtakingly captured in this account. In a way that inspires reverence, it reveals the mind and spirit of those who engage and persevere in sustained dialogue to make and consolidate peace. It also captures both the fear and suspicion that characterize potential participants in Stage One as described in Chapter Six and the remarkable experience of a civil society in which dialogues are proliferating beyond capacity to number them. It particularly highlights the special contribution and characteristics of dialogue among women.

A PERSONAL INTRODUCTION

This chapter is itself an exercise in dialogue. The authors are both women who have been active in the search for peace and in dialogue between the people of their two communities for many years: A Palestinian and an Israeli, a Muslim and a Jew, both deeply involved in the political and social lives of their own societies. Having met some ten years ago through Palestinian-Israeli dialogues in Jerusalem, we have gradually come to know each other and something about each other's lives; through some very difficult times and bloody crises in our region (and between our peoples), we have come to trust and like each other. In a sense, it is as a test of this understanding and friendship that we

have undertaken to write this chapter together, rather than produce two separate chapters—each from her own point of view. In jointly analyzing and evaluating our experience, we hope to take the dialogue one step further, as a
symbol of our commitment to the resolution of the conflict dividing our two
peoples.

HISTORY

At the heart of the Arab-Israeli conflict lies the dispute between Palestinians
and Jews over the former British mandate of Palestine, known by the Jews as
the Land of Israel. This dispute could be dated back to the time of the first
Zionist settlements in the area in the nineteenth century and, with Arab national awakening in the early part of the twentieth century, to the open conflict that occurred between the two communities in the Holy Land in the
1920s and 1930s.

The dispute became most acute, however, after the 1947 U.N. decision
to partition the land between Jews and Arabs and the subsequent creation of
the State of Israel in 1948. In the war that ensued, Israel expanded the area
allotted to it by the United Nations Partition Plan; the eastern part of
Jerusalem and the West Bank of the Jordan River were annexed by Jordan.
(According to the Partition Plan, the city of Jerusalem was to have been in-
ternationally controlled under a U.N. committee.)

Israel existed within the borders of the 1949 Armistice Agreements with
the Arab states until the June 1967 Six-Day War, at which time Israel occupied the Jordanian-controlled West Bank (with a Palestinian population of
roughly one million), the Egyptian-controlled Sinai Peninsula (including the
Gaza Strip, with a Palestinian population of 750,000)[1] and the Syrian-con-
trolled Golan Heights. Also, Israel dismantled the physical barriers between
East and West Jerusalem, officially annexing the eastern part in 1980 and at-
taching it to West Jerusalem, which had been the capital of Israel since the
founding of the state. Some 160,000 Palestinians were living in East
Jerusalem at this time, and an estimated two million to three million Palestinian refugees were living outside the occupied lands.[2] Thus, with the 1967
war, the conflict between Israelis and the Palestinians became one of Israel's
control over the occupied West Bank and Gaza and Israel's annexation of
East Jerusalem, as well as of the older issues regarding the fate of the Palestinian refugees and Palestinian claims to all of historic Palestine.[3]

The brief history described above is itself the product of years of dialogue.
Agreement between a Palestinian and an Israeli on one version of the history
of the conflict cannot be taken for granted and, indeed, is not easily

achieved. It is not only a matter of different versions but even the questions of where to begin the history, how (or if) to try to resolve the matter of which "people" was in the land first, for how long (and we may be speaking of hundreds, even thousands, of years), in what numbers and by what authority—that is, who has the "right" to the land—and where we should begin in trying to resolve the conflict. As we shall see below, the very difference in attitude toward the relevance of history was a factor in early dialogues. For now, this brief history will serve merely as background to the beginning of dialogue in the post-1967 context.

THE BEGINNING OF DIALOGUE

The very idea of dialogue was controversial, in both publics. The first to begin on the Israeli side, in the early 1970s, were people from the extreme Left of the Israeli political spectrum. These included the minuscule anti-Zionist organization Matzpen and two groups less antagonistic toward Zionism, though not generally described as Zionist: the New Communist Party (Rakah) and the Council for an Israeli-Palestinian Peace (composed of Zionists and non-Zionists).

The one common factor among these three pioneers of dialogue was their advocacy of the Palestinians' right to a state of their own. Both the Council and Rakah, a Soviet-supported Communist Party, adopted the two-state solution advocated by Moscow. These two organizations engaged in dialogue out of the belief that a Palestinian state next to Israel (rather than instead of Israel) meant, by implication, acceptance of each other—Palestinians and Israelis—and, therefore, a large degree of coexistence requiring at least the beginning of communication. Rakah members were the strongest advocates of dialogue and even pressed for inclusion of more mainstream[4] but dovish Zionists from the Mapam and Labor parties. On the whole, however, they found few advocates outside their own ranks. Indeed, all three groups were severely criticized within Israeli society and regarded with much suspicion; their phones were tapped, and they were victims of minor harassment.

Dialogue was regarded with equal, if not more, suspicion on the Palestinian side, for speaking with a legal Israeli entity might imply acceptance of the status quo—that is, of the occupation. Nonetheless, a small number of individuals began such a dialogue with the above-mentioned Israelis. These individuals, mainly from Bir Zeit University, were not affiliated with a particular organization within the Palestine Liberation Organization (PLO); they might best be described as Independents with strong leanings toward the Communists (not yet officially separate from the Jordanian Communist

Party) or the Marxist Democratic Front for the Liberation of Palestine (DFLP), led by Nayif Hawatmeh. These were the two groups that accepted the idea of a two-state solution and, therefore, condoned communication. When, for example, the individuals engaged in dialogue came under severe criticism from their peers at Bir Zeit, their only supporters came from the ranks of the DFLP.

In 1974, however, prominent PLO members outside the occupied territories from Fatah—the core organization in the PLO headed by PLO Chairman Yasser Arafat—began meeting with Israelis, including dovish Zionists from the Labor Party as well as from the Left. These contacts had Arafat's support, although some of their advocates, notably Dr. Issam Sartawi and Sa'id Hammami, were later assassinated by the Abu Nidal "rejectionist" organization because of their moderation.[5] A bitter dispute erupted in the PLO over these contacts, leading to an official decision at the 1977 Palestine National Council (PNC) meeting to permit contacts with anti-Zionist Israelis.[6] In practice, this decision was expanded to include meetings with Zionist Israelis as well, often organized with the help of the Israeli Communists (Rakah) and usually conducted in Europe at public meetings or academic gatherings.

In both societies, dialogue was viewed as fraternizing with the enemy. By entering into dialogue, you were according the enemy legitimacy and, possibly, dulling your fighting spirit, perhaps crippling your own ability to fight. For Palestinians, it might prove an obstacle to struggling for a state; for Israelis, it might form an obstacle to fighting in the army. Both societies and most of their political bodies feared the possible effects of dialogue: How can you kill if you are friends? Indeed, even Palestinians who supported the early dialogues argued that these contacts should be given minimum publicity lest they be emulated, while some of the Israelis involved even initiated (and won) a slander suit in the courts to prove that they were Zionists. As perhaps is natural for people locked in a life-or-death struggle, there was ambivalence on both sides.

Contacts remained quite limited for some time, but, by the mid-1980s, various third parties abroad, as well as more mainstream[7] Palestinians and Israelis, came to the conclusion that the absence of communication at the official level was detrimental to the future of both peoples. In the eyes of moderate Israelis, developments within the PLO following the Lebanon war of 1982 strongly suggested an opening toward compromise and peaceful resolution of the conflict. There was the concern that the Israeli government was either ignorant of these developments or, more likely, unwilling to acknowledge them. For many Palestinians, such as Sartawi, the Lebanon war further demonstrated the need to find a compromise solution rather than rely on armed struggle to end the occupation. PLO Chairman Arafat's decision to hold a PNC meeting in Jordan and to enter an agreement with Jordan's King Hussein as a step toward an American-brokered settlement split the movement, but it also gave the green light to broader contacts with Israelis on the part of prominent Fatah people inside and outside the occupied territories.

A number of dialogues, sometimes with overlapping participants, began at this time, including small, confidential workshops organized in the United States by Harvard Professor Herbert Kelman that brought together leading Israelis and Palestinians for several days, usually on a one-time basis; and a dialogue begun by the Israeli peace movement, Peace Now, with leading Palestinians in the occupied territories, joined occasionally by PLO officials at meetings in Europe.

While these were among the most sustained mainstream dialogues, a tentative women's dialogue was begun in Nairobi, Kenya, in 1985 (behind the scenes of the Third U.N. Women's Conference). This dialogue was initiated by American women who had been conducting an African American and Jewish American dialogue prior to Nairobi and who broadened it to include several Israeli and Palestinian women at the Nairobi conference. The Palestinian and Israeli women continued the dialogue upon their return home, meeting in East Jerusalem and at the home of one of the participants in Gaza. This dialogue broke down when the group planned a much broader public meeting: The Palestinian women backed down, explaining that they needed and preferred to work within their own community before working with Israelis. A small effort was made to revive the women's dialogue at a Kelman workshop at Radcliffe College in 1987. It was, in fact, successfully revived and greatly enlarged only after the beginning of the Intifada—the Palestinian uprising in the West Bank and Gaza that began in December 1987. The women's dialogue was reborn at a large, public meeting in Brussels, Belgium, organized by the Belgian Jewish leader Simone Susskind, who, with her husband, David Susskind, was the organizer of many Israeli-Palestinian activities and peace efforts.

THE NATURE OF DIALOGUE CHANGES: THE GOALS

The Intifada marked a major turning point for both societies and led to a significant change with regard to dialogue and communication between Palestinians and Israelis. For the Palestinians, the uprising in the occupied territories was a determined step by the people themselves toward independence and statehood. It brought about the creation of a cohesive Palestinian community while, at the same time, galvanizing the leadership abroad to bold and decisive political action. For the Palestinians in the occupied territories, the Intifada represented the revolution that would, in fact, attain the goal of statehood. It was the two-state solution in the making, and, for those who believed in this solution, it became clear that now was the time to create the conditions for coexistence. Thus, the belief that statehood was near brought Palestinians to the realization that coexistence would be virtually impossible if the only way Palestinians and Israelis related to each other was through violence and killing. Something, they believed, must be done to break down the wall of hatred and to change the way in which the two peoples viewed each other.

The purpose of the dialogue, therefore, was to be, first of all, a differentiation between the Israeli government and the Israeli people in the eyes of Palestinians. The intention of the Palestinians involved in dialogue was to demonstrate to their own people that not all Israelis were the Israeli government, the army, the occupier. Together with this, the Palestinians wanted to acquaint Israelis with the Palestinian plight, to show them the suffering and toll of the occupation. They wanted to have Israelis see them as people, just as they sought to have Palestinians see Israelis as people.

The Intifada was viewed in various ways by Israelis. In general, the uprising inspired fear in the already chronically insecure Israelis. Yet, it had two positive effects. For the average Israeli, who felt a threat to personal security, the Intifada brought about the realization that the status quo—continued occupation—was untenable; the Palestinians were not going to sit quietly and accept indefinite Israeli rule over them. The political conclusion—apparent in the 1992 Israeli elections—was that a peace settlement must be sought with the Palestinians. For many Israelis, the Intifada instilled the beginning of an awareness of the Palestinians as people. Everyday, one saw on television a civilian uprising. This was not a war being fought by armies with tanks and planes but, rather, women and children throwing rocks and stones and occasionally Molotov cocktails. Many Israelis were repulsed by what they saw their army—their own sons—doing against this rebellion, and women, in particular, tended to empathize or identify with these civilians who were boldly resisting oppression.

The Israeli peace camp was greatly expanded; an extremely large number of protest groups emerged—most notably, for virtually the first time, among women. Numerous and major dialogues were begun as Israelis sought both to understand the phenomenon of the Intifada and to communicate a certain sympathy, if not agreement, with the Palestinians' efforts. For some, there may well have been the element of guilt or a sense of shame for what they felt that they, as a people, were doing to another people. There was also the sense that each side must begin to see the other's view of things if they were ever going to be able to reach agreement. The explicit intention of the dialogue, on the part of the Israelis, was, first, to demonstrate to the Palestinians that there were moderate, mainstream Zionists with whom they could speak, who believed that the Palestinians had a right to self-determination; and, second, to demonstrate to the Israeli public that there were moderate, mainstream Palestinians with whom they could speak, who were willing to accept Israel's existence as a state.

The immediate goals of both sides were, therefore, identical: to undo the demonization that had occurred in both communities regarding the other, to see and demonstrate that the "other" was not necessarily "terrorist" or "occupier," poised to kill or oppress. Put in different words, the idea was to demonstrate that neither side wanted necessarily to annihilate the other, that there was something to talk about and someone with whom to speak. The longer-range goal was to create, among as broad a public as possible, at both the elite and grass-roots levels, an acceptance of the idea of a negotiated solution on the basis of mutual recognition and mutual compromise. Thus, the objective was not only to put pressure on the political leaderships to enter such negotiations, but also to "educate" the elites who were part of, or connected with, the political leaderships. And this was to be accomplished through participation in, exposure to or at least awareness of the developing dialogue.

TYPES OF DIALOGUE AND PARTICIPANTS

In keeping with the multifaceted nature of these goals, both the participants and the forms of dialogue varied. Thus, there were dialogues that were public or private, open groups or closed, specialized (women only; former military; by occupation, such as social workers, academics, mental-health workers, students), one-time meetings (one or more days) or sustained over time, in Israel/Palestine or abroad, direct or through third parties, large or small (less than 12 people), with or without facilitators, between elites or at the grass-roots level, political, social, with joint action, or with joint statement. There may even have been still other types of dialogue; groups did not necessarily know about each other. Obviously, many of the above types overlapped, as did their participants in many instances. At the same time, there were very clear distinctions between many of the types, producing quite different effects or results. The authors have participated in almost every type of dialogue, from the mid-1980s onward.

The participants on both sides were mainly educated, middle class and upper middle class, secular and largely male. Most of the Palestinians were Muslim, but Christians participated in a larger proportion than their percentage in the general Palestinian population. A very large number of the Palestinians were academics or members of the free professions, including the arts. They tended to be associated with one or another of the Palestinian political movements, although there was an almost equal number of Independents. In the later period of dialogue, as the Intifada progressed, more grass-roots people became involved in certain cities and villages. When this occurred, somewhat more women participated, as did lesser-educated and lower-income people, often including local notables. On the Israeli side, participants remained the more educated, middle class, mainly from cities and kibbutzim. They, too, included many academics and members of the free professions, including the arts. The Israeli participants were almost all of Ashkenazi origin (roughly defined as of European descent or European born), although, as the dialogue expanded, Sephardi Jews (from North African, Arab and Asian countries) became somewhat more numerous. They perpetuated, however, the highly educated profile of the Israeli participant. For the most part, Israeli Arabs did not participate in the dialogues; only occasionally did they act as mediators between the two groups. Israeli participants tended not to be members of political parties but were associated with either extraparliamentary or professional organizations.

While on the Palestinian side the political leadership with clear representation of all or nearly all of the political streams participated, their interlocutors on the Israeli side varied much more, with each Israeli group coming from a different organization or, in some cases, political party. Only at the grass-roots level were the Palestinian groups as varied and "ad hoc" as the Israeli. Indeed, at the grass-roots level, the reverse situation was more prevalent: varied local Palestinian organizations or groups meeting with Israelis from the countrywide peace movement. More significant, until 1992, virtually all of the Israeli participants identified themselves with the opposition, albeit in many, if not most, cases, the mainstream Zionist opposition (Labor, Mapam, the civil-rights movement, Peace Now, Shinui, the religious peace movement Oz v'Shalom, the East for Peace). The Palestinian participants were identified with, and, indeed, included the PLO leadership (mainly from Fatah, but also the Palestinians' Democratic Party [FIDA]—which broke off from the DFLP—the Communists and Independents).

PROBLEMS AND OBSTACLES

Although most of the participants shared the overall objectives discussed above, there were certainly people on both sides who came merely out of curiosity or because their organization, colleagues or a third party urged them to participate. Some, therefore, came reluctantly or with a great deal of skepticism. There was not only skepticism regarding the method of dialogue and its potential effect, particularly among those accustomed to official political or governmental activity as distinct from second-track diplomacy; there was also a great deal of mutual suspicion as to the other side's expectations and motives for participating—the possibility that one side merely intended to exploit the other side for political or other purposes. At the same time, in some cases participation carried with it certain risks. There might be a degree of risk in terms of a person's professional, political or social life, depending upon the situation at the time, the general atmosphere or the context of the dialogue itself. In the case of the more vulnerable, participation was often kept confidential, but, also, the commitment was particularly strong.

For example, Palestinians were loathe to drive to a meeting on a strike day declared by Hamas (because Hamas might employ violence against people found out on the streets in violation of the strike). Palestinians were also in danger of arrest or other punishment if found in Israel without a permit (at night, for example, or during periods of closures of various areas or of all of the occupied territories). Inasmuch as Palestinian political gatherings were forbidden by the occupation, their very getting together could cause them trouble. Israelis were often afraid to be on the roads in the occupied territories or in certain locations in the West Bank or Gaza because of stone throwing, or worse, during the Intifada.[8] For participants on both sides, there were risks of criticism from their colleagues, friends or even family—accusations that they were being "taken in" or used by the other side, that they cared more for the other side than for their own people. Some were afraid their employers would disapprove and possibly take action; others were concerned that their political standing might be compromised or their professional "objectivity" called into question.[9] Participation became particularly risky or difficult at times of crisis, such as an especially harsh action against Palestinians and killings, or after a terrorist attack or, most notably, during the Gulf War.

Even as we try to find examples from both sides, we do not mean to imply symmetry. Indeed, the absence of symmetry was the very first and most persistent obstacle that had to be faced—and, we hope, overcome—in dialogue. There was and is no symmetry between the two sides; their situations are not analogous. The Palestinians were under occupation. That meant that they had no political rights or recourse; they were subject to administrative detention, arrest, imprisonment with or without trial, house arrest, town arrest, harassment, land confiscation, curfews, searches, humiliations, deportation, blowing up of houses, interrogation, torture, deprivation of livelihood, family separation, censorship, closure of schools and more. Their partners in dialogue, Jewish Israelis, lived in an open, democratic society, protected by police, army, independent courts of law, elected representatives and all of the rights and privileges of citizenship in their own state.

These differences created strong psychological barriers, even if only unconsciously. Self-image and self-confidence were clearly different for the two sides; the independence of individual participants—how freely each felt himself or herself able to take an independent position—was clearly different for the two. Israelis had to be wary of patronizing or appearing to be patronizing, while Palestinians were wary of assuming the role of victim. Also at the psychological level, there was still, at least in first encounters, the tendency to see each Israeli participant as a soldier with a gun and each Palestinian participant as a terrorist with a bomb. The demonized stereotypes were not easy to discard, even for those whose objective was just that.

Suspicions ran high with regard to each side's motives, sincerity and commitment. Trust was a generally elusive commodity, sometimes never gained. There were Palestinians who believed that their Israeli partners were merely using them in the pursuit of personal political aspirations or in order to divide, perhaps embarrass, the Palestinian political elite or wrest from it verbal concessions beyond those generally accepted or agreed upon on their side. There were Israelis, too, who believed exactly the same things of their Palestinian partners, or that they were merely being used to provide assistance in gaining permits for family reunion or to assist in dealing with other hardships of the occupation. Israelis often thought that they were being called upon by the Palestinians to "prove" their sincerity and commitment, as if continuation of the dialogue were a concession the Palestinians were granting and, therefore, contingent upon certain behavior by the Israelis.

Each side, obviously, was loyal to its own people, aware of representing at least parts of its own society and liable to judgment by that society. Quite pragmatic political considerations often governed the discussions, as each side often felt compelled to consider how its joint actions or statements might be perceived or what effect they might have on the person's or group's standing or on other sectors or processes taking place outside the dialogue.

There were, therefore, often questions on each side such as how much, if any, publicity should be sought, how innovative or accommodating to be in joint statements or activities and how much would be gained or risked by any of these things in terms of efficacy or influence.

Contributing to these obstacles, and creating a barrier in itself, was the problem of language. The dialogues were conducted in a third language, English, since very few of the Israelis spoke Arabic and very few of the Palestinians spoke Hebrew. The use of English highlighted the cultural differences between the two peoples, suggesting, in the eyes of the Palestinians, the European background (foreign to the region) of the Israelis (despite the fact that most of the Israeli participants were born in Israel). In fact, the use of English was difficult for both sides, although it was more difficult for the Palestinians. This language problem impeded the ability to express oneself. It also greatly limited the numbers of people who could participate. More people might have been supportive of dialogue and even participated had the language problem not existed. Certainly, the language was a major problem in expanding the dialogue at the grass-roots level. Interpreters were used at various times, but, on the whole, sustained dialogue was impossible on the basis of interpreters.

Language was but one part of the cultural differences. Israelis, particularly younger ones, tended to be direct and frank; Palestinians were far more polite and formal. The background of living in an open and free society made for Israeli self-confidence (sometimes arrogance); a background of persecution and underground activity made for a certain cautiousness on the part of the Palestinians. Members of neither group were likely to be emotional or personal in their comments in a group; in this they were culturally more similar to each other than to Americans, for example. The Palestinians—whether because of their political affiliations, or leadership positions or vulnerability as the group without protection and freedom—tended to be uniform in their comments, at least in the early stages of dialogue. In contrast, Israeli participants often expressed different opinions from each other, even contradictory views.

In addition, more as a result of circumstances than cultural differences, Israelis tended to seek a social, as well as political, aspect to the dialogue, whereas Palestinians tended to maintain an exclusively political orientation. Nonetheless, although it was usually the Israelis who suggested or initiated social contact, the Palestinians invariably responded positively and generously, in keeping with traditional customs of hospitality.

One cultural difference that was not particularly evident in the dialogue was the different status of women in the two societies. Despite the fact that

Palestinian society is more traditional than Israeli society, and, therefore, many fewer women work outside the home or take part in public life, Israeli women were not to be found in any greater numbers at the level of political elites. There were more women participants on both sides at the grass-roots level, but there the cultural differences were felt in that more Israeli women participated than Palestinian. Yet, at all levels of dialogue, males far out-numbered females on both sides. This may be one of the reasons women created their own dialogue, which we discuss below.

<h2 style="text-align:center">CONTENT</h2>

With regard to the substance of the dialogues, there were certain persistent problems. In the eyes of the Palestinians, the Israelis always sought to focus on the issue of Israeli security. This tendency was threatening from the Palestinian point of view, for it indicated a one-sidedness and failure to understand that both sides had security concerns. The topic should, therefore, have been: how to make both sides feel secure. Moreover, Palestinians felt that the way in which the Israelis raised this issue and others was often degrading to the Palestinians. A constant Israeli refrain was: "You have to understand . . . ," a phrase that Palestinians believed tended to maintain the occupier/occupied rubric and immediately shifted the discussion from one between equals to one between two levels of people. A similar attitude was often reflected in the approach to the peace process. In the Palestinian view, Israelis often appeared to consider that peace was an Israeli gift to the Palestinians and that, if peace were a gift given by one side, it should be rewarded with something from the other side. Instead, peace should have been seen as in the interest and to the benefit of both peoples. Thus, once again, the occupier/occupied distinction was created. Each side continued to look only at itself and to view the other side from different levels.

In the first years of dialogue, Israelis were set aback by the Palestinian tendency to open every discussion with a litany of the historical injustices committed by Israel against the Palestinians. By going back into history, it appeared to the Israelis that the Palestinians were frozen in the impossible-to-resolve question of who took what from whom, who has a right to the land and other related questions that denied Israel's very right to exist. Instead, Israelis believed the two sides should have been working together to resolve the question of the future. In time, the recounting of history gave way to an opening litany of present injustices and crimes of the occupation. This often appeared one-sided to Israelis, as if Palestinians could do no wrong and as if the Israeli partners in dialogue must somehow compensate by agreeing to whatever joint action or statement was proposed.

At the grass-roots level, mainly in the one-time meetings, participants were far more direct and accusatory. Israelis asked Palestinians how they could send their children out to throw stones at Israeli soldiers—how they could do this to their children. Such insulting and hostile (though often sincere) questions frequently found their counterpart (though not necessarily with the same interlocutors) in Palestinian accounts of humiliations and alleged atrocities inflicted by Israel. Israeli hostility of this type, when experienced, appeared at public and some private meetings held inside Israel. Palestinians tended to be far less hostile in private meetings, particularly if they were the host. There is no doubt, however, that this type of hostility tended to disappear once a dialogue became an ongoing affair.

THE LEARNING PROCESS

Indeed, at the level of the elites and, to some degree, in the sustained grass-roots dialogue, many of the problems became less acute. Unable to change the approach of the other side, both parties came simply to accept each other's sensitivities and insensitivities. Without agreeing or necessarily seeing the justification for the Israelis' chronic sense of insecurity and continued reference to what Israeli society could or could not accept, Palestinians came to understand Israeli attitudes. They also came to understand that these were not merely political positions or manipulative rationalizations but, rather, genuine, if nonetheless incomprehensible, fears that could not be ignored. Israelis, for their part, came to understand the importance of history as the basis for the Palestinians' claim to rights and the depth of their commitment to independence. They also came to understand that the hardships of the occupation were not merely political propaganda or devices to create sympathy or guilt but genuine, sometimes intolerable, suffering on a day-to-day basis.

On a personal note, the Palestinian author of this chapter, Zahira Kamal, was touched by visits of Israeli participants to her home when she was under town arrest. At a time when her faith in the possibility of peace was severely tested, she came to realize that not all Israelis were the same. The Israeli author, Galia Golan, despite years of peace activity, including demonstrations in the West Bank against settlements, began to understand just what the occupation meant on a daily basis in human terms. By hearing of things from a Palestinian woman lawyer—a person of similar education, values and pride—

she began to see things from a different point of view. At the broader level of the dialogue, Palestinians came to understand Israelis' sensitivity to any attempt to compare the occupation with the Holocaust; Israelis came to understand the importance and meaning of the right of return for Palestinians.

Neither side liked the tit-for-tat expression of grievances or fears, but a learning process was, nonetheless, in progress. Each side learned that the other was not a monolithic society as represented by its official leadership. Drawing from our personal experience, we can say that we got to know the political and social complexities of each society, the different parties and organizations, who was who, with whom and in what way or at what level one could cooperate, the limits beyond which certain groups or individuals could not make concessions, what issues were of particular sensitivity, what issues were absolutely not negotiable, what issues lacked consensus in the society, what issues were most central. We came to understand something of the daily life of each other, to see each other as people, and we learned that we were not necessarily so different from each other. Indeed, one of the great surprises and perhaps the most valuable lesson learned was that we have many of the same values, care about the same things and want similar things for ourselves and our families. At the same time, in most cases we also learned to respect our differences in culture, in history, in life experiences, in points of view and ideologies, in loyalties and national sentiments.

JOINT ACTIVITY

Our acceptance of these differences and our eventual ability to agree to disagree, to progress and compromise even when full understanding was not attainable, were the result of the trust that developed over time. This was because most participants were not involved in dialogue for the sake of dialogue but to achieve an end, a political end. Therefore, some kind of joint action, such as a demonstration, vigil, conference, symposium or public discussion, was sought, with or without a joint statement. Joint statements were particularly important, not only to establish the positions of each side but, primarily, to take the public discourse and, hopefully, the officials of each side one or more steps forward.

For example, an early joint statement spoke of "self-determination" and "security" for both peoples and the necessity of exchanges between their "genuine representatives," a reference to the PLO on the Palestinian side. For the Israelis, it was too early to refer openly to Palestinian statehood, though this was understood by the term "self-determination." Security was included to accommodate the Israeli side; speaking with the PLO, to accommodate the Palestinian. Both sides were limited in these statements by what they thought their public and leadership might be led to accept or tolerate. For this reason, it was not always possible to agree on a statement or, in the same vein, a public action (which would necessitate agreed-upon slogans). Palestinians were particularly keen to have Israelis come out in favor of a state and talks with the PLO, as well as to condemn certain acts of the Israeli government. The Israelis were particularly keen to have the Palestinians come out in favor of recognition of Israel's right to exist (that a Palestinian state was not sought *instead of* Israel but next to it), as well as condemnation of terrorism. There were many other specific issues (refugees, Jerusalem) for which the two sides sought declared solutions or, at the very least, discussion of various solutions. Both sides believed that, by bringing issues into the public discourse, both the public and the leadership might be sensitized toward acceptance tomorrow of what may have been unthinkable yesterday. For this reason, publicity of the dialogue and joint actions became increasingly important and sought by both Israeli and Palestinian participants.

Perhaps the most dramatic and successful of these was Hands Around Jerusalem, an event at the end of 1989 in which 30,000 Israelis and Palestinians formed a human chain around the city walls of Jerusalem. Organized jointly by Peace Now and the local PLO-affiliated leadership, it brought together people from towns and villages and of all ages and backgrounds— from women in traditional dress and clergymen to students in jeans and politicians—in a call to make 1990 the year of peace.[10]

REACHING THE OSLO ACCORDS

The sought-after sensitization of the publics did eventually occur, and progress was made on both sides, leading to the Oslo Agreement of Principles signed on the White House lawn in Washington, D.C., September 13, 1993, which opened the official peace process between the PLO and the government of Israel. This is not to say that Oslo was the direct result of the dialogue or even that the sensitization that occurred was due solely to the dialogue. The "peace camp" on both sides was active in many ways designing and bringing about these changes. The dialogue, however, served as one of the vehicles, for it brought people together in a pseudo-negotiating situation, at a time when the official leaderships were unable or unwilling to meet. Israel had refused to speak with the PLO (there was even a law banning any contact), so the only contact was through these informal—often illegal—meetings.[11] It was not that the official positions were worked out in the dialogue. Rather, participants in the dialogue, who tended to be closely connected with, if not actually part of, the leadership circle on each side, learned in the process of the dialogue the various substantive matters, nuances, sensitive points and problems that were to be central to the official negotiations once they took place. The very language, phrases and formulae they used evolved in response to each other, and these, in turn, found their way into the official pronouncements once official contact did occur.

Moreover, the publics, too, were more accustomed to the contacts, or at least the idea of contact, as well as to the language and substantive aspects learned through the dialogue. Employing the newly acquired understanding, and also the statements often hammered out in the dialogue, the participants could and did work in their own communities—on the Israeli side through demonstrations and the like and on the Palestinian side, where such activities were forbidden, through other means of communication.

This was possible because, on both sides, civil society was highly developed. On the Palestinian side, the absence of independence and, therefore, of governmental organs had meant the creation of numerous organizations, unions and groups—that is, a highly developed, though in some cases underground, civil society reinforced and extended by the Intifada. Israel, as a Western-style democracy, had also developed a variegated, articulate civil society whereby parliamentary and governmental actions were amply supplemented by nonofficial bodies.

In the situation of years of hostility, violence and isolation, as well as political paralysis due to refusal at the official level to take the steps necessary toward the beginning of negotiations, the role of dialogue could be summed up as path-breaking, educating the two sides, making the contact and providing a bridge between the two peoples, thereby both creating pressure on, and eventually assisting, the official leaderships. Once the Oslo accords were signed and the official negotiations had begun, the nature and purpose of the dialogue changed somewhat.

AFTER THE OSLO ACCORDS

Almost immediately after the signing of these accords, Palestinians primarily from Fatah and Israelis primarily from Peace Now launched an effort to greatly broaden the dialogue to reach significantly more people at the grassroots level. Now that it was clear that the two peoples were on the road to coexistence, the need to gain popular support for peace and break down hostility became particularly acute.

A new element added at this time was the participation of Palestinian peace groups that formed spontaneously in small towns and villages and contacted Peace Now and other Israelis for the purpose of dialogue. A second new feature was the leadership on the Palestinian side of men who spoke in Hebrew—because they had spent years in Israeli prisons, released now as a result of the peace process. In some cases, deportees permitted now to return also became champions of dialogue. Both of these phenomena were amazing (at least in the eyes of the Israelis). The ex-prisoners, some of whom had spent 15–20 years in Israeli prison, had not only learned the language of the Israelis, they had also studied Israelis' history, society and culture and had come to know them through both television and exposure to Israeli citizens from all walks of life who, as part of the reserve duty required for almost all Jewish male adults, had served as guards in these prisons. In prison, many of these Palestinians had become "peaceniks," adding a certain legitimacy (in the eyes of Palestinians) to the dialogues they joined or initiated.

YOUTH DIALOGUE

A third new element in the post-Oslo period was the expansion of the dialogue to young people and children. Both sides, but in particular the Palestinians, believed that the place to begin now was to change the stereotypes that were being inculcated in children and young people. Peace Now on the Israeli side and numerous peace groups and organizations on the Palestinian side began a dialogue between young people (age 12 to 18, for the most part) that grew to include thousands of Israeli and Palestinian youngsters from all over Israel and the West Bank and Gaza.

The Israeli youngsters came from the Peace Now youth movement (which itself grew in an extraordinary fashion after the Oslo accords) and tended to be the children of middle-class, often politically aware, families. There were many, though, whose parents were right-wing—a few youngsters even came from Jewish settlements in the occupied territories. As the dialogue expanded, the sociological makeup of the participants became somewhat more representative of Israeli society as a whole.

The Palestinian youngsters tended to come from families that fully supported the peace process, both in the cities and increasingly in smaller towns and villages. They were often chosen by their teachers, and, while they, too, tended to be of middle-class, highly educated backgrounds, their numbers also increasingly contained a more representative sample of Palestinian society, including a handful of religious youngsters.

The initial stages of the youth dialogue were not easy. The Palestinians were more often than not the very youths who had been throwing stones and rocks at Israeli soldiers during the Intifada; the Israelis, both girls and

boys, were about to go into the army and might, as it was clear to all concerned, be called upon to arrest or otherwise constrain these Palestinian
youths. The Palestinian youngsters were, on the whole, far more politically
aware and involved than the Israelis; Israeli youngsters often lacked the political sophistication and articulation of the Palestinians. Both sides were
more straightforward than their adult counterparts, speaking their minds directly, often with no holds barred, as youngsters are prone to do: "Why do
you throw stones and Molotov cocktails?" "Why do you beat us up and close
our schools?" "Because you commit terrorism." "Because you rule over us."

Given the language barrier and the ages of the participants, the dialogue
often began with or included joint *activities*—communication through art,
drama, sports and games. For example, couples, Palestinian with Israeli, had
to place plaster of paris around their mutual handshake; in the ten-minute
wait until the material hardened, they could hardly refrain from relating to
each other, talking to each other. Or they engaged in a football game in
which the facilitator kept changing the rules every three minutes. There were
cultural differences and problems, particularly with regard to the freedom allotted girls and the attitude of boys to girls, which differed significantly in
the two cultures. Nonetheless, sustained dialogue was established, hampered
only by travel restrictions placed upon the Palestinians (periodic Israeli-im-
posed closures on the occupied territories or the near-constant closure of
Jerusalem to Palestinians living outside the city). Both sides increasingly related to each other with greater respect and a greater sense of cooperation
rather than suspicion. Friendships developed; the young people visited each
others' homes and spoke on the telephone. Their attitudes of tolerance and
openness surpassed those of their elders, and the numbers of eager participants expanded beyond the means or facilities to accommodate them.

THIRD PARTIES

In looking at the whole process of dialogue, it is difficult to determine the
importance of the role of third parties. Clearly, third parties were not needed
in the post-Oslo period—close contacts had already been established, and,
for the most part, people at all levels of society were open to some degree of
contact. In the earlier, perhaps more critical stage, third parties were most
useful, though not essential. Closed, private dialogues were generally
arranged without the benefit of third parties, although those involving leading political figures (members of the Israeli Knesset, for example) did tend
to need the assistance of a third party. Both private and public meetings that
included PLO officials had to be conducted abroad, necessitating a third

party. On the whole, though not always, such meetings were even initiated by third parties. This was the case with the most outstanding joint activity, the Hands Around Jerusalem, which evolved in response to plans by European peace groups to conduct a march in the area.

The sustained dialogues held locally, however, including those that began with the use of a third party, invariably took place without the benefit of a third party. This was probably a measure of the commitment of the participants, for those willing to engage in sustained dialogue no longer needed the assistance of a third party. And, indeed, when third parties became involved in these ongoing dialogues, they tended to be ignored, for the participants already knew each other and had already progressed to an advanced level of dialogue, often feeling that they had more in common with each other (Israelis and Palestinians) than with their counterparts abroad. At this stage, the third party was no longer needed to break the ice or facilitate discussion.

This is not to belittle the role of third parties; many of the dialogues may never have taken place or would have taken place far later had it not been for third parties. Even the third party–initiated dialogues that did not develop into sustained dialogues were useful, often groundbreaking and enlightening. They played their part in educating and sensitizing the two sides so that sustained dialogue could eventually take place.

WOMEN'S DIALOGUE

The women's dialogue was typical of this, though it varied from the general dialogue in certain ways. The early attempt at dialogue, begun at the Nairobi conference, failed to develop into a sustained dialogue for a number of reasons. The Israeli women believed that the primary basis for their dialogue would be feminism—that is, their shared interest in women's rights. However, it was made clear to them by their Palestinian counterparts that the latter were interested only in their national rights; women's rights were to await independence. While it might have been possible to continue despite this difference (and some personal contacts did continue), the Palestinian women apparently felt too vulnerable in their own society to engage in the expanded, semipublic dialogue sought by the Israeli women at the time.

Both positions changed with the Intifada. When, in 1989, a third party brought the women together in Brussels (a public meeting that included Israeli members of parliament and PLO officials), other general dialogues had already begun. In 1988, the Palestine National Council (PNC) had officially accepted Israel's right to exist and the idea of the political path to a two-state solution. In addition, the local Palestinian leadership had decided to take its case to the Israeli public. The PLO decisions had, in turn, legitimized contact with the PLO for those more in the center of the Israeli political spectrum (for example, Labor members of Knesset). Moreover, as noted above, there was a significant expansion of political activity on the part of Israeli women during the Intifada, possibly because of a certain identification with the civilian nature of the uprising and the role women were playing in the conduct of the uprising. In the course of the Intifada, with the realistic approach of statehood, Palestinian women decided that women's rights must take their place alongside national rights. Thus, legitimized by decisions of the Palestinian leadership and facilitated by the mutual interest in women's struggle against oppression, a broad, sustained and often public women's dialogue was begun.

On the Israeli side, an organization called the Women's Network for the Promotion of Peace (Reshet) was established, working with the major Palestinian women's organizations plus individual Independents. Together, women from the two communities organized visits to the West Bank for Israeli women to meet Palestinian women; they brought Palestinian women into Israel for parlor meetings and public meetings with Israeli women. Large numbers of women at the grass-roots level were reached in this way on both sides. As with the mixed dialogues, public meetings and demonstrations were held, accompanied by a joint political statement establishing the points of basic agreement. A high point in these activities was a joint demonstration at the former border between East and West Jerusalem in March 1989, at which leading women public figures signed a joint declaration calling for Israel-PLO negotiations. A second, broader activity was a mass women's march through West and East Jerusalem one day before—and in anticipation of—the Hands Around Jerusalem at the end of 1989.

Following a second women's meeting in Brussels in 1992, it was decided to institutionalize the dialogue, and, shortly after the Oslo accords, the Jerusalem Link was created, consisting of two independent women's centers, one in East Jerusalem and one in West Jerusalem, led by a joint steering committee. The purpose of the Jerusalem Link was to continue the dialogue while working both together and in each community for the promotion of peace and women's rights. Activities included joint leadership-training workshops, student dialogues, joint activities and dialogue among high-school-age girls (including a joint stay in a conflict-resolution program at an American camp every summer), symposia on such topics as religion and family law, lectures, demonstrations, neighborhood meetings and political statements. In many ways, the Jerusalem Link was seen by its participants as a model for Israeli-Palestinian coexistence: two organizations, separate but linked, identical but independent. Indeed, the Link was presented at the Fifth U.N. Women's Conference, in Beijing, China, in 1995 by leading Palestinian and Israeli women (PLO officials and Israeli members of Knesset) as a model for bridging the abyss created by protracted conflicts.

The dialogue of women originally was meant to activate a part of both societies that had been relatively silent over the years but no less a victim of the continued strife in the area. By meeting exclusively as women, the intention was not only to emphasize the special nature of the dialogue as a "political gimmick," but also to give women a voice. In mixed groups, those few women who participated tended to let the men do all of the talking; in women's groups, such traditional inhibitions (no less apparent on the Israeli side than the Palestinian) were eliminated.

A major difference in the women's dialogue was the greater presence of emotion. Unlike the men, the women did not open with a history of the conflict and injustices but, rather, with personal histories and often moving accounts of personal experiences. Indeed, in some cases the first round of introductions in such a dialogue evoked tears and a great deal of shared emotions. This provided the immediate advantage of breaking down barriers. Women's dialogue also had an advantage in that women could start from a basis of mutual understanding at least of injustices they experienced as women, in any society; nor did they have the obstacle the men had to face in seeing the other automatically and first as a soldier or a terrorist. In fact, women's dialogues often took a jump forward during the breaks and meals when socializing occurred, and this socializing was frequently continued beyond or outside the dialogue.

On a less positive side, women, socialized to be less confrontational, tended to avoid the difficult issues lest they disrupt the dialogue. This became most apparent during very critical periods, among them the period of the 1991 Gulf War and the period of the severe closure following the Hamas terrorist bombings of February–March 1996. In both cases, the dialogue broke down, meetings were canceled and contact, particularly of a public nature, avoided. Just when communication for greater understanding and public reaffirmation of the desire for peace were most important, both sides hesitated because of the negative effect joint moves might have on the public at such a time. Personal contacts were continued, and there were even efforts to draft joint statements, but resumption of dialogue and cooperation were long in coming.

A similar situation existed in the mixed dialogues as well, but there appeared, generally, to be an additional problem for the women. On the Palestinian side, women seemed to feel more vulnerable and, therefore, in need of answering to or staying close to the positions of their leadership—in a word, less free than the men. This was true to a far lesser degree on the Israeli women's side. In both cases, however, women were aware of the fact that they had very limited influence in their respective leadership circles and far less ability than the men to have an impact on public opinion through the media or official channels. On the other hand, they did have very good access and, in some ways, more opportunities to penetrate at the grass-roots level, through women's organizations on both sides.

CONCLUSION AND EPILOGUE

It is difficult to measure the effects of dialogue—general or specialized—on the overall peace process. The impact on the leadership and the public was undoubtedly significant and possibly crucial, both in bringing the two sides to the negotiating table and eliciting support for a solution. The depth of the emotional road journeyed together was demonstrated the day of the signing of the Oslo accords in 1993. Peace Now and Palestinian leaders viewed the White House ceremony together on a giant screen at the American Colony Hotel in East Jerusalem. The tears, as well as the champagne, that flowed in response to the historic Rabin-Arafat handshake were a testimony to the mutual longing for an end to the years of bloodshed between our two peoples. Capped three years later by the Israeli withdrawal from West Bank cities, followed by the Palestinian elections, and then the removal of the rejection of a Palestinian state from the ruling Labor Party's platform and the abrogation by the PNC of its covenant's references to the destruction of Israel, the process appeared to be reaching fruition.

It was our belief that peace was within our reach. And, at such a stage, we believed that dialogue would be a necessary prerequisite for the coexistence critical for the two societies living so closely side by side. We understood that one does not undo generations of hatred, fear and violence easily. The official agreements reached by governments and leaders were not the result of trust. Trust could be created only by people seeking to implement and sustain these agreements. And trust can come only through understanding and communication. Thus, we believed, the next stage, that of free and equal coexistence, would rely heavily upon dialogue, no less—indeed, probably more—than along the long road to peace.

Unfortunately, the Israeli elections of May 29, 1996, produced an unexpected and most deleterious result. A right-wing government came to power in Israel, winning by only a narrow margin, promising, nonetheless, continuation of the peace process. This promise appears to have been in vain, offering only lip service to the struggle for peace so clearly desired by both populations. As a result, instead of preparing our two peoples for the end of conflict and the beginning of coexistence, we now find that we must labor to revive the peace process altogether. The political-action component of the dialogue must be resumed and strengthened. Minimally, the dialogue must serve to maintain channels open between the two peoples, to give voice to those who continue to believe that peace is possible despite the new hardships and tragic setback experienced.

Yet, because of the progress made in the past, our efforts are based on far more trust and understanding, as well as unity of purpose and determination. The historic breakthrough of the past has created a mass of people, particularly among the young, who have come to know each other through dialogue, and this may be the strongest bulwark against despair. This also may provide the link necessary to maintain the conviction that, ultimately, Israelis and Palestinians can reach free and equal coexistence in two states, side by side, at peace with each other.

Chapter Ten

Evaluating Sustained Dialogue

EVALUATION AS THE CITIZENS' INSTRUMENT

Anyone engaged in sustained dialogue will ask at some point: "Why am I doing this? What am I accomplishing?" Funders will ask: "What are we getting for our money? What is the impact of this project?" Participants will ask: "Why am I taking risks for this?" A moderator of conscience will ask: "Am I doing harm?"

Periodically taking stock and judging achievement are essential to this work. The question is how to evaluate it in ways consistent with the method of work. The experience of sustained dialogue opens the door to a different way of thinking about evaluation—as the citizens' instrument for making midcourse corrections in an ongoing political process. The purpose of this chapter is not to evaluate but to suggest a different way of thinking about evaluation. It draws its examples from the Inter-Tajik Dialogue, which was discussed in detail in Chapter Seven.

EVALUATION AS PART OF AN OPEN-ENDED POLITICAL PROCESS

Sustained dialogue itself—like the peace process of which it is a part—is an open-ended political process. One cannot know at the beginning exactly what the dialogue will produce; the agenda, goals and specific steps must come out of the interaction of the participants. Each time the group takes a concrete step forward, new goals will emerge; achievements may become possible that were not possible before. This progression of goals and achievements can be judged only as the dialogue unfolds. So evaluation becomes part of the process.

To say that dialogue is an open-ended process is *not* to say that it is "talk without purpose or destination," as the word connotes in some languages. The process is carefully defined stage by stage; the purpose is to learn how to change relationships that cause conflict; the destination is a plan of action for changing relationships in the larger body politic. It *is* to say that, from within a conflict, a group can become a participant in the political process of continuous interaction and change among elements of the body politic, which is the essence of the peace process.

If sustained dialogue is an open-ended political process, then evaluation can be considered part of that process—identifying an advancing sequence of goals, judging their achievement and adjusting course accordingly. Any evaluation must focus on *how* change happens, not just on whether it takes place. Only then can change experienced within a group be replicated outside the group or in a changed situation. Continuous judgment by the group is essential to enhancing the quality and reach of its work.

In evaluating such a political process in a deep-rooted human conflict in often unformed bodies politic, one must be realistic about what is knowable and what is unknowable. Ideal conditions for creating a social-science experiment do not exist. A deep-rooted human conflict in a complex body politic exhibits so many variables that mathematical measurement will fall short of explaining it. Human judgment may be more useful and insightful in the political context; no judgment is more authentic than that of those whose lives and futures depend on the peace process.

One must also be realistic about the time needed to change conflictual relationships. If it is necessary to evaluate a project within a short period, one must describe interim goals and achievements realistic in that period. Even in a longer period, it is essential to be honest about what any single instrument or project can accomplish in relation to the whole conflict and the whole body politic. Any such statement is likely to be inexact. In some cases, all one group can do is to demonstrate that an approach works.

Presenting the peace process as the overall framework for peacemaking and peace building permits realistic statements of how projects address some specific elements of a conflict and not others and how they contribute to moving it toward peace. The framework can provide benchmarks for pinpointing where a project is achieving results and change benchmarks as it evolves.

In contrast to the perspective from which this book is written, common methods of social-science evaluation are rooted in the traditional thinking described in Chapters One through Four. They continue to focus on institutions and on technically definable issues rather than on whole human beings and relationships; on states and their governments rather than on whole bodies politic; and on citizens as statistics in opinion polls rather than as political actors. Traditional methods often assume that the results of political acts by human beings are objectively measurable and that one can know precise cause and effect in a complex political situation. They tend to dismiss complexity and ambiguity when these do not fit the social-science research design.

Many such evaluators want participants to respond to interviews or answer questionnaires at a time when those participants may have risked their lives to talk to the enemy and fear that any stranger could send them to jail or worse. Many of the participants have never seen a questionnaire; the only pollsters they have met represented a central authority they distrust. The same might also be true of citizens in poor neighborhoods of many cities in the world.

The larger problem is that social and political capacity, relationships, political processes and interlocking networks in civil society do not respond to measurement in social-science research designs. It is extremely difficult, if not impossible, to measure change over a long period in a whole human being acting in a whole, complex body politic. It is even more difficult when one must take into account continuous change or determine who in the complex interaction of multiple actors "caused" an outcome.

Just as this book argues for larger ways of thinking about conflict, politics and relationships among groups and countries, so it argues for a larger context for judging the work of sustained dialogue. Judging progress—just as judging effective action—requires a conceptual framework large enough to analyze and address conflict and peace building in the context of whole bodies politic. In judging the achievements of the Inter-Tajik Dialogue, for instance, there are two frameworks. *The multi-level peace process,* described in Chapter One, defines the larger context in the country within which efforts to end violence and to develop a peaceful society and a more cohesive country are pursued. *The five-stage process of sustained dialogue,* described in Chapter Six, provides the carefully defined context within which a dialogue works and participants develop their capacities.

CRITERIA: WHAT IS VALUED?

Evaluation must begin with a clear statement of what is valued and what questions are to be asked. In studying the ongoing Inter-Tajik Dialogue two different kinds of questions could be asked. Someone from the traditional school, who looks at peace in terms of governments and institutions, would likely ask what the Dialogue has contributed to reaching a peace agreement, while someone who looks at peace as a process would likely ask what the Dialogue has taught participants about designing a long-term peace process for Tajikistan and incorporating it into the Tajikistani experience.

In this chapter I take the second approach. I write from a proposition born of more than 30 years of experience and reflection in peacemaking: Making peace is a continuous process, a way of life; peace is never *made* but is always in the making. In that context, an evaluator's preoccupation with measuring concrete results—for instance, producing a peace accord—risks diverting attention from a more fundamental effort to build an expanding capacity to design, generate and sustain a peace process. In a peace process, one agreement—milestone though it may be—is just one step and always a new starting point on the way toward deepening peace.

If the focus is on the peace process and not just on a peace agreement, the time horizon is much longer. Embedding a peace process in the life of any people requires perseverance. Learning and relearning in a continuous process is not a finite or measurable task.

A strategy of people within a conflict generating the capacity to change their own conflictual relationships through a multilevel peace process stands in sharp contrast with that of outsiders trying to train negotiators, to teach specific skills or to mediate a peace agreement. This objective of citizens learning the process of moving toward peace contrasts sharply to one of outsiders trying to "make peace." A process of evaluation must judge progress toward what participants value—in this case, the capacity to design a peace process and political steps for sustaining it.

The criteria for judging progress in building such a capacity in Tajikistan lie in these questions: To what extent have Dialogue participants, together, changed their relationships to become a microcosm of a united Tajikistan and developed the capacity to design a process of national reconciliation for the larger body politic? To what extent have they developed the capacity, together or individually, to put their design into practice or into the hands of those who could implement it? The more important underlying question may not be what they have done but what they have learned to do in designing a continuing process to sustain progress toward a peaceful society that they can pass on to others.

These questions do not hold the Dialogue group responsible for making peace; citizens outside government do not have authority to negotiate or enforce. But they do have the capacity and the authority to decide what kind of country they would like to build and to consider how citizens could contribute to that work.

Building that capacity is a continuous process of learning from doing. The vehicle for this learning in the Inter-Tajik Dialogue is sustained dialogue—a process of human interaction in which participants first learn how their own relationships change as they speak and listen carefully to each other. Their next task is to project what they learn into the larger political arena to help change the relationships that fuel conflict there.

Sustained dialogue contrasts sharply to conventional conflict-resolution training. An outside trainer or moderator cannot tell parties to a conflict how to change their relationships. Those relationships are too deeply rooted; the outsider can only glimpse their surface. An outside moderator can provide a safe space and can model how to think about some problems in the course of dialogue. He or she can nourish participants' capacity to change by providing them an opportunity to probe the relationships underlying the conflict and to design realistic steps for dealing with a succession of current problems that they define in their changing lives. But even with effective and sensitive help from outside, participants learn only from experience the capacity to change their relationships; there is no mechanistic technique that can be handed to them.

For the participants, continuous evaluation is their instrument for making repeated midcourse corrections as they experiment and learn and as the situation changes. That capacity is essential to a political actor.

MAKING JUDGMENTS ABOUT THE INTER-TAJIK DIALOGUE

Because of the particular strategy pursued by the organizers of the Inter-Tajik Dialogue recounted in Chapter Seven—placing heavy responsibility for analysis, strategy and tactics on a Dialogue group from within Tajikistan—I suggest in this chapter that evaluation take place on two levels: The first is examining the soundness of the concept, strategy and methodology of the project's designers. Are the analytical, strategic and tactical frameworks solidly based? The second is judging the Dialogue itself—especially the method of work and the consequences of the steps designed by the Tajik group—in a way that is realistic given the complexity of the situation.

Level One: The Organizers' Analytical, Strategic and Tactical Frameworks

When, in December 1992, the Dartmouth Conference Regional Conflicts Task Force decided to try to start the Inter-Tajik Dialogue, the joint article by the co-chairs of the task force conceptualizing the process of sustained dialogue was about to be published, so the rationale and the approach had been fully agreed upon by the management team.[1] Since then, I have introduced the peace process as an overall conceptual framework for planning and evaluating sustained dialogue. That framework is the larger context within which sustained dialogue is one possible vehicle for progress toward peace. It includes analytical, strategic and tactical frameworks.

That framework of a political process of continuous multilevel interaction in which change takes place shifts the focus to how—not whether—change happens. Participants know they have changed; others can see the change. The challenge is to know how the change came about so that process of change can be replicated in the larger body politic. Evaluation, in this case, is an analysis of the process of change.

Analytical Framework

Relationships, Causes and Dynamics.   Working from long experience with the elements of a peace process and of a sustained dialogue, the initiators of the Inter-Tajik Dialogue determined that their task was to generate analysis from within the conflict itself, not to impose their own analytical framework on the conflict. Therefore, they worked to identify individuals who could reflect most of the main views and relationships in the conflict and provide insight into the conflict from firsthand experience to develop their own analytical framework from that experience.

The organizers started from these hypotheses:

- The most effective way to change deep-rooted conflictual relationships is from within. This can be done by creating in one dialogue a microcosm of the groups in conflict.
- Such a group will produce its own analytical, strategic and tactical frameworks, implicitly if not explicitly. Participants will set their own unfolding series of goals as the dialogue progresses and identify key actors in a potential peace process.
- Outsiders can help them get started, provide a safe public space for their meetings, offer guidance and help support their actions. Outsiders cannot know how to change their relationships.
- Whereas officials may be reluctant to negotiate, citizens outside government participate in dialogue any time they feel the need to do so.
- Ending a civil war and building a civil society, even in a relatively small country, will not be an ordered process. A group of citizens may have only limited influence. Cause and effect are not always fully knowable.

From these analytical propositions, the organizers hypothesized that establishing a sustained dialogue in Tajikistan could:

- provide in a first full-scale test the experience necessary for refining and judging the five-stage process;
- demonstrate for transfer to other situations the effectiveness of a dialogue as an agent for changing conflictual relationships and building peace;
- contribute to a peace process in Tajikistan, especially by creating a lasting group within the country whose members could talk, think and work together even in tense times;
- enlarge the field of conflict prevention and resolution by adding an approach to deep-rooted human conflicts not ready for formal mediation and negotiation and by focusing on peace building.

This analysis was captured at the beginning of the Dialogue in these summary words written by the U.S. organizers in 1993 to a potential funder:

> The task is to create a relationship [among] such groups in conflict that will permit them to recognize a common destiny together and the need to find common ground on which to work out ways of living together to deal with problems that affect them all. Often the best approach in a dialogue is to get at the overall relationship by focusing on specific problems. . . .
>
> This is often work that needs to be done before negotiation is ever possible. Such a process cannot be mediated in a mechanical way by outsiders because it has to evolve from within the groups to be legitimate. A third party may play a role in bringing a group together and getting them started, but in order for the process to survive the vagaries of ethnic conflict, it has to take root in the political context within which it operates.
>
> The long-term aim of such a process is to leave in place an institution of sorts—a way of talking and thinking together and a space for meeting so that in the future if the conflict re-emerges, as many ethnic conflicts do, the communities would have developed the capacities and experience within themselves either to preempt the threatened outbreak or to tackle it in a non-violent way.[2]

Actors in the Peace Process.   In the Tajik case, the organizers chose to focus on citizens at the second or third levels in nongovernmental organizations—not officials and not visible and controversial but close enough to the top to be heard and to speak authoritatively. These are the deputy chairmen of parties, organizations or movements or the vice chancellors and senior professors in the universities. When, after 13 months, official negotiations began and three Dialogue participants became delegates, the unanticipated opportunity presented itself to study through their experience in both groups the interaction between the official and the public processes.

Societal Context.   Decades under the Soviet system had—except perhaps at the village level—left citizens with little experience in thinking of themselves as political actors in building their new country. Most of the characteristics of civil society, described in Chapter Three, seemed lacking. Some exceptions existed, including a democratic movement that began during the Soviet opening up in the late 1980s and some aspiration to a free press. Part of our initial grant proposal quoted above was that the Charles F. Kettering Foundation would provide fellowships and workshops for individuals who wanted to work in organizations for citizenship education. Acknowledging that even thinking in terms of building civil society may be an objective with only a remote chance of success, a realistic attempt is at least possible.

The Strategic Framework

For reasons laid out earlier in this book and in the analysis above, the strategy was to create a dialogue involving parties within the Tajikistani conflict with the capacity to analyze the relationships, causes and dynamics of the conflict in great depth. We hoped it could show in microcosm how a unified country working together might function.

For the organizers, the Inter-Tajik Dialogue began against the background of a decade's experience with sustained dialogue at the heart of the Soviet-U.S.—later the Russian-U.S.—relationship. This experience showed that a dialogue group could act as a continuing "mind at work" at the heart of a relationship, absorbing developments and offering perspectives and approaches for dealing with them.

What does it mean to create a dialogue group as a "mind at work" in such a situation? One answer is to contrast that characterization to a group formed to accomplish a particular task and then to disband. The kind of group the organizers envisioned for Tajikistan was one in which the parties involved would develop the ability to work together as a group and then stay together to absorb, process and respond together to developments as they occurred in the country.

The organizers hoped that the Dialogue could also spin off institutions and ways of working that would become embedded in the life of the country. This idea is key to the strategy—to create the capacity, however small, in parties within the conflict to change its course by enabling participants to learn how to change fundamental relationships and to build new associations and networks that might, over time, establish the sinews of cohesion.

If the Inter-Tajik Dialogue could be consolidated, it had the potential of becoming one of the lasting institutions that the project's initiators envisioned at the core of Tajikistan's movement toward peace and independent identity. Tajikistan was, to be sure, a very different setting from the Cold War superpower context of the Soviet-U.S. dialogue—an intrastate rather than an interstate conflict in a country struggling to define its identity and build the foundations of a state that had never before existed independently within present boundaries. The ultimate aim was to set up a clearly public group that could relate both to official processes and to civil-society development.

For purposes of evaluation, this strategy draws a vague line between the organizers' efforts to create and tutor the group and the group's own struggle to gain confidence to think and work on its own. That is why assessing the project on two levels seems desirable.

The Tactical Framework

The elements of sustained dialogue—the form of dialogue chosen for this project—are rooted in more than two decades of experience in a variety of settings and workshops conducted by a half-dozen professionals and should not require new proof. But this was the first time the five-stage process as such had been tested. Its foundations, conceptualization and construction rest on the following assumptions from earlier cumulative experience:

- Experience mainly in Soviet-U.S., Israeli-Palestinian and Indo-Pakistani dialogues has demonstrated that it is possible to form a dialogue group of about a dozen people who reflect the mainstream perceptions and interests of groups in conflict. Normally, extremists will not join and would probably be disruptive if they did. So the group is a selected sample of those willing to consider engaging in a joint effort to solve common problems.
- It is possible to bring the same group together at regular intervals over extended periods of time. Many early workshops were one- or two-time events because it was necessary to establish simply that such meetings among adversaries could take place and could generate serious dialogue. Extensive experience has shown that continuity through many meetings is possible and productive.
- Experience has further shown that the talk in such a series of dialogues moves naturally through a sequence of stages, such as the five-stage

process described in this book. The process is a conceptualization of that experience, not a theoretical construct. Throughout this process, changed patterns of communication and interaction can be observed. Participants do not change identity. They do not necessarily change their own points of view; developments outside the dialogue, such as the performance of a government or a deteriorating economic or security situation, are more likely to cause such changes. But participants do learn respect for those with different views and demonstrate a growing capacity to work with them. They also show the capacity to take a range of interests beyond their own into account in designing solutions.

All of these points seem to be established. They do not need to be proved again by outside evaluators unfamiliar with the process. Although the elements of sustained dialogue presented in Chapter Six seem well established, experience in the Inter-Tajik Dialogue—the first full test of the whole process—leads to judgments such as these:

- A dialogue *can* become a creative "mind at work" at the center of a conflict. The highly substantive memoranda produced by the group and the associations created by individual participants demonstrate that.[3]
- The five-stage process is a valuable guide to diagnosing a group's progress and helping moderators formulate their own agendas—always subject to change by the dialogue group. At the same time, experience in the Inter-Tajik Dialogue demonstrates how a well-established group can return in each meeting to a quick mapping of the latest situation, focus on a problem, probe it in depth and produce a written analysis and recommendations—all within a three-day meeting.
- Cultures impose limits on how explicit a group can be in talking about relationships themselves. That is just as true of black-white dialogue in the United States as of intergroup dialogue in Central Asia. But moderators can distill what they hear as key characteristics of the relationships in conflict and check them with participants as a way of putting them on the table.
- Introducing the dimension of building civil society into the overall task of resolving conflict tangibly changes the character of a dialogue. Adding thought about the kind of society or relationships participants envision enlarges their options in making peace. For instance, the rec-

ommendation to establish a Consultative Forum for the Peoples of Tajikistan would probably not have emerged from a group concentrating only on ending violence.

- A most difficult challenge in Tajikistan—exacerbated by the insecurity of life and the actions of a government not fully credible on human or civil rights—has been for participants to act together or individually in political ways outside the Dialogue. That is the primary challenge as the Dialogue proceeds.

In sum, 23 meetings over more than five years (as of this writing in late 1998) and the work accomplished on the basis of participants' evolving analysis demonstrate that the choice of participants, the strategy of relying on their judgments and the tactical framework of the five-stage process are viable.

Level Two: The Inter-Tajik Dialogue's Contribution to the Peace Process

Having analyzed the purposes of the initiators of the Inter-Tajik Dialogue, the evaluators' task at the second level is to assess the work of the Dialogue itself. The five-stage process provides one context for describing the evolution of a group's capacity to talk, think and work together. Perhaps even more important, participants develop their own framework—at least implicitly—as they produce their own analysis, set their own strategy, design an advancing sequence of goals and set in motion steps in that direction. The peace process described in Chapter One also provides a framework for assessment here, perhaps even more significantly than at the first level.

The Analytical Framework

Relationships and Causes. Stage Two of the five-stage process—the first stage after participants in a dialogue sit down together—allows participants to get out on the table their views of the causes of the conflict and the relationships underlying them. The Inter-Tajik Dialogue began with a moderator's question: "What do you see as the causes of the conflict?" In the second meeting, a second question was added: "What are the interests of the group(s) with which you identify?" The group's responses showed participants' capacity for in-depth analysis.

Participants' analysis began with acknowledgment that there is little sense of Tajikistani national identity. They described relationships in Tajikistan along a number of fault lines. The most obvious are the tensions between clan-based regional power centers and the shifting alliances between regions.

Second is the ideological and human tension between those who were bred in the Soviet system and are most comfortable with some form of tight central control and those with inclinations toward a more "democratic" system. A third line of tension exists among nationalities, especially the Tajik majority and the quarter of the population that is Uzbek and, thus, often seen as pawns of the leader of Uzbekistan. Finally, the economic crisis in Tajikistan creates tensions among stakeholders themselves and between citizens suffering hardship and those judged responsible.

With these fault lines and the lack of a Tajikistani identity at the core of their analysis, participants at first blamed the civil war on their lack of preparation for independence. The power struggle followed the sudden disappearance of an understood center of power—the Soviet system. Later, their analysis deepened. On two occasions (Dialogues 8 in June 1994 and 16 in May 1996), they explicitly named the core cause of continuing fragmentation and insecurity as "the absence of an understanding on sharing power among the regions, the political movements and the nationalities in Tajikistan. . . ."

Underlying that continuing fragmentation and the lack of agreement on sharing power are deep suspicions and lack of functional relationships that could bridge those gulfs. That analysis was clear in the Dialogue group's proposals in Dialogues 12 and 13 (June and September 1995) to create a Consultative Forum of the Peoples of Tajikistan. The purpose of the forum was to provide space for people from across these dividing lines to come together to help strengthen a process of national reconciliation. In May 1996, the Dialogue group wrote a memorandum restating its analysis that the lack of agreement on power sharing threatened the security, the integrity and the sovereignty of the state. Participants underscored their analysis by urging that both the government and the two official negotiating teams broaden public participation.

Dynamics of the Conflict.   The Dialogue group has worked with sensitivity to the dynamics of the conflict and to the balance and composition of forces, but it has not been as constrained by them as the official negotiators are. The Dialogue began in March 1993 while the civil war was still going on and there was no apparent possibility of official negotiation. As described in Chapter Seven, the Dialogue played a role in the move from stalemate to negotiation. Official negotiations began in April 1994, but violence continued, albeit punctuated by a series of imperfect cease-fire agreements. The official negotiations continued, but they were often blocked by an open power struggle between the government and the opposition. As one opposition participant said in Dialogue 16 (May 1996), both negotiating teams realized that neither would get all of what it wanted on the battlefield. That feeling was presumably a significant factor in moving the parties toward a peace accord.

No study of the relationship between the dynamics of a conflict and the possibility of peacemaking is complete if it does not take into account the different capacities of the official and the public peace processes. The Inter-Tajik Dialogue has provided opportunities to study the interaction between the official negotiations and the public dialogue.

First, the fact that the Dialogue began during the civil war demonstrated that a public dialogue can begin even when formal negotiations are still judged by officials to be impossible. The record of the first year provides a close look at the role of the Dialogue in paving the way from stalemate to negotiation, one of the most important functions of sustained dialogue.

Second, as negotiations proceeded, it became possible to distinguish clearly the work of formal negotiations from that of a public dialogue. Between one and three members of the Dialogue group participated in the negotiations, one throughout. The Dialogue group made a careful choice—and communicated it to Tajikistan's foreign minister—that it would not attempt to duplicate the work of the negotiating teams. Instead, it would focus on the process of national reconciliation that would be needed to support decisions from the negotiations. Ideas flowed from the public to the official peace process, but participants in the public peace process made no attempt to negotiate differences.

Third, the official and the public peace processes have provided insight into how the timing of events external to a dialogue affect what a dialogue group can accomplish. This opens the door to understanding what constrains taking actions designed in a dialogue into the larger body politic.

Actors in the Peace Process. When the Dialogue began, participants assumed they had little choice but to focus on government and on beginning an official peace process. Some of the participants had been threatened for their political activity, and it was not realistic for any of them to work openly inside the country. Two participants regularly briefed officials at the top level of the government, and others briefed opposition political authorities in exile.

The Strategic Framework
From the early elements of this analytical base, in Dialogue 3 (August 1993) participants set as a priority goal "starting a negotiation between government

and opposition on creating conditions for the return of the refugees to their homes." That became their midterm strategy until negotiations began.

In Dialogues 8 and 9 (June and September 1994)—after formal negotiations had begun—they restated their focus. They began to speak of creating "a process of national reconciliation" as the longer-term framework for their thinking. That formulation has become a fundamental articulation of their long-term strategy. As it became more possible to work in the public arena, they broadened the range of actors to include both quasi-official citizens' bodies such as the Consultative Forum of the Peoples of Tajikistan and their own work in the universities and in other parts of the civil society. This refinement of strategy gives evidence that participants will judge the progress of their initiatives as well as new opportunities and then reshape strategy in the light of experience.

In Dialogue 16 (May 1996)—the first meeting in Tajikistan—participants were ready to reflect on the state of the official peace process. Their memorandum—one of their most somber statements—stated the need for a more broadly based national understanding on power sharing across the main dividing lines in the country. They set this as a further priority. In Dialogue 17 (October 1996), they defined their call for broadened participation in terms of a "multi-level peace process." As the signing of the final peace agreement approached, in Dialogue 19 (May 1997) participants set a new goal: "identifying and overcoming obstacles to building democracy and civil society in Tajikistan." Participants' repeated reshaping of objectives as the situation unfolded reflected their continuing evaluation of their own progress.

Moderators have repeatedly encouraged participants to discuss how they visualize the Dialogue itself moving forward. In Dialogue 14 (November 1995), one participant proposed creating in Tajikistan a "standing committee of the Dartmouth Conference to begin micro-dialogues." An emerging element in their explicit strategy became working in the civil society in the name of the Dialogue as well as individually. Circumstances in the country made that difficult initially, but by late 1996 that work had begun.

The Tactical Framework

How Have Relationships Changed and Capacities Grown? Any evaluation must begin by taking note that an effective dialogue group has been solidly established. By the end of 1998, a core group of eight or nine people had come to all but four or five of 23 Dialogue meetings.

Barely able to look at each other in the first meeting, participants have demonstrated beyond question their capacity to think, talk and work together—a capacity they learned over time through their interactions. In the words of participants at the fourth-anniversary meeting in Dialogue 18 (February 1997):

- "The Dialogue made me realize the complexity of the situation."
- "My opponents had problems of their own and I saw in them at last not enemies but suffering human beings."
- "The Dialogue has managed to make an objective evaluation of the essence of the conflict in Tajikistan, the reasons of its emergence and ways of its regulation."
- "I personally acquired experience in conducting discussions and learned how to reach a compromise."
- "I am a newcomer to this Dialogue, but I have already noticed that veterans learned to debate in the spirit of mutual respect."
- "Through the exchange of opinions, I also came to the understanding that we should work together to build our common future."

Beyond these words, authentic as they are, the concrete evidence of the group members' capacity to work together is their production of a series of 13 joint memoranda. These have articulated the unfolding elements and strategy of a multilevel peace process for Tajikistan. The Dialogue group has repeatedly defined current problems facing the country and written ways of thinking about those problems and of dealing with them. Participants have both originated approaches and put ideas already "in the air" into a larger strategic context. Their contribution has been to shape, over time, a cumulative philosophy and strategy for a political process of national reconciliation that could bring the fragmented regions of Tajikistan together into an ultimately unified country.

The participants' decision during Dialogue 19 (May 1997) to publish those memoranda in Tajiki, Russian and English following an introduction telling the story of the Dialogue reflects their judgment that the memoranda make a statement of continuing value to the people of Tajikistan. They also hoped their achievement would encourage others to become engaged in the process. The philosophy and strategy that participants have articulated show far greater breadth and originality than those of the prevailing political forces in the country. They reveal a way of working that differs from the confrontation and compromise of negotiation. They reveal a sense of ownership of the peace process by these citizens of different factions working together as a microcosm of what a unified Tajikistan might become.

These comments by the participants and their joint memoranda offer evidence on two levels of the group's capacities. On one level, the words of participants above demonstrate that they are able to articulate the capacities they have developed within the Dialogue. Second, the joint memoranda demonstrate clearly their analytical capacity to assess together how the country is doing—to define its evolving problems, to internalize them and to design strategies and steps for dealing with them across the spectrum of the whole body politic.

The participants are not as explicit as the co-moderators in using the design of the five-stage process of sustained dialogue itself as a framework for evaluating their own work within the group. Although they have, on two occasions, been given the written description of that process, they act out the process without using it explicitly to judge their performance. Before participants can take over the Dialogue or replicate it, they must think more explicitly in terms of the five-stage framework.

The co-moderators would say that participants—having been through the five stages in one form or another numerous times—start each meeting at the end of Stage Two or at the beginning of Stage Three as they assess their country's experience since they last met and define the problem or problems they most need to work on at that meeting. The memoranda they have produced demonstrate their capacity to move through Stages Three, Four and Five repeatedly. In Stage Three, they are excellent at probing the dynamics of a problem and identifying a strategy for dealing with it. Their work in Stage Four has not been detailed in developing an interactive tactical scenario of steps, but their memoranda have often presented the ingredients of a plan of action in detail. In Stage Five, they put their ideas and memoranda into the hands of government, opposition and U.N. leaders. They have also shown a capacity to act individually and together within the civil society in ways described below.

Impact: Taking the Design into the Body Politic.   In their memorandum from Dialogue 17 (October 1996), participants declared their framework to be the multilevel peace process.[4] The Dialogue group has gradually but steadily extended its reach across the multilevel peace process—into both the official peace process and what we would call the civil society.

Chapter Seven describes how, for its first 13 months, the Inter-Tajik Dialogue provided the only systematic exchange between pro-government and opposition figures. The group is credited by former Tajik and U.S. officials with playing a significant role in the beginning of formal U.N.-mediated negotiations by demonstrating the possibility of dialogue and by pressing opposition forces to coalesce. "After six meetings of the Dialogue it was no longer possible to argue credibly that negotiation between government and opposition was impossible," said a key Tajikistani official.[5]

In Dialogue 4 (October 1993), participants argued that negotiations were not possible as long as the opposition was fragmented and dispersed. Six weeks later, two Dialogue group members participated in formation of a united opposition; those two participants were among the signers of the first unified opposition platform; four, including those who signed the platform, became members of the Steering Committee of the opposition Coordinating Center in Moscow. Two Dialogue members provided a critical channel through which the Tajik government was briefed on that platform.

As stated earlier, beginning in Dialogue 6 (March 1994), the group produced and placed in the hands of key people in the official negotiations a series of memoranda on the strategy and elements of the unfolding peace process. The June 1997 peace agreement included four major concepts or organs formulated in those memoranda:

- In its first memorandum (Dialogue 6 in March 1994), the group introduced the idea of a negotiating process that would itself become the engine of a broad peace process in Tajikistan by working through four coordinating committees with comprehensive powers. Although that idea was only partly implemented during the period of negotiation, it is the design for the commission charged with implementation of the peace accords.
- In Dialogue 11 (March 1995), after the just-concluded elections, which excluded the opposition, the group introduced the idea of a "transitional period," that would lead toward a more inclusive political system. The peace agreement incorporates that concept to describe the first phase of the postaccord period.
- In Dialogue 12 (June 1995), the group took an opposition proposal for a supragovernmental Coordinating Council and recommended repositioning the council under the authority of the negotiating teams. The council would oversee implementation of decisions agreed to in the negotiations. This repositioning was intended to reduce the government's fear that the council would try to replace the government. This approach is included in the peace agreement as the Commission on National Reconciliation, which acts through the four working groups mentioned above as the key organization to oversee implementation of the peace accords.

- The concept of a Consultative Forum of the Peoples of Tajikistan was an "idea in the air"—its exact origins are unclear. Dialogue 12 (June 1995) included it among three options for transitional organs to oversee a process of national reconciliation. The president and the leader of the opposition agreed in July 1995 to the creation of the Consultative Forum. The Dialogue spelled out the forum's composition, functions and methods of work in its memorandum of September 1995 and has repeatedly pressed for its early convening so as to broaden public participation in the peace process. The Consultative Forum is included in the peace agreement, although it is not likely to be established until after the transitional period, if at all.

The organizers do not know whether anyone would attribute any of these outcomes directly to the memoranda written by Dialogue participants or whether each idea simply became one of the "ideas in the air" to be plucked down at the appropriate time. In either case, some clearly originated in the Dialogue.

When the official negotiations began, three Dialogue participants became delegates: two on the opposition side and one on the government side. The delegate on the government team was the vice chair of an association of one of the nationalities; he had been one of the Dialogue participants who briefed top-level government officials on the Dialogue meetings.

In Dialogue 8 (June 1994), the group named as its next focus after negotiations began designing a political process of national reconciliation to broaden public participation in the peace process. In the period following the peace agreement, that focus remains critical. In its joint memoranda, the Dialogue group has recommended bringing citizens together under the auspices of nongovernmental organizations to deliberate on proposed constitutional amendments and changes in the electoral laws. Their aim is to engage citizens who have been left out of the political process.

From the Dialogue during this period, other interactions in the civil society have developed. The University of Nebraska at Omaha (UNO), where the third U.S. team member is dean of international affairs, formed a relationship with the new private Technological University of Tajikistan. Some 30 UNO faculty have worked at the Tajikistani university, and about the same number of Tajikistanis have since studied at UNO.

Two participants formed their own nongovernmental organizations (NGOs) to teach citizenship and democratic thought and practice and to establish a position in civil society. One of these organizations, The Tajikistan Center for Civic Education, in December 1996 began a series of cross-regional symposia on the subject of regionalism, which is perhaps the biggest obstacle to national reconciliation and formation of a unified country. Center staff planned to extend this process to other areas in 1999 to promote dialogue across regional lines. The other NGO, the Oli Somon Foundation, initially probed the roots of democratic thought and practice in traditional Tajik culture and then formed the Independent University to teach management and other economic practices.

In July 1996, one participant became a member of a joint commission of representatives of the government and the opposition to negotiate local cease-fire arrangements. As described in Chapter Seven, his involvement in an important local negotiation helped open a critical east-west road and dramatized to Dialogue participants the importance of drawing local people explicitly into the work of the larger peace process. In Dialogue 17 (October 1996), participants reflected their colleague's grass-roots experience by stressing again the importance of broadening public participation in the peace process, which they then named a "multi-level peace process."

Dialogue participants are well positioned at all levels of the multilevel peace process. They are leaders in promoting the concept and in creating new organs in the budding civil society. These accomplishments are visible, but I am, of course, speaking of the work of a small number of citizens outside of government.

In any complex political situation, it is often difficult to know precisely where ideas originated, how they emerged from the shadows to center stage or what combination of influences actually produced a decision. Even participants in the official negotiations cannot know exactly what role the joint memoranda played. It is accurate to say that there is no other set of papers produced by citizens outside government—perhaps not even by government officials—articulating in such detail both the philosophy and the practicalities of the peace process.

One of the continuing shortcomings—and needs—of the Dialogue in the transitional postaccord phase concerns the involvement of a broader range of voices. At various times, the failure to widen the net to the fullest extent has resulted from a calculated decision to involve only those committed to joint problem solving, thereby excluding extremists; the difficulty of traveling from isolated parts of the country; and the outright fear for personal security of self and family in a country in which individual assassinations have been, and are still, frequent.

It would also be desirable to integrate the Dialogue more fully into the life of the country by holding meetings in Tajikistan regularly. As of the end of 1998, all but one of the Dialogue sessions had been convened elsewhere, primarily because threats to the lives of some opposition participants have forced them to live in exile. The peace agreement has permitted them to return to Tajikistan, but the movement toward real peace has been slow in improving the security situation.

EVALUATING ACHIEVEMENTS AND ANALYZING PROBLEMS

The organizers have taken a number of steps to ensure that full records of the Dialogue are available to assist in evaluation, albeit not always in the way some social scientists would wish. Even though the achievements are well documented and identified, problems remain in evaluating exactly what the impact of the Dialogue's work has been.

Documentation

A rapporteur's record exists for each session. In addition, the U.S. co-moderator has produced after each meeting an analytical memorandum of about ten pages, with the joint memorandum attached. Each of these memoranda by the U.S. co-moderator analyzes the Dialogue's progress, up to that point, within the setting of the five-stage process and reflects on the substantive matters discussed and how the discussion in each session seems to shape the agenda for the next one. One of the points that quickly emerges from this analysis is the importance of what happens between meetings. It is these events—as processed by participants—that highlight the group's role as a "mind at work" in the middle of a rapidly changing situation.

Participants' Judgments

At several points, the organizers have asked participants to write their own assessments of the value of the Dialogue to them. It has been interesting to see how many have cited the value of learning a different way of relating and talking. Some have reflected that new political bodies in Tajikistan need to learn to talk and work together as the participants have. On the occasion of particular events such as approval of the Consultative Forum of the Peoples of Tajikistan, the organizers have recorded interviews with the participants to get the story right while memory is fresh.

Interviews and Letters from Others

The organizers have a record of an interview with a former high Tajikistani official who described the "significant" role of the Dialogue in the government's decision to negotiate, as well as a letter on the same subject from the former U.S. deputy chief of mission in Tajikistan. In April 1995, the under secretary general of the United Nations for political affairs, who oversaw the official negotiations, gave a speech in which he cited the Dialogue as the most important nonofficial group complementing U.N.-sponsored negotiations. A range of accounts provides evidence that the work of the Dialogue is known to top governmental and international officials involved in the U.N.-sponsored negotiations.

Publications

Some of the organizers have written articles on the Dialogue. Now Chapters Seven and Ten of this book lay out how the process has worked and how the Dialogue has related to developments in Tajikistan.

One of the most difficult *problems* in evaluating work of this kind stems from questions about causality. In the case of the Inter-Tajik Dialogue, these arise even in the seemingly most clear-cut cases. For example, as the sequence of events described above suggests, the Dialogue played some role in the government's decision to negotiate. But anyone who has experienced government decision making understands the multitude of influences and actors at work in any decision. Often, even those who make decisions cannot say what influenced them most or what influenced other key figures in the decision making. Despite an impressive coincidence of interactions, it is not realistic to claim direct cause and effect.

The same is true of the agreement between the president of Tajikistan and the leader of the opposition on the Consultative Forum. Even though the agreement was recorded in the hand of a Dialogue member—and the organizers have a copy of the handwritten document—who can say for sure what the total range of influences on that decision was? Did the Dialogue play a role? Almost certainly. Was its role decisive? That may be unknowable.

The organizers have come to see evaluation as *a process within the process of sustained dialogue.* Moderators have often encouraged participants to express their goals for the Dialogue, but those moments have to arise naturally. When hostile groups or individuals first come together from the heat of a civil war—or even the latent tension in a racially divided city—they are intent on downloading what is on their minds. It is difficult to stop them in order to engage in a mechanical goal-setting exercise. When moderators are trying to establish the Dialogue as a safe place for participants to say what they really think and feel, allowing an outsider to come in and impose a mechanical exercise or series of interviews could be destructive.

That having been said, the dialogue process offers a continuous opportunity to set interim goals within a larger strategy and to discover that meeting those goals naturally opens the door to the next set of potential achievements. It is possible for moderators to build into the process of sustained dialogue a series of touchstones for judging progress if they exercise care in developing the analytical, the strategic and the tactical frameworks that are the essential elements of the peace process.

A CONCLUDING WORD

My first judgment is that experience in the Inter-Tajik Dialogue proves that the process of sustained dialogue is ready for use in other conflicts and tense situations. The elements of that process were well grounded in prior experience, but experience in the Dialogue has progressed well beyond the organizers' ability to predict. That experience has enriched the process both in detail and in concept through the intense interaction among participants and by adding the dimension of building civil society to the work of conflict resolution.

The Dialogue has clearly established itself and has become widely recognized for its work. It helped pave the way for negotiation. It produced highly substantive memoranda which reflect a philosophy of what would be required for a political process of national reconciliation. It has designed several possible candidates for institutional development: a Consultative Forum of the Peoples of Tajikistan, local dialogues modeled on its own and the Commission for National Reconciliation to implement decisions from the negotiations by pulling together different factions, university courses on conflict resolution and building civil society, and even a possible NGO to perpetuate its own work. The next phase of the project will determine which of these or others it may be possible to leave in place when the project ends. The ongoing record of this work will continue to unfold.

Epilogue

Sustained Dialogue:
A Public Space for Learning

In reprise, I replay Czech President Václav Havel's words: "It is not that we should simply seek new and better ways of managing society, the economy, and the world. The point is that we should fundamentally change how we behave."[1]

If citizens are to change the way they behave, they must choose, learn and practice new ways of thinking, talking and working together. Sustained dialogue can be a vehicle for that learning and practice—both in real-world situations and in the classroom.

This sounds like a utopian statement about changing human nature. That is not its intent. Our whole practice of child rearing and education intends to teach human beings to behave in socially acceptable and productive ways. We constantly teach and train people to use their minds more effectively and to interact with others in ways that enhance the capacities of groups and organizations to work more efficiently. The issue is not *whether* we should think about changing human behavior but *how* and to what end.

Sustained dialogue teaches a different way of behaving. That different way of relating is the foundation for a peaceful society. Why should we not aspire to embed that different way of relating in the fabric of our society from schoolroom to workplace, from church to community, from office to factory, from neighborhood association to government council?

Has the time not come to accelerate teaching the ways of peace instead of leaving it to chance that children will learn them through "socialization" on the playground or in the preschool? This is not a new idea. Across the United States, schools have programs to teach "conflict-resolution skills" so students can mediate disputes in the schoolyard. Around the world, organizations are generating opportunities for citizens to experience deliberation on public issues. Why not build from this work and intensify it?

CHANGING A CULTURE OF CONFRONTATION AND VIOLENCE

As Havel says, people need to change the way they behave. The American people—not to mention those in other parts of the world—are becoming increasingly confrontational. The use of violence to dismiss problems, to express dissent and to vent anger has reached a frightening level. The tendency of human beings to wall themselves off into their own ethnic, racial and national ghettos is destructive, especially just as a globalizing economy and dramatic new ways of interacting offer staggering opportunities to create new power for good. To repeat the words of Daniel Yankelovich: "Along with other observers of American life, I am troubled by the growing power of the forces dividing Americans from one another, fragmenting our culture, causing us to grow apart."[2]

Deborah Tannen puts this tendency in an even starker context. She speaks of

> a pervasive warlike atmosphere that makes us approach public dialogue, and just about anything we need to accomplish, as if it were a fight. It is a tendency in Western culture in general, and in the United States in particular, that has a long history and a deep, thick, and far-ranging root system. It has served us well in many ways but in recent years has become so exaggerated that it is getting in the way of solving our problems. Our spirits are corroded by living in an atmosphere of unrelenting contention—an argument culture.
>
> The argument culture urges us to approach the world—and the people in it—in an adversarial frame of mind. It rests on the assumption that opposition is the best way to get anything done. The best way to discuss an idea is to set up a debate; the best way to cover news is to find spokespeople who express the most extreme, polarized views and present them as 'both sides'; the best way to settle disputes is litigation that pits one party against the other; the best way to begin an essay is to attack someone; and the best way to show you're really thinking is to criticize.[3]

Only the active pursuit of a different way of relating can deal with the rage in our society that is barely beneath the surface and threatens to tear us apart. Only a different way of relating can undermine the growing assumption of an increasing number of Americans that violence is the solution to any problem. Only a different way of conducting our relationships will re-

verse the degradation of our political discourse and restore thoughtful interaction.

Only a different way of relating can inject power into the pursuit of
peace. Experience has taught us that peace is not just a condition; it is not
just the absence of war or violence; it is not just the absence of social or personal turmoil. Peace is a way of relating; it is a way of acting. Peacemaking
is a way of life. Peace is never made; it is always in the making. Unless we
work at it, there is no peace.

The twentieth century has been called the most destructive in history. At
the same time, it is one of the century's achievements that we have gone beyond defining peace simply as the absence of violence. We have proclaimed
that, to be genuine, peace must be linked with justice. We have learned that
the quiet enforced by totalitarian regimes and military occupation is no
peace. We have learned that oppressive social systems such as segregation or
sweatshop labor do not produce real peace.

The link between peace and justice, to be sure, has roots in the centuries,
but in the twentieth century, our pursuit of civil and human rights has become
broader, more focused and more intense. It has been directed at transforming
unjust relationships. It has aimed at changing how people relate to each other.

To say that we will not experience real peace until we change our way of
relating is to place the pursuit of peace at the center of day-to-day life. Peace
is no longer an abstraction; it is no longer something that only governments
are responsible for; it is no longer a social or political condition that one citizen personally can do nothing about. Peace starts with how citizens relate;
it is built from choices about ways of living that citizens can make. Those
choices are part of everyday experience.

Why care about this kind of peace? Because this active definition of peace
can determine the quality of life, fairness and decency in our world. This
way of relating will affect our pursuit of achievement and happiness. One vehicle for teaching this way of relating is sustained dialogue.

THE POWER OF SUSTAINED DIALOGUE

The experiences of sustained dialogue recounted in this book, along with
countless such experiences in everyday lives, demonstrate that dialogue creates a space for changing how we behave toward each other. To recall Dan
Yankelovich's words:

> [T]o a surprising extent a certain kind of dialogue can counterbalance the
> worst effects of the isolation and fragmentation that threaten to overwhelm

us. It can create better understanding among people with divergent views, help to overcome the mistrust that increasingly separates Americans from their institutions (e.g., government, business, the media, educators), connect cultural, professional and business interests, bring leaders and their constituents closer together, and create new possibilities in personal relationships and community.[4]

An important strategy that emerges from experience with sustained dialogue is that of proliferating dialogue. Twenty years of Israeli-Palestinian dialogues have unquestionably played a critical role in changing relationships between the two peoples. After a gradual start in the 1970s, they became so numerous that they could not be counted in the 1980s. Since the fresh peace agreement in Tajikistan, participants in the sustained dialogue there began talking about how to engage others in dialogue. That will presumably be a next step for the sustained dialogue in Baton Rouge.

The challenge now is to learn how to proliferate dialogue systematically with a well-defined purpose as a commonplace way of relating in daily life. A critical piece of that process must be increasing the number of dialogues, but part of it must also be teaching dialogue in the same way we teach other arts of living to our children.

The opportunity and the experience of choosing to step across the threshold into dialogue as an adult reflects the choice—often unconscious—of a citizen to become a political actor. We need to know much more about what causes citizens to decide to engage—to reach out to others to deal with common problems. We know the choice involves at least two elements: a judgment that a situation hurts personal and group interests intolerably and a sense that it may be possible to change the situation.

We need to know more about how to bring people to the judgment that a situation cannot be allowed to continue. Sometimes that involves encouraging them to think more vividly and analytically about where they are going—the potential costs for themselves, their group and their children. Sometimes, when the pain is already sharp enough, it involves helping people with little hope discover the capacities within themselves and their group to work together for change. This thinking is part of a citizen's education.

We have an increasing body of experience that can give people hope that they can change even an intolerable relationship. Making those sometimes difficult choices to engage in dialogue is more likely if people have experienced a different way of thinking, talking and working together—and *when* people have learned that change is possible and need not be threatening.

The goal is to make dialogue a natural way to behave and to help people experience its rewards. To do that, we must make dialogue part of education and experience.

The learning and practice of dialogue begin with two lessons that evolve hand in hand.

- First, learning to talk *with* rather than *at* others enables participants in a dialogue to begin experiencing the mutual respect that comes from listening carefully and talking together with increasing openness. Feeling mutual respect gradually opens the door to insight into relationships. As a rabbi friend told me: "Dialogue can create one of the holiest moments human beings experience."
- Second, learning a different, more disciplined and purposeful way of thinking and talking together makes it possible for members of a group to find shared interests and shared concern about where a situation is heading. It permits participants to assess the costs of inaction against the costs of trying to change; it permits them to design together steps to change relationships; it permits them to act together.

The logo of the National Issues Forums includes these words: "A different kind of talk. Another way to act."

As members of a group begin to think together about their capacities to design action to change the course of events, they think together about the processes of interaction—the dynamics of their relationships—that could be changed by specific steps. Figuratively, they step into the "space between" them and explore how they might learn to behave differently toward each other.

Putting the possible steps together in a scenario of interactions, they begin to feel the power inherent in the multilevel peace process. Acting reinforces learning. That kind of learning can take place in the classroom as well as in the body politic.

But what is actually happening in our schools and universities? Listen again to Deborah Tannen:

The teacher sits at the head of the classroom, feeling pleased with herself and her class. The students are engaged in a heated debate. The very noise level re-assures the teacher that the students are participating, taking responsibility for their own learning. Education is going on. The class is a success.

But look again, cautions Patricia Rosof, a high school history teacher who admits to having experienced that wave of satisfaction with herself and the job she is doing. On closer inspection, you notice that only a few students are participating in the debate; the majority of the class is sitting silently, maybe attentive but perhaps either indifferent or actively turned off. And the students who are arguing are not addressing the subtleties, nuances or complexities of the points they are making or disputing. They do not have that luxury because they want to win the argument. . . . [5]

What are the roots of this way of teaching? There are many, says Tannen, but among them: "Valuing attack as a sign of respect is part of the argument culture—our conception of intellectual interchange as a metaphorical battle." She goes on:

Perhaps . . . it is time to question our glorification of debate as the best, if not the only, means of inquiry. . . . What's wrong is that it obscures aspects of disparate work that overlap and can enlighten each other. . . . What's wrong is that it obscures the complexity of research. . . . What's wrong is that it implies that only one framework can apply, when in most cases many can.

If you limit your view of a problem to choosing between two sides, you inevitably reject much that is true, and you narrow your field of vision to the limits of those two sides, making it unlikely you'll pull back, widen your field of vision, and discover the paradigm shift that will permit truly new understanding.[6]

Sustained dialogue can provide space for a different approach to teaching and learning. It can open a door to a different way of knowing.

Teaching Dialogue: A Key to the Citizens' Century

A friend and colleague—Raymond Shonholtz, president of Partners for Democratic Change—has written of the twenty-first century as "the mediating future":

Currently and continually through the early years of the twenty-first century, citizens, organizations, and governments will be confronted with an ever increasing number of issues and conflicts that are beyond the jurisdiction of any one country and beyond the capacity of any nation, regional structure, or global organization to mandate a solution. . . .

The mediating future is about developing and expanding a twenty-first-century definition of international civil society to embrace the formation of nonstate, nonadversarial, cooperative mediating forums. . . . Within countries with an Anglo-Saxon tradition, conflict is generally resolved outside of governmental institutions and within the domain of civil society. . . . In the democracies of Central and Eastern Europe and the newly independent states that are in transition, conflict is a vehicle for building in civil society new institutions and structures for the orderly channeling of disputes into forums for their early and peaceful settlement. . . .

In the mediating future, conflict will be managed in international civil society through culturally sensitive mediating norms and modalities that encourage disputant participation, are confidence building in nature, and establish a context for relationship building and understanding between asymmetric cultures.[7]

Where will these "culturally sensitive mediating norms and modalities" come from? I have argued in this book that deep-rooted human conflicts will be transformed into peaceful relationships only in the context of a multilevel peace process conducted by whole human beings acting in whole bodies politic. Important as governments and formal mediation and negotiation will remain, lasting peaceful relationships will not be built until citizens outside government are deeply engaged and until the civil societies in which they work provide public space in which they can span the divisions in those societies.

In this book, I have presented a public peace process with sustained dialogue at its heart as the instrument for citizens to use in their work of ending violence and building the sinews of peace. I do not argue that a public peace process will become the primary vehicle for peacemaking. I do place that instrument for citizens outside government alongside formal diplomacy, mediation and negotiation as equally appropriate for study and practice. I argue that governments will not succeed in making and building peace unless citizens outside government do their essential part of changing human relationships. Above all, I argue that the multilevel peace process is the context for peacemaking in which all parts of a society can interact.

This work is done in the political arena. Its challenge in today's world is that no single academic or professional discipline is designed to educate the whole human being to participate in this whole political process. The thinking required will not come from combining existing disciplines; it will emerge only from large new perspectives. It will be "supradisciplinary." As Havel says: "The point is that we should fundamentally change how we behave." The peace process as a human process for peacemaking and peace-building offers a place to learn the practices of peace—the disciplined, systematic ways of thinking, talking and working together differently in pursuing peace.

"A different kind of talk. Another way to act." Why not teach them to our children?

Appendix

---~ツビン~---

The Process in Outline: A Brochure
Organizers' and Moderators' Manual

Those who would like to put sustained dialogue into practice may find the two documents in this Appendix useful. Although they repeat the substance and some of the wording of Chapter Six, they put the process presented there into a form addressed directly to potential organizers, participants and moderators.

Both documents are written for use in communities and organizations in the United States, but they are readily adaptable for other places and situations.

First is a text that can be printed as a four-fold brochure on normal U.S. paper. "The Process in Outline: A Brochure" is written to introduce potential users to the sustained-dialogue approach so they can make a quick judgment on whether the process is worth exploring more deeply. It follows a short statement of the rationale with a brief overview of the five-stage process and what it might be expected to produce. In Baton Rouge, Louisiana, the co-moderators gave it to potential participants.

The much longer "Organizers' and Moderators' Manual" is addressed in an operational voice to those who may be working to organize and conduct a sustained dialogue. It is rooted in the conceptual framework and the explanations of the process in this book, but it translates them into practical suggestions.

Even after reading this material, organizers and moderators will need to make their own adaptations to suit their particular situations. Hopefully, their experience will eventually enrich the experience of all who may work in this field.

Readers are particularly urged to go back and reread Chapters Two (on relationship), Five (on dialogue) and Six (the five-stage process). They put the material here in a larger context and provide a fuller rationale. Credits for material here are in the notes for those chapters.

THE PROCESS IN OUTLINE: A BROCHURE

Sustained Dialogue

A Process for Changing Strained Community Relationships

Uneasy race relations and ethnic tensions that plague many American communities seriously undermine their ability to solve an array of social, economic and political problems. This brochure introduces you to a process for thinking and talking together that defuses conflict and builds mutual respect and the capacity to work together.

THE CONCEPT

The approach offered here is an interactive process designed to change the very nature of troublesome relationships. It is not designed to bring together contending parties to negotiate for equal pieces of a pie. Rather, participants probe the dynamics of contentious relationships that cause problems. They gradually develop a capacity for designing actions to change those relationships for the better. Then they decide how to take those steps into the wider community.

It is essential to keep the focus on relationships—not just on specific problems between groups. Relationships exist when the actions of one person or group affect another—positively or negatively—on a continuing basis. Probing the dynamics of relationships creates the possibility of changing them.

The process begins with identification of a dozen or so individuals who are concerned enough about the situation in their community to be willing to talk about it in depth under the guidance of an experienced moderator. Participants should be respected representatives of conflicting groups and must be willing to commit to a series of regular meetings that could extend over many months. They will meet in a space that is comfortable to all.

The key to sustained dialogue is careful listening to others to discover common interests and explore reasons for unresolved differences. Relationships change when groups discover they need each other. The participants will have succeeded if, by the end of the process, they have:

- brought out the misperceptions, fears, mistrust and suspicions that lie at the heart of the difficulties between their groups;
- experienced changes in their own relationships within the dialogue group;
- worked out a scenario of interdependent steps that they think could begin to change the foundations of the relationships that exist among groups in the community;
- begun implementing the scenario in the wider community.

PUTTING THE CONCEPT TO WORK

The process develops in five parts, though the stages do not have rigidly defined boundaries. Each may take more than one meeting. Participants move back and forth across the stages when they need to update a changing situation, rethink an earlier question or tackle a new problem. The framework outlined below gives you an idea of the work that must be done and the central questions that must be addressed if the dialogue is to produce the desired results. A team—rather than one person—may be needed to initiate, organize, convene and moderate the process.

Stage One: Deciding to Engage in Dialogue

The purpose at this stage, normally before people come to the table, is twofold: to find respected participants who reflect key viewpoints in their communities and who agree to meet regularly over months, and to agree on the nature, purpose and rules of the dialogue:

- to discuss openly both problems and the relationships that cause them for the purpose of changing those relationships;
- to listen thoughtfully and speak briefly with respect for others;
- to speak only for yourself and not for any organizations;
- not to quote anyone outside the room.

People are often reluctant to talk about relationships like this. Those who decide to take the risk have weighed questions such as: What will my children and grandchildren face if relationships continue as they are?

Stage Two: Mapping and Naming Problems and Relationships

The purposes when participants first come together are: (1) to get out on the table the array of problems and relationships among them and to examine how those problems affect real interests; (2) to share their personal experiences with the relationships that have created those problems and that would need to be changed to resolve those problems; and (3) to identify and choose the two or three problems on which they will focus in-depth attention one at a time.

It may be difficult to share personal experiences involving racial or ethnic tensions, but this is key. Probing the dynamics of the relationships that cause problems is essential to changing those relationships.

Between sessions, each participant might be asked to:

- Write carefully worded descriptions of the problems that were identified.
- Explain how those problems affect them.
- Decide which problem the group should work on first and why.

Stage Three: Probing Problems and Relationships to Choose a Direction

In this stage, participants probe deeply the specific problems they decided to work on. The aims are to see how relationships affect interests, to glimpse how relationships might be changed, and to decide whether to try. There is always a dual agenda: to determine why participants really care about this problem; and to discuss the problem in a way that reveals the dynamics of the relationships that cause it.

First, participants will share the problem descriptions they wrote between meetings and write definitions that the whole group can accept.

Second, they will probe one problem at a time to bring to the surface the dynamics of relationships that create the problems, focusing on such questions and tasks as:

- What are the main elements of the problem?
- Describe the main people and/or groups involved in this problem.
- How does this problem affect what you and/or your group value most? Can you explain this in a personal story?

Third, participants suggest possible directions to take in tackling the problem. The purpose is not to detail a course of action but to frame broad choices.

Fourth, they will weigh those choices and try to come to a sense of direction that they think should guide next steps.

Fifth, after full discussion of each problem, participants should step back and take stock of where they are headed by asking:

- Where is the situation going? What future would we prefer?
- Would we like to change course? What are the costs?
- What changes in relationships would be needed to move to the kind of community that would deal effectively with this problem?
- Where could we find common ground for changing relationships?

The key question is whether participants are ready to work together to design a series of interactive steps that could change relationships. If that seems like too big a step to take right now, it is worth talking about why it is difficult. If the group seems ready:

Between sessions, each participant might be asked to:

- List obstacles to moving in the direction in which you want to move.
- State what you need from others to overcome those obstacles.
- List possible steps for overcoming those obstacles.

Stage Four: Scenario-Building— *Experiencing a Changing Relationship*

In a sense, the group is a microcosm of the larger community, and, by this stage, relationships within the group have changed. Figuratively, participants are no longer sitting across the table talking to each other; they are sitting side by side, thinking *together* about how to generate changes they all agree should occur. Their task now is to develop a series of interactive steps—a scenario—that can gradually change how groups feel about each other. To do this, they should:

- List the main obstacles to change. Remember: These can be feelings as well as practical factors.
- List steps to overcome each obstacle.
- List who can take those steps. What steps could you persuade your group to take? What steps would you be personally responsible for?
- Now list those steps in an order to show both their sequence and how steps by different groups can interact.
- Consider how the dialogue group—after the scenario begins—can create public recognition that something different is happening.

Between sessions, each participant might be asked to:

- Write down what can be done with this scenario.
- Review your expectations for these meetings and list ways in which they were met and not met.

Stage Five: Acting Together to Make Change Happen

The purpose in this stage is to decide whether to act in the larger community and, if so, to develop practical ways that the scenarios developed in Stage Four might be put into action. Participants will focus on such questions as:

- Do conditions in the community permit implementing the scenario?
- Do capacities exist for carrying it through?
- Who needs to take what steps?

THE BOTTOM LINE

The purpose of this process—sustained dialogue—is to probe the dynamics of contentious relationships in order to develop gradually a capacity for taking actions to change those relationships for the better. Over time, the group might continue to develop ideas and practical steps for reducing tensions by improving relationships.

Organizers' and Moderators' Manual

̶ ̴̗̰̰ ̶

Sustained Dialogue

A Process for Changing Strained Community Relationships

Uneasy race relations and ethnic tensions that plague many American communities seriously undermine their ability to solve an array of social, economic and political problems. This booklet presents a process for thinking and talking together that defuses conflict and builds mutual respect as well as the capacity to change destructive relationships and to work together. It provides a guide to organizers and moderators of such a process.

Introduction

The Approach

The approach offered here is sustained dialogue—an interactive process designed to change conflictual relationships over time. This approach differs from other public-policy discussions in focusing on the underlying relationships that cause divisive problems—not just on the problems.

This kind of dialogue is more structured than a good conversation or study group and less structured than a negotiation. It promises results—but by changing relationships rather than through precisely negotiated agreements. It is designed for communities in tension.

Relationships exist when the actions of persons or groups affect each other—positively or negatively—on a continuing basis. Sustained dialogue is a human and, eventually, a political process in which participants probe the dynamics of even the most difficult relationships that cause problems and gradually develop the capacity *together* to design steps to change them. Then they decide how to take those steps into the community.

The key to dialogue is listening carefully to another person's interests and feelings so as to discover where common ground exists for pursuing common interests and why differences remain. Dialogue brings to the surface real fears, misperceptions and interests and can establish ground for mutual respect. It produces insight into how groups can interact so as to change their relationship.

This process involves identifying a dozen or so individuals who are concerned enough about the situation in their community to be willing to talk about it in depth in a series of regular meetings over a considerable period of time. Participants must be respected and must reflect key viewpoints in their groups. They must be willing to meet for several hours at a time—four or five at a minimum—regularly over months. (In conflict situations abroad, three-day meetings are common.) An experienced moderator or co-moderators will lead the dialogue. It is essential to provide a safe space to meet—some place in or near the community where all feel comfortable and safe.

The commitment of time is critical. This process is not do-able in a few short sessions. Participants must somehow free themselves of a sense that time is pressing on them. They must commit minds and hearts to devote whatever time a compelling task requires.

The organization and management of a process can best be thought of in terms of the functions to be performed. Someone must launch the idea. Someone must identify able and willing participants. Someone must get their agreement to participate. Someone must fund. Someone must convene. Someone must moderate the meetings. Often, these functions will be performed by different persons, so a team effort may be most natural. Each situation will determine what will work best.

The Process

Above all, this is a process that aims at changing relationships. What makes this process different is its dual agenda: Participants have to talk about the practical problems between them, but always the real purpose is to use that discussion to learn what it reveals about the underlying relationships that cause the problems. Probing the dynamics of key relationships can bring to the surface insights into how these relationships might be changed.

These pages describe a process of dialogue that grows and deepens through five stages:

- One: People decide to engage in dialogue because they feel a compelling need to build or change a relationship to resolve problems that hurt or could hurt their interests intolerably. These participants are themselves a microcosm of their communities.

- Two: They come together to talk—to map and name the elements of those problems and the relationships responsible for creating and dealing with them.
- Three: They probe specific problems to uncover the dynamics of underlying relationships with these aims: (1) to define the most pressing problems; (2) to probe the dynamics of the relationships underlying these problems; (3) to lay out broadly possible ways into those relationships to change them; (4) to weigh those choices and to come to a sense of direction to guide next steps; (5) to weigh the consequences of moving in that direction against the consequences of doing nothing; and (6) to decide whether to try designing such change.
- Four: Together, they design a scenario of interacting steps to be taken in the political arena to change troublesome relationships and to precipitate practical steps.
- Five: They devise ways to put that scenario into action.

By the end of the dialogue, participants have moved from wariness of each other to a working relationship and insight into how to share their experience together more widely. The group will have succeeded if, by the end of this process, participants have:

- probed the misperceptions, fears, mistrust and suspicions that they see as lying at the heart of their groups' relationship;
- experienced changes in their own relationships within the group by talking openly and listening carefully and then by working out a scenario of interdependent steps that they think could begin to change the foundations of their groups' relationship;
- shared their dialogue with a wider number of community members and begun implementing the scenario.

The bottom line: Your purpose is to create an ongoing idea-producing group reflecting tense relationships in the community that can design and spin off into the community ideas and practical steps for reducing tension and improving those relationships. This happens as participants take these ideas out into their own sectors of the community and cause them to be implemented.

Why Stages?

You must understand that these five stages are not rigid, and that the process is anything but neat and orderly. One stage does not fully end before the next begins. Participants move back and forth across the stages often when they need to update a changed situation, rethink an earlier judgment or tackle a new problem. Or their minds may be all over the place when they are groping for focus. When they do go back, it is at a deeper level because they are continuously deepening their experience with their relationships through the course of the dialogue. The real purpose of the five-stage framework suggested is to give you some touchstones and to provide a checklist of the work that needs to be done if the dialogue is to have a rigorous sense of purpose and direction and if it is to produce fundamental change in conflictual relationships. For instance:

- A group may well find in Stages Two or Three—or even after the dialogue has been working for some time—that some crucial voices are missing, so someone will go back to Stage One to recruit additional participants.
- You may find the group periodically or even regularly returning to Stage Three as the dialogue moves along because participants need to redefine the key problems they want to work on as the situation develops or they need to tackle a new problem in a situation that has changed.
- When a group is designing a scenario of interdependent steps in Stage Four, participants may want to go back to the questions they addressed in Stage Three to probe the dynamics of relationships more deeply for further insight into steps that might change interactions.
- You may see a group jump quickly to solutions. Recognizing that participants have skipped over probing the dynamics of underlying relationships that cause the problems can help you pull them back in a way that will eventually enlarge their options.

Retracing steps in such ways is normal and often necessary. You will find Guideposts throughout this manual to help you. The key is to make sure that movement serves a purpose.

Depending on how you have scheduled and paced your dialogue, you might spend several sessions in a particular stage before the group is ready to move on. Especially in the early stages, participants need to say what is in their hearts—often, long-pent-up feelings and perceptions that many feel have never really been heard and absorbed. Helping participants hear and work with these thoughts is what makes this dialogue different from public-policy discussions. Difficult and drawn out as this may be, it does not make sense to cut off prematurely insights that will eventually offer clues to changing relationships. U.S. moderators are all too prone to be impatient with such talk and to cut people off.

Getting Stuck

You should also expect to get "stuck" at particular points because some subjects are scary to talk about in depth. Most often, these points occur as a group tries to move from one stage to the next. Both individuals and the group will need to mature and gather courage to step across some thresholds. These points are identified and discussed in the detailed presentation of the five stages that follows this Introduction, but some broad comments may be helpful here.

The variety of possible resistances is as wide as the number of situations confronted, so there can be no comprehensive guide for responding to all possible situations. The best help is establishing a proper attitude toward resistance to movement.

Perhaps the most useful thought to keep in mind is this: Treasure the participants' resistance to moving forward because you will learn much from it. It is not a nuisance or a hindrance but a concentrated opportunity for unlocking another door to further progress.

Resistance is an almost inevitable response to the possibility of change at every stage. People are often reluctant to change for good reason. The most productive approach is not to try to persuade participants to give up their reluctance: "Trust me. It will be OK. You are safe in this group." The most productive approach is to say and demonstrate that you understand that reasons for resistance are real for the participant: "You wouldn't feel that way without good reasons. Let's see if we can understand those reasons." If you accept the participants' reasons without judgment and work together to analyze as much as you can, participants may gradually come to feel safe enough to move to the next level.

Psychologists have learned that their most important work is helping patients understand their internal obstacles to change. They have also learned that the best approach is to work with a patient to unravel those resistances as they come up, not to try to roll over them.

Remember, resistance and reluctance will come up at every step toward deepening the dialogue. It is normal. Becoming frustrated with such obstacles is the moderator's greatest enemy. Learn from them what is really going on in a dysfunctional relationship by probing as deeply as you can for the reasons. An attitude of patient exploration is most likely to produce useful insight.

One other point to keep in the front of your mind is that the time between meetings is often the period when participants work through their resistance to going on. There is something about thinking over the problem when there is no time pressure and when one can talk over aspects of the situation indirectly with friends. Often, groups that are at an impasse at the end of one meeting will return to the next ready to move forward in an exciting way.

The Moderator(s)

Choice of moderator(s) depends very much on each situation. In some cases, the persons who take the initiative to form a dialogue will naturally become its leaders. In others, the moderator(s) may not play a role in organizing the dialogue. In those situations, it may be wise for the organizers not to settle on a moderator or co-moderators until they have a sense from their soundings how potential participants feel about who should moderate. Even in those cases, organizers will do well to have some ideas in the back of their minds to test subtly.

The unique character of each group will suggest particular qualities in a moderator. Some qualities that seem essential whoever the participants may be:

- sensitivity to the human dimension of problems—why people hurt, what participants as human beings really need, why people may be understandably angry—and ability to relate to participants on that level rather than as trainees to be instructed;
- commitment to the overall purpose of reconciliation between groups that have real grievances with each other;
- ability to convey genuine caring and commitment at a human level;
- realism about the pace at which people can change;
- some depth of experience with related problems and ability to conceptualize that experience so as to draw on it in this group;
- ability to help people see common elements in their experiences and views;
- sensitivity to the cultural uniqueness of the groups involved;
- capacity to design agendas that build from previously expressed ideas to advance and deepen the process;
- a sense of political and social process—ability to see the whole picture, keep a destination in sight and not take sides;
- respect from participants as a caring person and as an experienced professional.

A word of perspective on the process: Those chosen as moderators may have played comparable roles in other processes. However, this process is different.

This is not like moderating a community forum or policy discussion. This process is sustained over a longer period of time. Participants focus not just on problems, but—even more important—also on the relationships that cause them. In focusing on changing relationships, moderators will need to welcome expressions of emotion within reason and try to help the group learn from them.

This is not mediation. While many of a mediator's abilities may be helpful in this process, the mediator is usually invited to help participants—perhaps from many groups—reach a specific agreement about one defined problem or complex of problems. Sustained dialogue may also involve a number of viewpoints within a community, but it also involves the full range of problems that affect relationships within the community. Its purpose is not to seek agreement on a specific problem but to change relationships so participants can deal with whatever problems arise, using whatever methods seem appropriate.

This is not negotiation. People in deep-rooted human conflict have little to negotiate—at least initially—because identity, historic grievances, fears and stereotypes are not negotiable.

This is not a training or skills-building exercise or an academic seminar, although participants may learn a lot from how a moderator conducts herself or himself, poses questions, draws on broader experience, expresses care and concern and demonstrates respect and sincerity. Moderators should not approach their role as teachers or trainers. At most, they should share experiences as equals.

THE DIALOGUE

Now we turn to a detailed presentation of each of the five stages. Please remember: They are presented to describe a sequence of tasks and the progress of relationships. The important thing for you to do now is, first, to study each as a stepping-stone and then to see them all together to understand the whole process. When you think you have some grasp of the process, try describing it to yourself; then go back and study each stage, outlining for yourself how you would use this material and the ideas behind it in your situation. Your aim is not to follow the course laid out here word for word; your aim is to internalize it and to make it your own instrument.

A word of comfort to the moderator: This may look like a complicated process. It is. Not only that, people can be painfully frustrating—even offensive and dense—in an experience like this. But the dialogue process is also exciting, challenging and immensely rewarding as you move deeply into it and feel relationships change. You would not have been asked to moderate if you were not the kind of person who has the human capacity to absorb and help channel the fears, grievances, hurts and hopes of the people you will be working with. You will grow as they change. You will make this process your own, sculpt it creatively to your use and contribute your own experience to its enrichment. This manual is only to help you think about what you want to do and how to get into the process.

In this manual, the comments and questions that appear in italics are suggestions for your guidance. You will need to select and to internalize them and make them appropriate for your particular group. Please be reassured: There are more points and questions here than you can ever go through in a dialogue. They are here to help you get a full sense of the approach and to give you a pool of resources to call on. They are guides to the ground that needs to be covered. You will draw on them and shape them to meet your needs.

Remember, too, that you will occasionally find Guideposts as you move through this manual. These are intended as guides in moving back and forth between stages and in reflecting on what kind of interaction you may be facing.

STAGE ONE: DECIDING TO ENGAGE IN DIALOGUE

This stage is sometimes described as the easiest to talk about and hardest to do. Yet, it can be the most important. Selecting the right participants is critical, and bringing them together can sometimes be very difficult.

The purposes at this stage—before people ever come to the table—are: (1) to find appropriate and willing participants; (2) to reach agreement that they will meet; and (3) to produce understanding on the nature, purpose and rules of the dialogue. Five questions must be addressed:

- Who will take the initiative?
- Who will the participants be?

- How can you try to overcome the resistance of potential participants to meeting and talking with persons they fear, suspect or think they don't like?
- Under what conditions will the dialogue take place?
- How can you precipitate a decision to meet?

Everyone must understand that the aim is to start a series of meetings that will continue over a considerable period—not just one meeting. Everyone must also understand that this is different from other meetings: Participants will focus on the overall relationships for the purpose of improving them rather than only on specific issues.

It may be useful to think of the tasks to be handled: taking the initiative, sounding out potential participants, selecting individuals and helping them decide to participate, arranging space, convening, funding and moderating. Most often, a team of several members will work together to make a dialogue happen. It may take some time just for this group to form itself, since different organizations may have to make decisions and come together.

Who Will Take the Initiative?

A dialogue can start in one of two ways: Either one or more concerned individuals from within the communities in tension can seek out like-minded people in the other community, or an interested person or group from outside the immediate field of tension can try to bring people together.

From Within

Sometimes, a person or a group inside one community takes the initiative, or individuals from each group cautiously reach out to the other. The advantage of this approach is that participants take ownership of their dialogue from the beginning. Experience shows that, as long as two parties avoid accepting joint ownership of their dialogue, they can slough off responsibility for progress onto the third party. When one or two people reach out to people in an adversary group, they will usually speak from serious concerns or commitments that they believe the other people share. Whatever the exact situation, a dialogue is formed as a few individuals talk quietly with others and carefully reach an understanding, one by one, that a dialogue group will form.

From Outside

Since it is often difficult for groups to come together on their own, a catalyst from outside is sometimes needed. A person or group who would play the role of catalyst normally begins by talking in depth with as many directly involved individuals as possible to gather knowledge about the interests, feelings and positions of each group. Through these conversations, the willingness of individuals to commit themselves and their qualities as participants will lead to an invitation to commit themselves to a dialogue. This effort is sometimes called a fact-finding mission.

How you explain why you are there is critical; the people you will "interview" can be very suspicious of who sent you or what you will get out of any involvement. The best approach is to explain simply and straightforwardly why you care.

The two main goals at this point are: identifying individuals who might be good participants in the dialogue and learning the key problems and how each group sees them.

The identity of the convener or convener team or organizations can also make a big difference. One possibility is co-conveners from within the communities in tension—a person or an organization from each community who is respected by the other side(s). Alternatively, one person from within or outside trusted by all involved could serve this function. If there is an outside convener, a team with broad experience across communities can bring to the discussions different perspectives and impart a neutral character.

Who Will the Participants Be?

One might start by speaking with two-dozen or three-dozen people but for the initial dialogue select about a dozen who represent main perspectives in the communities, noting that there are divisions within groups as well as between them. It may not be possible to enlist a fully representative group at first, but it may be better to begin than to seek perfection. Eventually, the aim is to spread the dialogue experience in the community to lay foundations for changing relationships, but now the aim is to select a core group whose members can work together and seem likely to stay together over time.

The participants must be individuals who are respected and listened to in their communities. They should not be selected just because of their title or position. Participants come because of themselves, not to represent any organization. Where organizations are involved, often participants are at the number-two level, listened to by top decision makers but less visible and more free to listen and to share—less compelled to defend or posture. But all participants speak only for themselves.

Whatever the participants' roles in the community, one human characteristic is essential: Each must be willing to listen to others' views and feelings—not just to pronounce her or his own position. This normally rules out extremists and fanatics, although at some point those viewpoints must be taken into account.

Usually, participants are individuals who have concluded that the present situation hurts their interests to an extent that is becoming intolerable. As individuals, they are ready to say "Enough!" and to risk working toward a solution, but they need to enlarge the credibility of their perspective in the community. (Learning what brings people to this conclusion in a situation is crucial.) In other instances, a third party may try to precipitate a sense of need for dialogue by dramatizing the costs of letting the situation drag on or by offering inducements to meet.

Participants often need some kind of political "permission" from within their communities to engage. Or they must have the stature or courage to engage despite opposition. A third party can help create legitimacy.

How wide a range of views should be represented? Should extremists be included? Normally, those willing to participate fall in the middle of a spectrum. A dialogue probably needs to start there and work its way toward the edges of the spectrum. Eventually, those extremists who will not talk may need to be contained by as broad a centrist group as possible.

In addition to willing partners, comparable partners must be found. All must believe that serious dialogue is possible among authentic representatives—in the nonofficial sense—of each group who are of comparable abilities and standing in their communities. Each individual must believe that the quality of the interaction will justify any risk.

How Can You Overcome Resistance to Dialogue?

Often, potential participants are reluctant or even fearful—with good reason—to meet with people who may seem threatening in some way. Some feel safer with a known situation or are not ready to face others' pain. Some deny that a problem exists at all because they are not ready to deal with it. Others blame the other group for being unwilling to talk. The challenge is to cause people to see a long-term problem as warranting a systematic dialogue before it reaches a violent stage or to cause people to acknowledge that suffering has gone on long enough. If there is no overt violence, people often deny that there is a problem.

Questions such as these may help in overcoming resistance:

The situation seems calm now, but do you want to leave it to your children this way?

*Do you see tensions under the surface that could cause trouble? Should
an effort be made now to try to head them off? What would your children
face if relationships continue as they are? How do others feel?
Why don't people want to talk? What are they afraid of?*

Another challenge—even when people are talking—is to get them to realize that they are not really talking about the problems in their relationships
that cause trouble. Groups may have learned that it is in their own self-interest to work together in common projects or workplaces but carefully
avoid talking about underlying tensions in their relationships so as not to
disrupt minimal necessary cooperation. "But we do talk," they say.

*If you think seriously about present relationships, could you tell some sto-
ries about underlying tensions? Or do you really believe that no tensions
exist?
    Can you give examples of what kind of talking goes on now? Does it go
to the heart of the underlying relationships that cause tensions? Or does it
skirt around them?*

When tensions have risen or already erupted in some way, people on both
sides may believe that time is on their side and that its passing will reduce
tensions. Some may even need conflict to define their identity. The problem
is how to convince people that tensions usually deepen rather than disappear
with time if not dealt with.

*What are the costs of continuing tension to you and your community? Does
anyone gain from this tension? If so, who and how?
    What will your children and grandchildren face if relationships con-
tinue as they are? How much longer can you tolerate this situation? When
is enough enough? Is this the kind of community/country you want your
children to grow up in?*

Later, if tensions are already escalating, some might believe that they have
already invested too much in pressing their positions to give up now. Talking to the other community could even be seen as "selling out" in some way.
The question is how to cause people to see that they are interdependent with
the other community and that it serves their own interests to engage in a systematic dialogue with them.

How much longer can this go on? When is it time to say "enough"?

Do you believe there are individuals in the other community who want to talk?

Are there influential people in your community who would like to explore ways of dealing with underlying tensions and improving relationships? Would the potential benefits of quiet exploration outweigh the costs? What kind of "permission" would you need in order to explore the other community's views? From whom would you gain this permission?

What Are the Conditions for Dialogue? The Compact or Covenant

It is important to explain to participants that the dialogue will take place in a space "owned" by all and safe for all. You are asking them to take some risks. Often, meeting in a familiar neutral site in which all participants will feel comfortable will help participants feel safe.

What will be discussed? A detailed agenda can grow only out of the dialogue itself, but some general statement of purpose needs to be understood. At this stage, the simplest possible statement that reassures participants that their needs will be heard is most likely to bring participants into dialogue.

To give the dialogue purpose and direction, the primary condition the parties must agree upon is that the purpose—whatever the specific subject being discussed—is to probe for underlying elements of tense or conflictual relationships between them that must be changed to improve conditions or resolve conflict.

Participants should be aware that they are being invited to a series of meetings that may continue over a considerable period—not just to a single meeting.

Everything possible should be said to get across the point that the quality of behavior and discussion in this space is expected to be quite different from the confrontational characteristic of other interactions in a conflictual situation. Certain ground rules should be agreed upon in advance.

Participants need to ponder the special character of the experience they are about to begin to judge whether they want to get involved. They should know what will be expected of them and what they may expect of others. Talking about these ground rules will also permit organizers to assess the capacity of potential participants to learn to work with others in the ways that will be required. Talking in this way can also provide organizers with a vehicle for explaining that the group will deal with both problems and the dynamics of the relationships behind the problems and gaining some sense of potential participants' capacity to respond to that dual agenda.

COVENANT

- The purpose of this dialogue is to work on changing the relationships among the groups with which participants identify.
- There will always be two items in the agenda: the particular problems participants need to talk about and the underlying feelings and relationships that cause these problems.
- Because of the importance of this work, participants commit themselves to meet regularly over a period of months—at least four to five hours in each meeting, although international meetings may last two to three days. The duration of the series will be open-ended. Participants will wait until they are well into the dialogue to agree on when to finish the series of meetings.
- Participants represent only themselves. They reflect views in their communities, but, in these dialogue sessions, they do not formally represent organizations or groups.
- Participants will observe time limits on their statements to allow genuine dialogue.
- Participants will speak from their hearts as well as from their minds.
- Participants will interact civilly, listen actively to each other with attention and respect, not interrupt and allow each to present her or his views fully.
- Because participants will need to speak about the feelings and relationships behind the specific problems that bother them, feelings will be expressed and heard with mutual respect. Participants will try to learn from these expressions.
- Participants will try to respond as directly and as fully as possible to points made and questions asked. Each will make a real effort to put herself or himself in others' shoes and speak with sensitivity for others' views and feelings.
- To facilitate serious work, participants will listen carefully to the issues and questions posed by the moderator and try to stick to them.
- Nobody in the dialogue will be quoted outside the meeting room.
- No one will speak publicly about the substantive discussion in the dialogue unless all agree.

To highlight the importance of these ground rules, you may want to prepare them—adapting them to your situation—on a separate paper to discuss them individually and with the group when it first meets. That paper could be titled "Covenant" or "Compact." Depending on what is possible, participants would be asked to commit themselves personally to something like the accompanying statement.

Group Size

A critical factor in determining how a group will talk will be its size. Often at the beginning of a discourse, you might be working against a background in which previous groups assembled looked more like conferences than like a task force in format. There may have been two- or three-dozen people in the room in which there was little opportunity for any form of communication other than a sequential statement of views as people raised their hands without much direct interaction. For parties who are leery of the greater intimacy of dialogue, this conference mode may have been the only acceptable way of meeting. In some cases, that very experience may have caused participants to recognize the value of a more intensive exchange in a smaller group. Some of them may be ready to try a different format for meeting.

Often when a group has begun in that conference mode, it can prove a breakthrough in the way the group works when it moves to a small-group or task-force format. Usually, the task force involves a dozen individuals at most in each group, and the agenda becomes more focused. If it is essential to have a larger group at the outset in order to represent many points of view, that may produce useful insights at an early stage, but it is more likely that participants will work effectively together only after moving into the dialogue format.

Product and Transition: Precipitating a Decision to Meet

Any such list of tasks is intimidating and suggests more formality and rigidity than will be the case in the real world. But these tasks need to be handled somehow for dialogue to begin.

When the groundwork has been laid, a decision to meet must be precipitated. This may require a traumatic event, a conciliatory gesture by a group or simply an invitation to meet. Whatever the situation, someone needs to propose: "Shall we meet and try to talk about our relationship?"

The product at the end of Stage One is an agreement among prospective participants to engage in a dialogue over some period for particular purposes. The understanding will set time, place, convening authority, financial responsibility if necessary and ground rules.

It should be repeated here that the person or persons who have completed the tasks in this stage to make a meeting happen may or may not moderate the meetings. Quite often, different experiences and abilities make different individuals appropriate to the two jobs. If the task of moderating falls to someone else, that person should be briefed on the full experience in Stage One and should be given a copy of this "Organizers' and Moderators' Manual" to begin Stage Two.

Separate Meetings with Each Team?

It is often desirable for the moderator to get together separately before the first meeting with the individual groups or subgroups in the dialogue. Such a meeting can serve several purposes:

- It can help participants begin to develop a relationship of mutual trust and respect.
- It can provide the moderator direct initial insight into what is on each group's and individual's minds.
- It can provide a preliminary sense of who are leaders, idea producers, negative factors and reconcilers in each group.
- It can help moderator and participants begin to identify the most divisive issues, as well as glimmers of common ground.
- It can provide a preview of potential sources of resistance to deepening working relationships as the dialogue progresses.
- It can reinforce the ground rules and forge parts of an alliance to make them work.

Please note: As you begin an actual dialogue, you will find it immensely helpful if you can take good notes yourself or arrange for a careful record of the dialogue to be kept. As soon as a meeting ends, you will also find it helpful to write an analysis for yourself of how far the group has progressed, what the obstacles are and what might be a useful takeoff point for the next session. The purpose of these notes is to give you an opportunity to review main thoughts and feelings so you can think in retrospect about the flow of the interaction. The purpose is not just to record who said what. In fact, it is important *not* to have a paper with names of speakers that could embarrass anyone if it were accidentally to reach people outside the group.

STAGE TWO: MAPPING AND NAMING
PROBLEMS AND RELATIONSHIPS

GUIDEPOST: Each group will normally go through this stage only once, so it is important to do a thorough job. Groups that cycle back from later stages will usually come back to the beginning of Stage Three—or at most to an abbreviated mapping exercise around one problem or situation.

BACKGROUND FOR THE MODERATOR

The purposes when participants first come together are: (1) to set the tone and habits of dialogue; (2) to get out on the table the main problems that affect relationships among them; and (3) to be sure the group identifies all of the significant relationships that are responsible for creating these problems and would need to be changed to resolve them. We speak of "mapping"—or drawing a mental picture—of the whole complex of relationships involved in the important problems participants face.

In addition to these specific purposes, you will want to keep certain overall aims in an ever-present back-of-the-mind agenda. The art of moderating depends on looking constantly for opportunities to move this underlying agenda forward.

First, when a group comes together, it is important to give character to this space by reiterating, consolidating and affirming the agreement on ground rules that was reached in the previous stage. The purpose, agenda and ground rules should be reaffirmed by all members of the group together. The "covenant" or "compact" shared with participants might be placed in front of each participant to be amended or confirmed by the whole group as the meeting begins.

Second, it is particularly important—because it is not the usual way of talking about issues—to restate the dual agenda.

We will always have two subjects on the agenda at the same time. One will be the specific problems we need to talk about. But, at the same time, we want to talk directly about the relationships underneath those problems. Trying to talk straightforwardly about our relationships is what makes this meeting different from others. Remember, relationships can be good or bad, healthy or unhealthy, constructive or destructive. But wherever people interact regularly over time, some kind of relationship exists.

You need continuously to help participants learn how talking about concrete problems can reveal the dynamics of the relationships underlying them.

Third, to enhance a full sense of the relationships involved, you must find ways to help participants become aware of each other as human beings and to dispel abstractions and stereotypes. Dialogue requires that each individual develop respect for the other persons and some trust that the dialogue is sincere. "Storytelling" can be a powerful way of introducing a human element. It can transform enemies into human beings. It can often project authenticity and power in ways that no analytical statement could. "Storytelling" can often become the only experience vivid enough to cause some participants to recognize the reality of others' problems and pain.

Fourth, to make each person come alive to the others, you must accept strong expressions of feeling, try to keep them within the bounds of mutual respect and try to channel them into fuller understanding. It is important to acknowledge them.

Expressions of feeling are understandable in this situation. The challenge is not to respond to them directly but to ask ourselves what we can learn from them about the dynamics of these relationships.

Fifth, at a more analytical level, the parties must learn to delve beneath initial positions to underlying interests. Most important, you should ask participants to explain why their interests are important to them.

Finally, you will need to find appropriate moments—"teaching time-outs"—to introduce certain concepts so participants can learn to use them to enlarge their way of approaching problems. Some of these in this first meeting might be: (1) dialogue as a way of talking that is different from argument, debate, mediation or negotiation; (2) the overall relationship between groups; and (3) interests.

CONDUCTING THE DIALOGUE

Mapping the Problems and the Relationships Underlying Them

It may be desirable as a group sits down to spend some time in which participants would begin getting to know each other in the context of the problems on the agenda.

In introducing yourselves, could each of you please share with the group some experience you have had with the relationships we are going to discuss?

After substantive introductions, you might begin the dialogue with the three questions below. The word "problem" refers to conditions, situations, practices, behaviors or obstacles that cause tension between groups.

What are the main problems you face and would like to resolve? Can you capture them in the story of an experience you have had?

How do these problems affect the interests of the group with which you identify? What are those interests? Why are they important to you?

What are the important relationships responsible for creating these problems that would need to be changed in order to resolve them?

You should tailor the questions to address the specific problems the group faces. But their aim is to help participants identify and define both the critical problems and the relationships underlying them. You cannot repeat that dual agenda too often because it is not a familiar one to most participants.

Responses to these questions will include a mix of analytical and emotional statements about events in the distant past and in recent time. Although you will have to curb lengthy recitals of history, everything people need to say has some relevance in their minds and is part of the picture, so you must treat it—and them—delicately.

As each problem is discussed, it is also essential to probe real interests—not just the objectively defined interests, but also the underlying explanations of why something is important to a person or group. You should ask some variation of the following question often enough to make the point that this dialogue is different from the usual academic or policy discussion:

Why do you really care? Why is that so important to your group?

Through most of this discussion, as participants lay out what is on their minds, you will play a relatively permissive role at this stage—except for encouraging participants to respect the right and time of each to speak and asking them to reflect on what lies beneath the points they are making. On these two points—identifying underlying relationships and probing deeply into interests—you will need to press harder.

A Thought for You, the Moderator

As participants discuss problems, they will often mention conditions they would like to see evolve that would better serve the interests of all. Developing a picture of preferred alternative relationships is work that will be done more systematically at the end of the next stage. But it can help lighten the atmosphere in the group to encourage hope. Without losing the main focus of this stage, it may be useful to focus such comments for later use with questions such as the following:

> *What kind of relationships would better serve your interests?*
> *What would you have to change to create those relationships?*
> *What would you want or need to preserve from the present situation? Why?*
> *Who else would have to be involved if you were to make those changes?*

Again without losing the main purpose of identifying problems and the relationships that cause them, you may find it helpful to seek a few brief responses to these questions:

> *Given the kind of relationships you would like to create, what are the main obstacles standing in the way of moving in that direction? We'll note them for later use.*
>
> *Given the direction in which you would like relationships to move and the barriers in the way, how would you define the main obstacles you face? We'll note them.*

Hope is part of a present situation. These questions are not intended to throw the group into focusing on solutions. That should be avoided at this stage. They simply help participants start thinking about the costs of the present situation. Obstacles are also part of the present situation; identifying them helps define key problems. But you may feel that it is safer to skip these questions at this stage.

Transition

Defining Key Problems
When a relatively full picture of key problems and the relationships behind them has emerged, you will begin shifting gears to bring this stage to a close. The task is to cluster problems and to select one to three for the group to talk about in greater depth. One way to start this transition to the next stage is to ask questions such as these:

> *Given the problems you have identified, what are the problems you most need to work on in greater depth?*
>
> *Can you define these problems concisely so as to reflect all major interests in the room?*

> *Given the realities of the situation, which problem should you work on first? What can you learn from the order in which you have placed these problems?*

The aim is to produce an agreed-upon list of the one to three carefully defined problems that the group considers most important. In this stage, the purpose has been to map the field—to identify a broad range of problems and the relationships underneath them that would have to be changed to deal with those problems. This has been a survey; that is why it is called "mapping." In contrast, in the next stage the group will take one problem at a time and probe it deeply and systematically. Often, group members will agree that they must deal with one problem before they can consider others seriously. There will be more time in the next meeting(s) to discuss the substance of each problem and more time to probe deeply into the dynamics of the relationships responsible for creating that problem.

In the next stage, you as the moderator will play a more active role in keeping the dialogue to the point and in helping the group address the difficult probing questions.

Overcoming Resistance

You should be prepared for the group to get "stuck" for a time at this point. Resistance can take unexpected forms. After a vigorous discussion, you may find participants lapsing into silence, going off on tangents, talking around a problem—that is, taking whatever tack they can to avoid the subject.

Much more difficult sometimes than reaching agreement on a list of specific problems for focusing the next stage of the dialogue is actually moving forward to talk about them in depth. Participants may be able to identify a problem and walk up to it—and then not be able to talk about it seriously. It is important for you to conduct a short trial run to see whether the group is ready.

> *If we tackle this problem, what are the elements you will talk about?*
> *Are you really willing to explore new ideas—to go beyond fixed positions? What might some of those ideas be?*

Resistance is likely when dialogue focuses on problems that participants know will involve their reaching out to others in ways that acknowledge the legitimacy of some of the other participants' views or make themselves vulnerable. It is one thing to agree on subjects to be discussed but quite another to be ready to talk about those subjects in a way that shows understanding of the other's feelings and way of thinking—or reveals one's own.

Resistance can result from a number of feelings. Some participants are unable to accept that others have serious needs or, even if they do, cannot reexamine their own positions in the light of others' needs. Other participants may realize that the discussion could trigger such deep feelings of injustice, grievance and anger that they fear they will lash out in a way they are afraid of; they may think that the risk is not worth taking. They may be frightened of the emotions they know could be released. Still others may fear that reaching out could cause their own group to ostracize them.

Overcoming such resistance is critical to the transition to Stage Three. Here are two possible approaches group members could take together:

Option One: Take a "Walk through History."   The more radical approach is to stop and deal with the resistance head-on—to have participants listen respectfully as each pours out her or his experiences, grievances, and hurts. Each participant tells her or his own story.

> *Tell us how the problem began for you or your group. What happened? How were you affected? Who was responsible?*
>
> *Can you tell us how your group thinks the other group would tell this story.*

The purpose is to begin a change in perceptions and stereotypes: "I didn't know that's how it looked to you. . . . We should forgive each other and try to start our relationship again." This approach tackles resistance at its heart and can open the door to changed relationships, but it requires a block of time and risks bogging down in recriminations and might even trigger an outburst of emotion that could destroy the dialogue. If carried through with mutual respect and human concern, it can produce a transforming experience and lay a foundation for reconciliation. But many moderators are afraid—sometimes with good reason this early in the dialogue—that they cannot constructively channel the emotions that may be turned loose.

Option Two: Address Obstacles through Concrete Problems.   Some groups may not be ready for such an intense experience this early in their relationship. In such cases, some variant of the "walk through history" may be reserved for later, if at all. Meanwhile, an alternative is to march ahead with discussion of the practical problems identified to the extent possible but actively seek out and use the moments when feeling is expressed and might be dealt with constructively to probe a particular obstacle to dialogue.

If the participants remain "stuck" in holding to present positions and unable to rethink their positions in the light of others' needs, you may need to state as clearly as possible that participants are closing their minds and hearts to others' concerns and adjourn the session, asking participants to reflect between meetings on why it is so difficult to open up to others' views and feelings.

This may be a point when a moderator should arrange to meet with individuals separately between meetings if that is possible. Since moments of resistance are moments of real potential insight if the moderator can start an honest conversation on the subject, it may well be worth the effort to try this. It could help participants in thinking through this problem to talk it out in a setting that is safer than the whole group. These feelings will have to be shared in the full group later, but maybe not the first time around.

Products

The first product of Stage Two is your judgment as moderator that resistance has been sufficiently overcome and that the quality of the dialogue has begun to change—that the participants can talk with each other instead of just stating views and that they show a readiness to settle down to an in-depth discussion of specific problems, one at a time. It is essential that they show a readiness to think honestly about the implications of others' interests for their own positions. Until they can, they are not ready to move solidly into Stage Three.

The second product is a clear definition and understanding of one to three concrete problems to be discussed in depth one at a time. This should be an agreed-upon list. These are problems that—if discussed in detail—will reveal the dynamics of the relationships that must be changed if the problems are to be dealt with. They must be defined concisely but in a way that reflects the main interests of all participants.

Homework Assignment

It often proves useful to provide participants a way of channeling their reflections as they evolve between meetings. At this stage, you might simply ask participants:

We have identified one or more specific problems to discuss more deeply at our next meeting. Could you come next time with a carefully worded statement of the problem(s) as you would describe it (them)? Could you list the most important ways in which these problems affect you? Come prepared to state which problem you think needs to be discussed first and why.

Or: *It seems difficult for you to reach out to each other. Could you try before the next meeting as fully and honestly as possible to describe why you don't feel comfortable opening up?*

GUIDEPOST: Once a group leaves Stage Two, it will normally not return. As participants work through later stages, they will continuously refine and deepen their map of their relationships. If they need to circle back, they will usually pick up with redefining the problem they want to work on at the beginning of Stage Three.

STAGE THREE: PROBING PROBLEMS AND RELATIONSHIPS TO CHOOSE A DIRECTION FOR CHANGE

GUIDEPOST: Beginning groups will enter this stage in natural progression from Stage Two. Groups that have been at work longer often need to circle back from later stages to tackle a new problem or an old task in a changed situation. These groups will normally pick up here by defining quickly the task they must work on now rather than go back to Stage Two. Their experience in dialogue will provide the full sense of their relationships that they need here.

BACKGROUND FOR THE MODERATOR

The purposes in this stage are: (1) to use in-depth probing of specific problems to reveal the dynamics of the conflictual relationships that cause those problems and—on the basis of that work—(2) to frame possible choices among approaches to changing those relationships so the group (3) can weigh those choices to set a general direction for action. At the end of Stage Three, participants will decide whether they have generated the will to change relationships. Only when they feel a compelling need for change and accept personal responsibility for trying to make change happen can the dialogue move beyond this stage.

To begin moving toward that objective, you will need to shift the way of talking from explaining positions and stating views to genuine dialogue, in which participants talk with each other, listen openly to each other, respond directly to each other and ask each other clarifying questions about why they feel as they do. You can state this as an objective in your opening remarks, but you will have to continue coaching throughout the session. Coaching can take the form of asking participants to respond directly to each other's points or posing questions for clarification yourself to model direct exchange.

You can think of the work in this stage as progressing through these phases:

First, you need to confirm the definition of the problem the group intends to work on. If it is a starting group moving from Stage Two, you will build from the homework participants have done. If this is a group circling back from a later stage, you will help participants redefine their starting point for moving on.

Second, you will help participants probe the problems that they have agreed they most need to work on in a way that helps bring to the surface the dynamics of the relationships that are responsible for creating the problem and that must be changed if the problem is to be dealt with.

Third, you will ask participants to suggest possible directions to take in tackling the problem. The purpose at this point is not to lay out a detailed course of action; that is the work of Stage Four. The purpose here is to frame the broad choices.

Fourth, you will then move participants to weigh those choices and to try to come to some sense of direction that they agree should guide their next steps.

Fifth, by asking the participants to assess where present relationships are leading, you will help them face up to the questions: Do we have the will to change the situation? Can we muster the determination to design ways of changing the destructive relationships that stand in the way of change? Spotlighting the dynamics of key relationships serves two purposes: Participants connect relationships to their real interests, and they also glimpse how those relationships might be changed. Again, asking participants to share personal experiences about how their interests are affected will be an important part of helping them reach judgments on the cost of allowing present relationships to go on as they are.

You as the moderator will need to play a more directive role in this stage. For example, strong feelings may flare up. You should control some and choose others to probe the dynamics of the interactions involved. You will also need to discipline the dialogue to keep it focused on the dual agenda— one problem at a time and the relationships that underlie the problems.

CONDUCTING THE DIALOGUE

Setting the Tone for a New Stage in the Dialogue

At the start of each session, you have the opportunity in an opening comment to consolidate and advance the pattern and substance of work. These are "teaching moments" in which repetition of purposes and methods helps participants become more conscious that they are engaged in a process with purpose and direction. They also become conscious of the concepts that can become useful tools as they proceed. Repetition is an important part of the teaching. These are some of the points that could be made explicit:

> *Until now, the discussion was largely an exchange of viewpoints. Now we want to shift to genuine dialogue. The purpose now is not to present views but to explore what others think and why. The key is really listening.*
>
> *We must now give greater attention to the relationships behind problems and situations.*
>
> *It's not enough to have a good analytical discussion of problems. We need to get at the underlying relationships that cause the problems. Those relationships are our real targets because we can't really resolve these problems until we can get at their roots.*
>
> *In order to help keep our talk focused on one subject at a time and to help probe the relationships behind the problems, I will be playing a more active role as moderator.*

Because the work in this stage needs to follow a particular logic—and this is key—it may be useful to offer a preview before ending your introductory remarks and plunging in:

> *In this meeting, we will try to follow a more logical sequence in our work than we have so far. When we were "mapping" the range of issues and relationships we need to deal with, it was natural to encourage you to say what was on your minds.*
>
> *Now, as we try to work our way through one problem at a time, we will go through five steps with each problem:*
>
> - *First, you need to agree on your definition of the problem you want to work on.*
> - *Second, you need to lay out the elements of the problem and the dynamics of the relationships that cause it.*

- *Third, you need to think of enough steps that might change those relationships to permit you to frame some general choices among different approaches. This does not have to be an elaborate exercise— just enough to help you choose the general direction you want to take.*
- *Fourth, you will need to spend some time weighing those choices together to come to an understanding on a general direction for action.*
- *Fifth, you will want to step back and look at where this situation is going in order to decide whether your interests are being hurt badly enough to cause you to want to try to design ways to change it.*

Each of these steps is presented in more detail below. For your background only, it will be helpful to keep in mind one way of diagnosing relationships. It is useful to think of relationships as breaking down into six components: (1) identity—not just physical characteristics, but also the human experience that has shaped a group's way of looking at the world; (2) interests— not just physical needs, but psychological needs and priorities as well; (3) a pattern and process of interaction—interdependence—that provides a context for change; (4) the way power operates—not just as material resources, but also as capacity to influence the course of events using human resources; (5) limits on behavior toward each other accepted at least tacitly by both sides; and (6) perceptions, misperceptions and stereotypes.

Confirming the Agenda

In groups just beginning a dialogue, an agenda—a list of problems—was agreed upon in general terms at the end of the last session. For homework, participants were asked to write their definitions of those problems. Since some time will probably have passed, it is a good idea to reach precise agreement on the definition of those problems. In groups circling back, the nature of the problem will probably be obvious from previous conversation, but it will be important for group members to say how they see the problem in the light of developments that have caused them to circle back.

I asked you to state carefully the problems the group agreed to work on. Would you share your definitions? Can we agree on a definition of each? We will hold off on discussing how these problems affect you until we move to the next step.

Can we list these problems in some logical order? What are the reasons behind this ordering? These reasons can give a sense of how problems interact.

Do we agree to stick with each subject long enough to reach under-standing?

Do we all understand the two related subjects on our agenda? We will be talking about specific problems, but we also want to probe the rela-tionships behind them.

(To the group circling back: How do recent developments cause you to restate this problem? How have they affected it?)

Probing Problems and Relationships

Once an agenda of one to three problems is agreed, the dialogue group turns to them one at a time. (Often, one problem is of such importance that a group will want to work on that problem through to the end of the process before tackling others. Sometimes, one may be an "umbrella" for others.) Dialogue begins with concrete problems because that is what people can most easily get their hands on. But the questions you will be asking are designed to begin getting at the relationships behind the prob-lems. You can draw now on the second round of questions below to deepen the probing of those relationships, or you can save them for a sec-ond round of probing.

GUIDEPOST: What follows will be a whole conversation with points popping out as they come to participants' minds. You will need all of this, but it won't come out in an orderly way in response to a neatly ordered set of questions. Let the talk flow. Use the questions to deepen it and to help or-ganize what you hear.

Possible first-round questions, built around the elements of relationship described above:

How would you describe this problem in the present situation?

What are its main elements?

Describe the main people and/or groups involved in this problem. What do they really want and need?

How does this problem affect what you and/or your group values most? How have you seen individuals in your group personally hurt by this prob-lem? Can you capture your point in a personal story?

What do you need from other groups to further your interests?

How do these groups normally interact: Do they fight, bargain, pos-ture, talk? Do they accept limits on how they act toward each other (for example, use of violence)?

> *How does each group perceive the others?*
> *What is the basis of each group's power?*

Some moderators may use a blackboard or flip charts to keep responses visible. A word or two can be used to capture each of these questions: elements, groups' interests and identity, interdependence, interaction, limits, perception, power. Using these words has the advantage of familiarizing the group with concepts that may be useful to them.

In a first round of responses to these questions, the talk may be similar to a thoughtful public deliberation about a serious subject that affects a community—with one significant difference: The participants come from communities that may fear, hate, despise, dehumanize and sometimes even kill each other. No problem will be constructively dealt with unless the conflictual relationships beneath it are changed.

Once the board or flip chart shows a reasonable number of ideas, you may have to go back and press in some areas for the underlying interests, feelings, experience, perceptions and relationships. Often, the handle for doing this is to pick up on a story someone has told and ask that participant to elaborate. Time and again, picking up on a remark that has gone unnoticed can open up a flood of comments about the dynamics of relationships—the feelings—involved. You must listen for these and make the most of them.

The usefulness of urging people to tell stories to elaborate on their points cannot be stressed enough. They will be especially important in setting the scene for the final exercise in this stage—deciding whether the problem is serious enough to cause participants to want to change course. Often, it is only stories of personal experience—rather than analytically stated points—that are gripping enough to cause participants to understand another person's plight. These stories are essential and should be encouraged at every natural opportunity for their cumulative impact.

In probing underlying relationships further, if you think you need to, you can use questions such as those below—some of them repeat. There will not be time or patience for a complete analysis; you simply need to be satisfied that participants have gone beyond a surface discussion of the problem to the underlying human relationships.

> *From your group's perspective, can you describe how other groups see themselves?*
> *What experience and heritage have produced their self-interest?*
> *Could you describe the other groups' interests in your own words? Can you see why those interests are important to them?*

Can you explain why these groups normally interact as they do?
What groups seem powerful to you? What is power in this situation? If
power is the capacity to influence events, who is really powerful? Why?
Do you sense any way in which parties to some of these relationships
observe certain limits in dealing with each other?
How does each group perceive the other? Why do you think that is the
case? In what ways does your group hold others responsible for your situa-
tion? Do you see ways of changing those perceptions?
Do these groups have any significant common interests? What are they?

GUIDEPOST: Sometimes, participants themselves will move the conversation to the next phase. "This has gone on long enough. People are really being hurt. It shouldn't be/doesn't have to be this way." Sometimes, you
may think that the talk is becoming repetitive and needs to move on. Don't
worry if you end up moving too soon. You can always circle back. Reminder:
Shifting gears is often easiest after a break.

Framing Approaches to Changing Relationships

The next step is to explore the range of possible actions that the dialogue
about problems and relationships suggests for changing the situation. Your
objective at this point is not to develop a detailed plan of action but rather
to distill a general sense of direction from the conversation.

It is important at this stage to stay at a level of broad human approaches
that reflect what participants consider important. As experts would define a
course of action, it would be built around a series of specific, technically defined actions. As citizens choose a sense of direction, it reflects their views of
human nature, their feelings of what is valuable to them and their hopes for
an improved life—a judgment that a strategy must include certain fundamental elements.

The reason for doing this now is to give participants choices to weigh together. That work can deepen their understanding of each other's concerns
and interests. If they can reach some broad view together, it will widen the
reservoir of actions from which they can work when they come—in Stage
Four—to designing a scenario of interactive steps.

The way to arrive at these broadly stated choices among approaches is to
look at the list of possible actions that have emerged in the conversation and
to cluster actions that seem to reflect a similar approach. Usually, they can
be characterized by the analysis of the problem that underlies them. Working in that way, you can help the group describe possible approaches clearly

enough to permit a discussion about the advantages and disadvantages of each and a statement of a general direction in which the group thinks the larger body politic should move.

A progression of questions such as the following would lead in this direction:

> *You have done a good job of laying out the elements of the problems and relationships you face. What kinds of actions can you see taking to deal with them? We don't want to spend time developing a detailed course of action. We just want to see what directions you might move in.*
>
> *(After a number of suggestions have been made): These suggestions seem to me to cluster in such ways as to suggest two or three possible broad approaches. Is that how it seems to you? Would this characterization of the choices give you enough to discuss in trying to choose a general direction for action?*

Remember, at this stage there need not be precision. The purpose is simply to set the stage for discussion of alternatives to the present situation.

Choosing a Direction for Action

The discussion of possible directions to move in dealing with problems and relationships will have framed deliberation on how to state the general direction in which the group would like to move. In fact, the discussion of possibilities will probably flow into formulating a choice.

The choice can be broadly or precisely stated. If there is no possible ground for even a broad agreement at this point, the group may want to stop here and go back to pick up another problem it has defined and bring consideration of that subject down to this point in the hope that the experience would open new doors.

> *Given the choices among possible directions that we identified, how do you feel about each? How would each affect your group's interests?*
>
> *Can you describe a broad approach to the problem as a basis for further discussion?*
>
> *If not, perhaps it would help to go back and pick up another problem and work it through the same kind of dialogue we have pursued to this point and see whether that opens new doors.*
>
> *Or we could step back and reflect on the present situation to see what doors that opens.*

It may be useful just to declare a moment of stock taking on the basis of the dialogue so far. Such reflection on the situation as the group has now described it may sharpen participants' thinking and encourage them to make another try at moving forward.

Assessing Where Relationships Are Going and Generating the Will to Change

Generating the will to change is the ultimate goal in Stage Three. Only the participants can do that, but you can set the stage so they can explore.

To begin moving in that direction, you will bring the group to a pause for an assessment of where present relationships are taking the situation. Building on their discussion so far, they need to think about whether they like what they see ahead. The key to moving to the next stage in the dialogue is a judgment that change is decidedly necessary and worth the cost. Then participants need to judge that the kind of change they would like cannot be achieved as long as the present state of relationships persists and that the costs of not changing are greater.

Where is the Situation Going?

This dialogue should have prompted thought about the consequences of continuing the present situation. At some point—perhaps after a break— you will need to shift gears by asking the group to imagine how the present situation might unfold. The participants could visualize a number of paths along which the situation might develop if nothing is done in the interim to reverse current trends. Once a trajectory is established, ask participants to assess the costs of that future to each party. It is not necessary that participants agree on the likelihood of any of these developments. It is essential that each hear the other's perspectives about how the current situation might unfold.

> *Given the present interactions between groups, where is the situation going?*
> *How would each line of development affect each group's interests?*
> *How would each line of development affect the capacities of each group to deal effectively with this problem—or to work with other groups where outcomes depend on collaboration?*
> *Can you live with what you see developing? Can your children live with it? Or do you see a serious need for change?*

Is Change Possible? What Would It Require?

If a will to change seems to be emerging, your next questions will be:

Is change possible?
Are others interested in change? Why? Is there some common ground?
What changes in relationships would be needed to move to the kind of community/country that would deal effectively with this problem and better serve your interests?
What changes in the mix of elements in these relationships would be needed?
What does each group do to perpetuate this situation?
What would you be willing to do to promote a desire for change among all who are affected?
What can you change in your own group's actions?
Bottom line: Are you really ready to work toward change? Can you now see a direction for action?

Attempting Transition: Is the Group Thinking Together? Is There a Will to Change?

The main task in bringing Stage Three to closure and moving to the next level of dialogue is to determine whether group members are ready and able to think and work together in an operational way. Do they really show the will to take that next step and begin talking together about how to design change? Often in a first burst of enthusiasm, participants will express determination to move ahead, but, when faced with the demands that step will require, they will back off. So even if they seem ready, you will want to probe to satisfy yourself.

Since you seem to feel that some change in the way your groups relate to each other would serve the interests of most groups, would you be willing to think together about the obstacles to change and about steps each group could take to make change possible?

If the group sounds ready to move on, you might want to take a very few minutes to try them out.

What do you see as the main obstacles to change?
What steps might help to overcome them?

GUIDEPOST: This is the most common place to get stuck—sometimes for a considerable period. See the discussion of overcoming resistance below.

Don't feel pressed to go on if the group doesn't seem able yet. Have a good discussion of why change is still difficult and adjourn with good feeling that the group has talked about that question honestly.

Depending on your judgment of the response:

If you would consider such a task, we would begin our next session with a working agenda to help you design a series of interactive steps. Is that agreed?

If not, why is it still difficult for your group to change or to work with others?

Transition: Overcoming Resistance

This is perhaps the most difficult transition in the whole process. To take the next step, participants must shift from being adversaries—however civilized they may have learned to be with each other—to becoming coworkers. That is asking a lot. It can be frightening.

Despite stories that dramatize pain caused by the present situation, some participants deep down may actually find practical advantages in it. In particularly tense situations, opposition and confrontation may elevate some individuals to positions of leadership they probably would not enjoy to the same extent if the confrontation ended. Others might lose a livelihood, a way of life or unusual material gain. At a minimum, living with a situation one knows—even if it causes some pain—may provide certainties, whereas moving to an unknown situation could leave individuals uncertain of their capacity to meet the challenge.

Enemies may genuinely fear what the adversary represents. They may really believe that the other side is so committed to holding or gaining power in self-defense that no real change in the relationship is possible. If there is no possibility of compromise, the only alternative might seem capitulation that would threaten what is most valued.

Cooperating with an adversary requires giving up one's worst picture of her or him. That worst picture may boost one's own self-esteem. Each of us defines her or his own identity in terms of not being someone else—for example, our enemy. Giving up that worst picture may cause uncertainty about who we are.

These are only a few of the factors that may be at work. They are mentioned here only to stimulate your own thoughts. Since you may be able to go only so far in a discussion with the whole group together, this may be another occasion for separate meetings with the individual groups.

Products

The products of this stage are: (1) the experience of an increasingly direct and probing dialogue that deepens and begins to change relationships within the group; (2) a new body of insight into the perceptions, feelings and conceptual frameworks of others; (3) an outline of how present relationships between the parties need to change in order to produce conditions that might lead to a more desirable way of dealing with problems; and (4) above all—at some point—a judgment that the costs of continuing the present situation and relationships outweigh the costs of trying to change them. The critical product—and Stage Three cannot end without it—is the generation of a will to change.

GUIDEPOST: At the end of Stage Two, the group may have identified one paramount problem it wanted to work on—a problem that needed to be dealt with before others could be tackled. If so, participants will push ahead, leaving other problems to return to later. Alternatively, if they identified two or three problems of close-to-equal importance, they may want to go back now to the beginning of Stage Three and bring their dialogue on these up to this point. One possible advantage is that seeing the problems together can produce new insight.

Homework Assignments

If the group is not ready to move on:

> *Before the next meeting, would you please think seriously and write your answers to these questions:*
> *Why is it still difficult for the group to think together about designing change?*
> *Is the situation still not really bad enough?*
> *What would have to happen to persuade you—and other members of your groups—that the situation can't go on any longer?*

GUIDEPOST: If the group is not ready to move on, you will come back to the next meeting and start from the questions above. You can supplement these by going back through the phases of Stage Three at a deeper level. Again, think about how the discussion of overcoming resistance above applies to your group.

If the group is ready to move on:

> *Before the next meeting, would you please write three lists:*
> *List obstacles to moving in the direction you want to move.*

State what you need from other groups to overcome those obstacles.
List possible steps for overcoming those obstacles.
Who can take those steps?

STAGE FOUR: SCENARIO-BUILDING—
EXPERIENCING A CHANGING RELATIONSHIP

BACKGROUND FOR THE MODERATOR

The purposes in this stage are twofold: to bring members of the group into a new way of thinking together about how to generate the change they would like to see happen and to design a scenario for change. In a sense, the group is a microcosm of the larger relationships involved, and its task is to project the change that members are experiencing into the larger community.

Figuratively, they are no longer sitting across the table talking to each other. They are sitting side by side to design ways to change relationships they all agree need to be changed to deal with problems in the interests of each.

The vehicle for change is posing a task that requires participants to design steps to change relationships between their groups. By thinking together about how to change a situation and the relationships that cause it, they themselves experience what the relationship would have to become in the larger society if the desired changes were to be accomplished. Each participant also experiences the internal obstacles to change and agonizes over how individuals and groups in the community will overcome those obstacles.

We call this task "scenario-building" because participants are asked to list obstacles to change, to think of steps to overcome those obstacles and to identify actors who can take those steps. Then they are asked to arrange these steps so that they interact—one responding to another—so the steps work to reinforce each other, build momentum and gradually create a new atmosphere. This interactive sequence of steps is like an unfolding scene in a drama.

CONDUCTING THE DIALOGUE

Scenario-Building: The Vehicle for Change

Establishing the starting point can stem from previous dialogue.

At the end of the last session, we asked: "What changes in relationships are needed to deal with the problems we have discussed?" Would someone review the responses? In what direction do you want to move?

With a starting point established, participants are then asked to perform four tasks that they have begun in their homework assignments:

First, they are to identify obstacles to moving in the direction they have determined that they want to pursue. They will certainly identify tangible obstacles, such as the positions of opposing parties, the lack of resources, the opposing objectives of different groups, the inflamed emotions in a heated conflict. But they will also need to probe beneath those to be sure they have brought to the surface the underlying human dimension of those obstacles—the fears, the historic grievances, the misperceptions, the stereotypes, the wounds from the past, the human interests. Often, these are greater obstacles to change than objective components of a situation, for which there may well be technical solutions.

> *What are the main obstacles to changing relationships in the ways needed?*
> *Are those the real obstacles or are there also other deeper-rooted obstacles?*
> *Are you addressing the fears, misperceptions, grievances, animosities?*

Second, once the group has developed a full list of obstacles, members need to develop a parallel list of steps that could help overcome those obstacles. Some of these may be official steps. Others may be steps taken by non-governmental organizations. All of them are steps designed for the purpose of removing the obstacles identified. These steps will include concrete measures to change conditions that one group finds unjust or harmful. The steps also need to include ways of dealing with misperceptions and underlying human fears and hurts. That area is not as often thought of in political life. It may include public statements or acts that symbolize contrition and forgiveness—recognition of harm that has been done and apology for it—or simply an acknowledgment of another group's suffering.

> *Name as many steps as you can think of to remove each of the obstacles you have listed.*
> *Since no single action may be enough to change long-standing relationships, a series of steps may be needed for cumulative impact.*
> *You need to pay special attention to the human obstacles. They are often the most serious obstacles, but we are least familiar with how to respond to them. You also need to pay attention to the obstacles your group poses or is responsible for.*

Third, once the participants have developed a significant list of obstacles and steps to overcome them, they need to identify who can take those steps.

Often, the first attempt at a list of actors reveals that participants are naming steps for others to take—none that they themselves will take responsibility for initiating. The exercise has little real meaning until participants themselves are personally engaged. They will not experience the cost of changing critical relationships until they struggle with those costs inside themselves.

Who can take the steps you have listed?
What steps could you persuade your own group to take?
What steps would you personally take responsibility for?

Fourth, the group needs to arrange these steps in some realistic interactive sequence. If they are to have the impact of changing a relationship and/or the dynamics of the interaction among groups, these steps must be placed in a pattern of action, response and further response. For instance, Party A may be able to take step one only if it is assured that Party B will respond; Party B may agree, but only if Party A will respond with step three. We have often called this sequence of interactive steps a "scenario" because it resembles the way a playwright builds an act in a play, with the interactions among the characters on the stage building a situation and then moving it forward.

What steps could your group take first? What is the exact objective?
What responses from other groups are required to make your steps possible? Must those responses be agreed upon before the first steps can be taken? Why?
How must your group respond to make their steps possible?
What other groups could be brought into the scenario?
Is it possible to cluster steps to enhance impact? What impact do you want?
When several significant steps have been taken, is there a way to create public recognition that something different is beginning to happen?
Is a cluster of steps possible to dramatize and consolidate the new trend?

Products and Transition

It is difficult to say which is the more important product of this thinking together—the scenario itself as a plan for future action or the relationships within the group that have been changed by creating the scenario. The scenario does provide a plan that could be taken out of the group into organizations in which participants are influential or into governments as suggestions for a new course of action. But the experience with key relationships within the participants themselves may lead them to insights into change that are even more important.

This stage ends when participants are satisfied with the scenario, but the delicate question hanging over the group will be: "What do we do with this plan?" They have a choice: They may want to treat their experience as a learning exercise within the group, perhaps to be shared with only a few close colleagues outside the group. Or the group could say: "This is too important to leave where it is. We have to find a way to put this into action."

The choice of whether to go on to act together to put these insights into play in the political arena may be difficult for many. So there may be, at the end of this stage, a deep discussion of the dangers and advantages of taking the next step. The participants may have very difficult personal and group choices to make. You should not try to influence this deliberation. Participants may need time before a next meeting to decide. Determining what to do is the work of Stage Five.

Homework Assignments

Before the next meeting, would you please:
Write down what you think can and should be done with this scenario.
Review your expectations for these meetings and list ways in which they were met and not met.

STAGE FIVE: ACTING TOGETHER
TO MAKE CHANGE HAPPEN

BACKGROUND FOR THE MODERATOR

One of the greatest challenges in this process is how to take the transforming insights and experiences generated within the dialogue into the larger community. The work in this stage goes well beyond what was done in Stage Four. Then participants were thinking about what *should* be done; now they must think about what *can* be done. How can a small group translate personal experiences of changed relationships into societal change? You must be realistic about expectations. At the same time, you must ask yourself: "How far can this process reach?"

Within the progress of this dialogue, the purpose at this stage is to determine whether the scenarios developed in Stage Four are realistic in the present situation and, if so, what practical steps might be developed for putting them into action. Whether and how participants will take action may still be a matter of difficult choice for each of them.

In the larger context of the whole dialogue, however, individual participants will have—between meetings—already carefully taken their insights back into their communities and councils in some way. During this dialogue—if it has continued over time—participants may have taken new, more influential positions, founded new organizations or formed new networks. It is worth asking as soon as a group moves into Stage Five: "What might each of you do to develop dialogues like this in your own communities or groups?"

The immediate task at this stage is for the participants to reflect together on what is possible for them. They need to deal with two sets of questions: Is the situation in the community such that an attempt at change seems workable? What capacities and resources can the group marshal?

CONDUCTING THE DIALOGUE

Assessing Conditions and Capacities

Conditions

In designing their scenario, perhaps without talking much about the situation in which implementation would take place, participants will have instinctively taken those conditions into account. But now they need to engage in a more systematic assessment:

> *What conditions in the society are favorable for the actions that you propose?*
> *What conditions are unfavorable?*
> *Do you see a chance of change?*
> *What risks, if any, would individuals take in their community if they were to pursue some of the actions that you suggest?*
> *Do they risk negative reaction and even social or physical danger by seeming to get out in front of the group in suggesting reaching out to the other community?*
> *Is there a risk of government retaliation if individuals or groups seem to be acting in ways that would change political or social behavior in the society?*

Capacities
Beyond assessing basic questions of possibility and security, participants will have to grapple with their doubts about what they can accomplish. One way to help put doubts into perspective is to ask participants to consider their own capacities to marshal resources for change. Often, as individuals think about the associations and networks of which they are a part, they begin to see what results old and new relationships might produce. They may begin to visualize what citizens outside government can accomplish simply by committing themselves to work together. That will be even more true if some are already in influential positions.

What capacities are there in the society to carry out actions such as those suggested?

At what level of development is the experience of citizens in creating associations in the public arena to accomplish their purposes? Are citizens accustomed to taking such initiative? Or is there so little experience with such citizen action that it seems impossible or dangerous to take such initiative? Does the problem begin with generating such capacity among citizens, or is there already a tradition of citizen action?

Do groups exist that already work across present lines of conflict or cleavage between groups in tension? At what stage of development are they?

This is essentially a process of assessing the situation in which the group will attempt to work and assessing what it has to work with. What capacities exist and what needs to be changed or created before action can be taken? At the end of this discussion, the bottom-line questions are:

Do the basic conditions of personal security exist that will permit individuals or groups to feel safe in taking the actions suggested? If not, what prior actions must be taken to create such conditions?

Do capacities exist in the society to work with? Are there citizens and associations already in place to work with or do those capacities need to be created before change is possible?

What can you personally—or organizations and groups you relate to— do to carry out parts of the scenario you have developed?

A Strategy for Implementation

Having worked through an assessment of conditions and capacities in the society, participants are ready to determine what opportunities and instruments exist for implementing the scenario they developed in Stage Four. They must now decide what steps they can and are willing to take to begin implementing that scenario.

To start laying out a strategy for implementation, group members must go back to their assessment of conditions and capacities within the society and grapple with such questions as:

Are conditions ripe for launching the first steps of the scenario we developed? Or are some preparatory steps necessary?

The scenario developed in Stage Four identified people and groups who might take the steps identified. Are those people or groups able and ready to take such steps? If not, can those groups be persuaded to act? How? If existing groups seem, in the light of our assessment, to be inadequate, can they be changed in some ways?

If some preparatory steps are necessary, can some of those steps be taken interactively so as to begin changing relationships even in this preparatory period? Could those steps usefully be added as a new beginning of the scenario?

In some situations prior to the evolution of a more developed civil society, the only option may be to work through existing institutions or organizations, such as agencies of government, political parties or established educational institutions. Even in highly developed civil societies, perhaps the most usual objective of nonofficial dialogue has been to influence government policies. Often, participants in such dialogues have been chosen because they are close to government policymakers.

Beyond working with existing institutions is the objective of influencing the direction of established nongovernmental organizations or associations where they exist, or creating them where they do not. Some nongovernmental organizations serve essential functions in the society that are almost quasi-governmental. Others put significant distance between themselves and official policies, but their operating practices give them a character and degree of stability that make many of them seem part of the Establishment. Still others are loose associations of citizens that have come together to accomplish a particular purpose and have very little permanent structure.

This public arena outside governmental structures provides the greatest opportunity for citizens to bring people together to pursue their purposes.

To implement the whole scenario, who could take what steps?
How could those who must take those steps be persuaded to take them?

What Responsibilities Will Participants Assume?

Once participants have a sense of what steps need to be taken to persuade larger elements of the society to act, they need to pause and talk seriously about what course they as individuals and the group as a whole might take. The group might consider a range of options such as the following, but these are laid out here only as a framework for you to have in mind; the options need to come from participants:

Option One

Individuals might make what personal use they can of the ideas generated in the group. Some members of the group may already have pursued this approach. It involves sharing insights with governments or discussing possible actions within participants' individual organizations. That, of course, can continue.

Option Two

Participants might act individually or as a group according to a plan agreed upon by the group to distribute its detailed scenarios systematically to appropriate authorities in government and in public organizations without lobbying them persistently to act. The rationale would be the importance of preserving their capacity—by not getting involved as implementers—to reflect on the changing situation, to call attention to growing problems in the relationship and to design new scenarios for heading them off or taking advantage of them.

Option Three

The group might constitute itself as an action group outside the dialogue meetings. It would actually assume responsibility for making steps in the scenario happen. Even if it were not itself the agent of action in all cases, it would undertake efforts to encourage governments or other organizations to take the steps involved.

Option Four

The group might remain a place in which ideas are generated but also draw individuals who have authority to act into this space for periods of time to equip them with the means of acting outside a group. Examples might include drawing individuals from action organizations into a series of workshops to experience designing political scenarios, then encouraging them to return to their organizations to implement those scenarios, or drawing others into a workshop on conducting dialogues, then encouraging them to go out to start comparable dialogues.

Since it is often difficult to bring individuals into a group that has been together for a long time, a preferable alternative can be for members of the original group to create new groups in their own communities. As such dialogue groups proliferate, participants could create a steering group to consolidate a scenario and encourage member groups and others to carry it out. The mere act of proliferating groups is itself an important action.

Option Five

The group might enlarge the space for a time to include participants from government and/or conflicting groups for the purpose of briefing them on the dialogue's experience. This would not involve them in the dialogue as such but would provide an opportunity to explain insights from the dialogue. The purpose would be to open the door to new partnerships between governments and the public. The original group could preserve its ability to remain a space in which people come together to think through basic problems and approaches to them, leaving action to be taken in other contexts when participants leave that space.

In this option, it would be possible for a dialogue group to create a subset of itself to discuss a particular problem. Participants could, for example, create a working group with membership designed to work on a particular conflictual relationship, while preserving the integrity of the original group itself. This way, the base group would have both a capacity for reflection and an opportunity to work operationally to help others deal with their conflict.

To bring participants' discussion of next steps to closure, these questions might be helpful:

What must happen first? Who will do it? How will it be connected to the next step?

What step must be taken in response? Who will take it? How will it be made clear that this step responds directly to the first and deliberately opens the door to a follow-up step?

What steps can be taken to generate wider public awareness of changing behaviors?

Will members of the group assure that the motivations behind steps are understood by all involved groups?

Concluding Reflections

The ultimate benefit from this stage is the experience of working together over time. Confronting unexpected obstacles in implementing a course of action together and designing ways of overcoming them deepens understanding of the relationship.

Whatever mechanism a group uses to put its insights into action, attention must also be given to the character and purpose of the action designed. If the fundamental work of this group is to design a change in the relationship among the parties they come from, then the actions must be directed at changing the relationship.

That will have been the purpose of the scenario, which lays out a series of steps in a way that contributes to enhancing interaction among the parties involved. It is in that interaction that relationships begin to change. What is important in taking those steps into the political arena is remembering that the basic purpose of generating interaction is to change relationships. The aim is not just persuading one party to take certain steps; the aim is to motivate that group to take its steps with the conscious purpose of facilitating or encouraging interaction with another party.

Keeping an eye on this underlying purpose can significantly change the way in which actions are taken. Many times in political experience, one party will have taken a step only to discover to their puzzlement that it has had no effect in the other body politic; perhaps they have not noticed it, or, just as likely, they have had their own internal reasons for not wanting to notice it.

The art then is both to design a scenario of interactive steps that makes sense analytically and—in the stage of acting together—to make sure that responses to such actions set in motion a cumulative interaction. This is not an abstract exercise. A relationship begins to change when one party—to use the words of a Russian colleague—is able to "penetrate the consciousness" of the other. A relationship begins to change when one group can cause the other to see it in a different way or hear it with new understanding. The purpose is to design actions that jolt Group B into taking notice that Group A's behavior is different from what Group B expected.

Much has been made in diplomatic literature of "signaling." Actions by one side are wafted into the air much as the smoke signals of Native Americans. Little attention has been given to assuring that those signals are read—and read correctly—by those for whom the signals are intended. The stage of acting together must give primary attention to creating an *inter*action and using that interaction as the context within which change in a relationship is gradually brought about.

As individuals from the two groups begin working together in this way, it is essential to recognize the full importance of what is happening. Individuals coming from groups that regard each other with suspicion—or even as adversaries—are trying together to design steps that would begin to create new relationships. In a sense, they are conspiring with individuals from a group many of their friends see as hostile to stimulate actions in each group that would change perceptions of the other.

As they begin to work together to generate actions that will change perceptions or even create the possibility of groups working together to change some aspect of the relationship, they will do well to think in terms of how to generate a response from the bottom up. They will not be directing their actions primarily at governments; they will be attempting to persuade citizens and groups of citizens on each side to take responsibility from the ground up to change the way the two groups interact. Because members of a group like this are citizens outside government, their actions must be designed to influence other citizens outside government.

Finally, it is important to remember that it is possible—even after a group has reached this point—to circle back to Stage Three to define further problems and to move with them through scenario building to action.

Endnotes

Preface

1. For example, Jürgen Habermas, *Knowledge and Human Interests* (1968), translated by Jeremy Shapiro (Boston: Beacon, 1971).
2. For more on the origins of the Dartmouth Conference, see the Introduction under the heading "A Public Peace Process: The Citizens' Instrument."
3. The other was Joseph J. Sisco, then assistant secretary of state for Near Eastern and South Asian affairs, soon to become undersecretary for political affairs.
4. *The Book of Confessions* (New York, now Louisville, KY: United Presbyterian Church, Office of the General Assembly, 1967), paras. 9.31, 9.44, 9.45.
5. *Peacemaking: The Believers' Calling* (New York, now Louisville, KY: United Presbyterian Church, Office of the General Assembly, 1980), p. 5.
6. "Joint Statement Issued by President Carter, President Anwar al-Sadat of Egypt, and Prime Minister Menachem Begin of Israel," September 6, 1978, in *Weekly Compilation of Presidential Documents*, Vol. 14, No. 36 (September 11, 1978), p. 1501.
7. Harold H. Saunders, "The Group Concept in American Sociology and Political Science, 1883–1929: A Study of Changing Views of the Nature of Society" (Ph.D. diss., Yale University, 1956).
8. Thomas Smerling, now president of the Israel Policy Forum in Washington, D.C.
9. These lists appeared as a work in progress in "Beyond 'We' and 'They': Conducting International Relationships," *Negotiation Journal* (Vol. 3, No. 3, July 1987), pp. 245–277.
10. Gennady I. Chufrin and Harold H. Saunders, "A Public Peace Process," *Negotiation Journal* (Vol. 9, No. 2, April 1993), pp. 155–177.
11. Rodrigo Botero, former Colombian finance minister.

Introduction

1. I have decided not to name the speaker because of the potentially unfavorable comparison—despite the excellent work of this organization—with approaches in other cities.

2. Mark Miller and Marc Peyser, "Black Churches: 'We Live in Daily Fear . . . ,'" *Newsweek*, (September 2, 1996), international ed., France, p. 4.

3. I first coined the name "a public peace process" in the title of a document, "Framework for a Public Peace Process: Toward an Israeli-Palestinian Peace," produced by a group of Israelis and Palestinians in a 1991 meeting that I moderated under the sponsorship of the Beyond War Foundation (since renamed the Foundation for Global Community) of Palo Alto, California, and the Stanford University Center on Conflict and Negotiation. It was next used as the title of an article by Gennady I. Chufrin and Harold H. Saunders, "A Public Peace Process," *Negotiation Journal* (Vol. 9, No. 2, April 1993), pp. 155–177. An elaboration of that article, in Russian, produced by Chufrin was published by the Charles F. Kettering Foundation, Dayton, Ohio, in 1995. A translation into Tajiki was published by the Tajikistan Center for Citizenship Education in Dushanbe in 1998.

4. During the 1960s, Norman Cousins organized, and the Rockefeller and Ford Foundations funded, the U.S. side of the Dartmouth Conference, while the Soviet Peace Committee served that role in Moscow. By the early 1970s, the Kettering Foundation, working closely with Cousins, who was a trustee, became the U.S. sponsor, and the Institute of U.S.A./Canada Studies of the Soviet Academy of Sciences became the Soviet cosponsor with the Peace Committee. As of this writing (in December 1998), James Voorhees was writing a monograph on the history of the Dartmouth Conference, principally from U.S. archives. Alice Bobrysheva, who interpreted for Cousins's first meetings in Moscow and then worked with Georgi Arbatov, director of the U.S.A./Canada Institute, for the 30 years of the Dartmouth Conference plenaries, is the source of the information about Khrushchev's approval. The origins of the Dartmouth Conference Regional Conflicts Task Force are described in the Preface under the heading "A Career Focused on Conflict Management, Peacemaking and Reconciliation."

5. Dwight D. Eisenhower, *Public Papers of the Presidents: 1959* (Washington, D.C.: GPO, 1959), p. 625.

6. John Burton, after a career in the Australian diplomatic service, turned to academic work, first in England and then in the United States, where he played a formative role in shaping the Institute for Conflict Analysis and Resolution at George Mason University. The late Edward Azar was a professor at the University of Maryland. Herbert Kelman is professor of social ethics at Harvard University. Vamik Volkan, a Turkish Cypriot by birth, is a psychoanalyst and professor at the University of Virginia's Health Sciences Center and founder of the Center for the Study of Mind and Human Inter-

action there. Christopher Mitchell is a professor at George Mason University. All have pioneered in developing, both in practice and in conceptualization, nonofficial dialogue among citizens in conflict. Please see the Acknowledgments for a fuller statement and the Suggested Readings for some of their writings relevant to the focus of this book.

7. See Ronald Fisher, *Interactive Conflict Resolution* (Syracuse, NY: Syracuse University Press, 1997) for a comprehensive account of these approaches.

8. Boutros Boutros-Ghali, *An Agenda for Peace: Preventive Diplomacy, Peacemaking and Peace-Keeping*, report of the secretary general pursuant to the statement adopted by the Summit Meeting of the Security Council on January 31, 1992 (New York: United Nations, 1992), VI, pp. 32–34.

9. When extended families in some societies grow into clans that act as such in the formal political and economic arenas, they also become part of the civil society. While ethnicity, race and religion define identities that may reach beyond state borders, organizations built around those identities and operating within a state are also normally part of the civil society.

10. See Sara M. Evans and Harry C. Boyte, *Free Spaces: The Sources of Democratic Change in America* (Chicago: University of Chicago Press, 1992 ed.), especially pp. 17–25; and David Mathews, *Politics for People* (Urbana and Chicago: University of Illinois Press, 1994), pp. 159–160.

11. This point is developed in *Meaningful Chaos: How People Form Relationships with Public Concerns*, report prepared for the Kettering Foundation by The Harwood Group (Dayton, OH: Kettering Foundation, 1993).

12. Daniel Yankelovich, draft manuscript of the Introduction in *The Magic of Dialogue: The Art of Turning Transactions into Successful Relationships* (New York: Simon and Schuster, 1999).

Chapter One

1. Almost my first publication on the Arab-Israeli peace process after leaving government called attention to the need to break down the human obstacles to peace before negotiation can begin: Harold H. Saunders, "We Need a Larger Theory of Negotiation: The Importance of Pre-Negotiating Phases," *Negotiation Journal* (Vol. 1, No. 3, July 1985), pp. 249–262. But my original book-length conceptualization of that peace process still strongly reflected my government experience: Harold H. Saunders, *The Other Walls: The Politics of the Arab-Israeli Peace Process* (Washington, D.C.: American Enterprise Institute, 1986), especially Chapters 1 and 2. The second edition, with the new subtitle *The Arab-Israeli Peace Process in a Global Perspective* (Princeton, NJ: Princeton University Press, 1991), includes an Epilogue placing the official peace process in the context of changes in our world that throw the spotlight on citizens. "Prenegotiation and Circum-Negotiation: Arenas of the Peace Process," in Chester A. Crocker and Fen

Osler Hampson, eds., with Pamela Aall, *Managing Global Chaos: Sources of and Responses to International Conflict* (Washington, D.C.: U.S. Institute of Peace, 1996), Chapter 28 returns explicitly to the larger political environment in which negotiation takes place. This present book is my next major step in developing the idea of a comprehensive—a multilevel—peace process large enough to embrace the whole body politic.

2. The Helsinki Final Act, signed in 1975, was the capstone of several years of East-West negotiations designed to reduce unpredictability and increase interactions and confidence across Cold War boundaries in Europe. The Conference on Security Cooperation in Europe became a permanent institution; now named the Organization of Security and Cooperation in Europe (OSCE), it comprises most of the countries of Europe and the former Soviet Union.

Chapter Two

1. The full text of President Anwar al-Sadat's speech, "Statement Before the Israeli Knesset, Jerusalem, November 20, 1977," appears in Harold H. Saunders, *The Other Walls*, (Princeton, NJ: Princeton University Press, 1991), Appendix VI, pp. 171–182. This excerpt is found on p. 177.
2. Mikhail Gorbachev, "Address to the Forty-Third Session of the United Nations General Assembly" (New York: TASS, December 7, 1988).
3. The concept is developed more fully in Harold H. Saunders, *The Concept of Relationship: A Perspective on the Future Between the United States and the Successor States to the Soviet Union* (Columbus, OH: Mershon Center, Ohio State University, 1993).
4. See Vamik D. Volkan, *The Need to Have Enemies and Allies: From Clinical Practice to International Relationships* (Northvale, NJ: Jason Aronson, 1988), for discussion of identity in intergroup relationships. A most helpful capsule discussion of the concept of identity appears in Erik H. Erikson, "Prologue," in *Identity: Youth and Crisis* (New York: Norton, 1968), Chapter 1.
5. See Harold H. Kelley, Ellen Berscheid, Andrew Christensen, John H. Harney, Ted L. Huston, Georges Levinger, Evie McClintock, Letitia Anne Peplau, Donald R. Peterson, *Close Relationships* (New York: W.H. Freeman, 1983), Chapters 1 and 2, especially pp. 12–13 and 31–40.
6. See I. William Zartman, *Ripe for Resolution: Conflict and Intervention in Africa* (New York: Oxford University Press, 1989, 2nd ed.); *Elusive Peace: Negotiating an End to Civil Wars* (Washington, D.C.: Brookings Institution, 1995); with Timothy Sisk, "Beyond the Hurting Stalemate" (National Research Council Paper, 1996).
7. See, for instance, John Paul Lederach, "Process: The Dynamics and Progression of Conflict," in *Building Peace: Sustainable Reconciliation in Divided Societies* (Washington, D.C.: U.S. Institute of Peace, 1997), Chapter 5.

8. This traditional Arab process is also described as "the indigenous Lebanese ritual of *sulha* ('peacemaking' or 'reconciliation'), which is an integral part of ancient communal traditions, whether Muslim, Christian or Druse, throughout the Arab world," in Laurie E. King-Irani, "The Power of Transformation and the Transformation of Power: Rituals of Forgiveness and Processes of Empowerment in Post-War Lebanon," in *Lessons from Lebanon* (Boulder, CO: Westview, forthcoming).

9. Many accounts of acknowledgment-contrition-forgiveness exchanges appear in Michael Henderson, *The Forgiveness Factor: Stories of Hope in a World of Conflict* (Salem, OR, and London: Grosvenor Books, 1996), with Forewords by Rajmohan Gandhi and Joseph V. Montville. See also Edward Luttwak, "Franco-German Reconciliation: The Overlooked Role of the Moral Re-Armament Movement," in Douglas Johnston and Cynthia Sampson, eds., *Religion: The Missing Dimension of Statecraft* (New York: Oxford University Press, 1994), Chapter 4.

10. This account appears in Joseph V. Montville, "The Healing Function in Political Conflict Resolution," in Dennis Sandole and Hugo van der Merwe, eds., *Conflict Resolution Theory and Practice* (Manchester, England: Manchester University Press, 1993), pp. 112–127. Montville, a former U.S. Foreign Service officer who worked primarily in the Middle East, is director of the preventive diplomacy program at the Center for Strategic and International Studies in Washington, D.C. He is the author of the phrase "track two diplomacy" and a practitioner of the "walk through history"—an exercise in which participants in a dialogue or other program talk or walk their way through painful moments in their shared history as a way of broadening their perspective on their relationship. He has been one of the pioneers in focusing operationally on acknowledgment, contrition and forgiveness.

11. For other discussions of the acknowledgment-contrition-forgiveness transaction and of reconciliation, see John Paul Lederach, *Building Peace,* Chapter 3; and Donald W. Shriver Jr., *An Ethic for Enemies: Forgiveness in Politics* (New York: Oxford University Press, 1995).

Chapter Three

1. Part of the text of this section, "Civil Society: A Context of Peacemaking and Peace-Building," originated as a letter dated January 4, 1996, from David Mathews and Harold H. Saunders to David Hamburg and Cyrus Vance, co-chairs of the Carnegie Commission on Preventing Deadly Conflict. The idea of two interrelated strategies—the five-stage process of sustained dialogue and a civil-society strategy—had been developed in Randa M. Slim and Harold H. Saunders, "Managing Conflict in Divided Societies: Lessons from Tajikistan," *Negotiation Journal* (Vol. 12, No. 1, January 1996), pp. 31–46.

2. The International Civil Society Exchange is an annual gathering of individuals working to strengthen citizenship, civil society and democratic practice in their countries. It originated as the Western Hemisphere Exchange, first formally organized by the Charles F. Kettering Foundation in 1989 following three years of exploration. It was expanded beyond the Western Hemisphere in 1994 to include participants from East-Central Europe, Russia and Lebanon. Participating organizations formed the International Civil Society Consortium for Public Deliberation in 1995. It is the practice of the exchange not to identify individual speakers outside the meeting room.

3. This picture of U.S. citizens' feelings was reported in The Harwood Group, *Citizens and Politics: A View from Main Street America* (Dayton, OH: Kettering Foundation, 1991), a study conducted for the Kettering Foundation. Its findings are also described and elaborated in David Mathews, *Politics for People* (Urbana and Chicago: University of Illinois Press, 1994), Chapter 1.

4. CIVICUS is "an international alliance dedicated to strengthening citizen action and civil society throughout the world" that was formally launched in 1993 after two years of exploratory work. CIVICUS's founders, according to the group's brochure, have pursued a strategy based on five building blocks: (1) preparing seven regional reports on the status of civil society around the world; (2) producing and distributing a world report (1995); (3) convening regional consultations in six regions of the world; (4) convening the first world assembly of CIVICUS (1995); and (5) building CIVICUS's membership. CIVITAS, an international consortium for civic education, was inaugurated at an international conference of civic educators held in Prague in June 1995. In the words of its brochure: "CIVITAS works to improve the capacities of its members through the exchange of ideas, techniques and materials. In the view of CIVITAS and its supporters, the mechanisms of democracy can function only when they are infused with a vigorous culture of democracy, and education is the well-spring of democratic culture."

5. See Robert D. Putnam, with Robert Leonardi and Rafaella Y. Nanetti, *Making Democracy Work: Civic Traditions in Modern Italy* (Princeton, NJ: Princeton University Press, 1993).

6. Personal letter, dated July 16, 1997, from Vaughn Grisham to the author. See also his book, *Tupelo: The Evolution of a Community* (Dayton, OH: Kettering Foundation, 1999).

7. The phrase "putting a responsible public back into politics" is central to Mathews's *Politics for People*. My Chapter Three is rooted deeply in the analysis laid out in this and previous books by Mathews and in the programs of the Kettering Foundation.

8. See Jane Mansbridge, *Beyond Adversary Democracy* (New York: Basic Books, 1980); David Mathews, *The Promise of Democracy* (Dayton, OH: Kettering Foundation, 1988); and Mathews, *Politics for People*, pp. 52–64.

9. Mathews, *Politics for People*, p. 99.
10. The Harwood Group, *Citizens and Politics*.
11. Mathews, *Politics for People*, pp. 100–101. He cites Hannah Arendt, *On Revolution* (New York: Penguin, 1963), pp. 118 and 133. The quotes from John Adams are hers.
12. Mathews, *Politics for People*, p. 105. He cites Arendt, *On Revolution*, p. 145, for the quote from Thomas Paine.
13. Alexis de Tocqueville, *Democracy in America*, edited by J.P. Mayer, translated by George Lawrence (Garden City: Doubleday, 1969), p. 513.
14. This attention to the small group as the principal unit of social organization is documented in my unpublished doctoral dissertation: Harold H. Saunders, "The Group Concept in American Sociology and Political Science, 1883–1929" (Ph. D. diss., Yale University, 1956). The impact of urbanization and industrialization on the individual as seen through the eyes of American authors in the late nineteenth and early twentieth centuries is captured in an unpublished essay by Harold H. Saunders, "In His Image" (B.A. Thesis, Princeton University, 1952).
15. Mathews, *Politics for People*, p. 167–168. He cites Daniel J. Elazar and John Kincaid, "Covenant and Polity," *New Conversations* (Vol. 4, 1979), pp. 4–8.
16. See Sara M. Evans and Harry C. Boyte, *Free Spaces: The Sources of Democratic Change in America*, (Chicago: University of Chicago Press, 1992 ed.).
17. Mathews, *Politics for People*, pp. 151–152. He cites Stanley J. Hallet, "Communities Can Plan Future on Their Own Terms," *Regeneration* (Vol. 6, January–February 1990), p. 8.
18. Mathews, *Politics for People*, p. 147, citing Hallet, "Communities Can Plan," p. 9.
19. Mary Parker Follett, *The New State: Group Organization: The Solution of Popular Government* (originally 1920; Gloucester: Peter Smith, 1965, reprint), cited in Mathews, *Politics for People*, p. 143.
20. Vaclav Havel, "The End of the Modern Era," *New York Times* (March 1, 1992), p. E15, quoted in Mathews, *Politics for People*, p. 163.
21. Putnam, with Leonardi and Nanetti, *Making Democracy Work*, p. 172.

Chapter Four

1. The source is the author's recollection from his own participation in mediation of the Egyptian-Israeli Peace Treaty. Other discussions of this point appear in Jimmy Carter, *Keeping Faith: Memoirs of a President* (New York: Bantam Books, 1982), pp. 282–284; and William B. Quandt, *Camp David: Peacemaking and Politics* (Washington, D.C.: Brookings Institution, 1986), pp. 51–52.

2. Independent Commission on Disarmament and Security Issues (the Palme Commission), *Common Security: A Blueprint for Survival* (New York: Simon and Schuster, 1982).

Chapter Five

1. This is the phrase used at the Charles F. Kettering Foundation to describe a situation in which each group in a community argues its favorite solution without stepping back to consider the deeper underlying causes of the problem or the various community interests involved.
2. David Bohm, *On Dialogue*, edited by Lee Nichol (London and New York: Routledge, 1996), pp. 6–7.
3. Drawn from a paper prepared by Shelley Berman, based on discussions of the Dialogue Group of the Boston chapter of Educators for Social Responsibility (ESR), National ESR Office.
4. Daniel Yankelovich, Introduction, in *The Magic of Dialogue: The Art of Turning Transactions into Successful Relationships* (New York: Simon and Schuster, 1999).
5. Bohm, *On Dialogue*, pp. 9–28, especially pp. 9, 20–21, 26, 28.
6. Bernard Murchland, ed., *Higher Education and the Practice of Democratic Politics: A Political Education Reader* (Dayton, OH: Kettering Foundation, 1991), p. 7.
7. According to the practices of the Dartmouth Conference Regional Conflicts Task Force, comments are not attributed to individuals outside the meeting room.
8. The Institute for Multi-Track Diplomacy in Washington, D.C., was founded by John McDonald and Louise Diamond.
9. These formulations on resistance were suggested in a personal letter to me by J. Anderson Thomson Jr. of the Center for the Study of Mind and Human Interaction in the Health Sciences Center of the University of Virginia, Charlottesville, Virginia. Extended conversations with Maurice Apprey of the same center also deepened my understanding of resistance.
10. The paragraphs that follow are drawn from an unpublished paper by Vamik Volkan, "Methodology for Reduction of Ethnic Tension, and Promotion of Democratization and Institution Building" (Center for the Study of Mind and Human Interaction, University of Virginia, March 1995), especially pp. 2–3 and 8–13.

Chapter Six

1. See Christopher R. Mitchell, "Intra-National Mediation: Person or Process? Alternative Models of Third Party Involvement in Protracted Internal Conflicts," paper prepared for delivery at the International Society of Political

Psychology Annual Conference, Helsinki, Finland, July 1–6, 1991. This was later published as "The Progress and Stages of Mediation: Two Sudanese Cases," in David Smock, ed., *Making War and Waging Peace: Foreign Intervention in Africa* (Washington, D.C.: United States Institute of Peace Press, 1993), especially pp. 139–160.

2. See Chapter Eight for the story of the Baton Rouge sustained dialogue.

3. David Bohm, *On Dialogue,* edited by Lee Nichol (London and New York: Routledge, 1996), pp. 13–14.

4. Herbert Kelman, who has developed this practice most fully in his problem-solving workshops with Arabs and Israelis, will normally hold a meeting of three or four hours with each team before the opening session. He systematically repeats the ground rules but spends most of the time hearing what problems are of deepest concern to each.

5. Harry C. Boyte, "Concepts and the Five-Stage Process," personal memo, dated June 23, 1993, to the author.

6. This point about the need to teach concepts was developed in Boyte's personal memo to the author, "Concepts and the Five-Stage Process," cited above. The concepts are rooted in the work with citizens' organizations of the Center for Democracy and Citizenship at the Hubert H. Humphrey Institute of Public Affairs of the University of Minnesota. The point made throughout these chapters about the value of teaching concepts draws on this memo.

7. For more on the "acknowledgment-contrition-forgiveness transaction," please see Chapter Two, notes 9–11.

8. See Chapter Five under the heading "Some Human Experiences in Dialogue."

9. The subjects of framing issues for public deliberation and deliberation itself are dealt with in David Mathews, *Politics for People* (Urbana and Chicago: University of Illinois Press, 1994), Chapter 6 and pp. 151–153. The Charles F. Kettering Foundation has produced a considerable collection of booklets and working papers on these subjects. These are available from the Kettering Foundation, 200 Commons Road, Dayton, OH 45459, U.S.A. A careful reader may note that my presentation in Chapter Three of a citizens' political process places the framing of issues in Stage Two rather than in Stage Three, as is the case here in Chapter Six. That difference illustrates two points: First, breaking political processes into stages is not an act of rigid doctrine but a reflection of what is happening in particular circumstances. Second, in the citizens' political process, in which there may be more focus on concrete issues through deliberation, I find it natural to place the preparations for deliberation in a prior stage and to make deliberation an act of its own. In contrast, in the public peace process, in which mapping and naming issues necessarily requires so much time, it seems logical to present the naming of a problem as a transition point. It is here that some groups get stuck and need more time before they are ready to move on. This reflects the

way in which the work seemed to organize itself in the Inter-Tajik Dialogue described in Chapter Seven.

10. As noted earlier (see the Introduction, note 3), this meeting took place under the auspices of the Beyond War Foundation (now the Foundation for Global Community) of Palo Alto, California, and the Stanford University Center on Negotiation and Conflict. The document produced in this meeting was built around a vision of a peaceful relationship between Israeli and, eventually, Palestinian states as well as a number of steps that individuals in that meeting or organizations of which they were a part could take in their respective bodies politic to change perceptions of each other's communities. The document was not so much a scenario of interactive steps as an inventory of programs and actions that could be taken. The relevant point here is that a network of organizations through which group members could act—a developed civil society—already existed despite military occupation. The group itself did not take responsibility for follow-up, but the individuals returning to their own lives did commit themselves to work in those directions through larger organizations. They also committed themselves to inviting others to think of their organizations' activities as being part of the public peace process and as contributing to it. In effect, they made themselves an informal center for enhancing the cumulative impact of all of these actions.

Chapter Seven

1. The origins of the Dartmouth Conference Regional Conflicts Task Force are described in the Preface under the heading "A Career Focused on Conflict Management, Peacemaking and Reconciliation." The origins of the Dartmouth Conference are described in the Introduction under the heading "A Public Peace Process: The Citizens' Instrument."

2. The two-part strategy is described in Randa M. Slim and Harold H. Saunders, "Managing Conflict in Divided Societies: Lessons from Tajikistan," *Negotiation Journal* (Vol. 12, No. 1, January 1996), pp. 31–46. The background section on the civil war in Tajikistan and the section on the civil-society strategy are adapted from that article.

3. For the steps leading to the constitutional formation of the USSR, please see Anatole G. Mazour, *Russia Past and Present* (New York: D. Van Nostrand Company, Inc., 1951), pp. 450–451 and 479–481. For a brief history of Tajikistan's formation, see Martha Brill Olcott, *Central Asia's New States: Independence, Foreign Policy, and Regional Security* (Washington, D.C.: United States Institute of Peace), pp. 121–128.

4. For a fuller account, please see Irina Zviagelskaya, *The Tajik Conflict* (Moscow: Russian Center for Strategic Research and International Studies and Reading, England: Ithaca, 1997).

5. The team includes Gennady I. Chufrin (corresponding member, Russian Academy of Sciences, and former deputy director of the Institute of Oriental Studies) and Harold H. Saunders, co-moderators; Vitaly Naumkin and Irina Zviagelskaya (president and vice president, respectively, Russian Center for Strategic Research and International Studies, and senior scholars in the Institute of Oriental Studies); Thomas E. Gouttierre (dean of international programs, University of Nebraska at Omaha) and Randa Slim (program officer, Charles F. Kettering Foundation, when the Dialogue began).

6. An earlier account of the Inter-Tajik Dialogue appeared in Harold H. Saunders, "Sustained Dialogue on Tajikistan," *Mind and Human Interaction* (Vol. 6, No. 3, August 1995), pp. 123–135.

7. One of the rules of the Dialogue is that individuals will not be quoted by name outside the room. The sources for all such quotes in this chapter are my notes, my analytical memoranda written after each meeting or the rapporteur's confidential record.

8. This and the next nine joint memoranda produced during meetings of the Dialogue were later published in Tajiki, Russian and English: Gennady I. Chufrin, Ashurboi Imomov and Harold H. Saunders, eds., *Memoranda and Appeals of the Inter-Tajik Dialogue Within the Framework of the Dartmouth Conference* (1993–1997) (Moscow: Russian Center for Strategic Research and International Studies, 1997). This also includes a short account of the Dialogue. All quotes from joint memoranda may be found in this volume.

9. This was a translation of a revised version of the article by Gennady I. Chufrin and Harold H. Saunders, "A Public Peace Process," originally published in *Negotiation Journal.* The revised version is available only in Russian and Tajiki.

10. David Mathews, *Politics for People* (Urbana and Chicago: University of Illinois Press, 1994).

Chapter Eight

1. David Duke had run in 1990 against Bennett Johnson in the election for U.S. Senate. In 1991, he had been in a runoff election for governor against Edwin Edwards. It was the belief of many participants, according to Reverend Jeff Day, that the racial fallout from these campaigns provided some of the incendiary material—along with crime and its racial overtones and public education—that set the stage for the decision to focus the town meeting on race, as it had triggered the conversations leading to the formation of the black-white clergy group in early 1992.

2. Cary Prejean, "Leadership and Team Building," at the time of its use in the committee, an unpublished draft.

Chapter Nine

1. The Sinai, without Gaza, was returned to Egypt as part of the Israeli-Egyptian Peace Treaty of 1979.
2. These included refugees from both the 1948 and the 1967 wars, as well as Palestinians who were outside the area at the time of the 1967 war. Some of the latter were permitted to return over the years under the rubric of family reunification. In addition, there were, by 1998, close to one million Arab citizens of Israel; these are Palestinians who remained in Israel after the 1948 war.
3. Historic Palestine includes not only Israel of the 1949–1967 borders (armistice lines) and the West Bank of the Jordan (annexed by Jordan in 1951 and occupied by Israel in the 1967 Six-Day War), but also the East Bank of the Jordan. This East Bank became known as TransJordan, created as a separate entity by the British in 1921. TransJordan, today the Hashemite Kingdom of Jordan, is not part of the Israeli-Palestinian dispute; moreover, King Hussein of Jordan relinquished all claims to the (occupied) West Bank in favor of the Palestine Liberation Organization (PLO) in 1988.
4. By "mainstream" is meant Israelis associated with the Zionist parties, movements or organizations, the most mainstream being those of the Labor Zionist persuasion.
5. Hammami, while the PLO representative in London, was assassinated in 1978; Sartawi was assassinated at a meeting of the Socialist International in 1983 in Lisbon.
6. At the PNC meeting, Arafat came out in favor of contacts "with all personages who recognize our rights as a people to self-determination and the establishment of an independent Palestinian state." See Galia Golan, *The Soviet Union and the Palestine Liberation Organization: An Uneasy Alliance* (New York: Praeger, 1980), p. 175, citing MENA (Middle East News Agency) (March 17, 1977). These remarks, which would include Zionists, were said to have received applause (Golan, *Uneasy Alliance*, citing *Middle East International* [May 1977], p. 10). See also Alain Gresh, *The PLO: The Struggle Within* (London: Zed Books, 1988), pp. 196–199.
7. "Mainstream" in the Palestinian context refers to those identifying with the PLO, the most mainstream being Fatah and the large number describing themselves as Independents.
8. The Israeli author remembers the day of the second or third meeting of the early women's dialogue, held at a Palestinian woman's home in Gaza. She did not even tell her husband she was going to Gaza because of the danger involved in being there in the 1980s. Indeed, while she was there, an Israeli was knifed to death in the town market.
9. Then Bir Zeit Professor Dr. Sari Nusseibeh, for example, was beaten up by Bir Zeit students on one occasion because of his activities with Israelis, and Professor Galia Golan's regular appearances before the Knesset Foreign and

Security Affairs Committee (as a Soviet expert) were canceled because of her participation in meetings with Palestinians abroad.

10. Apparently to sabotage the event, Israel declared a closure of the territories for the day of the Hands Around Jerusalem. Nonetheless, 15,000 Palestinians managed to get there, many from outside Jerusalem.

11. The law was abrogated by the Knesset after the 1992 elections that brought in a left-center majority in the Knesset. It had banned contact with members of "terrorist organizations," which was the way the government described the PLO. The ban basically applied only abroad, where PLO officials could and did meet with Israelis. Inside the occupied territories, Israel, as the occupying power, forbade membership in a political organization, so Palestinians kept any such membership secret. In the meetings abroad, which were, indeed, illegal, a number of devices were used to keep within the letter of the law and to protect the Israelis involved: Participants from the two sides might refrain from sitting next to each other in public sessions; a third party might stand or sit between Palestinians and Israelis during breaks or in smaller sessions. Many absurd situations resulted until the ban was, in fact, totally ignored (although one Israeli, Abie Nathan, was jailed for this activity, and a group of others was brought to trial). The Israeli author remembers going over to a PLO official whom she had met in numerous previous dialogues and giving him a greeting kiss on the cheek—wondering if that were included in the "contact" banned by the Israeli law.

Chapter Ten

1. Gennady I. Chufrin and Harold H. Saunders, "A Public Peace Process," *Negotiation Journal* (Vol. 9, No. 2, April 1993), pp. 155–177.

2. Randa M. Slim and Harold H. Saunders, "Proposal for a Financial Partnership in Developing Political Processes for the Resolution of Conflict and Strengthening Civil Society: A Public Peace Process," memo, dated January 27, 1993, to the William and Flora Hewlett Foundation, pp. 6–7.

3. Gennady Chufrin, Ashurboi Imomov and Harold Saunders, eds., *Memoranda and Appeals of the Inter-Tajik Dialogue Within the Framework of the Dartmouth Conference* (1993–1997) (Moscow: Russian Center for Strategic Research and International Studies, 1997). As noted in Chapter Seven, one participant chartered the Tajikistan Center for Citizenship Education; another, the Oli Somon Foundation.

4. This framework provides the organization of the substantial collection of reading materials on conflict resolution and civil society—the portable library—assembled for the three-dozen university professors and administrators who asked for help in starting courses in conflict resolution. It provided the starting point for their curricula. In this way, the philosophy and experience of the Dialogue will be embedded in the teaching of five universities.

The publications on the five-stage process and on the story of the Dialogue and its memoranda will also become part of the canon of readings on conflict resolution. The collaboration with the universities to develop courses in conflict resolution has been partly funded by the United States Institute of Peace and the William and Flora Hewlett Foundation.

5. This comment was made in a later off-the-record conversation between that official and the American-Russian team, recorded in a formal confidential memorandum for the file.

Epilogue

1. See Chapter Three, note 20.
2. See Introduction, note 12.
3. Deborah Tannen, *The Argument Culture: Moving from Debate to Dialogue* (New York: Random House, 1998), pp. 3–4.
4. See Introduction, note 12.
5. Tannen, *The Argument Culture*, p. 256.
6. Tannen, *The Argument Culture*, pp. 267 and 289–290.
7. Raymond Shonholtz, "The Mediating Future," in Raymond Shonholtz and Ilana Shapiro, special editors, *Annals of the American Academy of Political and Social Science* (Vol. 552, July 1997), "Strengthening Transitional Democracies Through Conflict Resolution," pp. 144–145, 147, and 149.

Suggested Readings

Axelrod, Robert, *The Evolution of Cooperation* (New York: Basic Books, 1984).

Azar, Edward E., *The Management of Protracted Social Conflict: Theory and Cases* (Hampshire, England: Dartmouth, 1990).

Azar, Edward E., and Burton, John, eds., *International Conflict Resolution: Theory and Practice* (England: Wheatsheaf, 1986).

Bercovitch, Jacob, and Rubin, Jeffery Z., *Mediation in International Relations* (London: Macmillan, 1992).

Bunker, B., and Rubin, Jeffery Z., *Conflict, Cooperation, and Justice: Essays Inspired by the Work of Morton Deutsch* (San Francisco: Jossey-Bass, 1995).

Berman, Maureen R., and Johnson, Joseph E., *Unofficial Diplomats* (New York: Columbia University Press, 1990).

Burton, John, *Resolving Deep-Rooted Conflict: A Handbook* (Washington, D.C.: University Press of America, 1987).

————, *Conflict: Human Needs Theory* (New York: St. Martin's Press, 1990).

————, *Conflict Resolution and Provention* (New York: St. Martin's Press, 1990).

Bush, Robert A. Baruch, and Folger, Joseph P., *The Promise of Mediation: Responding to Conflict Through Empowerment and Recognition* (San Francisco: Jossey-Bass, 1994).

Chufrin, Gennady I., and Saunders, Harold H., "A Public Peace Process," *Negotiation Journal* (Vol. 9, No. 2, April 1993), pp. 155–177.

Crocker, Chester A., and Hampson, Fen Osler, eds., with Aall, Pamela, *Managing Global Chaos: Sources of and Responses to International Conflict* (Washington, D.C.: United States Institute of Peace Press, 1996).

Deutsch, Morton, *The Resolution of Conflict: Constructive and Destructive Processes* (New Haven, CT: Yale University Press, 1973).

Diamond, Louise, *Peacemakers in a War Zone* (Occasional Paper No. 1) (Washington, D.C.: Institute for Multi-Track Diplomacy, 1993).

————, *Beyond Win/Win: The Heroic Journey of Conflict Transformation* (Occasional Paper No. 4) (Washington, D.C.: Institute for Multi-Track Diplomacy, 1994).

Diamond, Louise, and McDonald, John, *Multi-Track Diplomacy: A Systems Approach to Peace* (Washington, D.C.: Institute for Multi-Track Diplomacy, 1993; West Hartford, CT: Kumarian, 1996, rev. ed.).

Doob, Leonard W., ed., *Resolving Conflict in Africa: The Fermeda Workshop* (New Haven, CT: Yale University Press, 1970).

Faure, G.O., and Rubin, Jeffery Z., *Culture and Negotiation* (Newbury Park, CA: Sage, 1993).

Fisher, Roger, and Ury, William, *Getting to Yes: Negotiating Agreement Without Giving In* (Boston: Houghton-Mifflin, 1981).

Fisher, Ronald, "Third Party Consultation as a Method of Intergroup Conflict Resolution: A Review of Studies," *Journal of Conflict Resolution* (Vol. 27, No. 2, June 1983), pp. 301–334.

———, *The Social Psychology of Intergroup and International Conflict Resolution* (New York: Springer-Verlag, 1990), particularly the chapter on third-party consultation.

———, "Developing the Field of Interactive Conflict Resolution: Issues in Training, Funding, and Institutionalization," *Political Psychology* (Vol. 14, No. 1, March 1993), pp. 123–138.

———, "Generic Principles for Resolving Intergroup Conflict," *Journal of Social Issues* (Vol. 50, No. 1, 1994), pp. 47–66.

———, *Interactive Conflict Resolution* (Syracuse, NY: Syracuse University Press, 1997).

Jervis, Robert, *Perception and Misperception in International Politics* (Princeton, NJ: Princeton University Press, 1976).

Kelman, Herbert C., "An Interactional Approach to Conflict Resolution and Its Application to Israeli-Palestinian Relations," *International Interactions* (Vol. 6, 1979), pp. 99–122.

———, "Interactive Problem Solving: The Uses and Limits of a Therapeutic Model for the Resolution of International Conflicts," in Volkan, Vamik D., Montville, Joseph V., and Julius, Demetrios A., *The Psychodynamics of International Relationships, Vol. 2: Unofficial Diplomacy at Work* (Lexington, MA: Lexington Books, 1991), Chapter 8.

———, "Acknowledging the Other's Nationhood: How to Create a Momentum for the Israeli-Palestinian Negotiations," *Journal of Palestine Studies* (Vol. 22, No. 1, Autumn 1992), pp. 18–38.

———, "Informal Mediation by the Scholar/Practitioner," in Percovitch, J., and Rubin, J., eds., *Mediation in International Relations: Multiple Approaches to Conflict Management* (New York: St. Martin's Press, 1992).

———, "Coalitions Across Conflict Lines: The Interplay of Conflicts Within and Between the Israeli and Palestinian Communities," in Worchel, S., and Simpson, J., eds., *Conflict Between People and Groups* (Chicago: Nelson-Hall, 1993), Chapter 14, pp. 236–258.

———, "In Practice: Contributions of an Unofficial Conflict Resolution Effort to the Israeli-Palestinian Breakthrough," *Negotiation Journal* (Vol. 11, No. 1, January 1995), pp. 19–27.

Kriesberg, Louis, *Social Conflicts* (Englewood Cliffs, NJ: Prentice-Hall, 1973, 1982).

————, *Constructive Conflicts: From Escalation to Resolution* (New York: Rowman and Littlefield, 1998).

Lederach, John Paul, *Preparing for Peace: Conflict Transformation Across Cultures* (Syracuse, NY: Syracuse University Press, 1995).

————, *Building Peace: Sustainable Reconciliation in Divided Societies* (Washington, D.C.: United States Institute of Peace Press, 1997).

Lund, Michael S., *Preventing Violent Conflicts: A Strategy for Preventive Diplomacy* (Washington, D.C.: United States Institute of Peace Press, 1996).

McDonald, John W., "Further Exploration of Track Two Diplomacy," in Kriesberg, Louis, ed., *Timing and the De-Escalation of International Conflicts* (Syracuse, NY: Syracuse University Press, 1991), Chapter 8.

————, *Guidelines for Newcomers to Track Two Diplomacy* (Occasional Paper No. 2) (Washington, D.C.: Institute for Multi-Track Diplomacy, 1993).

McDonald, John W., and Bendahmane, Diane B., *Conflict Resolution: Track Two Diplomacy* (Washington, D.C.: GPO, Department of State, Center for the Study of Foreign Affairs, March 1987; Washington, D.C.: Institute for Multi-Track Diplomacy, 1995, rev. ed.).

Mitchell, Christopher R., *Peacemaking and the Consultant's Role* (Farnborough: Gower, and New York: Nicholls, 1981).

————, *The Structure of International Conflict* (London: Macmillan, 1981).

————, "A Willingness to Talk: Conciliatory Gestures and De-Escalation," *Negotiation Journal* (Vol. 7, No. 4, October 1991), pp. 405–429.

————, "The Progress and Stages of Mediation: Two Sudanese Cases," in Smock, David, ed., *Making War and Waging Peace: Foreign Intervention in Africa* (Washington, D.C.: United States Institute of Peace Press, 1993), especially pp. 139–160.

————, "Conflict Research," in Groom, A.J.R., and Light, Margot, eds., *Contemporary International Relations: A Guide to Theory* (London: Frances Pinter, 1994), pp. 128–141.

Montville, Joseph, "Psychoanalytic Enlightenment and the Greening of Diplomacy," *Journal of the American Psychoanalytic Association* (Vol. 37, No. 2, 1989), pp. 297–318.

————, "Transnationalism and the Role of Track Two Diplomacy," in Thompson, W., and Jensen, K., eds., *Approaches to Peace: An Intellectual Map* (Washington, D.C.: United States Institute of Peace Press, 1991), Chapter 10.

————, "The Healing Function in Political Conflict Resolution," in Sandole, Dennis, and van der Merwe, Hugo, eds., *Conflict Resolution: Theory and Practice,* (Manchester, England: Manchester University Press, 1994), pp. 112–127.

————, "Complicated Mourning and Mobilization for Nationalism," in Braun, Jerome, ed., *Social Pathology in Comparative Perspective: The Nature and Psychology of Civil Society* (New York: Praeger, 1995), Chapter 8.

————, "Ethnic Conflict," in Powers, Roger S., and Vogele, William B., eds., *Protest, Power and Change: An Encyclopedia of Nonviolent Action from ACT-Up to Women's Suffrage* (New York: Garland, 1997), pp. 169–173.

——, ed., *Conflict and Peacemaking in Multiethnic Societies* (Lexington, MA: Lexington Books, 1989).

Montville, Joseph, and Davidson, William D., "Foreign Policy According to Freud," *Foreign Policy* (No. 45, Winter 1981–1982), pp. 145–157.

Moore, Christopher W., *The Mediation Process: Practical Strategies for Resolving Conflict* (San Francisco: Jossey-Bass, 1986).

——, "Dispute Systems Design: A Pragmatic Approach for the Development of Procedures and Structures to Manage Ethnic and Political Conflicts," *Pacifica Review* (Vol. 6, No. 2, 1994), pp. 43–55.

Nader, L., and Todd, H.F., "The Dynamic of Identity in Personal and Social Conflict," in Kriesberg, L., Northrup, T.A., and Thorson, S.J., eds., *Intractable Conflicts and Their Transformation* (Syracuse, NY: Syracuse University Press, 1989).

Raiffa, Howard, *The Art and Science of Negotiation* (Cambridge, MA: Belknap, 1982).

Ross, Marc Howard, *The Culture of Conflict: Interpretations and Interests in Comparative Perspectives* (New Haven, CT: Yale University Press, 1993).

——, *The Management of Conflict: Interpretations and Interests in Comparative Perspectives* (New Haven, CT: Yale University Press, 1993).

Rouhana, Nadim N., "The Dynamics of Joint Thinking Between Adversaries in International Conflict: Phases of the Continuing Problem-Solving Workshop," *Political Psychology* (Vol. 16, No. 2, June 1995), pp. 321–345.

——, "Unofficial Third-Party Intervention in International Conflict: Between Legitimacy and Disarray," *Negotiation Journal* (Vol. 11, No. 3, July 1995), pp. 255–270.

Rouhana, Nadim N., and Kelman, Herbert C., "Promoting Joint Thinking in International Conflict: An Israeli-Palestinian Continuing Workshop," *Journal of Social Issues* (Vol. 50, No. 1, 1994), pp. 157–178.

Rubin, Jeffery Z., "Some Wise and Mistaken Assumptions About Conflict and Negotiation," *Journal of Social Issues* (Vol. 45, No. 2, 1989), pp. 195–209.

Rubin, Jeffery Z., Pruitt, Dean G., and Kim, S.H., *Social Conflict: Escalation, Stalemate, and Settlement* (New York: McGraw-Hill, 1994, 2nd ed.).

Saunders, Harold H.: Please see Acknowledgments for a list of publications. In addition to that list:

——, "We Need a Larger Theory of Negotiation: The Importance of Pre-Negotiating Phases," *Negotiation Journal* (Vol. 1, No. 3, July 1985), pp. 249–262.

——, "Officials and Citizens in International Relationships," in Volkan, Vamik D., Julius, Demetrius A., and Montville, Joseph V., eds., *The Psychodynamics of International Relationships, Vol. 2: Unofficial Diplomacy at Work* (Lexington, MA: Lexington Books, 1991), Chapter 4.

Saunders, Harold H., and Slim, Randa M., "Dialogue to Change Conflictual Relationships," in *Higher Education Exchange* (Dayton, OH: Kettering Foundation, 1994), pp. 43–56.

Volkan, Vamik D., *The Need to Have Enemies and Allies: From Clinical Practice to International Relationships* (Northvale, NJ: Jason Aronson, 1988).

————, "Ethnonationalistic Rituals: An Introduction," *Mind and Human Interaction* (Vol. 4, No. 1, December 1992), pp. 3–19.

————, *Blood Lines: From Ethnic Pride to Ethnic Terrorism* (New York: Farrar Strauss and Giroux, 1997).

Volkan, Vamik D., and Itzkowitz, Norman, *Turks and Greeks: Neighbours in Conflict* (Cambridgeshire, England: Eothen, 1994), especially Chapter 1, pp. 1–12.

Volkan, Vamik D., Julius, Demetrius A., and Montville, Joseph V., eds., *The Psychodynamics of International Relationships, Vol. 1: Concepts and Theories* and *Vol. 2: Unofficial Diplomacy at Work* (Lexington, MA: Lexington Books, 1990 and 1991).

Volkan, Vamik D., and Harris, Max, "Vaccinating the Political Process: A Psychological Analysis of Relationships Between Russia and the Baltic States," *Mind and Human Interaction* (Vol. 4, No. 4, November 1993), pp. 169–190.

Index

Printed in the United States
19465LVS00001B/318